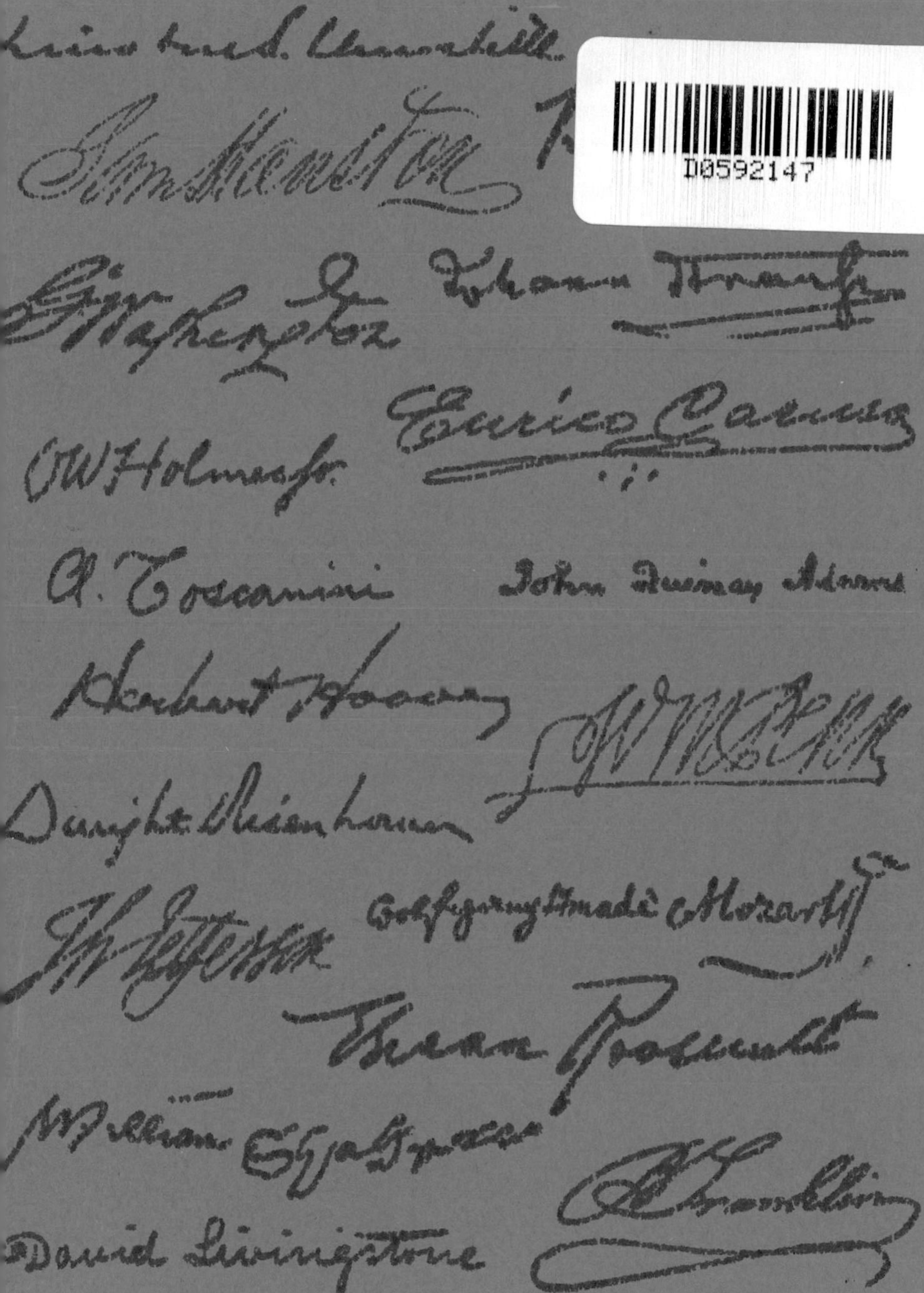
Enrico Caruso
O W Holmes Jr.
A. Toscanini
John Quincy Adams
Herbert Hoover
Dwight Eisenhower
Wolfgang Amadè Mozart
David Livingstone

GREAT LIVES, GREAT DEEDS

THE READER'S DIGEST ASSOCIATION, PLEASANTVILLE, NEW YORK

CORONET SERIES

Illustrations by

Kenneth Riley
Robert Abbett
Len Goldberg

CONTENTS

For alphabetical index of great people, see page v

Introduction—Lives of the Great • *Fred Eastman* 7
A Thrill That Swept the World (Charles A. Lindbergh)
Francis and Katharine Drake 11
The Adventures of Mark Twain • *Jerry Allen* 17
The Steady Light of Helen Keller • *Ishbel Ross* 34
Mozart, Music's Wonder Child • *Donald Culross Peattie* 43
The Uncommon Will Rogers • *Eddie Cantor* 51
A Good Soldier (Dwight D. Eisenhower) • *Grace Perkins Oursler* . . . 56
The Wisest One (Socrates) • *Max Eastman* 59
Prophet in Poetry (Carl Sandburg) • *Ralph McGill* 65
The Victorious Madame Curie • *Eve Curie* 69
Architect of Democracy (Thomas Jefferson)
Donald Culross Peattie 81
Terror of the World (Genghis Khan) • *Edwin Muller* 87
King of the Road (Henry Ford) • *Joe McCarthy* 94
The Microbe Slayer (Louis Pasteur) • *J. D. Ratcliff* 102
The F.D.R. Legend (Franklin Delano Roosevelt)
Hamilton Basso 108
Jungle Philosopher (Albert Schweitzer) • *John Gunther* 113
A Visit with Gandhi • *Louis Fischer* 119
Wilderness Trail Blazer (Daniel Boone) • *Donald Culross Peattie* . . . 123
Bulldog Warrior (Sir Winston Churchill) • *Robert Lewis Taylor* . . . 131
Prince of Storytellers (Hans Christian Andersen)
Donald and Louise Peattie 142
The Incomparable Ben Franklin • *Bruce Bliven* 147
Poet of Our Land (Walt Whitman) • *Max Eastman* 157
The Fabulous Queen (Cleopatra) • *Don Wharton* 163
Pioneer of Freedom (William Penn) • *Donald Culross Peattie* . . . 169
Heavenly Genius (Johann Sebastian Bach) • *Peter Farb* 175
Bold Discoverer (Galileo) • *Donald Culross Peattie* 180
A Lady Who Never Stopped (Eleanor Roosevelt)
Emma Bugbee 187

The Epic of Michelangelo • *Donald Culross Peattie* 194
The Electric Thomas Edison • *Charles Edison* 200
Everybody's Saint (Francis of Assisi) • *Donald Culross Peattie* . . . 206
Great Liberator (Simón Bolívar) • *Thomas Rourke* 214
The Astonishing World of Picasso • *Malcolm Vaughan* 224
Rough-Riding President (Theodore Roosevelt) • *Time* 226
Hail, Caesar! • *Donald Culross Peattie* 233
He Charted the Cosmos (Albert Einstein) • *Joseph Phillips* 241
Inspired Justice (John Marshall) • *Donald Culross Peattie* 246
The Midnight Rider (Paul Revere) • *Esther Forbes* 255
Beethoven the Incredible • *George R. Marek* 273
Mighty Traveler (Marco Polo) • *Donald Culross Peattie* 278
Apostle of Goodwill (Booker T. Washington)
    O. K. Armstrong 284
Nurse Cavell, the Life-Giver • *Jacqueline van Til* 292
All the World's His Stage (William Shakespeare) • *Time* 298
Cavalier of the Wild (La Salle) • *Donald Culross Peattie* 303
Her Book Brewed a War (Harriet Beecher Stowe)
    Forrest Wilson 309
The Evolution of Charles Darwin • *Donald Culross Peattie* 317
Conqueror of the Seas (Ferdinand Magellan) • *Stefan Zweig* . . . 323
A Gentleman of Virginia (Robert E. Lee) • *Robert W. Winston* . . 337
The Westward Voyager (Henry Hudson) • *Llewelyn Powys* 345
The Widow of Windsor (Queen Victoria) • *André Maurois* . . . 349
Voice of Liberty (Patrick Henry) • *Donald and Louise Peattie* . . . 355
The Peace That Lies Within (Buddha) • *Max Eastman* 362
He Lighted the Dark Continent (David Livingstone)
    O. K. Armstrong 367
Sam Houston's Magnificent Last Stand • *John F. Kennedy* 374
He Knew the World Was Round (Christopher Columbus)
    George Kent 381
Our Unknown Ex-President (Herbert Hoover) • *Eugene Lyons* . . 388
Maid of Orléans (Joan of Arc) • *Louise Redfield Peattie* 399
He'd Rather Be Right (John Quincy Adams) • *John F. Kennedy* . . 407
Explorer of the Universe (Sir Isaac Newton) • *Robert Strother* . . . 413
The Wisdom of Confucius • *Max Eastman* 419
Pirate-Knight (Sir Francis Drake) • *Donald Culross Peattie* 423
A Man to Remember (George Washington) • *Time* 430

iv

What Plato Says • *Max Eastman* 437
Teller of Tales (Cervantes) • *Donald Culross Peattie* 443
The MacArthur I Knew (General Douglas MacArthur)
    General George C. Kenney 449
Heroic Preacher (John Wesley) • *William F. McDermott* 462
Spark of Reason (Voltaire) • *Donald Culross Peattie* 467
The Sultan of Swat (Babe Ruth) • *Jack Sher* 474
Crusader for Common Sense (Tom Paine) • *Max Eastman* 481
The Maestro (Arturo Toscanini) • *Ann M. Lingg* 490
Discoverer Supreme (Captain James Cook)
    Donald Culross Peattie 495
Portrait of an Old Master (Rembrandt) • *Malcolm Vaughan* . . . 502
The Rail-Splitter (Abraham Lincoln) • *G. Lynn Sumner* 505
Emperors of the Waltz (Johann Strauss, Sr. and Jr.)
    Donald Culross Peattie 511
The Great Dissenter (Oliver Wendell Holmes) • *Beverly Smith* . . 517
The Magician of Liberty Hall (Charles Steinmetz) • *Floyd Miller* . . 523
Aristotle, the Master Mind • *Will Durant* 540
Old Hickory (Andrew Jackson) • *Donald Culross Peattie* 544
The Soldiers' Angel (Florence Nightingale)
    Mary Raymond Shipman Andrews 551
The Grand Caruso • *George Kent* 557
Peary of the Pole (Admiral Robert E. Peary) • *Jo Chamberlin* . . . 564
Mr. Alice in Wonderland (Lewis Carroll) • *Lancelot Robson* . . . 570

ALPHABETICAL INDEX

Adams, John Quincy . . . 407
Andersen, Hans Christian . 142
Aristotle 540
Bach, Johann Sebastian . . 175
Beethoven, Ludwig van . . 273
Bolívar, Simón 214
Boone, Daniel 123
Buddha 362

Caesar, Julius 233
Carroll, Lewis 570
Caruso, Enrico 557
Cavell, Edith 292
Cervantes, Miguel de . . . 443
Churchill, Sir Winston . . 131
Cleopatra 163
Columbus, Christopher . . 381

v

Confucius	419	Mozart, Wolfgang Amadeus	43
Cook, Captain James	495	Newton, Sir Isaac	413
Curie, Marie	69	Nightingale, Florence	551
Darwin, Charles	317	Paine, Tom	481
Drake, Sir Francis	423	Pasteur, Louis	102
Edison, Thomas	200	Peary, Admiral Robert E.	564
Einstein, Albert	241	Penn, William	169
Eisenhower, Dwight D.	56	Picasso, Pablo	224
Ford, Henry	94	Plato	437
Francis of Assisi, Saint	206	Polo, Marco	278
Franklin, Benjamin	147	Rembrandt	502
Galileo	180	Revere, Paul	255
Gandhi, Mohandas K.	119	Rogers, Will	51
Henry, Patrick	355	Roosevelt, Eleanor	187
Holmes, Oliver Wendell	517	Roosevelt, Franklin Delano	108
Hoover, Herbert	388	Roosevelt, Theodore	226
Houston, Sam	374	Ruth, George Herman (Babe)	474
Hudson, Henry	345	Sandburg, Carl	65
Jackson, Andrew	544	Schweitzer, Albert	113
Jefferson, Thomas	81	Shakespeare, William	298
Joan of Arc	399	Socrates	59
Keller, Helen	34	Steinmetz, Charles	523
Khan, Genghis	87	Stowe, Harriet Beecher	309
La Salle, Sieur de	303	Strauss, Johann, Sr. and Jr.	511
Lee, Robert E.	337	Toscanini, Arturo	490
Lincoln, Abraham	505	Twain, Mark	17
Lindbergh, Charles A.	11	Victoria, Queen	349
Livingstone, David	367	Voltaire	467
MacArthur, General Douglas	449	Washington, Booker T.	284
Magellan, Ferdinand	323	Washington, George	430
Marshall, John	246	Wesley, John	462
Michelangelo	194	Whitman, Walt	157

Introduction by Fred Eastman

LIVES OF THE GREAT

IT'S FUN TO read about young Charles Darwin eagerly holding one rare beetle in his right fist, another in his left, and then suddenly catching sight of a third which he simply must have for his collection. What to do? In a flash he puts one of the beetles in his mouth and reaches for the third. But the mouth-imprisoned beetle squirts its acid down Charles's throat, so that in a fit of coughing he loses all three.

It's fun to turn a page and see Ralph Waldo Emerson and his son trying to get a rebellious calf into a barn. Ralph Waldo pushes and his son pulls, but the calf stubbornly stiffens its legs. Along comes an Irish servingmaid who giggles at their dilemma, then puts a maternal finger into the calf's mouth and leads it gently to the barn. That night Emerson writes in his journal, "I like people who can *do* things!"

But biographies offer more than the fun of anecdote and incident. You start out to discover that illusive thing, a man's personality; not merely the outer facts about his life—when he was born, where he went to school, what titles he won—but the inner man, the soul that hides behind the facts, why he wanted to do what he did and where he got his power.

That's only one of the joys of reading biographies. Here's another: to make new friends. You may not be able to make friends with a neighbor and he may not be worthy of your friendship. But go down to the bookshop or the public library. Ask for a life of St. Francis of Assisi, and in two evenings' time you will be walking shoulder to shoulder with one of the humblest and quaintest and most inspiring souls of all human history. Or ask for a biography of Thomas Jefferson and soon you will be going around an inch taller as you try to keep the stride of that giant. Such reading, to quote the New England clergyman, George Gordon, "gives one a place in the best society of the world."

And here's another joy: to see how others have faced experiences of life that are common to us all and have mastered them or compromised with them. Open an autobiography such as John Ruskin's *Praeterita*, and you have at once an unforgettable picture:

> I had been taught the perfect meaning of *peace*, in thought, act and word. I never had heard my father's or mother's voice once raised in any question with each other; nor seen an angry, or even slightly hurt or offended glance in the eyes of either. I had never heard a servant scolded. I had never seen a moment's trouble or disorder in any household matter; nor anything whatever done in a hurry. Nothing was ever promised me that was not given; nothing ever threatened me that was not inflicted, and nothing ever told me that was not true.

Compare that home with young Byron's. See Byron's emotionally unstable mother flying into a fit of rage, chasing the lad around the room and calling him a "lame brat." You know now why Byron grew up with such undisciplined passions that they well-nigh wrecked his body, so that he sang at the age of 36:

> My days are in the yellow leaf,
>   The flowers and fruits of love are gone,
> The worm, the canker, and the grief
>   Are mine alone.

Or take the common experience of trying to face life with a handicap. In biographies you shall find comfort. Yes, and shame for self-pity. Deafness? Beethoven composed his Ninth Symphony

when he was so deaf that he never heard a note of it. Ill health?
Darwin, Disraeli, Carlyle, Dickens, Emerson, John Burroughs
had it. Queen Elizabeth I had a high batting average among the
queens, but she has been described in books as suffering from
eyestrain, fits, "achy" teeth, smallpox, stomach disorders, ulcers,
dropsy and rheumatism, not to mention occasional complete
breakdowns! Michelangelo had a urinary disorder, Molière had
weak lungs, Ibsen had a nervous illness, Handel became blind,
Rubens had gout and neuralgia.

Poverty? The list of the financially handicapped among the
great is so long that one wonders if the first step toward permanent achievement might be securing release from all bondage to
property and things. Charles Lamb supported himself by a clerk-
ship. Matthew Arnold earned his daily bread as an inspector of
schools—a task whose drudgery must have galled his sensitive spirit. Name your handicap—whatever it is, you have but
to open the door of biographies to find others with the same
symptoms. Or is it the opposition of your fellowmen, rather than
physical and economic handicaps, that troubles you? See St.
Francis of Assisi haled to court by his own father. Look at
Savonarola carrying on single-handed a battle against the powerful Lorenzo de' Medici and his allies. Behold Joan of Arc cast
to the flames. Or in more modern times observe the scientists
pouncing upon Darwin, the literary critics upon Browning and
Kingsley, and the politicians upon Lincoln and Woodrow Wilson
and Herbert Hoover.

Greatest of all the joys in reading biographies is the joy of
discovering courage—courage in action. Courage facing handicaps. Courage bucking the opposition. Courage venturing across
unknown seas with Columbus, or into icy wastes with Peary, or
through the jungles with Livingstone, or out upon the social
frontiers with Jane Addams. Here is Captain Scott in the Antarctic,
feet frozen, food exhausted, lying down in his tent to die, writing
in a quavering hand at the conclusion of his diary that heartrending last appeal to the public, "For God's sake, look after our
people!" Courage—to forget self and think of others!

A THRILL THAT SWEPT THE WORLD

By Francis and Katharine Drake

EVERY DAY hundreds of people in warm, comfortable planes work, eat, sleep, read or play gin rummy high in the heavens over the Atlantic Ocean. A protective network of weather stations keeps lynx-eyed vigil over their course, while crews of pilots, engineers, navigators and radiomen transport them to Europe safely in less than seven hours.

Yet less than four decades ago the skies over the sullen Atlantic held but one small plane, crawling along the empty air from New York to Paris in 33½ hours. It is amazing that it was there at all— a single-engined monoplane of 220 h.p., carrying a single occupant. It had no deicers, no lights, no heat, no radio, no automatic pilot. Its wings were made of wood and fabric, and its total weight was less than that of the electrical equipment of a modern airliner. Yet it flew on into the brilliant light of history and bore its pilot to unimagined fame.

In 1919 Raymond Orteig, a New York hotelman, offered a prize of $25,000 for the first nonstop flight between New York and Paris, a distance of 3600 miles. Eight years passed before progress in plane and engine design brought such a venture within the borderline of possibility. The beginning of 1927 found a number of famous pilots on both sides of the Atlantic making ready. Almost at the last moment, an obscure final entrant flew into New York.

It was no last-minute impulse that brought Charles A. Lindbergh to the starting line. At 25, a seasoned airmail pilot and captain in the Air Corps Reserve, he had carefully worked out in 1926 the plane, engine, navigation and financial requirements for flying the Atlantic. But he had only $2000, and the New Year had come and gone when a group of St. Louis businessmen raised this to $15,000. (Total expenditure from drawing board to Paris proved to be $13,500.)

Construction on the plane—a Ryan with special fuel tanks and a Wright Whirlwind engine—was begun on February 28. With other entries preparing for spring takeoffs, a 60-day limit was set for its completion. Superhuman effort on the part of all concerned enabled Lindbergh to check in at Curtiss Field, Long Island, on May 12, 1927. That was the week in which Charles Nungesser and François Coli, the two French airmen bound nonstop from Paris, disappeared at sea, that found Richard E. Byrd and his three-man crew, and Clarence Chamberlin and Charles Levine also ready to take off from New York. Death and disaster had eliminated the other entrants.

All week the weather was bad. But on the rainy evening of May 19, as Lindbergh and his helpers were on their way to dinner, a forecast indicated a radical weather change—storms and fog belts lifting over the Great Circle route to France. Thirteen hours of furious activity followed. It ranged from picking up five sandwiches, a quart of water and—as a courtesy—several letters of introduction, to towing the *Spirit of St. Louis* to Roosevelt Field, with its longer runway. When he climbed into the cockpit early next morning, Lindbergh had had no sleep for 24 hours.

The pilot's expression as he listened to the engine gave no hint that the most dangerous part of the whole flight stared him in the face—the takeoff. A crash on takeoff had eliminated contenders René Fonck and Noel Davis and Stanton Wooster. Few engines of such small horsepower as Lindbergh's had ever lifted such a heavy load. Moreover, Lindbergh would have to take off with a slight tail wind from a slow, muddy runway. Telephone wires, trees and a hill loomed at the far end.

He ran up the engine to full power, while an engine expert

listened. She was still 30 revolutions shy—but, said the expert, running as well as could be expected on a damp day. Lindbergh thanked him and fastened his safety belt. He gestured for the blocks to be pulled away from in front of the wheels.

Fire-fighting apparatus had been sent to the end of the runway. The crowd tensed, remembering the flames that had consumed Davis and Wooster a month before. They felt a swift compulsion to stop this youth. It was too late—the wheels had begun to roll. Five seconds, ten, fifteen—and the tail skid was still trailing in the mud. Watching pilots urged the straining plane along with body English. *Get the tail up! Slam that throttle against the stop!* Twenty-five seconds, thirty—past the safety mark now, too late to cut the gun and try again. *Now!* A harder patch of runway, a sudden quickening—a bounce, another, a long bound, a cheer from the crowd. *She's up!*

Up, up, inch by inch, flashing past the fire truck. Ten feet to spare over a tractor. Twenty over the telephone wires. Enough speed to clear the trees and squeak around the hillside. Lindbergh described it thus: "About 7:40 a.m. the motor was started, and at 7:52 I took off on the flight to Paris."

The day dragged through noon and had faded into evening before the first note of cheer came to millions hanging breathless on the fate of the young flier. At 7:15 p.m. word flashed from Newfoundland that the *Spirit of St. Louis* had passed St. John's. At the Maloney-Sharkey fight in Yankee Stadium, 40,000 fans rose as one man as the announcement came over the loudspeakers. They uncovered their heads and prayed for Lindbergh.

Far out over the dark sea the lone pilot was bracing himself for the battle of his life. A clammy shroud of fog reached up incessantly for his wing tips. He coaxed his loaded plane higher and higher. Spectrally, the fog rose after him. Just as he skimmed the summit a great storm mass lay spread across his route, its towering peaks like sentries challenging his right to pass.

Even as the storm front rushed at him, Lindbergh had come to a decision. His eyes moved to his instruments. He took a deep breath and bored ahead—straight into the storm. Up and down the plane slammed, pushed about by monstrous forces. But worse was to come—*ice*, prime murderer of pilots in those days. The plane gave a warning shudder. Lindbergh realized that there might be hours of this ahead. "I was forced to turn around and get back to clear air immediately, and then fly around any clouds which I could not get over." Holding a true course through so many confusing detours was later acclaimed an outstanding piece of navigation.

Dawn, moving toward him from the Old World, extended the first friendly hand. Eighteen hours out of New York, about halfway, the sun rose and with it the temperature. No need to dodge and detour any longer. But the need of sleep was paralyzing. To combat it, Lindbergh checked instruments, checked course. He took his numbed feet off the rudder and stamped them; he hit his face stinging blows with the palm of his hand—anything to create diversion. The sun was fairly high when the first breaks began to show in the blanket layers below. A few more minutes and there, at the bottom of a vast hole, streaked the sea. The *Spirit of St. Louis* swooped to greet it, plunging to within a hundred feet of the gray, tossing waste. Whitecaps! The navigator's instinct knew a glow of satisfaction, for the spray was driving from the northwest. A tail wind! But as if begrudging him even this miserly respite, the cloud curtain closed down again, forcing him to fly blind for two more unbroken hours.

Lindbergh had no way of knowing that he and the *Spirit of St. Louis* were already in every headline, on every tongue; that fear clutched at every heart as radio announcers' voices cut into programs throughout that interminable Saturday: "There is still no word. . . ." Waning afternoon brought Lindbergh a fresh burden of anxiety. He was 27 hours out of New York. Surely if he were on course a landfall was nearly due. Now came the classical ordeal which, in mythology, tries mortals who have hitched their wagon to too bright a star: mirages. "Numerous shorelines appeared, with mountains, bays, trees perfectly outlined against the horizon." Land beckoned the tired pilot from all directions—all but the true one.

By this time Lindbergh had been more than two days and nights without sleep. He believes that the absence of window-panes—taken out for better visibility—may have saved his life. By kicking the rudder from time to time he brought a blast of cold sea air through the window openings. Meanwhile he stared with disfavor at the little patch of mud on the underside of each wing, pieces of Roosevelt Field scuffed up on the takeoff. Just beyond the reach of his arm, these few ounces of extra weight began to irritate him increasingly.

Suddenly a handful of specks came into view, a little south of his course. He could hardly trust his tired eyes. More mirages? He nosed the *Spirit of St. Louis* down. Fishing boats! That meant land in the offing. Lindbergh circled a boat and throttled down. On the boat a man stuck his head out a porthole and looked up. Lindbergh had waited a long time to ask his question. "Which way is Ireland?" he shouted. But the fisherman gave no sign that he had heard or understood. So Lindbergh gunned his engine and resumed his course.

Land! Even from a modern airliner the sight of that first strip of earth—so thoroughly secure after the immensity of sea—is a wonderful experience. As the coastline spread and the late sunshine flooded Dingle Bay, the tired pilot's cup of happiness must surely have spilled over. Valentia! The southwest tip of Ireland! He was dead on course.

Then those last five hours on weary but triumphant wings. In the thrill of achievement, sleep now seemed unimportant. Over Ireland, over neat, pretty England, across the Channel in the peaceful twilight—it was like following the evening chimes homeward. When dusk deepened to dark, the London-Paris airway beacons pointed steady fingers to journey's end.

Paris! There all at once was Charles Augustus Lindbergh, of St. Louis, Missouri, circling the Eiffel Tower, 3610 miles and 33½ hours out of New York. Spiraling down to Le Bourget Field, he marveled at the density of French Saturday-evening traffic, the incredible mass of people around the field, with every face turned up. As the *Spirit of St. Louis* rolled along the turf, the crowds surged toward it, thousands of voices lifting a deafening roar. Lindbergh cut the switch lest the propeller kill somebody. As the ship came to a halt, parts of it began to crack from human pressure. He edged open the door, yelled desperately for mechanics, but his voice was lost in the tumult. He was torn from the cockpit, passed from hand to hand. It was half an hour before his feet touched the ground. Then French pilots rushed him to safety.

Cables clicked to every corner of the world. Throughout America, radio and movie programs were interrupted. The boys in the Ryan aircraft plant yelled themselves hoarse. The stately New York *Times* crowned six solid pages of text with the most exuberant headline in its history: LINDBERGH DOES IT!

In the mad months that followed, it was no ordinary young man who kept his head level, who walked with kings and crowds, his genuine modesty untouched. He had an instinct for translating decent thoughts into simple, unaffected words—as in the first speech of his life, in which he offered the people of France his sympathy for the loss of Nungesser and Coli, their heroes who had attempted, he explained, a far more perilous feat than his own.

By the time he sailed home, on a cruiser sent by the President of the United States, movie and advertising offers alone had topped $2,500,000. He refused everything except the Orteig prize and a few hard-earned technical and writing awards. His flight had been made to advance aviation. That it did. Prejudice against flying crumbled, and passenger service expanded. Airmail rose 300 percent that year.

At a time in our history when it was sorely needed—a time of bootlegging, crime and scandal—Lindbergh brought back something bigger than fame. In the words of Charles Evans Hughes, he represented "all that we wish—a young American at his best." In the years that followed, Lindbergh was to know happiness and tragedy, to have good counsel and poor, to be right and to be wrong. But nothing ever marred the perfection of his greatest hour, when he stood forward with an integrity and dignity that merited the unstinted gratitude of his country.

THE ADVENTURES OF MARK TWAIN

Condensed from the book

By Jerry Allen

T HE TOWN revolved around the river. In summer, when the blazing sun beat down, it dozed under the weight of the sultry days. On Main Street a sow and her litter of pigs might root along the wooden sidewalk, sharing the deeply rutted roadway with foraging hens and a hound languidly scratching his fleas. None of them gave ground when wagons, drawn by plodding farm teams, creaked by on their way to market. On Water Street clerks in the stores listlessly awaited buyers for butter at six cents a pound, sugar and coffee at five cents, eggs at three cents a dozen, native corn whiskey at ten cents a gallon. At the foot of Market Street shipments of hemp and tobacco stood ready at the wharf. And beyond the levee, shining in the sun, the Mississippi rolled by in a majestic mile-wide tide.

The waterfront was as still as the town. Then one of the wharf loungers, discerning a plume of smoke on the river, would race to the street with the news. "S-t-e-a-m-boat a-comin'!" Instantly all was excitement and commotion. And all who could—men, boys and dogs—dashed pell-mell for the dock. The steamboat provided a brave and magnificent spectacle as it came alongside the landing. While passengers scrambled to get ashore and to get aboard, slaves carried freight on and off. For ten minutes the melee lasted. Then the *Big Missouri* pulled out, her chimneys puffing gray smoke. A few minutes later the town was asleep again.

This was Hannibal, Missouri, a little community on the edge of the wilderness. It was the home of "Judge" and Jane Clemens and their four children. And it was the playground of their troublesome son Sam, an incorrigible "imp of Satan" who was one day to become one of America's greatest writers, known and loved the world over as "Mark Twain"—the pen name he assumed. In the middle 1840's, when Sam was a boy, Hannibal held 1500 souls. But it was an important port on the great Mississippi. It was to become even more important when Mark Twain looked back at it to write fondly of remembered deviltry.

One Saturday young Sam Clemens sneaked off with his best friend, Tom Blankenship, to go swimming in Bear Creek. Sam, a lad of ten, was small for his age, with a massive head of curly red hair and slate-gray eyes. Tom was the son of a ne'er-do-well who drank up everything his fitful labor earned and so could not afford to send his eight children to school. Tom Blankenship (later to be immortalized as Huckleberry Finn) was the only really independent person in town. Tattered and woods-wise, he lived by his wits but lived well enough; for he knew where the berries were thickest, the watermelons ripest, where the catfish sunned and the rabbits burrowed. He was the envy of every boy in town.

Together Sam and Tom dived into the chilling water of Bear Creek, daring each other to bring up trophies from the bottom. After the swim they fished for their dinner, but the small one they caught wasn't enough for two. Sam decided to go home. He dressed slowly, carefully concealing the signs of forbidden pleasure. He resewed himself into his shirt with stitches that he thought were identical to his mother's, using a needle and thread cached under his jacket lapel. He tried to plaster down his stiffly curling hair, to look like the model boy of his mother's hopes. Minutes later he hurried into the kitchen of the Clemens' modest two-story frame house on Hill Street. "Dinner ready, Ma?" he asked.

Tiny, red-haired Jane Clemens, a former Kentucky belle, eyed her son with mingled love and despair. "Dinner indeed, Sam!" she said. "It's two hours since I called you. Just where have you been?"

"There was a terrible landslide up on Holliday's Hill, Ma, and . . ."

"That's likely," his mother said dryly, interrupting a whopper in mid-flow. Then she examined his shirt where the collar was still sewed securely. "You haven't been swimming, and that's one good thing."

"You sewed him up in white thread, Ma," said Sam's younger brother Henry with an honesty that so often brought Sam discomfort.

"White thread? That's right, I did. An' here you are a-wearin' black thread, little Sam. So just you march right outdoors and start whitewashin' the fence. It will keep you out of mischief for a while at any rate."

"But, Ma," Sam protested, "this is Saturday."

"Now do as I say!"

Sam shuffled outside. Slowly he carried the long-handled brush and the whitewash to the sidewalk. There he looked at the board fence, 30 yards long and higher than his head. He dipped his brush and started stroking. The brush got heavier and heavier, and he had painted only half a board when he heard John Robards coming down the street, acting the parts of boat, captain and engine bells of the *Big Missouri*, drawing nine feet of water.

Sam, now painting with zest, paid no attention to the vocal steamboat. He touched up each brushstroke, gazing at his work as if he were an artist.

"I'm goin' swimmin'," John said, "but I reckon you can't, 'cause you got work to do, huh?"

"You call this work? A boy doesn't get a chance to whitewash a fence every day," replied Sam, gingerly brushing a board with care. John watched for a few moments, then could stand it no longer. "Here, Sam, let me whitewash a little." Sam explained that he would not dare entrust the job to anyone else.

"I'll give you the core of my apple," John pleaded.

"I'd like to, John, but . . ."

"The whole of it?"

Sam turned over the brush, took the apple and sat down in the shade, watching John, happily honored, whitewash furiously. Boy after boy came by that afternoon, all heading for the swimmin' hole. Yet each one stayed to outdo the others in the craft of whitewashing—paying Sam well for the chance. The afternoon was still young when Sam ran out of whitewash. The fence had three coats on it, and Sam had acquired an enormous stock of payments— part of a jew's harp, a brass doorknob, a dead cat, 12 marbles, the handle of a knife and a kitten with one eye.

When he called his mother to inspect the job, she allowed that she had underestimated her boy and, feeling self-reproach for it, gave him a choice apple and sent him off to play. Her back was no more than turned when Sam, waylaying Henry, clobbered him for tattle-telling.

Years later, as a man of 40, Mark Twain was to record that whitewashing coup in *The Adventures of Tom Sawyer*—a juvenile (and adult) classic which was in great part the story of Sam's own boyhood. Many such episodes from his early life were to find their way into his books. There was, for example, the day Sam and his girl, Annie Laurie Hawkins, were lost in McDowell's Cave, a subterranean labyrinth in the banks of the Mississippi. Sam and his gang often played in the cave, groping their way with candles. But when Sam wandered off with little Annie Laurie, he got lost in the cave's endless passages. Their last candle was sputtering out before they heard the search party's echoing calls and saw lights flickering in a distant chamber.

There was the hot August day that Clint Levering, a boy of ten, was playing with Sam and Will Bowen and John Briggs at the river. The rolling Mississippi carried Clint away from shore, sweeping him downstream. He became panicky and went under; they saw his head bob up once or twice, and not again. Sam and Will and John saw Clint when he was found, and the corpse sent chills through each of them.

Sam was a sensitive boy, and all the violence and tragedy of Hannibal life remained deeply imprinted on his memory. And so did the fun and the adventure.

In March of 1847, when Sam was 11 years old, fate dealt a

disastrous blow. Sam's father, a none-too-successful lawyer everyone affectionately called "Judge," came down with pneumonia and died in two weeks. The family's only income now consisted of the meager sums Sam's older brother, Orion, could save from his printer's wages in St. Louis, and the small fees his sister Pamela collected from her piano pupils. Sam soon had a part-time job as errand boy for the Hannibal *Gazette*. The family crept along in genteel poverty.

Sam, chafing at school, won his mother's consent to leave it. He was 12 when he became a printer's devil, or general errand boy, on the *Missouri Courier*. For the two years he served as apprentice Sam's duties were endless: build the morning fire, sweep the office, sort out the good type, wet down the paper stock, hand-set type by candlelight, fold the printed papers, wrap 350 for mailing, and at dawn each Thursday deliver the weekly sheet to the hundred subscribers in the town. He finally left when Orion bought enough type to start his own newspaper in Hannibal, a weekly called the *Western Union*. The wage Orion handsomely promised Sam, a skilled printer of 15, was $3.50 a week. He rarely saw all of it, for Orion, an impractical dreamer, had a talent for failure.

Sam was always a restless boy and one day when he was 17 he read a newspaper item about the New York World's Fair. He had managed to scrape together a little money and he promptly decided to see the Fair for himself. When the downriver steamboat leaving for St. Louis clanged its bells and sent up its plume of gray smoke, Sam Clemens was aboard. It was his good-bye to Hannibal, but through 35 years of his writing he would ever be returning to that beloved port.

Toward the middle of 1853 Sam arrived in New York with $3 in change in his pocket and a $10 bill sewed inside the lining of his coat. He took in the sights of the World's Fair, spreading its wonders in the Crystal Palace which had been built at the city's northern limits, Fifth Avenue and 42nd Street—now the site of Bryant Park, adjoining the New York Public Library. Then, his pocket money quickly gone, he found a job in the printing establishment of John A. Gray & Green on downtown Cliff Street.

He might have stayed on in the East but for Orion, who had moved his mother and Henry to the small Mississippi River town of Keokuk, Iowa, 50 miles north of Hannibal. Sam decided to aid Orion with his new venture, a small commercial printing shop. It proved no more successful than his brother's earlier enterprises had been. For months Sam worked diligently as a typesetter for Orion, but his heart wasn't in it.

Sam greatly admired the pilots of the great river steamboats, the men who could "read the water," steer blindly in the night, sense the meaning in the wind. Horace Bixby, a pilot of the steamboat *Paul Jones*, was such a man. Sam went to him and pestered him for three days until he agreed to take Sam on as his cub, to make a steamboat pilot out of him. The cost would be $500; $100 down, the rest payable out of future wages. Sam borrowed the $100 from his sister Pamela's husband, Will Moffett. Then for 17 months he trained as a cub pilot. He learned the exact shape of the river, upstream and down; how the shoreline looked in the daylight, in starlight, in confusing gray mist, in bright moonlight and in blackness. He was guided over the bad stretches by leadsmen who sounded the depths for the *Paul Jones*, which would ground on a six-foot bottom. He listened as the calls rang out the safe margin of three fathoms, the still safe depth of two fathoms—12 feet—and on down to danger: "M-a-r-k three! Quarter less three! Half twain! Quarter twain! M-a-r-k twain! Eight and a half! E-i-g-h-t feet! Seven and a half!"

There was excitement in steamboating, and there was risk. Some boats went down with hull timbers raked open by submerged wrecks or reefs. Some smashed ashore in fog or storm. Many blew up. At the end of each upstream trip Sam laid over in St. Louis. The Moffetts bought a larger house there so Mrs. Clemens could live with them, and Sam and Henry when they could get home.

Sam stuck diligently to his apprenticeship, and in September 1858, shortly before his 23rd birthday, he was granted a pilot's license. The world changed for Sam with that document. He was now one of the great of the earth. An able pilot, he became the cockiest of them all, the one with the tallest tales. He played the piano, he sang the river songs, he was full of high spirits and tremendously popular.

Early in the summer of 1861, however, the Civil War brought an end to his Mississippi steamboating. Sam Clemens was then 25. He had been a pilot for almost three years, earning the regal sum of $250 a month. Both the Union and the Confederacy were calling for volunteers, and Missouri, like other border states, provided them for both sides. Sam returned to Hannibal to enlist. He joined a highly irregular guerrilla outfit formed by 15 of the town's young bloods who called themselves the Marion Rangers. One night when they were bivouacked in a corncrib, the sound of muffled hoofbeats brought every militiaman tensely awake. As they peered through chinks in the log wall of the crib, a lone horseman emerged on the footpath. War nerves, keyed up by recent rumors that the enemy was advancing, made him seem like a horde. They fired. The man fell dead.

When no battalion appeared, they crept out warily. The dead man was not in uniform, he was not armed. He was no enemy, only a stranger. Sam's had been one of the shots and he felt like a murderer. Sam had had his fill of war—three weeks of it—and with half of the other Rangers, he resigned.

Back in St. Louis, Sam received stupendous news from his older brother. Orion, through the influence of Edward Bates, an old St. Louis friend and a member of Lincoln's Cabinet, had been appointed secretary of the new Territory of Nevada. As secretary, Orion would be treasurer, secretary of state and—when the governor was away—acting governor. His salary would be $1800 a year, his residence, Carson City.

Orion wanted to take Sam with him to Nevada as his private secretary, and Sam leaped at the chance. Six days later, in St. Joseph, Missouri, he paid the expensive fares for himself and the secretary of Nevada Territory—$150 each—on the overland stagecoach. The driver cracked his whip, hostlers cheered and six fresh horses started the swaying coach on its journey westward. After twenty days, having averaged four miles an hour over prairie and mountains and seen the flying hoofs of innumerable relays of the newly established Pony Express, the stagecoach reached Carson City at last. •

The Territory of Nevada had been created only six months before, hewn from the vast land won from Mexico in the Mexican War. For three years it had been filling with miners drawn by the discovery of the Comstock silver lode. Now it was to have a government. It was to have law.

Sam and Orion soon found that every man in Carson City had his heart set on making a million from silver. Mining talk seethed all day long. Riches came fast to some. Incredible stories of sudden wealth were regular fare. And wagonloads of solid silver bricks came into the capital from the smelters and made the stories real. Sam, as eager as any for a fast fortune, could stand the talk no longer. He decided to give up his job with Orion and go to the Esmeralda region near Mono Lake to find his own mine.

Esmeralda was a camp of strong, eager young men, rowdy and tough. Sam threw in with a couple of sturdy partners, and week after week picked away at the mountains. The riches were there. But none of it came from any shaft he and his partners dug. The days were exciting, with the promise of a strike at every new digging, but the nights were long. To pass the time, Sam wrote far-fetched newsletters and sent them to the *Daily Territorial Enterprise*, Nevada's leading newspaper, published in Virginia City. The editor liked his exaggerated, humorous reports of mining-camp life, and when he asked him to come to Virginia City and be an *Enterprise* reporter—at $25 a week—Sam accepted. Sam's job was to fill two columns a day with local news. He covered the town and wrote its life story of mines, murders and desperadoes. He signed his stories with the name "Mark Twain." He was never to discard it. The Mark Twain pieces became highly popular, and Sam's pay was raised to $40 a week.

In 1864 Sam moved on to San Francisco. There he wrote pieces for the *Californian*, a literary weekly edited by Bret Harte. But he was still eager for adventure and when the Sacramento *Union* asked him to go to Hawaii as its special correspondent—writing four letters a month at $20 apiece—he jumped at the chance.

Sam spent four months in the Hawaiian Islands. On his return he decided to give a public lecture on his Hawaiian experiences and hired a theater in San Francisco. He was a natural-born actor and the project was a success from the start. Three weeks of lecturing brought him $1500, more than he had ever earned from writing or silver mining. The money represented one thing to Sam: funds enough for a chance to see the world.

He had read the prospectus of "Captain Duncan's Holy Land Pleasure Excursion," to leave from New York on the *Quaker City*, an 1800-ton coal-burning side-wheeler with sails. Passengers would spend six months on a cruise of the Mediterranean; the fare was $1250. The San Francisco *Daily Alta California* contracted to buy 50 Mark Twain travel letters from him at $20 each, and he faced a solid future—$1000 from his writing and untold lecture sums when he returned.

He left for New York and boarded the *Quaker City*. He made merry sport of the cruise in letters to the New York *Tribune*, the New York *Herald* and the *Daily Alta California*. He poked fun at the crew and passengers, including himself, and a world weary of sedate books reached for his skylarking stories.

Before the *Quaker City* returned him to New York, an event occurred which started Sam on the great adventure of his life. It happened when he came upon the picture of a girl. One day Sam strolled into the stateroom of Charlie Langdon, a young fellow passenger. Charlie talked about his family and showed Sam a picture of his only sister, Olivia. "Livy, everybody calls her," he said proudly.

Sam was struck by the picture. "Why, she has the most beautiful face that surely any mortal ever had. Goodness and gentleness and . . . I could worship a girl like that. I mean it, Charlie."

"Oh, you'd like her! Say, why couldn't we all meet in New York when my family goes there for Christmas week?"

After the return of the *Quaker City*, Sam worked as a newspaperman in Washington to finance writing the book he planned on his travels—*The Innocents Abroad*. But the Christmas holidays found him in New York, eager to meet the beautiful girl of the picture. Nervously he walked into the St. Nicholas, New York's most fashionable hotel at the time, where Mr. Jervis Langdon and family of Elmira, New York, were staying. Charlie introduced Sam to his sister Livy. She was everything Sam had pictured—a small, delicate girl of 22 with serious dark eyes, cameo features, straight black hair center-parted and caught in a knot at the back of her head.

After that first meeting, Sam waited the five days required by social custom of that time before he saw her again. Then on New Year's Day, when Livy was helping receive callers at a friend's New York house, he arrived at ten in the morning and stayed 13 hours. He had 34 New Year's calls on his list, but made only one that day.

After the holidays Sam settled down to write *The Innocents Abroad*. He finished the first draft by summer and took it to Elisha Bliss, head of the American Publishing Company, of Hartford, Connecticut. Then he confidently left for the Langdon home in Elmira. There he immediately proposed to Livy. Cautious and family-bound, she refused Sam but she did not refuse to see him or write to him.

Sam got a job as an editor on the Buffalo *Express*. Elmira was 145 miles from Buffalo and he commuted weekly for several months. Then *The Innocents Abroad* solved its author's problems. Soon after publication it became a best-seller. In one month— December 1869—12,000 copies were sold. Now with money enough for marriage, Sam was jubilant when Livy finally accepted him. He was 34 at the time.

Livy and Sam settled in a house in Buffalo. Sam worked with gay zest, editing the Buffalo *Express* and preparing a new book, *Roughing It*, based on his western days. But three months after the wedding, Livy's father became ill. Jervis Langdon died in August. Livy had nursed him through the hot summer, an ordeal that

caused her to give premature birth to a son in November. Langdon
Clemens was a delicate child who never grew strong. White-faced,
with a chronic cough, he was always to Sam the somewhat
frightening "cubbie."

Sam moved his sick wife and ailing son from Buffalo to a rented
house in Hartford, a town where he had many friends, and went on
the lecture circuit again for four months. Basing his talks on his
Nevada days, he journeyed from town to town making other people laugh. But night after night of telling humorous stories—his
"preaching" as he often called it—was a burdensome chore for a
man who longed for his family.

Shortly after the lecture season ended, on March 19, 1872,
Mark Twain's second child, Olivia Susan Clemens, was born. She
became the brilliant, fanciful, intense Susy her father was to adore.
Three months later the frail 19-month-old Langdon died of
diphtheria.

Roughing It proved a big success, and as new lecture audiences
were waiting, Sam became confident of his future as an author. He
decided it was time to build a substantial home. In the new house
in Hartford, Sam dropped anchor. He raised his children there:
Susy and two younger daughters—Clara and Jean. Twelve of his
books were written there or at Quarry Farm, the Langdon summer
place near Elmira. On the farm was a little octagonal cottage,
covered with ivy and surrounded by trees and wildflowers. Here
Mark Twain began *The Adventures of Tom Sawyer*, published in
1876 and a perennial favorite to this day.

On an afternoon in 1880, misfortune moved into Sam's life in
the form of a Hartford jeweler, Dwight Buell, who offered Sam
stock in a typesetting machine that its inventor, James W. Paige,
was working on and had almost finished. Sam was crazy about inventions, and as an ex-printer with no tenderness for the typecase,
he welcomed a tireless, mechanical hand that could set type. He
bought $2000 worth of stock. Sam was anxious to invest his earn-
ings to secure his family's future, for he believed that the income
from his books, hinging as it did on a public's wayward fancy,

might soon end. By now his six books—*The Innocents Abroad*, *Roughing It*, *The Gilded Age*, *Sketches New and Old*, *Tom Sawyer* and *A Tramp Abroad*—had sold several hundred thousand copies in the first 12 of his years as an author. He should have been in extremely comfortable circumstances. Instead he was always on the verge of ruin.

Sam knew that his affairs required management. To handle them he sent for Charles L. Webster, husband of Pamela's daughter Annie. Webster was then 30 and a civil engineer. He was totally inexperienced in business and publishing but Sam liked him because he was unselfish, energetic and married to Annie. Sam put Charley in complete charge of one firm he had bought outright—the Kaolatype Company, which had a chalk-plate process for engraving illustrations. In two years Kaolatype failed.

Sam now decided to become his own publisher and put Charley in charge of the Charles L. Webster Company, a firm which would issue the books of Mark Twain and other authors. In February 1885, *Huckleberry Finn* was published under the imprint of his firm. It gave the new house a solid start. *Huckleberry Finn* was an immediate and immense success, and was to become a classic and his best-paying novel.

The second book of the Webster Company, published the same year, was the *Memoirs* of General Ulysses S. Grant. In 1884 Grant was a poor man, dying of cancer of the throat. He agreed to write his personal history in order to provide for his wife, and completed the two-volume *Memoirs* only four days before he died. Orders for the book came in a deluge, and Sam set the wheels moving for his new company's gigantic task. Twenty presses and seven binderies worked night and day rolling out a story the country was impatient to read.

The generous publishing contract guaranteed General Grant 70 percent of the profits. From the *Memoirs*, his widow received the largest single royalty check that had ever been paid up to that time—a payment of $200,000. Her total royalties were $420,000. The Webster Company itself made a profit of $180,000. Mark

Twain led the campaign for public donations with which Grant's Tomb was erected in New York City.

The year 1885 was a financial peak for Sam. He drew $40,000 in profits from the Webster Company. But money ran through holes in his pockets. He had always liberally shared whatever bounty he had. He gave freely to many aspiring students, actors and artists. As his part "of the reparation due from every white man to every black man," he paid for the education of a Negro student, Charles W. Johnson, sending him through Yale Law School. Among those whom he helped at one time or another were Helen Keller and Bret Harte. Meanwhile chunks of his earnings were being drained into the Paige typesetter, which was still "almost completed." In 1887 the typesetter was using up Sam's funds at the rate of $3000 a month. He had borrowed heavily, had dumped $150,000 into the machine.

In June of 1891, Sam found that he did not have enough money to keep his big house open. Living in America was high, living in Europe was cheap. With his treasure chest empty, he took his family to Europe. For a year they settled in the rented Villa Viviani in Italy, outside Florence. In that 28-room house Mark Twain completed *Tom Sawyer Abroad*, *The Tragedy of Pudd'nhead Wilson* and part of *Personal Recollections of Joan of Arc*.

Every effort to save the publishing firm proved fruitless. In the panic of 1893-94 many business houses fell, creditors taking what assets there were. The Webster Company had unpaid debts totalling $94,000, and Mark Twain returned to New York to go through the legal proceedings of bankruptcy, determined to return every cent of the staggering sum, though not legally obligated to do so. At fifty-eight, he had become bankrupt—a late time to be starting life over. The humiliation of it burned.

Secretly, Sam thought the typesetter would be his salvation. It was a machine with 18,000 separate and delicately adjusted parts; repeated breakdowns made it too impractical, too costly. Eight months after the bankruptcy Sam, back in Paris writing *Joan of Arc*, heard the bad news. His investment, now amounting to $190,000, was gone completely, and with it the dream.

Sam made arrangements for a lecture tour that would take him for a year of speaking engagements around the world. Sam, his wife and daughter Clara left from Elmira on the westbound train. As he crossed America, the nation's newspapers carried Mark Twain's schedule, and lecture halls were crowded. Before he sailed for Australia from Vancouver, bolstered by the heartwarming, overwhelming reception, he sent back $5000 to whittle down the debt. From Sydney on around the continent "down under," Mark was everywhere hailed as an old friend. His lectures drew all the halls would hold, and two weeks after arriving he forwarded another payment on the debt. From Australia, Tasmania and New Zealand he sailed to India. Crowds gathered wherever he appeared, cheering, applauding.

When he reached England he rented a house in Guildford, a quiet town near London, where he planned to write the record of his journey, *Following the Equator*. Susy and Jean were to rejoin the family there. But Susy and Jean did not arrive. A letter came instead. It said that Susy was ill and their sailing would be delayed. Their family physician pronounced her run-down from driving herself too hard with singing practice. The news sounded ominous. Frantically, Sam cabled worried questions. The reply was that Susy's recovery would be long, but certain.

Livy and Clara immediately sailed for America. On August 18, while they were still in mid-Atlantic, Sam, waiting in England, received another cablegram: SUSY COULD NOT STAND BRAIN CONGESTION AND MENINGITIS AND WAS PEACEFULLY RELEASED TODAY.

The shock dazed him. He was not expecting anything like that; he had not believed that Susy was seriously ill. The cable report only three days before had said her recovery was certain, and he had had no doubt of it.

A few days after Susy was buried in Elmira, beside her small brother Langdon, Livy sailed for England with Clara and Jean. The family found a hideaway in London at an address known only to near relatives and close friends. During ten months of seclusion Sam wrote page after page of the long book *Following the Equator*, driving himself to exhausting work to hold off tormenting thoughts of Susy. Thanksgiving came and the family ignored it. Christmas came and they did not mention the day.

Searching for a haven where sorrow would not follow, they left London and for three restless years moved on and on— Switzerland, Sweden, Austria. They finally settled in Vienna because Clara, preparing for a career as a concert pianist, could study there to advantage.

Sam wrote with a surging drive, had four or five books going at once. Meanwhile the publishing debts were shrinking, and Sam was impatient to see the end of them. At last the account was balanced. Less than four years from the date of his bankruptcy Mark Twain paid the Webster Company's last creditor and, at the end of January 1898, was free of debt. Now he longed for no place so much as home. Ending a nine-year exile, he sailed for America in October 1900.

The last years of the life of America's greatest comic spirit were filled with sorrow. His youngest daughter Jean suffered from epilepsy and was often in hospitals for long stays. And Livy, who had always been frail, developed a heart condition that was to keep her bedridden for the last 22 months of her life.

The following winter Livy's physicians recommended that she be taken to the mild climate of Italy, and Sam rented a house near Florence. There Livy's health improved for a time. But the end was near. And on the evening of June 5, 1904, when Sam, Clara and Jean went into Livy's room to say good-night, she did not answer. Steeped in sorrow for "the loss of one whose memory is the only thing I worship," Sam returned with Jean and Clara to America. Brooding in his rented house at 21 Fifth Avenue in the downtown quiet of New York, he found solace in writing *Eve's Diary*, a tribute to Livy; and in music, listening for hours to recordings of Beethoven's symphonies.

With age had come recurrent bronchitis and a heart ailment like Livy's, and for relief he began to spend his winters in Bermuda. But he had had enough of wandering, and out of the timeworn wish for a home again he had a new house built at Redding, Connecticut. Named Stormfield, it was to be a home for Clara, when she was free from concert tours, and for Jean, when she was freed from hospitals, and for him, a tired man and old.

And so for a short while it was. But the home was still new in October 1909, when Clara married and sailed for Europe with her husband, Ossip Gabrilowitsch, the concert pianist and conductor, whom she had met in Vienna. And that same year on the morning before Christmas, a servant awakened Mark Twain to impart the shattering news that his daughter Jean was dead.

On Christmas Eve—the so gaily planned Christmas Eve— Jean's body lay in the suddenly barren home, and throughout the deep silences of the night a father wandered from room to room. As he had written of Susy and of Livy in a release of grief, Sam now wrote of Jean. He wrote of his youngest child, whose going left him so finally alone, through the day of Christmas. He told the tragic story and laid aside his pen when it was finished.

"I shall never write any more."

It was as he said. "The Death of Jean" was Mark Twain's last writing.

Release from his loneliness came less than five months later. He was in Bermuda when he sensed his time was near. "I don't want to die here," he wrote a friend. "I am growing more and more particular about the place." On the homeward journey, a race with time, his faltering heart caused him acute pain and only his determination to reach home kept it beating. But once there he welcomed death as "the most precious of all gifts."

Late in the afternoon of a spring day, April 21, 1910, Mark Twain died at Stormfield, at the age of 74. For him who had made the world laugh the sad pilgrimage was ended.

The difference between the right word and the almost-right word is the difference between lightning and the lightning bug.
—*Mark Twain*

THE STEADY LIGHT OF HELEN KELLER

Condensed from Journey Into Light

By Ishbel Ross

HELEN KELLER has an ageless quality about her—inherent even in her looks—in keeping with her amazing life story. Blind, deaf and mute from early childhood, she rose above her triple handicap to become one of the best-known characters in the modern world and an inspiration to both the blind and the seeing everywhere. When she visited Japan after World War II, boys and girls in remote villages ran to greet her, crying, "Helen Keller!" Her name had penetrated jungles even before the days of radio or motion pictures. Although warmed by this human reaction, she has no wish to be set aside from the rest of mankind. She believes the blind should live and work like their fellows, with full responsibility.

Helen, at ten years old, already was reading Braille avidly and could communicate by means of the manual alphabet. That spring of 1890 she learned of a deaf, dumb and blind Norwegian girl who had been taught to talk. Like lightning Helen spelled into the hand of her teacher, Anne Sullivan: "I must speak."

Miss Sullivan took Helen to Miss Sarah Fuller, principal of the Horace Mann School for the Deaf in Boston. Miss Fuller went to work at once, passing Helen's hand lightly over the lower part of her face, and putting Helen's fingers into her mouth, so that she might feel the position of the teacher's tongue, her teeth and the movement of the lower jaw.

Miss Fuller then set her tongue just behind her lower front teeth for the sound of *i* in *it*. Next she put Helen's forefinger against her teeth, placed another finger on her throat and repeated the sound *i* several times. As soon as she had ceased, Helen's "fingers flew to her own mouth and throat and, after arranging her tongue and teeth, she uttered a sound so nearly like what I had made that it seemed an echo of it."

Then they practiced the vowels *a* and *o*, which Helen repeated distinctly. After this they tried the words *mamma* and *papa*. Miss Fuller delicately pronounced the word *mamma*, at the same time drawing her finger along the back of Helen's hand to indicate the relative length of the two syllables. After a few repetitions, *mamma* and *papa* came correctly and with "almost musical sweetness from her lips."

Going home in the streetcar after her seventh lesson, Helen turned to Miss Sullivan and said in "hollow, breathy tones": *I am not dumb now*. This was her first real use of words in conveying a thought, and it came within a month after her first lesson in articulation. It was human speech from the lips of one who, except for her early baby babblings, had reached the age of ten uttering only the uncouth sounds of the mute.

Helen took 11 lessons from Miss Fuller, but this was only the beginning of her long tussle with speech. Week after week, month after month, year after year, she labored to improve enunciation. She repeated words and sentences for hours, using her fingers to catch the vibrations of Miss Sullivan's throat, the movement of her tongue and lips, the expression of her face as she talked. She has never ceased to labor over her voice, to make speeches in public and to conduct much of her conversation by direct speech. Those closest to her observed that her articulation improved noticeably in her 60's. Her mastery of speech has been called "the greatest individual achievement in the history of education."

After years of practice, she became adept at reading lips by vibration. By placing the middle finger on the nose, her forefinger on the lips and her thumb on the larynx, she can "hear what others say," particularly if their speech is clear and resonant. She found Franklin D. Roosevelt an ideal subject in this respect. She caught Mark Twain's best jokes by vibration. With her fingers on his lips Enrico Caruso "poured his golden voice" into her hand. Feodor Chaliapin shouted the "Song of the Volga Boatman" with his arm encircling her tightly so that she could feel every vibration of his mighty voice. Jascha Heifetz played for her while her fingers rested lightly on his violin. She read Carl Sandburg's verses from his lips and old plantation folk songs from the rim of his guitar. With her hand resting on a piano she detected "tiny quavers, returns of melody and the rush that follows." She got some small response by vibration from radio, too.

The initial penetration of the dark mists that enshrouded Helen Keller dates back to 1886, when she was six years old. Born in the little Alabama town of Tuscumbia on June 27, 1880, she was a normal baby up to 19 months and seemed to enjoy the flowers, the flitting birds, the play of light and shadow. Then she was stricken with a "fever of brain and stomach." She was desperately ill, but the fever subsided almost as suddenly as it had begun.

Soon her mother noticed that Helen's eyes did not close when she bathed the child. She took her to an oculist and learned that Helen was blind. Next she noticed that the child did not respond to the loud ringing of a bell. Helen was deaf, too. Inevitably, by the age of three she was also mute, and such words as she had babbled at a year and a half were forgotten.

Helen grew fast and was physically strong and well formed, but her good nature dissolved in frantic tantrums. Her failure to make herself understood was followed by wild gusts of rage. She would fling herself on the grass and give way to uncontrollable fits of screaming. Her table manners were appalling. She would not wash her face or button her shoes. Years later she wrote: "I felt as if invisible hands were holding me. I made frantic efforts to free myself."

Her gentle mother, cowed by such violence, gave in to her at every point. There was great power in Helen, instead of the apathy that usually rests heavily on the triply handicapped child. Mrs.

Keller was close to despair when she picked up Charles Dickens'
American Notes and read of Laura Bridgman, the deaf, mute and
blind girl in New England whose mind had been reached by
Samuel Gridley Howe, head of Perkins Institution.

Finally Helen was taken to Michael Anagnos, who had succeeded Dr. Howe. He recommended as tutor an Irish girl who
had just been graduated. This was Anne Sullivan, who was to be
Helen Keller's inseparable companion for the next half-century.
She was the child of Irish immigrants and her own childhood had
a Dickensian touch. Her drunken father beat her. She was starved,
bruised, neglected, and finally was abandoned to the almshouse
as a state charge. She entered Perkins in 1880, blind from trachoma.
Two operations virtually restored her sight, although she had
trouble with her eyes all her life and became blind again in her
later years.

Anne Sullivan, arriving in Alabama, was struck by Helen
Keller's fine bearing and intelligent face. Helen rushed at her
as she stepped from the carriage, felt her dress and face, tried to
open her bag and staged a scene on the doorstep when Mrs.
Keller attempted to stop her. Miss Sullivan offered a doll sent by
the Perkins children. When Helen had played with it for some
time, Miss Sullivan spelled into her hand the letters *d-o-l-l*. The
child's attention was arrested by this unfamiliar maneuver and she
tried to imitate the finger motions. This was the first conscious
effort ever made to teach Helen Keller.

When Miss Sullivan tried to put away the doll, a tussle began.
It was the first of many. The new teacher moved Helen away from
her upset parents to a nearby cottage. A herculean battle of wills
raged for several days. It was a physical as well as a mental struggle, but Miss Sullivan won, even though she had to hold Helen
down by force for two hours at a time to quell her fierce resistance.
"Her restless spirit gropes in the dark," Teacher commented.
"Her untaught, unsatisfied hands destroy whatever they touch
because they do not know what else to do with things."

She noticed that the child already had several ways of indicating her wishes. If she longed for ice cream, she turned the handle

of an imaginary freezer. For bread and butter she went through the motions of cutting and spreading. She pretended to put on glasses to symbolize her father. She took to rocking the new doll, making a monotonous chanting sound with her lips and touching them lightly with her fingers. But she also learned to spell new words by the manual language—pin, hat, cup and verbs like sit, stand and walk.

Within two weeks a gleam of light dawned. Miss Sullivan took her to the pump house and drew water. As it flowed into the mug and over the child's right hand, she spelled *w-a-t-e-r* into the other. "The word, coming so close upon the sensation of cold water rushing over her hand, seemed to startle her," Miss Sullivan wrote. "She dropped the mug and stood as one transfixed. A new light came into her face."

Helen's own recollection is: "Somehow the mystery of language was revealed to me. I knew then that water meant the wonderful cool something that flowed over my hand. That living word awakened my soul; gave it light, hope, joy; set it free!" Helen returned to the house in a fever of excitement, touching everything as she moved, visibly seeking its name. The ground, the trellis, the bushes, the pump—she knew now that everything had a name and she wished to know what it was. Within the space of a few hours she had added 30 new words to her vocabulary. From that point on her education proceeded with uncanny speed.

Miss Sullivan taught her to read with little sentences slipped into a frame, after each separate word—raised on cardboard—had been placed beside its object, like *doll is on bed*. "When her fingers light on words she knows," Miss Sullivan wrote, "she fairly screams with pleasure and hugs and kisses me for joy. When I gave her my Braille slate to amuse her, the little witch soon was writing letters. I had no idea she knew what a letter was."

At the end of three months Helen knew 400 words and many idioms. That summer the game went on for hours at a time, outdoors and in. She learned to distinguish mountain laurel from honeysuckle, and a pig from a hen. Miss Sullivan made raised maps in clay for her pupil, with strings and orange sticks for equator, meridians and poles. She taught Helen to count by stringing beads in groups, and arranging kindergarten straws for addition and subtraction. It was the only subject the child disliked. Her pencil writing soon was excellent. Within a month after trying it, she wrote a correctly spelled and legible letter to her cousin.

Miss Sullivan took Helen back to Perkins when she was almost eight, and a whole new world opened up for her. She had Braille books to read and she could associate with other children who knew the manual alphabet. She soon displayed amazing abilities. She studied arithmetic, geography, zoology, botany and reading. These were days of great mental growth for Helen. As she and Miss Sullivan traveled, Teacher spelled into her hand fluent descriptions of the passing scene—the hills and rivers, the hamlets and cities, the way people looked and what they wore. They summered on Cape Cod and Helen learned to swim, but her first splash into the sea brought a great surprise. No one had thought to tell her that there was salt in the ocean! She learned to row and sail, to ride horseback and use a tandem bicycle. By this time she was tall and graceful, and showed charm and humor.

College was the next step, and Helen prepared with her usual thoroughness. She entered the Cambridge School for Young Ladies in Massachusetts and was tutored intensively, with Miss Sullivan always by her side to read the lectures into her hand. In 1900 she enrolled at Radcliffe, the first individual with a triple handicap to enter an institution of higher learning. But college was a disappointment to Helen. She did well, but felt the lack of time for meditation. She could not take notes during lectures because her hands were "busy listening." What she could remember, she jotted down when she got home. For algebra, geometry and physics she used a Braillewriter, but she had little aptitude for mathematics. Examinations were a nightmare. But she enjoyed some of her classes and she and Teacher worked with their usual wholehearted concentration. They got books in Braille from Germany and England, and Helen read until her fingers bled.

Helen was graduated in 1904, taking special honors in English.

She was 24 years old. Already requests were flowing in for appearances and for magazine articles. She was invited to the St. Louis Exposition in 1904 to awaken worldwide interest in the education of the deaf-blind. But on Helen Keller Day the crowds got out of hand. Her dress was torn and roses were snatched from her hat.

She prepared to lecture by taking special lessons with a music teacher. At times her voice would become unmanageable. It would dive down or go soaring up beyond her control. Rain, wind, dust or excitement affected its pitch. But in 1913 she made her first public-speaking appearance. "My mind froze," Helen commented at the time. She prayed. Words rose to her lips, but she could not utter a syllable. At last she forced out a sound that felt to her like a cannon going off. Later she was told it was only a whisper.

But after this Miss Keller and Teacher made many appearances in public. Teacher would demonstrate how she had taught young Helen. The pupil then would speak, winding up with the phrase: *I am not dumb now.* In 1914 they set out on the first of a number of transcontinental speaking tours. By this time a brisk and capable young Scottish girl, Polly Thomson, had joined them as secretary and manager. They went to Hollywood to make the film *Deliverance.* Then they embarked on a dignified vaudeville act, which caused a sensation at the Palace in New York. Helen loved it. She found vaudeville full of life, color and variety. She "felt the breath of the audience in her face."

Helen Keller was known now around the world. Her books were translated into many languages, as well as into Braille. In the 1930's she began her international traveling. She went repeatedly to Europe, then to the Orient—interested always in the blind, talking for the blind, raising money for the blind. Those who had read about her now turned out to see her. By this time she was a learned and composed young woman, equal to any emergency. She received honorary degrees and decorations in many lands.

But Teacher's health was failing. She was almost blind. No longer could she keep up with the vigorous and healthy Helen. She died in 1936, shortly after the last of a long series of eye operations. That year the Roosevelt medal for "Coöperative Achievement of Unique Character and Far-reaching Significance" was awarded to this remarkable pair.

Miss Keller lives in a graceful rambling house set in the Connecticut woods near Westport. A stone Japanese lantern, eight feet high, stands symbolically in one corner of the lawn with a constantly burning light—not to go out while Helen Keller lives. Around the walls of her study are her Braille books, which she reads until the fingertips that have traveled over so many miles of raised dots have to be bound with silk for protection. Her Braille Bible is still her most valued possession. She knows great stretches by heart. She reads in the dark or the daylight, like all the blind, who sleep poorly and do not know night from day.

Helen Keller is deeply spiritual. Her faith sustains her in the quiet hours when she retreats into the deep silence that only the deaf, blind and mute can know. "I look forward to the world to come," she says, "where all physical limitations will drop from me like shackles; where I shall again find my beloved Teacher, and engage joyously in greater service than I have yet known."

"The road is always better than the inn." These words by the great Spanish writer, Cervantes, mean a way of living. In my younger days I often aimed too hard to reach some goal, finish some job. "When this is done," I'd say, "I shall find real satisfaction and reward." But later I came to realize that each achievement, like each inn, is only a point along the road. The real goodness of living comes with the journey itself, with the striving and desire to keep moving. Now I find that I can look back on my 84 years with pleasure and, what is even more important to me, that I can still look to the future with hope and desire. I have learned to take each inn along the way with a traveler's stride—not as a stopping point, but a starting point for some new and better endeavor.   —*Maurice Maeterlinck*

MOZART, MUSIC'S WONDER CHILD

By Donald Culross Peattie

Positively the last concert! . . . The boy, not yet seven, will perform on the harpsichord, play a concerto for violin and accompany symphonies on the clavier, the keyboard being covered with a cloth, as easily as if he could see the keys. He will name all notes sounded at a distance, singly or in chords, and improvise on harpsichord and organ as long as desired. Tickets one-half taler.

THUS did a notice in a German newspaper in 1763 advertise, as if he were a sideshow freak, the most universal genius of music the world has ever known, Wolfgang Amadeus Mozart. In the audience sat another boy, the 14-year-old Goethe, destined too to become immortal. Years later he could still recall the far-off bright picture of the merry-faced little musician who ran to the bench before the harpsichord in his absurd, exquisite costume of lilac satin, with powdered wig and tiny sword, and flung his heart into the glittering notes.

Born with absolute pitch, infallible rhythm and natural comprehension of harmony, Master Mozart had come into this world with an inexplicably complete gift. That is how, at the age of four, the child began to learn to play the clavier (a forerunner of the modern piano) and at five picked up a violin and, reading at sight, staggered through six trios with his father and a friend.

This child read and wrote musical notes before he could do as much with letters. Compositions dating from his sixth year are recognizable from the opening bars as the music of Mozart and nobody else. Graceful and sure, spirited, precise and brave, they are the work of a unique stylist and a great soul.

Fingers and brain were equally endowed. At ten the boy astounded the Hollanders by playing superbly on the largest, most complicated organ in the world. At 14 he was taken to hear the Vatican choir sing a long, difficult *Miserere* which was kept so secret that the singers were forbidden to copy the parts on pain of excommunication. The boy drank in every note, walked home and wrote the entire thing out from memory. On a second hearing, he was distressed to find he had made three mistakes. Instead of excommunicating him, the Pope made him a Knight of the Golden Spur.

The father of this phenomenon was Leopold Mozart, a second-rate violinist and first-rate teacher of Salzburg, Austria. Always reverent before his child's genius, he nevertheless exploited it. With Wolfgang's sister, a talented young harpsichordist, he dragged the boy all over Europe. The children played before the rulers of France and England, and for the imperial family of Austria. On that occasion the boy slipped on the palace floor, got a bad bump and was comforted by a girl who helped him to his feet. By way of thanks, Wolfgang offered to marry her when they grew up. But ahead lay a different fate for Marie Antoinette.

Rumbling coach and miry road, wretched inn and long, hard hours could not exhaust the merriness and spirit of the boy. Delighted audiences often refused to leave their seats, and the obliging child would play on and on, seemingly in a spell of enchantment, inventing melody upon melody, the notes of the one rushing back and forth across the other like a spring shower dancing upon flowers. Until at last Papa Mozart would call a halt, and the fashionable ladies and gentlemen would shower the child with caresses and applause, none of which ever spoiled his natural sweetness.

The financial returns of the tours, however, always proved less than the expenses. The highborn listeners were likely to pay in snuffboxes, shoe buckles and trinkets. Papa Mozart took it all with a bow, and bundled the children off to play for their supper elsewhere. He was the boy's sole teacher. Wolfgang never went to school, but he flung himself joyfully on all forms of learning. Especially did arithmetic fascinate him, and he chalked sums all over the tables and walls, enchanted by a science which could be made to yield the one right and perfect answer. Here is a key to why his music is right, perfect, exactly satisfying.

In Mozart's time people found some of his music "too modern, too advanced." And to our ears a Mozart piece, heard for the first time, sounds as though you had known and loved it all your life. The reason is that Mozart profoundly influenced the music that came after him. Beethoven studied him constantly, and Haydn paid his young friend the sincere flattery of imitation. Chopin was deeply imbued with Mozart's spirit and said at his death, "Play Mozart in memory of me." Even the proud Wagner bowed his head to him. You can trace much of the gay spirit of Strauss waltzes, much of the music of Schubert's great songs back to the pure fountainhead of Wolfgang Amadeus Mozart.

Melodies sprang from his fingertips. He would sit in a rocking coach, drumming his fingers on his knee, delight on his face, until the theme was worked out in his head and he could scribble it on a scrap of paper. At 14 his newest opera was produced in Milan, Italy, under his own direction, by the largest orchestra in Europe. At 15 he was the author of 20 symphonies and six short operas.

In the years from 15 to 21 he invaded the most technically difficult fields of composition, where to step at all is to invite comparison with past masters. He showed that he was the master of them all. Every year his gifts, like a new star rushing toward the earth, grew brighter. In all justice he should have been given the highest musical post that his emperor, Joseph II of Austria, could bestow.

Instead he was neglected by the Emperor, whose hirelings were fearful and jealous of the extraordinary greatness of Mozart's gift. Rival musicians prevented his works from being played, or when they were produced the performers were often bribed to ruin the music. There was no copyright to protect a composer; once a

piece of music was known it could be freely performed, or even
appropriated into another man's work.

The only security for a composer was to be taken into the
employ of some court or person of wealth. Mozart did get such an
appointment—at about $67 a year! His employer, the Archbishop
of Salzburg, had Mozart eat with the servants, and supposed that
by grossly insulting him he could keep him properly humble.
Resigning, Mozart settled in Vienna as a free-lance artist.

When the celebrated musician Christoph von Gluck died,
Wolfgang was given his post—"chamber composer" to the
court—but at less than half von Gluck's pension. Yet he was
humbly glad to get even this, for he had married at the age of 26,
and the babies came promptly.

His wife was Constanze Weber, one of four pretty girls in a
family where everyone was musical. Constanze was a giggly 13
when he first saw her, or rather looked past her at her older sister
Aloysia, a 15-year-old with a gorgeous figure and singing voice.
Aloysia promised to wait for him while he went off to Paris seeking his fortune. When he returned, unsuccessful, hers was already
made in the opera. Long after, asked why she turned down
Mozart, she confessed, "I thought he was such a *little* man."

Constanze picked up the pieces of his broken heart, and, to the
unforgiving rage of Papa Mozart, they were married. "Stanzi" was
a tuneful little blonde, an ideal companion for picnics in the
Vienna woods. As a wife she lacked all domestic capabilities.
Mozart could see the pathos of her fun-loving disposition caught
in the wheels of poverty and childbearing. So her "Wolfi" extrava-
gantly spent money on little luxuries to coax back the smile of
childish delight he had married. Worse, her health was frail, her
childbirths were agonizing, and five of her seven children were
swept into an early grave.

Mozart had troubles enough to have set any other musician to
writing dirges. But into his music he never brought the sorrow,
grime and humiliations of his life. The worse things got, the more
he poured his courage into his art. And it is never grim courage,
but blithe as bird song.

In order to pay the butcher and even stave off the sheriff (who called frequently and took away pieces of furniture), Mozart got up concert after concert. For each one he composed a fresh work. Frequently it was finished only at the last moment; some of his greatest works were written in a matter of days.

Sometimes in the notoriously dank Vienna winters it was difficult for Mozart to keep warm enough to practice. A man called to find Wolfi and Stanzi dancing about. This story has been told as if they were waltzing gaily and regarded it as a joke. Actually they were almost paralyzed by cold and were throwing themselves about hysterically. The friend rushed out and got them fuel.

But the friend to whom the world owes most was a businessman named Puchberg, who repeatedly let Mozart have small sums when the distracted composer was driven to the wall. Reading Mozart's letters imploring his friend's aid, we burn with indignation to think that this radiant genius was reduced to begging.

In Prague, Bohemia, at least, Mozart was understood in his lifetime and adored. When he was invited there to conduct his gay opera *The Marriage of Figaro*, which had been coolly received in Vienna, he found that nothing but *Figaro* was whistled in the streets. While there he wrote the beautiful "Prague" Symphony, and presently he returned to prepare an opera especially for that music-loving town.

It was one of the good times for Wolfgang and Constanze when they journeyed over the mountains to the mellow Bohemian capital where Mozart worked on *Don Giovanni*, often called "the perfect opera." Da Ponte, the poet who wrote the text for the opera, was a merry scamp who lodged across the narrow street from the Mozarts. From time to time one man would shout across to the other with a request to come and hear new pages. Or, to the delight of all Prague, they would swing down the street together, singing, to the tavern for a bottle of wine. Admirers entertained the Mozarts everywhere, so much so that time ran short. Not until the evening before the dress rehearsal was the overture written.

Never had comedy been expressed in music with such delicious effect. But the *Don* is also a tragedy, and showed Mozart for a writer of superhuman power and dramatic instinct. Applause and encores stretched three hours of music into six. The box-office receipts saved the theater owner from bankruptcy, but the composer received only a flat—a very flat—sum.

As the brief star of Mozart's life rushed toward perpetual darkness, it seemed to gather speed and to glow more dazzlingly. His last nine symphonies, some of which never got a hearing in his lifetime, are worthy to stand with Beethoven's nine. Too often people dismiss Mozart as dainty, knowing only the minuets and little sonatas taught to children; but you cannot hear his music to the end without discovering his depth.

In the 36th year of his life, though he was very ill in Vienna, he composed the famous fairy opera, *The Magic Flute*, filled with wonderful melodies. A fly-by-night producer brought it out in a ramshackle theater. News of it got about and all Vienna flocked to hear it. The producer made so much money he built a new theater. But Mozart was too ill to see the performances; he would lie eyeing his watch, saying, "Now the curtain is going up. . . . Now they are walking unhurt through the flames, to the sound of the magic flute."

A few months before, Mozart had been visited by a stranger, a grim fellow who was empowered by his employer, he said, to commission Mozart to write a Requiem Mass for male and female voices, in honor of his employer's deceased wife. The messenger would not give his master's name. It is now known that the employer, Count Walsegg, was fond of commissioning musical works secretly and then having them performed as his own.

Many interruptions prevented Mozart from delivering the piece. At intervals the messenger reappeared to hurry the composer. As Mozart became ill he imagined that this emissary came from the Other World and that the *Requiem* was for his own death. Feverishly he strove to finish it. With terrifying power the *Requiem* sounds the very depths of grief and shuddering repentance, explores the furthest horizons of our human longing for immortality, and ends in a clear, serene chord of faith. On his deathbed, with his best friends about him, the composer's lips shaped the notes of the Judgment Day trumpet that rings through the *Requiem*.

A few friends gathered in the gloom of a coming storm to hear a brief Mass said over Mozart's casket. As they set out toward the cemetery; lightning flashed and lashing rain and wind bent them double. They turned back, and the hearse went on alone. Into a pauper's grave was lowered the slight form that had housed the most singing spirit which ever dwelt on earth.

Mozart triumphed over injustice, sickness, debt and death itself. To all that was ignoble or appalling, he returned an answer that tingles still with the rapture of living.

So dependent on the adulation of his audiences was Franz Liszt that he is said to have paid women 25 francs to faint at his concerts. The swoon was always timed to occur just before the climax of his most popular run. Liszt would leap from his piano stool, pick up the swooner and leave the rest of the audience impressed by his brilliance and dismayed by their own stolidity. Once, however, the hired fainter forgot to faint. Liszt's fingers flew up the keys—but he could not finish the run. So he fainted himself.   —*Lilliput*

After his concert in a midwestern town, Paderewski was found backstage in a silent, preoccupied mood. One of his aides asked if he were ill.

"No, no," the great musician replied, "but some friends were missing. The gray-haired couple. They were not in their usual seats in the fourth row."

The aide was surprised. "I didn't know you had friends in this town. Did you know them well?"

"I knew them very well," Paderewski explained, "but I never met them. I liked the way they listened. Every time I have played here for 20 years I have always played for them." He shook his head gravely. "I hope there's nothing seriously wrong."   —*Howard Taubman*

THE UNCOMMON WILL ROGERS

By Eddie Cantor

EVER SINCE that tragic day in 1935 when Will Rogers crashed to his death in Alaska on a round-the-world flight, America has been searching for someone to take his place. So sorely missed is Will's way of making us laugh at ourselves that anyone with the slightest hint of his sharp, dry humor is quickly dubbed "the new Will Rogers."

Impossible! Will was irreplaceable.

I first met Will Rogers in 1912 when we were on the same vaudeville bill at the Orpheum Theater in Winnipeg, Canada. Right away I knew this Oklahoma cowboy was like no other actor I'd ever met. He actually enjoyed listening as much as talking. Before I knew it, I had told him how I'd grown up in a New York tenement, how I'd gotten into show business, and on and on. I think I realized then that the day was to come when I would love him more than any other man I'd ever known, with the kind of deep and admiring love I might have had for a father or older brother.

Once, trying to muster nerve to make a radical change in my act, I asked his advice. He gave me that wonderful squinty smile of his and said in his casual way, "Why not go out on a limb? That's where the fruit is." His own success as a performer, and as a man, was the result of a lifetime "out on a limb"—never hesitating when instinct impelled action, always saying what he thought.

Born William Penn Adair Rogers in Oologah, Indian Territory, near Claremore, Oklahoma, he was proud of his 5/16 Indian blood. In the early days he billed himself "The Cherokee Kid," and he later originated the classic comment, "My ancestors didn't come over on the *Mayflower*—they met the boat."

By the time I met Will he had already made a name for himself. He was the ridin'est, ropin'est, broncobustin'est cowboy anywhere. Will had left home in his early twenties and gone to Argentina to look for a job. From there he traveled to South Africa, and was punching cattle in Ladysmith in 1902 when he first turned his hand (literally his rope) to performing in Texas Jack's Wild West Circus.

It was at the old Hammerstein Theater in New York that Will began talking during his trick-roping act. One night when he found himself snared by the lariat, he drawled, "A rope ain't bad to get tangled up in if it ain't around your neck." His casual humor made a hit. Soon he was ad-libbing about what he'd read in the papers, and his fame as a homespun philosopher began to grow. There was an enduring quality about what Will Rogers said or wrote:

"Our foreign dealings are an open book—a checkbook."

"I reckon some folks figure it's a compliment to be called 'broad-minded.' Back home, 'broad-minded' is just another way of sayin' a feller's too lazy to form an opinion."

"Too many people spend money they haven't earned to buy things they don't want, to impress people they don't like."

Perhaps his best-known quip was made at a dinner in New York. I sat on the dais next to Will, who was toastmaster. All of us who were to speak had agreed that each would "get on and off" in eight minutes. But one man kept rolling along for 45 minutes before he wound up with, "Mr. Toastmaster, I'm sorry if I overstayed my time, but I left my watch at home."

Rogers hunched forward, furrowed his brow and said, friendly-like, "There was a calendar right behind you." Will Rogers poked fun at people only if they were riding the crest of the wave and could take it.

With his daily column in hundreds of newspapers, his stage and radio appearances and his motion pictures, Will had enough success to swell any man's head. But he continued to wear a wrinkled "store" suit and a ready-made shirt. He used his time and money for more important things. During World War I, a good part of his salary went to the Red Cross. He always had needy actors on his payroll. As a speaker he received hefty fees, which he turned over to various charities.

He never had a written contract with Florenz Ziegfeld. In 1915 they just shook hands and that was it. Until Rogers, Ziegfeld looked upon all comedians as mere parsley around his main dish—the girls. Will didn't hesitate to kid him about this. The first words he uttered on a Ziegfeld stage were: "Y'know, folks, I'm just out here while the girls make a change. Imagine, changin' from nothin' to nothin'!"

On one of Will's radio broadcasts he announced a surprise guest, "the President of the United States, Calvin Coolidge." Then, imitating Coolidge's voice, he began: "It gives me great pleasure to report on the state of the nation. The nation is prosperous on the whole, but how much prosperity is there in a hole?" Many listeners thought it really was the President and were incensed later when they learned it had been Rogers. Will felt bad about the misunderstanding, but President and Mrs. Coolidge enjoyed the gag and invited him to the White House for dinner.

Just before Will was to meet Coolidge, a friend bet him that he couldn't make dour Cal laugh in two minutes. "I'll bet he laughs in 20 seconds," answered Will. Then came the introduction: "Mr. Coolidge, I want to introduce Mr. Will Rogers."

Will held out his hand, looked confused and said, "Excuse me, I didn't quite get the name." He won his bet.

During the White House dinner, Mrs. Coolidge said there was only one person who could do a better impersonation of Calvin Coolidge than Will—and that was herself. She went into a monologue that won Will's applause. "Yes, that's mighty fine, Mrs. Coolidge," he conceded. "But think what you had to go through to learn it." .

Will liked making motion pictures because it gave him a chance to spend more time with his family. By 1934 he was the top favorite on the screen. One of his great hits was *State Fair*, in which a prize boar called "Blue Boy" was used. The last day of shooting, the studio suggested that Rogers buy the boar for the family larder. Rogers declined. "I wouldn't feel right eatin' a fellow actor," he said.

Blessed with rugged health, Will never thought of consulting a doctor, much less an eye specialist. One day his fellow star, Thomas Meighan, saw him holding a paper at arm's length. "For heaven's sake, Will, take my glasses," he said. Will put them on, finished his paper and walked away with the glasses in his pocket. He used them from then on.

Rogers got into his famous gumchewing routine quite by chance. One matinee, he walked on stage, chewing gum by mistake. The audience burst into laughter as Will parked the gum on the proscenium arch. He went into his act, and when he'd taken his last bow and was about to walk off, he got another laugh as he retrieved the wad and said, "It ain't that I'm stingy, but there's a lot of mileage left in this."

Will was an early flying enthusiast. And when the famous pilot Wiley Post invited him to fly around the world in the summer of 1935, Will eagerly accepted. The trip brought death to both men when the plane crashed near Point Barrow, Alaska.

Not long after Will was killed I went to Claremore, where a Will Rogers Memorial Museum had been established. Walking through the museum, I noticed the churchlike silence. People were speaking in whispers, a moving tribute to a man whose goodness had been as eloquent as his wit. In glass cases were mementos which Will had given some of his friends and which we, in turn, had sent to the museum. I lingered in front of one containing a heavy silver filigreë belt and gun. I remembered how happy I was the day he gave them to me and how sad I was when I shipped them off.

Set apart from the rest of the treasures was the most poignant object of all: his typewriter, with a page still in the roller. The smashed keys told the story of the crash more graphically than if they had pecked out the words. Will had been typing his daily column when the end came. It's small comfort, but at least he died doing what he liked best—writing and flying.

As I left the building I looked back, and there was Will—a likeness so real you could hardly believe it was bronze. Jo Davidson, the sculptor, had captured everything—even to the twinkle in Will's eyes. He almost seemed to be speaking. And in a way he was, for carved at the base of the statue were the words that are the key to his personality: "I never met a man I didn't like."

Years ago, when many people were saying Hoover should be denied a second nomination and that Calvin Coolidge should be drafted, George Horace Lorimer, of the *Saturday Evening Post*, received a telephone call from Mr. Coolidge. Mr. Coolidge wondered if Mr. Lorimer would be interested in buying an article from him stating his attitude toward Mr. Hoover and the Republican convention. Mr. Lorimer was definitely interested and sent Thomas Costain to Northampton to talk with Mr. Coolidge.

"How much are you prepared to pay me?" asked Mr. Coolidge right off the reel.

"Ten thousand dollars," said Mr. Costain.

Mr. Coolidge studied his shoes for a while, then left the room. Five minutes later he returned. "Ten thousand two hundred and fifty dollars," he said, "and not a penny less." And walked out again.

Mr. Costain swooned. Had Mr. Coolidge asked for $12,000 or $15,000—but $10,250. . . . He looked helplessly at Mr. Coolidge's secretary. The latter smiled. "You don't seem to realize," he explained, "that Mr. Coolidge comes from Vermont. He figures that a thing worth $10,000 can be sold for at least 2½ percent more."   —*Frederick Van Ryn*

A GOOD SOLDIER

By Grace Perkins Oursler

THE BOY had fallen, running home after school, and skinned his left knee. It was no more than a scratch—there wasn't even a rent in his trousers—but by night the knee started to ache. Nothing much, he thought, being 13 and the sturdy son of a frontiersman. Ignoring the pain, he knelt in his nightgown and said his prayers, then climbed into bed in the room where he and his five brothers slept.

His leg was painful the next morning, but he still did not tell anyone. The farm kept the whole family relentlessly busy; always he had to be up at six to do his chores before school. And he must be thorough about them or he would be sent back to do them over again, no matter what else he had to miss, including meals. In their household, discipline was fair but stern.

Two mornings later the leg ached too badly for him to drag himself to the barn. It was Sunday and he could remain behind while the rest of the family drove to town. He sat in the parlor and half dozed until his brothers returned from Sunday school. Mom and Dad did not come home with them because Sunday was parents' day off; the boys did the housework and cooked the big meal of the week, while father and mother stayed on for church service. But by the time dinner was ready the boy had climbed into bed. The shoe had to be cut off his swollen and discolored leg. Why on earth hadn't he told somebody? Go quick and fetch the doctor!

Mother bathed knee and foot and thigh, applied poultices and wiped the boy's sweating forehead with a moist, cool cloth. She was an intense and vital woman. Confronted with this angry infection, she remained serene. Mom had nursed her brood through accidents and ailments from toothaches to scarlet fever; one son she had lost, but that only made her calmer and more determined when she had to fight for the others.

Old Dr. Conklin examined the leg and pursed his lips. "It's not likely we can save it!"

The invalid sat up stiffly. "What's that mean?" he asked huskily.

"It means," explained the doctor gently, "if things get worse we'll have to amputate."

"Not me!" stormed the boy. "I won't have it! I'd rather die!"

"The longer we wait, the more we will have to take off," urged the doctor.

"You won't take *any* off!" The boy's voice broke with an adolescent crack, as his mother turned away, shaken. But there was no adolescence in the eyes that defied the doctor's reproachful gaze. Dr. Conklin stalked out, nodding to the mother to follow him. As he stood in the hallway explaining to both parents about what could and probably would happen, they could hear the boy calling for his brother: "Ed! *Ed!* Come up here, will you?"

The brother stamped in and then they heard the sick lad's voice, high-pitched with pain: "If I go out of my head, Ed, don't let them cut off my leg. Promise me, Ed—*promise!*"

In a moment Ed came out and ran to the kitchen. When he returned his mother said, "Ed, what's your brother asking for?"

"Fork! To bite on; keep from screaming."

Then Edgar stood outside the bedroom door, his arms folded. Quite clearly he was standing on guard. Ed looked straight at old Dr. Conklin. "Nobody's going to saw off that leg!" he announced.

"But, Ed—you'll be sorry," gasped the doctor.

"Maybe so, Doc. But I gave him my word." And nothing changed that. If Ed had not stood his ground, father and mother might have yielded. They were not yet convinced that amputation was necessary; they were doubtful. The unshakable attitude first of the sick boy and then of his brother was incredible, for defiance of parental authority was unknown in this household. Yet there was Ed, standing before the sickroom door. "Guess we'll wait and see how he looks by tonight, eh, Doc?" said the father.

For two days and nights Ed stood guard, sleeping at the threshold, not leaving even to eat. The fever mounted, and the suffering boy babbled in torment, but the older brother showed no weakening of resolve, even though the discoloration of the swollen leg was creeping toward the pelvis, just as the doctor had predicted. Ed remained firm because he had given his promise, and also because he shared the frontiersmen's horror of being less than physically perfect.

The parents knew that their son would never forgive an amputation, and Ed's attitude continued to be decisive, time after time, when the doctor returned. Once, in helpless rage, Dr. Conklin shouted, "It's murder!" and slammed the front door. Nothing but a miracle could save the boy now!

Mother, father and watchful brother Ed shared the same thought, as their anxious eyes turned from the doorway. Had they forgotten their faith in the turmoil of their fears? Why, this sick boy's grandfather, that vigorous and inspiring old farmer-minister who had been leader of the River Brethren colony in Pennsylvania, had always believed in healings wrought by faith. Now, in this desperate hour, the three went to their knees at the bedside. They prayed, taking turns in leading one another. Father, mother— and at last Edgar—would rise and go about the farmwork and rejoin the continual prayer. During the second night the other four brothers would join in the prayers from time to time.

The next morning, when the old doctor stopped by again, his experienced eye saw a sign. The swelling was going down! Dr. Conklin closed his eyes and made a rusty prayer of his own—a prayer of thanksgiving. Even after the boy dropped into a normal sleep, one member of the family after another kept the prayer vigil.

It was nightfall again and the lamps were lighted when the boy opened his eyes. The swelling was way down now, and the discoloration had almost faded. In three weeks—pale and weak, but with eyes clear and voice strong—the boy could stand up.

And Ike Eisenhower was ready to face life.

THE WISEST ONE

By Max Eastman

HE WAS a funny-looking man with a high bald dome, a face very small in comparison, a round upturned nose and a long wavy beard that didn't seem to belong to such a perky face. His ugliness was a standing joke among his friends and he helped them enjoy the joke. He was a poor man and something of a loafer—a stonecutter by trade, a sort of second-string sculptor. But he didn't work any more than was necessary to keep his wife and three boys alive. He preferred to talk. And since his wife was a complaining woman who used her tongue the way an angry teamster used a horsewhip, he loved above all things to be away from home.

He would get up before dawn, eat a hasty breakfast of bread dipped in wine, slip on a tunic and throw a coarse cloak over it, and be off in search of a shop, or a temple, or a friend's house, or the public bath, or perhaps just a familiar street corner, where he could get into an argument. The whole town he lived in was seething with discussions and arguments. The town was Athens, and the man we are talking about was Socrates.

Not only was he funny-looking, but he had funny ways and notions, and a good-natured magnetic stubbornness in sticking to them. One of his friends had asked the oracle at Delphi who was the wisest man in Athens. To the astonishment of all, the priestess had mentioned this loafer, Socrates. "The oracle," he said, "picked me for the wisest Athenian because I am the only one who knows that he doesn't know anything."

This attitude of sly and slightly mischievous humbleness gave

him a terrific advantage in an argument. It made him something of a pest, really. Pretending that he himself didn't know the answers, he would badger people with questions, like a district attorney, and lead them to make astounding admissions.

Socrates was the evangelist of clear thinking. He went about the streets of Athens preaching logic—just as 400 years later Jesus would go about the villages of Palestine preaching love. And like Jesus, without ever writing down a word, he exercised an influence over the minds of men that a library of books could not surpass. He would go right up to the most prominent citizen, a great orator or anybody, and ask him if he really knew what he was talking about. A distinguished statesman, for instance, would have wound up a patriotic speech with a conclusion about courage, about the glory of dying for one's country. Socrates would step up to him and say, "Pardon my intrusion, but just what do you mean by courage?"

"Courage is sticking to your post in danger!" would be the curt reply.

"But suppose good strategy demands that you retire?" Socrates would ask.

"Oh well, then, that's different. You wouldn't stay there in that case, of course."

"Then courage isn't either sticking to your post or retiring, is it? What *would* you say courage is?"

The orator would knit his brow. "You've got me—I'm afraid I don't exactly know."

"I don't either," Socrates would say. "But I wonder if it is anything different from just using your brains. That is, doing the *reasonable* thing regardless of danger."

"That sounds more like it," someone in the crowd would say, and Socrates would turn toward the new voice.

"Shall we agree then—tentatively, of course, for it's a difficult question—that courage is steadfast good judgment? Courage is presence of mind. And the opposite thing, in this case, would be presence of emotion in such force that the mind is blotted out?"

Socrates knew from personal experience about courage, and the listeners knew he knew, for his cool and sturdy behavior in the Battle of Delium in the Peloponnesian War was, like his physical endurance, a matter of wide note. And he had moral courage too. Everybody remembered how he alone had defied the public hysteria which followed the naval battle at Arginusae in the Aegean Sea, when ten commanders were condemned to death for failure to rescue drowning soldiers. Guilty or not, it was unjust, he had insisted, to try or to condemn men in a group.

The above conversation was, of course, in its details imaginary. But it illustrates the essential thing that made this enchantingly frog-faced and persuasive man, Socrates, a turning point in the history of civilization. He taught that all good conduct is conduct controlled by the mind, that all the virtues consist at bottom in the prevailing of mind over emotion.

Besides insisting on the moral importance of clear thinking, Socrates took the first great step toward teaching men how to do it. He introduced the idea of defining your terms. He would say, "Before we start talking, let's decide what we are talking about." This undoubtedly had been said before in private conversations, but Socrates made a gospel of it.

For three generations before Socrates, Greek philosophers had studied nature and the stars, giving birth in a magnificent intellectual flowering to what we call *science*. Socrates turned scientific method to the study of the art of living. In his day the marvelous world of Greek city-states and Greek culture stretched around the Mediterranean Basin and across the Black Sea to the coast of Russia. Greek merchant ships dominated Mediterranean trade. Under the leadership of the great commercial city Athens, the Greeks had just defeated the armies of Persia. To Athens there now flocked, from all over the world, artists, poets, scientists and philosophers, students and teachers. Rich men from as far away as Sicily sent their sons to follow Socrates on his walks and listen to his peculiar arguments. The old man refused to charge a fee.

All the great schools of philosophy that sprang up in the Greek and, later, Roman worlds claimed descent from him. Plato was his pupil and Aristotle was Plato's pupil. We are still living in the

Socratic heritage. The teaching of Socrates might not have impressed the world so deeply had he not died a martyr to it. It seems strange to put a man to death for "introducing general definitions." And yet, if you think what that new technique, when stubbornly pursued to its logical conclusions, can do to time-honored emotional beliefs, Socrates' fate is not surprising. To his young and progressive friends Socrates seemed the mildest of men, but he must have been regarded as a troublemaker by thousands of old fogies and even by many thoughtful, moderate persons. There were two formal charges against Socrates: he did not believe in the gods recognized by the city, and he "corrupted the young."

It is not clear today exactly what Socrates' accusers meant, but certainly young people loved this old man. The lure of new ideas, the invitation to think for themselves drew them to him, but their parents feared they were learning revolutionary doctrines. Then, too, one of his students, the hotheaded and unstable Alcibiades, had gone over to the enemy during the war with Sparta. It was no fault of Socrates'. But Athens, smarting under defeat, was looking for scapegoats.

Socrates was tried by a jury of 501 citizens, and condemned to death by a margin of only 60. Probably very few of them expected him to die. He had the legal privilege, for one thing, of proposing a milder penalty and calling for a vote on that. If he had done this humbly, lamenting and imploring as was customary, more than 30 would doubtless have changed their votes. But he insisted on being rational about it.

"One of the things I believe in," he said to the disciples who came to him in prison urging escape, "is the reign of law. A good citizen, as I've often told you, is one who obeys the laws of his city. The laws of Athens have condemned me to death, and the logical inference is that as a good citizen I must die."

This must have seemed a little cantankerous to his anxious friends. "Isn't that carrying logic a little too far?" they protested. But the old man was firm.

Plato has described Socrates' last night on earth in the dialogue *Phaedo*. Socrates spent that night, as he had most of the others, discussing philosophy with his young friends. The subject was: Is there a life after death? Socrates was inclined to think so, but he kept his mind open and listened thoughtfully to the objections of his students who took the opposing view. To the end, Socrates kept his head and did not let his emotions influence his thinking. Though he was to die in a few hours, he argued calmly about the chances of a future life.

As the hour approached, his friends gathered around and prepared their hearts to see their beloved teacher drink the cup of poison. He sent for it himself a little before the sun set over the western mountains. When the attendant brought it in, Socrates said to him in a calm and practical tone, "Now you know all about this business, and you must tell me what to do."

"You drink the hemlock and then you get up and walk around," the attendant said, "until your legs feel heavy. Then you lie down and the numbness will travel toward your heart."

Socrates very deliberately and coolly did as he had been told, only pausing to rebuke his friends for sobbing and crying out as though he were not doing the wise and right thing. His last thought was of a small obligation he had forgotten. He removed the cloth that had been placed over his face and said, "Crito, I owe a cock to Asclepius—be sure to see that it is paid."

Then he closed his eyes and replaced the cloth, and when Crito asked him if he had any other final directions, he made no answer.

"Such was the end," said Plato, who described this death scene in unforgettable language, "of our friend, who was of all whom we have known the best and most just and wisest man."

By all means marry. If you get a good wife, you will become very happy; if you get a bad one, you will become a philosopher—and that is good for every man.   —*Socrates*

The shortest way to live with honor in the world is to be in reality what we appear to be.   —*Socrates*

PROPHET IN POETRY

By Ralph McGill

Until he was 35 Carl Sandburg was totally unknown to the literary world. Since then his prose and poetry have achieved wide recognition and renown. He has won two Pulitzer Prizes—one in 1940 for his four-volume Abraham Lincoln: The War Years, *the other in 1951 for his* Complete Poems. *Also well known are his* Abraham Lincoln: The Prairie Years *(1926),* Mary Lincoln, Wife and Widow *(1932),* Remembrance Rock *(1948).*

CARL," said Lillian Steichen Sandburg, "will be down any minute now. Even when he works till dawn he is up by lunchtime." I waited on the porch on that day in 1953, rocking in one of the big, old-fashioned chairs. My thoughts were on the man with the boyish heart who, at 76, still poured forth writing and song possessing the simple beauty and strength of the marching blue mountain ranges of the Appalachians on which I looked.

Soon there was a booming voice and Carl Sandburg came out. We sat and talked. As always on a visit to Connemara, the first subject was the view. It stretched across miles of tumbled ranges all the way to towering Mount Mitchell, clothed in the haze of blue which the Indians said was the shadow of the Great Spirit.

The Sandburgs came to the North Carolina mountains in 1945 from Harbert, Michigan. The cold and winds of winter had moved them to decision, and one summer they drove southward. They found the house called Connemara about a mile and a half up from Flat Rock, sitting alone, surrounded by pine, hemlock and rhododendron. Perhaps it was just chance—though it is easy to believe it a sort of destiny—that brought this son of a Swedish immigrant, internationally famous as the biographer of Abraham Lincoln, to the pillared house built by one of the "rebel chieftains" of Lincoln's war years. Connemara had been the home of Christopher Gustavus Memminger, secretary of the Confederacy's treasury.

Sandburg and his family took Connemara to their hearts. First there was much carpentering and plastering to do. "There came a time," said Sandburg, "when I began to look in the crannies and under old stones to see if the Secretary of the Treasury had left any money around—even Confederate—to help pay the contractor." But at last the work was done.

"Then came the great move," Sandburg recalls, "mostly books and goats." Goats? In Michigan there had been a shed. It was too small for a cow, which Carl wanted. "We'll get a goat, then," he said. And they did. From that one milk goat the herd grew to 160 purebreds, known and respected by all the nation's goatkeepers. This was later reduced by sale to a nearby dairy, leaving only enough goats to supply the Sandburgs' needs.

When I visited him, Carl Sandburg's working quarters at Connemara consisted of a neat, Spartanlike bedroom and a small workroom with a window which looked out on the ancient mountains. His habit was to begin work in the late afternoon and often keep at it into the dawn. He wore an old-fashioned green eyeshade, such as newspaper editors once used, and most of the time there was the stub of a "seegar" in his mouth. Sandburg liked to relax with his old guitar, used in hundreds of lectures in which he sang folk ballads or some of his poems. He would sit on the front porch and make up songs as the mood came to him, about the hills, the visitors or a big news story of the day.

He has always had the natural simplicity of a truly great person. It might be said that he inherited this simplicity and faith. Among Sandburg's earliest recollections is that of his father, who toiled ten hours a day in the railroad shops at Galesburg, Illinois. The elder Sandburg couldn't write, but could read a little. The son remembers him bent over the Bible—a Swedish Bible from the old country—and he remembers, too, his mother's prayers and her whole way of life, which was, in a very real sense, a living testament of faith.

A letter his mother wrote in 1926, a few days before her death, helps to explain Sandburg's gentleness and humility and deep feeling for humanity. In her groping words can be seen the foundations for some of her son's poems. "Life is short if early days are lost. . . . With thought and love in the home so much can be overcome. . . . I find so much comfort in the thought of wise men; the Bible is full of it. . . . Crushed I am many times, but not to death. The apron of silence is with me. Silence is a gift. Be silent."

During one of my visits with Sandburg, our talk turned to his six Lincoln books. And then he was off: "You take Lincoln when he floated a flatboat down the Sangamon River in the summer of 1831—going to New Salem. It was a town of just about a dozen families at the time, yet for the young man from the prairie it was a great metropolis. Think what it meant to him, the rawboned young fellow out of the backwoods!

"At New Salem there was a gristmill run by the Rutledges and Camerons. [Sandburg spoke as if they were actual acquaintances of his.] A man could hear all sorts of talk there as the farmers, from all parts of the new country and the old, came to grind their corn and wheat. And there was a school taught by Mentor Graham, a college graduate. Graham developed a special friendship for young Lincoln and soon had him devouring books. A debating society was organized, and Lincoln made his first real speech before it. There was talk and enterprise there to sharpen the mind. It was in New Salem that young Lincoln began to find himself, to take on polish and to react to the best in his environment. When he moved on to Springfield he was ready for life."

There was more about Lincoln. Sandburg seemingly has never forgotten a single scrap of information discovered in many years of research on Lincoln. He felt so near to his subject that when he wrote the last chapters of *The War Years* he had to stop work from time to time to control his tears. Now and then people come to him and ask somewhat plaintively: "What would Abe Lincoln do now?"

"Well," he will tell them, "all I can say for sure is that he would eat, sleep and think a lot . . . especially the latter."

People mean much to Sandburg: he thinks of them as human beings, not as problems or statistics. He is patient with all persons with dreams—especially young writers. (He has never forgotten the friends who encouraged him, and who listened to him read and sing.)

Being with Carl Sandburg, listening to him or just sitting looking at the blue ridges, one was apt to forget that this famous, gentle man was once a poor, lonely and bewildered boy; was once a barbershop bootblack; was once a hobo, a dishwasher, a day laborer. Sometimes he seemed almost like one of the old prophets who came out of the desert's loneliness with a vision.

Now in his advanced years, he faces the future with a faith from the pages of his father's old Swedish Bible and from his mother's life. "The Chinese," he says, "have a saying that after 70 a man is like a candle in the wind . . . but sometimes the winds are soft . . . and if, when a man comes to die, he has a boy's heart, is that a bad thing?"

President Lincoln was asked if it were true that he had said, when someone complained to him that General Grant was drinking, "I must find what brand of whisky he drinks, so I can send a few barrels to the other generals."

Lincoln replied, "No, I didn't happen to say it—but it's a good story, a hardy perennial. I've traced that story as far back as George II and General Wolfe. When certain persons complained to George that Wolfe was mad, George said: 'I wish he'd bite some of the others.'" —*Clara E. Laughlin*

THE VICTORIOUS
MADAME CURIE

Condensed from Madame Curie

By Eve Curie

Translated by Vincent Sheean

IN THE FALL of 1891 a young Polish girl named Marie Sklodowska excitedly registered for the science course at the
Sorbonne in Paris. Often in the corridors young men would
pass this shy and stubborn-faced girl who dressed with poverty-
stricken simplicity, and would ask: "Who is it?" But the answer
was vague. "It's a foreigner with an impossible name. She is always in the first row at the physics courses." The boys' eyes would
follow her graceful outline down the corridor, and they would
conclude: "Fine hair!" The ash-blonde hair and the little Slavic
head were, for a long time, the only identification the students at
the Sorbonne had for their timid comrade.

But young men were what interested this girl least. She was entirely fascinated by her scientific studies and worked as if in a
fever. Every minute she did not study was a minute lost. Too shy
to make friends with the French, Marie Sklodowska took refuge
among her fellow countrymen in the colony which formed a little
island of free Poland in the Latin Quarter of Paris. There her life
was one of stark simplicity, devoted to study alone. Her income—
made up by her own savings from her work as a governess in
Poland, and the small sums her father, an obscure but cultured
teacher of mathematics, could send her, was but 40 rubles a

month. From this slim amount—*three francs* a day—she had to pay for her room, meals, clothes and all expenses at the university.

Marie did not admit that she could be cold or hungry. In order not to buy coal she often neglected to light her stove, and she wrote figures and equations without noticing that her fingers were numb and her shoulders shaking. For weeks at a time she ate nothing but buttered bread and tea. When she wanted a feast, she bought two eggs, or a piece of chocolate or some fruit. On this diet the fresh, solid girl who had left Warsaw a few months before grew anemic. Often, as she stood up, her head would go round. She had just time to get to her bed when she would lose consciousness. Coming to, she would think herself ill and ignore her illness as she did everything else that interfered with her work. It never occurred to her that her only disease was starvation.

Marie had ruled love and marriage out of her life's program. Dominated by the passion for science, at 26 she still clung fiercely to her independence. Then came Pierre Curie. A French scientist of genius, he was devoting body and soul to scientific research, and was unmarried at 35. He was tall, possessed long sensitive hands, a rough beard and an expression of rare intelligence and distinction. Their first meeting occurred in 1894 in the laboratory, and immediate sympathy brought them together. Pierre Curie found Mlle. Sklodowska truly an astonishing person. How strange to talk to a young and charming woman, using technical terms, complicated formulas. . . . How sweet it was!

Pierre Curie tried to get on friendly terms with the girl. He asked if he could visit her. Friendly but reserved, she received him in her little room. In an almost empty attic, with her threadbare dress and her stubborn expression, Marie had never seemed more beautiful. What fascinated Pierre was not only her total devotion to her work, but also her courage and nobility. In a few months Pierre Curie asked Marie to be his wife. But to marry a Frenchman, leave her family forever and abandon her beloved Poland seemed to Mlle. Sklodowska unthinkable. Ten months had to pass before she finally accepted the idea of marriage. The first days of their life together Pierre and Marie roamed the country-side on bicycles purchased with money given them as a wedding present. They lunched on bread and cheese and fruit, stopped at unknown inns, and at the cost of some thousands of pedal strokes and a few francs for village lodgings, had the luxury of solitude for long enchanted days and nights.

The young couple settled in a little flat at 24 rue de la Glacière. The bare walls were furnished only with books; there were two chairs and a white wooden table. On the table were treatises on physics, an oil lamp, a bunch of flowers, and that was all. Little by little Marie improved in housekeeping wisdom. She invented dishes which needed little preparation or could be left to "cook themselves." Before going out, Marie would regulate the flame with a physicist's precision: then, casting one last worried glance at the stewpans she was entrusting to the fire, she would fly down the stairs and catch up with her husband. In a quarter of an hour, bent over other containers, she would regulate the flame on a laboratory burner with the same careful gesture.

In the second year of their marriage, Marie gave birth to a daughter: Irène, a beautiful baby and a future Nobel Prize winner. The idea of choosing between family and the scientific career did not even cross Marie's mind. She kept house, washed her baby daughter and put pans on the fire, but she also kept on working in a laboratory—working toward the most important discovery of modern science up to that time.

At the end of 1897 the balance sheet of Marie's activity showed two university degrees, a fellowship and a monograph on the magnetization of tempered steel. The next goal was a doctor's degree. Casting about for a research project for this, Marie was attracted by a recent publication of the French scientist Antoine Henri Becquerel, who had discovered that uranium salts *spontaneously* emitted, without exposure to light, some rays of unknown nature. A compound of uranium, placed on a photographic plate surrounded by black paper, made an impression on the plate through the paper. It was the first observation of the strange and unusual occurrence to which Marie later gave the name of *radio-*

activity, but the nature of the radiation and its origin remained a mystery. Becquerel's discovery fascinated the Curies. What was the source of the energy which uranium compounds constantly released as radiation, they wondered. Here was an absorbing subject of research—a leap into an unknown realm.

Thanks to the director of the School of Physics where Pierre taught, Marie was given the use of a little ground-floor storeroom for her experiments. Scientific research in this hole was not easy. And the climate there, fatal to sensitive precision instruments, was not much better for Marie's health.

While deep in her studies of uranium rays, Marie discovered that compounds of another element, thorium, also emitted spontaneous rays like those of uranium. Moreover, in each case the radioactivity was a great deal stronger than seemed justified by the quantity of uranium or thorium contained in the products examined! Where did this abnormal radiation come from? Only one explanation was possible: the minerals must contain, in small quantity, a *much more powerfully radioactive substance* than uranium and thorium. But what substance? In her experiments, Marie had examined *all known chemical elements*. Then minerals must contain a radioactive substance which must be a hitherto unknown chemical element.

A new element! Pierre Curie, who had followed the rapid progress of his wife's experiments with deep interest, now abandoned his own experiments in order to aid hers. In the damp workroom, two brains, four hands, now sought the unknown element. They separated and measured the radioactivity of all the elements in pitchblende, an ore of uranium. As the field of investigation narrowed, their findings indicated the existence of two new elements instead of one. By July 1898, they were able to announce the discovery of one of these substances. Marie named it *polonium*, after her beloved Poland.

In December 1898, the Curies announced the existence of a second new chemical element in pitchblende which they called *radium*—an element whose radioactivity they believed to be enormous. Now, nobody had ever *seen* radium. Nobody knew its atomic weight. To prove the existence of polonium and radium, the Curies were now to labor for four years. They already knew the method by which they hoped to isolate the new metals, but it meant handling very large quantities of crude material.

Pitchblende, in which polonium and radium were hidden, was treated at the Joachimsthal mines in Bohemia to extract uranium salts used in making glass. It was a costly ore, but according to the Curies' calculations, the extraction of uranium should leave polonium and radium intact. Then why not work the surplus, which had very slight value?

From the Austrian government they obtained a ton of the substance, and began work on it in an abandoned shed close by the little room where Marie had done her first experiments. It had no floor and was furnished with some worn kitchen tables, a blackboard and an old cast-iron stove. "And yet," Marie wrote later, "it was in this miserable old shed that the best and happiest years of our life were spent, entirely consecrated to work. I sometimes passed the whole day stirring a boiling mass with an iron rod nearly as big as myself. In the evening I was entirely broken with fatigue." In such conditions M. and Mme. Curie worked from 1898 to 1902. Dressed in her old dust-covered and acid-stained smock, her hair blown by the wind, surrounded by bitter smoke which stung her eyes and throat, Marie was a virtual factory all by herself. Finally in 1902, 45 months after the day on which the Curies announced the probable existence of radium, Marie achieved victory: she succeeded in preparing a decigram of pure radium and determined its atomic weight. Radium now officially existed.

Unfortunately, the Curies had other struggles. Pierre's salary at the School of Physics was $1200 a year, and after Irène's birth the cost of a nurse made heavy inroads on the budget. New resources had to be found. In 1898, a chair of physical chemistry fell vacant at the Sorbonne and Pierre decided to ask for it. It paid $2000 a year and would mean fewer hours of lessons; but he was rejected. Pierre was to obtain the post of professor only in 1904, after the whole world had acclaimed his worth. For the present he had to accept an inferior position at the Sorbonne. Meanwhile Marie secured a professorship at a girls' school near Versailles.

The Curies continued to teach, with a good will and without bitterness, giving to the job their best efforts. And torn between their own work and their jobs, they forgot to eat and sleep. On several occasions Pierre was obliged to take to his bed by attacks of intolerable pain in the legs. Marie was upheld by her tense nerves from a breakdown, but friends were startled by the pallor and gauntness of her face. Thus radioactivity grew and developed, meanwhile exhausting little by little the pair of physicists who had given it life.

Purified as a chloride, radium appeared to be a dull white powder, much like common kitchen salt. But its properties were stupefying. Its radiation passed all expectation in intensity; it proved to be two million times stronger than that of uranium. The rays traversed the hardest and most opaque matter. Only a thick screen of lead proved able to stop their treacherous penetration.

The last and most moving miracle was that radium could become the ally of human beings in the war against cancer. Radium was *useful*—and its extraction no longer had merely experimental interest. A radium industry was about to be born. Plans for making use of radioactive ores had been made in several countries, particularly in Belgium and in America. But engineers could produce the "fabulous metal" only if they knew the secret of the delicate operations involved.

Pierre explained these things to his wife one Sunday morning. He had just finished reading a letter from some technicians in the United States who wanted to use radium in America, and had asked for information. "We have two choices," Pierre told her. "We can describe the results of our research without reserve, including the processes of purification . . ." Marie made a mechanical gesture of approval and murmured: "Yes, naturally."

"Or else," Pierre went on, "we can consider ourselves to be the 'inventors' of radium, patent the technique of treating pitchblende, and assure ourselves of rights over the manufacture of radium throughout the world."

Marie reflected a few seconds. Then she said: "It is impossible. It would be contrary to the scientific spirit." Pierre's serious face lightened. "I shall write tonight, then, to the American engineers, and give them the information they ask for."

A quarter of an hour after this little Sunday-morning talk, Pierre and Marie headed for the woods on their beloved bicycles. They had chosen forever between poverty and fortune. In the evening they came back exhausted, their arms filled with leaves and field flowers.

In June 1903, the Royal Institution officially invited Pierre to London to lecture on radium. Following this came a deluge of invitations to dinners and banquets, for all London wanted to see the parents of radium. In November 1903, the Royal Society of London bestowed on Pierre and Marie one of its highest awards: the Davy Medal.

Next, recognition came from Sweden. On December 10, 1903, the Academy of Science of Stockholm announced that the Nobel Prize in Physics for the current year was awarded half to Antoine Henri Becquerel, half to M. and Mme. Curie for their discoveries in radioactivity. This Nobel Prize meant some $15,000, and it was not "contrary to the scientific spirit" to accept it. A unique chance to release Pierre from his hours of teaching, to save his health! When the check was paid, there were presents and loans to Pierre's brother, to Marie's sisters, subscriptions to scientific societies, gifts to Polish students, to a childhood friend of Marie's. Marie also installed a "modern" bathroom in their house and repapered a shabby room. But it never entered her head to mark the occasion by buying a new hat. And she kept on with her teaching, although she insisted on Pierre's leaving the School of Physics.

When fame opened her arms to them, telegrams piled up on the huge worktable, there were newspaper articles by thousands, hundreds of requests for autographs and photographs, letters from inventors, poems on radium. An American even wrote to inquire if he could name a racehorse after Marie. But, for the Curies, their mission was not finished; they wanted only to work.

Marie wrote in the spring of 1904: ". . . Always a hubbub. People are keeping us from work as much as they can. Now I have decided to be brave and I receive no visitors—but they disturb me just the same. Our life has been altogether spoiled by honors and fame. . . . Our peaceful and laborious existence is completely disorganized."

At the end of her second pregnancy, Marie was near exhaustion. On December 6, 1904, another daughter was born, crowned with shaggy black hair: Eve, the author of this biography. Marie soon resumed the routine of school and laboratory. The couple were never seen in society. But they could not always get out of official banquets in honor of foreign scientists. On such occasions Pierre would don evening clothes and Marie would put on her one evening dress.

On July 3, 1905, Pierre Curie was elected to France's Academy of Sciences. Meanwhile the Sorbonne had created a chair in physics for him—the post so long desired—but still there was no adequate laboratory. Eight more years of patience were required before Marie was to install radioactivity in a dwelling worthy of it—a dwelling which Pierre was never to see. Towards half past two on Thursday, April 19, 1906—a sultry, rainy day—Pierre took leave of the professors in the Faculty of Science, with whom he had been lunching, and went out into the downpour. As he attempted to cross the rue Dauphine, Pierre absentmindedly stepped from behind a cab into the path of a heavy wagon. Surprised, he attempted to hang on to the chest of the horse, which suddenly reared. The scientist's heels slipped on the wet pavement. The driver pulled on the reins, but the wagon, dragged on by its weight of six tons, continued for several yards. The left back wheel passed over Pierre.

Six o'clock: Marie, gay and vivid, appeared in the doorway of her home. She found callers, and vaguely perceived in their attitude the signs of compassion. As they gave an account of the facts, Marie remained motionless. After a long, haggard silence, her lips moved at last: "Pierre is dead? Dead? Absolutely dead?"

From the moment when those three words, "Pierre is dead," reached her consciousness, she became an incurably lonely woman.

After the funeral, the government officially proposed to award the widow and children of Pierre Curie a national pension. Marie refused flatly: "I don't want a pension," she said. "I am young enough to earn my living and that of my children."

On May 13, 1906, the council of the Faculty of Science unanimously decided to award Pierre's chair at the Sorbonne to Marie. This was the first time that a position in French higher education had been given to a woman. On the day of her first lecture at the Sorbonne, the crowd filled the amphitheater and overflowed into the corridors and into the square outside. Necks were craned so as not to miss Mme. Curie's entrance. What would be the new professor's first words? Would she thank the Minister, the university? Would she speak of Pierre Curie? Yes, undoubtedly: the custom was to begin by pronouncing a eulogy of one's predecessor. . . .

Half past one. . . . The door at the back opened, and Marie Curie walked to her place in a storm of applause. She inclined her head. It was a dry little movement intended as a salute. Standing, Marie waited for the ovation to cease. It ceased suddenly. Marie stared straight ahead of her and said: "When one considers the progress that has been made in physics in the past ten years, one is surprised at the advance that has taken place in our ideas concerning electricity and matter. . . ." Mme. Curie had resumed the course at the precise sentence where Pierre Curie had left it. Having reached the end of her arid exposition without flinching, Marie retired by the little door as rapidly as she had come in.

Now the personal fame of Mme. Curie mounted and spread like a rocket. Diplomas and honors from foreign academies arrived by the dozen. And although the Academy of Sciences failed to honor her with membership—Marie missed being elected by one vote—Sweden awarded her the Nobel Prize in Chemistry for the year 1911. Not for more than 50 years was another person judged worthy of receiving such a recompense twice.

The Sorbonne and the Pasteur Institute jointly founded the Curie Institute of Radium, comprised of two parts: a laboratory of radioactivity, directed by Marie Curie; and a laboratory for biological research and the study of cancer treatment, directed by an eminent physician. Against the advice of the family, Marie made the laboratory a gift of the radium, worth more than a million gold francs, which she and Pierre had prepared with their own hands. To the end of her life this laboratory remained the center of her existence.

In 1921 the women of America raised $100,000 to buy a gram of radium to be presented to Marie Curie. In exchange they asked her to visit them. Marie hesitated. But, touched by the magnificent generosity, she conquered her fears and accepted for the first time, at 54, the obligations of a great official journey. At the landing pier in New York an enormous mob waited five hours for her. From the moment of her arrival it was apparent how much the timid Mme. Curie meant to America. Even before knowing her, the Americans had surrounded her with an almost religious devotion; now that she was among them, their homage was boundless.

Most of the universities of America had invited Mme. Curie to visit them. Medals, honorary titles and degrees were awaiting her by the dozen. But she was stunned by the noise and the applause. The staring of countless people frightened her, as did the violent jostling. She was afraid of being crushed in one of these terrible eddies. Eventually she became too weak to continue her trip, and on the advice of her doctors she returned to France.

I believe the journey to America changed my mother's mind about her determined isolation. As a research worker she might cut herself off and concentrate entirely on her own work. But Mme. Curie at 55 was something other than a research worker: the prestige of her name was such that by her mere presence she could assure the success of some project dear to her. From now on she was to reserve a place in her life for these missions. Her journeys now were much alike. Scientific congresses, lectures, university ceremonies and visits to laboratories called Mme. Curie to a large number of capitals, where she was feted and acclaimed.

Warsaw built a radium institute—the Marie Sklodowska-Curie
Institute—and the women of America accomplished a new miracle by collecting the money for the purchase of a gram of radium
for it—the second gram given by America to Mme. Curie. The
events of 1921 repeated themselves: in October 1929, Marie
again sailed for New York, to thank America in the name of
Poland. She was the guest of President Hoover and stayed at the
White House for several days. But nothing in her had changed:
neither the physical fear of crowds nor her incurable modesty. It
was always the laboratory—and its young scientists—that held
first place in Marie Curie's heart. "I don't know whether I could
live without the laboratory," she once wrote.

Marie had always scorned the precautions which she imposed
on her pupils: to manipulate tubes of radioactive bodies with
pincers, never to touch unguarded tubes, to use leaden "bucklers"
or shields to ward off the harmful radiations. She barely consented
to submit to the blood tests which were the rule at the Institute of
Radium. Her blood content was abnormal. What of it? . . . For 35
years Mme. Curie had handled radium and breathed the substances given off by radium. During the four years of the war she
had been exposed to the even more dangerous radiation of the
Roentgen apparatus. Slight deterioration in the blood, annoying
and painful burns on the hands, were not, after all, such very
severe punishments for the number of risks she had run!

Marie paid little attention to the light fever which began to
trouble her. But in May 1934 she took to her bed after an attack
of the grippe and did not leave it again. When at last the robust
heart beat no more, science pronounced its verdict. The abnormal
symptoms, the strange, unprecedented blood tests, accused the
true criminal: radium.

On Friday, July 6, 1934, at noon, without speeches or processions, without a politician or an official present, Mme. Curie modestly took her place in the realm of the dead. She was buried beside Pierre in the cemetery at Sceaux, in the presence of her
relatives, her friends, and the co-workers who loved her.

ARCHITECT
OF DEMOCRACY

By Donald Culross Peattie

O NE OF our greatest Presidents of the past was born
at the foot of the Blue Ridge, near Charlottesville, Virginia, in 1743. Thomas Jefferson set the real American
standard of living when, at only 33, he penned the Declaration of
Independence. "I have sworn upon the altar of God," he said,
"eternal hostility against every form of tyranny over the mind of
man." Unlike Washington, he was never in battle; he was a civilian
hero. Though he could not free the slaves, he tried to, and succeeded as nearly as was possible without destroying the new nation by a civil war. Jefferson shoulders his way to a place with
Lincoln and Washington on the strength of moral greatness and
manifold genius. For he, the apostle of the common man, was one
of the most uncommon who ever lived.

His mother, a Randolph, brought the child blue blood; his
pioneer father, who died when Thomas was only 14, imparted a
sturdy, democratic strain. Entering the College of William and
Mary at 16, practically on his own, the tall, hazel-eyed boy with
the sandy-red hair went hard at his books. He specialized in English
law, which, uniquely then, regarded all men as equal before Justice.
His notebooks are a digest of profound reading on government,
law, ethics and philosophy. When his neighbors in Albemarle
County elected the 26-year-old, newly admitted lawyer to the colonial legislature of Virginia, he was already one of the most deeply
read and original thinkers in the land.

And already the people of America were rising to fulfill his ideal of them. In Williamsburg revolution seethed, until in 1774 the royal governor dismissed the rebellious legislature; Jefferson and other members proceeded without a governor. With Patrick Henry, George Mason, Francis Lightfoot Lee, Richard Henry Lee, Dabney Carr, Peyton Randolph and George Washington, Jefferson sent a call to the other colonies to meet in a Continental Congress. As a delegate to the congress, and a member of the committee to draw up a declaration of independence, Jefferson could now announce to the world that democratic philosophy which still guides us.

It is true that others, like Benjamin Franklin and John Adams, suggested some ideas for the great document. But the noblest and the newest were Jefferson's own. In an earlier statement Congress had claimed our rights to "life, liberty and *property*." Young Jefferson, himself a man of property, struck out the last word and, in the Declaration, substituted what was possible to even the poorest—"the pursuit of happiness." For he believed in happiness and in the people, and he saw that "it is the people's sweat that is to earn all the expenses of the war, and their blood which is to flow."

Refusing a third term in the Continental Congress, Jefferson modestly went back to the state legislature of Virginia, where, he said, he could "do the most good." While the Revolution was fought out on bloody fields, this rugged statesman worked to win the peace. Revising old feudal and strict moral laws to fit the new freedom, he conceived and executed revolutionary changes which became models. He abolished the decree by which the eldest son inherited all, although himself an eldest son; he established a system of free public education and—for the first time in the history of Christendom—separated church and state, thereby securing religious freedom on this continent. "It behooves every man who values liberty of conscience," he sternly warned, "to resist its invasion in others."

During the Revolution, Virginia twice made him its governor. And once he missed, by five minutes, capture at the hands of

Tarleton's raiders. But "Monticello," his home near Charlottes-ville, was spared by the British because of his humane and cour-teous treatment of war prisoners. The war over, Jefferson refused a third term as governor, and in 1783 entered the Congress of the United States. At each session he put in place new and precious building blocks of government. For pounds and shillings he in-troduced our present system of dollars and cents. He formulated the plan of government for territories not yet states. He, a Vir-ginian, got Virginia to cede to the federal government all her claims to the present Middle West that is east of the Mississippi. He succeeded in abolishing slavery at least north of the Ohio, and so probably tipped the balance that would one day save the Union in the Civil War.

Jefferson was made minister to France in 1785; there he saw the Bastille fall. Next it was as Secretary of State that Washington wanted him. Under Adams he was Vice President, and in 1801 he became the third President of the United States, the first to be inaugurated in Washington. When he went unguarded on foot from Conrad's boardinghouse to the Capitol to take the oath of office, the world saw that a new kind of ruler had appeared in it.

Under Jefferson we paid off a great proportion of the national debt and yet reduced taxes. On tax policy, "pay as you go" were his very words. The people had the leader they wanted, and they swept him back to a second term on a landslide. In return, he doubled for them the size of the United States. For 15 million dol-lars he bought from Napoleon everything between the Mississippi and the Rockies. His enemies screamed at the useless extravagance of the Louisiana Purchase. What he had bought was one of the richest parts of the earth—at less than three cents an acre. And he knew what to do with it; he sent Lewis and Clark to carry the flag to the very mouth of the Columbia River and so thwart the claims of Canada, Mexico and Russia to our Pacific Northwest.

He looked south of our continent too, and saw with rejoicing the beginning of Bolívar's great work of liberation from Spanish oppression. He looked into the future and foreshadowed the good-neighbor policy. He learned to speak Spanish fluently and thought all North Americans should. "I hope to see," he wrote, "a cordial fraternization among all the American nations . . . and their coalescing in an American system of policy. . . . I should rejoice to see the fleets of Brazil and the United States riding together as brethren of the same family, pursuing the same objects."

In 1809 Jefferson once more refused a third term of office, and retired forever from politics to his country estate of Monticello. There for 17 years he exercised his diverse gifts as architect, farmer, inventor, naturalist and philosopher. You may still see in the beautiful old mansion the clever gadgets he rigged up, the weather vane with the dial in the hall, the dumbwaiters and tunnels and private staircases, the machine which could write letters in duplicate, and the indoors-and-outdoors clock with cannonball counterweights, one for each day in the week. At Monticello he was happy, despite tragic losses; his beloved wife, Martha Skelton, and four of his six children had died. But Monticello remained to him as a lifelong passion. An ardent gardener and a scientific farmer, he was ahead of his time in soil conservation and contour plowing, by which furrows are formed to help prevent the washing away of soil by rainfall. Indeed, he invented an excellent plow, and introduced such plants as cork oaks, olives and upland rice, distributing them to experimenters all over the country.

The mansion itself, designed in detail by its master, took 35 years to build. Jefferson was a born architect; through this most civic and logical of the arts he visibly expressed that power to build which he showed in political form too. Monticello's domes and pillars and symmetrically balanced wings fathered the style called "southern plantation." The architect had early shown his gift when he assisted the French engineer L'Enfant in designing the federal city; his hand appears in the dome and columns of our national Capitol, and the mode thus set was copied in our state capitols and later taken up in Paris and London.

But his pet and pride was the University of Virginia. Not only did he plot its beautiful buildings and grounds (a model for campuses ever after) but he created the university itself. Breaking with the old classics-and-theology theory of higher education, he laid emphasis on modern languages, liberal arts, the sciences, and an administration free of any religion or sect. Teachers of the day were startled when he founded a chair of agriculture and provided an astronomical observatory; students were delighted when he instituted the honor system.

His belief in the students was of a piece with his main political faith: that if you give the American people the facts, they will act wisely. So he urged the establishment of free circulating libraries for every county in the land; the Library of Congress itself is built upon a nucleus of a personal collection of 13,000 volumes from Monticello. Of all books, he knew best and loved best the greatest one. Indeed, he created a sort of Reader's Digest version of it, known today as the "Jefferson Bible." This is simply the essence of the New Testament, arranged and condensed under the title *The Life and Morals of Jesus*. Thomas Jefferson quietly announced his own religion thus: "I am a Christian in the only sense Christ wished anyone to be—sincerely attached to His doctrine in preference to all others." Out of that simple Christianity was conceived the democracy that he blueprinted.

Yet "Long Tom," as the people affectionately called him, was a fellow livable and lovable. He reverenced women, adored children, delighted in flowers. He had a boy's curiosity and inventiveness; he had a frontier mind that looked always to the West, the direction of our future. Personally simple in habit, he was lavishly hospitable. Under bitter attack from the party of his political enemies, the Federalists, he never lost his smiling, quiet dignity. It was Abraham Lincoln, the first Republican President, who said, "The principles of Jefferson are the axioms of a free society." And, wise as Jefferson was in the ways of the world, he could yet say honestly, "The glow of one warm thought is worth more to me than money."

It has been said that it would take ten experts to evaluate Thomas Jefferson, to measure the breadth of his mind and the height of his spirit, and to appreciate the many kinds of man he was: Jefferson the architect, Jefferson the philosopher, Jefferson the lawmaker, the inventor, the farmer, the writer, the Bible student and moralist, the naturalist, the diplomat, and Jefferson the leader of what has been called "the second American revolution," the battle of those who believed in the people against those who feared them. But while we are listing experts to appraise our third President, we would need to call up a musician, a mathematician, a linguist, a humorist, a gardener, a lover—and still we haven't turned all the flashing facets of his genius.

History chose the Fourth of July, 1826—the 50th anniversary of the signing of the Declaration of Independence—for the day when Thomas Jefferson entered into immortality. Behind him he left these words: "I shall not die without a hope that light and liberty are on a steady advance. Even should the cloud of barbarism and despotism again obscure the science and liberties of Europe, this country remains to preserve and restore light and liberty to them. . . . The flames kindled on the Fourth of July, 1776, have spread over too much of the globe to be extinguished by the feeble engines of despotism; on the contrary, they will consume them and all who work them."

Tall, kindly, quizzical, a little stooped, he walks among us still, with that friendly but noble bearing. And words that he said when the United States was young are truer now than when he spoke them: "During the greatest of all wars . . . our country will require the union of all its friends to resist its enemies within and without. . . . The only contest between divided friends should be who will dare farthest into the ranks of the common enemy."

Man's mind stretched to a new idea never goes back to its original dimensions.   —*Oliver Wendell Holmes*

The tree of liberty must be refreshed from time to time with the blood of tyrants. It is its natural manure.—*Thomas Jefferson*

TERROR OF THE WORLD

By *Edwin Muller*

W ERE the accounts of all battles, save only those of Genghis Khan, effaced from the pages of history . . . the soldier would still possess a mine of untold wealth from which to extract nuggets of knowledge useful in molding an army." That was said by General Douglas MacArthur.

The soldier, General MacArthur explained, cannot learn his profession solely by practice. Though weapons change, he must go to the past to learn the basic elements of the art of war. Nowhere can he find them better illustrated than in the career of the Emperor of the Mongols—some 750 years ago.

Genghis Khan won by conquest the greatest empire that the world has ever seen. It extended from the Pacific to mid-Europe, including most of the then known world and more than half its population. His city of Karakorum, in central Mongolia, became the chief capital of the Oriental world, which threatened to engulf the forces of Christendom.

Napoleon ended in defeat; Genghis Khan never lost a decisive battle. He died an old man, at the peak of his victories and with his empire still vigorously expanding. Caesar and Alexander the Great owed much to their predecessors, who had perfected the Roman legion and the Macedonian phalanx; the Mongol Emperor developed his own military machine. His armies were nearly always greatly outnumbered. Probably he could never put more than 200,000 men in the field, but with that small force he crushed empires of many millions. He was perhaps the most successful soldier in all history. "Genghis Khan" means "Mightiest Ruler." He chose the name for himself, having been known in early years as Temujin.

When Temujin was 13 years old his father was poisoned by his enemies. Temujin already had the strength and stature of a man. He could stay in the saddle all day and could shoot a powerful arrow. And he was strong in spirit. He was resolved to succeed his father as chieftain of the tough tribe of nomads on the steppes, those harsh, treeless regions of high Asia. But the tribesmen would have none of him, and the other chieftains determined to get rid of this young rival. They hunted Temujin across the steppes like an animal, caught him and put a heavy wooden yoke on his neck and bound his wrists to it. One night he struck down his guard with the yoke and escaped. He hid in a stream while horsemen rode up and down the bank looking for him. Later he crept out and persuaded a roaming hunter to release him from the yoke.

The historical account of those early years is a record of hair-breadth escapes from pursuit and treachery; but he kept to his fixed purpose of fighting his way to leadership. He won loyal followers, and his father's men began to shift back to him. Before he was 20 he was a chieftain. Then he began to intrigue and fight to bring other tribes into a league with his own. Always he was the leader. Invariably he killed anyone who sought to share power with him. Jamuga was his cousin. In the lean days they had slept under the same blanket, had shared their last scraps of food. But Jamuga, not content to be a subordinate, gathered his own followers. The two clashed in battle. In the end Jamuga stood before his cousin, a prisoner. Temujin calmly ordered him strangled to death.

Togrul had been the friend of Temujin's father and had helped the boy at a critical period. But when the older chief was not willing to submit to the youth, Temujin had him killed. On the other hand, he lavishly rewarded leaders willing to serve under him. The years went by. He made his headquarters in Karakorum, the City

of the Black Sands—a city of tents on the great east-west caravan route. Temujin did not molest the caravans; they had a place in his scheme for the future.

He was a sturdy figure, clad in sheepskins and hardened leather, with the unwieldy gait of a man who had lived in the saddle. His face, deeply lined, leathery, had a coating of grease against the cold and the biting wind. It is likely that he never washed from one year's end to the next. His eyes, set far apart under a sloping forehead, red-rimmed from the blowing dust, glowed with a fierce intensity. He spoke little and then after long meditation.

At the age of 50 Temujin had welded the tribes of central Asia into one united force of which he was sole leader. His name spread far across the steppes. And yet, if at that time an enemy's arrow had found the right spot in his armor, history would scarcely have heard of him. The mighty deeds of his life were crowded into his last 16 years. He had built a military machine to conquer the world. Now he set out to use it.

To the east was China, the world's oldest civilization. It was divided then into two empires, the Kin and the Sung. To the west was Islam, the separate nations that had grown from the conquests of the great Mohammed. Farther west were Russia, then a mass of petty states, and middle Europe, a jumble of large and small powers. First the Khan attacked China. He forced his way through the Great Wall and hurled his columns across the vast spaces of the Kin, or northern empire. The capital, Yenking (now Peiping), was taken, the emperor put to flight. It was a complete rout.

Three years later Genghis Khan moved west. Within a few months Mongol troopers were plundering the lovely capital of Samarkand, and the Sultan was fleeing for his life. In the years that followed, the armies of the Khan overran the Middle East, went on through Russia into central Europe. Everywhere they were victorious. Why? Genghis Khan had an unconquerable will, a violent energy of body and mind, an utter ruthlessness. But his greatness lay in something more than that.

Genghis Khan had the ability to brush away all traditions, to go straight at a problem with a completely new approach. He could take all the available methods, techniques, weapons, and mold them, in infinite detail, to his purpose. He was the first to organize a nation for the exclusive purpose of waging war; some 750 years ago he had the supposedly modern concept of "total war." In the Mongol horse and rider he had magnificent raw material. The horse was tireless. It could get along if watered once in three days. It could find fodder under any conditions, pawing down through snow and ice for remnants of dry grass. The rider could stay in the saddle a day and a night, could sleep in the snow, keep going on little or no food. He was brought up on hand-to-hand combat, taught to shoot as soon as he learned to talk.

In equipping this natural soldier Genghis Khan showed his genius for planning and detail. The Mongol's armor was of rawhide, hardened and lacquered. Each man had two bows, one for use on horseback, one for greater precision on foot. He had three types of arrows: for long, medium and close range. The heavy, metal-tipped short-range arrows were designed to pierce armor. Each trooper carried an emergency ration of dried milk curd; half a pound would nourish him for a day's fighting. He had spare bowstrings, and wax and needle for repair work. He carried his equipment in a leather bag which could be inflated for crossing streams. The army was built in units of 10's, 100's, 1000's, and 10,000's. Besides the fighters there were supporting troops: the engineers and specialists who operated stone-throwing catapults and other siege machinery, the quartermaster corps, a remount service, arsenal keepers, a lost-and-found department. And back of the army was the nation, all working to produce food and equipment for the army while themselves living on as little as possible.

The tactics developed by Genghis Khan were a marvel of precision acquired by intensive training. The battle formation was in five ranks, the squadrons separated by wide intervals. In front were the shock troops. Heavily armored, they used sabers, lances and maces. At the rear were the mounted bowmen. The bowmen advanced at a gallop through the intervals between shock-troop squadrons and opened fire while riding at full tilt. At close range they would dismount, shift to their heavier bows and pour in volleys of the heavy arrows. The essence of the attack was an intensity and concentration of fire hitherto unknown.

Once the enemy was disorganized, the shock troops charged to complete the rout. It was a smooth-working combination, perfectly coördinated. There were no shouted commands. Orders were sent by waving black and white flags. The Mongol attack won by superiority in weapons, speed in bringing those weapons into contact with the enemy, and then by rapidity and accuracy of fire. The armies of China, the dashing warriors of Islam, the knights and men-at-arms of Christendom, all broke before the Mongol hail of arrows.

Although the armies of the Great Khan were outnumbered, he usually had the most troops on hand at the actual point of battle. He knew how to divide the enemy's forces and concentrate his own. He was a master of deception, turning up in one place when the foe expected him in another. He won by flanking movements rather than by costly direct attacks. His campaigns were based on speed and mobility, on his ability to outmarch the enemy two to one. His swift columns would penetrate the opposing armies, cut them into many parts, then destroy them one by one. He moved past the strongly held fortresses, leaving them to fall later.

Some of Genghis Khan's wars were half won by propaganda before he put an army in the field. In the use of words as weapons no commander has surpassed this barbarian who couldn't read or write. His secret supporters were the caravan merchants. Through them he hired agents in each country that he planned to attack. He studied the foe's geography, people, politics; he sought out discontented elements and set one against another. His spies in Islam reported that the Sultan's mother was jealous of her son's power. Genghis Khan dictated a letter to her. It pretended to be in answer to one of hers, thanked her for her offer of help. Then he saw to it that the messenger was captured by the Sultan. When Genghis Khan marched, his armies found the country not far short of civil war. He bribed dishonest politicians. His agents discovered that the Chinese war minister had been stealing funds.

When the news was spread, it caused a political crisis in China just as the Mongols were marching to the attack.

He also used propaganda as a weapon of terror. It was his regular practice to remind the country he planned to invade of the dreadful things that had happened to others who had resisted the Great Khan. Submit or be killed, he warned. If his foes submitted, he marched in and annihilated them anyway. He used propaganda skillfully at home to build up morale. He praised the soldier's profession, made it seem natural that all others should toil to keep the soldier in the field. He taught his people that the Mongols were a race apart, superior to all others.

With him terrorism was a cold and passionless policy. If a city resisted him, he burned the place and slaughtered men, women and children. It was a thorough process. When his army marched away, he left a few of his men and a handful of captives concealed in the ruins. Later the captives were forced to go about the city shouting that the Mongols had gone. When the few inhabitants who had escaped emerged from hiding, the Mongols killed them, too. Heads were cut off to prevent anyone from feigning death. In one city alone 500,000 civilians were slaughtered.

Such was the military machine with which Genghis Khan conquered the world. He died on a campaign in 1227, aged 66, at the height of his power. After his death the machine went rolling on. His successors became the lords of all Asia. They drove deeper into Europe, beat the Hungarians, Poles, Germans. None could stand against them. The Mongol power was still supreme under Kublai Khan, grandson of Genghis. It fell apart at last in the hands of less able descendants. Today the Mongols are again only a weak group of nomad tribes. Karakorum has vanished under the drifting sands of the Gobi Desert. Its name is almost forgotten.

But the name of Genghis Khan is not forgotten nor are the great Mongol's conceptions of "the unvarying necessities of war," as General MacArthur pointed out. Separated from "the ghastly practices of his butcheries, his barbarism and his ruthlessness, they stand revealed as kernels of eternal truth," as perilous to ignore in modern times as they were over seven centuries ago.

KING OF THE ROAD

By Joe McCarthy

AFTER THE death of Henry Ford, a cardboard shoe box containing personal belongings was found under a workbench in the experimental laboratory at his home. In it, among other things, was a tightly sealed test tube with a neatly printed label that said, "Thomas Edison's Last Breath."

Ford was devoted to Edison because the inventor encouraged him to go ahead with his gasoline-driven automobile back in 1896 when most people were scoffing at the idea. The horseless carriage had obsessed Ford since a fateful moment 20 years earlier when he was 13: he was riding beside his father on a farm wagon near Dearborn, Michigan, when he saw a steam engine moving along a country road under its own power, a chain attached from the engine to the rear wheels. Little Henry's eyes bulged. He had seen steam engines before—they were used on farms for threshing and sawing wood—but this was the first he had seen in motion without a horse pulling it. As Ford clearly recalled years later, the engine stopped to let his father's horses pass, and "I was off the wagon and talking to the engineer before my father knew what I was up to."

From that day on, Ford wanted no part of farming. He learned to be a mechanic, worked as a repairer of farm machinery, ran a sawmill. In 1891, when he was 28, he broke the news to his wife, Clara, that he was taking a job as night engineer at the Detroit power plant of the Edison Illuminating Company for $45 a month. He explained that it was a chance to learn about electricity, which he needed to use in his long-planned gasoline engine. The

thought of moving to the city and leaving her newly built house in Dearborn dismayed Clara, but she packed their things without complaint. Henry had outlined to her his scheme for a horseless carriage, and she believed in it as firmly as he did.

During the next two years, according to Ford's diaries, he was so engrossed in the gasoline engine that often he forgot to pick up his pay at the Edison plant. On Christmas Eve in 1893, when his son Edsel was seven weeks old and Clara was busy preparing to entertain her family at dinner the next day, Ford carried his first completed engine into their kitchen.

He mounted the engine in the sink and asked Clara to help him start it. He showed her how to pour gasoline from a cup into the metal container that served as a carburetor, and how to turn the screw that would feed the fuel into the intake valve while he turned the flywheel. He connected his crude spark plug with the electric current of the house and gave Clara the signal to start pouring.

The engine—it had one cylinder, made from a piece of gas pipe—coughed and shuddered, shaking the kitchen sink and throwing flames out of its exhaust valve. Ford watched it run for a few minutes. Then he waved Clara aside and let the engine die down. It worked; that was all he needed to know. He began work immediately on a two-cylinder engine.

Ford's rented home in Detroit was half of a two-family house. Behind it there was a brick shed for tenants' coal. Ford used his half of the shed as a workshop. It was here, at four o'clock in the morning of June 4, 1896, that he finished his first automobile and took it out for a drive down Grand River Avenue to Washington Boulevard, where it stalled from ignition trouble. Two months later, at an Edison convention in New York, Ford was introduced to Edison as a fellow who had made a gasoline car. Edison wanted to know more about it. He watched Ford make sketches on a menu, then said, "You have it—a self-contained unit that carries its own fuel. That's the thing! Keep at it!" Ford left the dinner walking on clouds.

Ford didn't invent the automobile, but he was the first motor-car maker to go after the mass market when most other automobile manufacturers were designing expensive playthings for rich men. The car Ford had in mind was to be a sturdy and simple mechanism, light in weight and easily assembled so that its cost would fit the average man's pocketbook. He found the answer in his wonderfully uncomplicated Model T—later known as the Tin Lizzie or the flivver—and in the assembly line, which cut the time required for putting together a chassis from 14 hours to 1 hour and 33 minutes. Setting up assembly plants all over the country, Ford turned out Model T's at the rate of 1.6 per minute, 15 million of them in 19 years. Between 1917 and 1927 nearly half the cars made in the United States were Fords. And Henry relentlessly lowered their prices so that still more people could buy them—from $850 in 1908 to $290 in 1925.

The Model T made the Ford Motor Company the most dazzling enterprise in American business. Its incredible success is summed up in the oft-told story of Rosetta Hauss, a sister of James Couzens, the company's first business manager. Couzens tried to sell Rosetta $200 worth of his shares, but she was full of doubts. Finally she invested $100. During the next 16 years she received $95,000 in dividends, and in 1919, when Ford bought out his minority stockholders, she sold her $100 share for $260,000.

Henry Ford was a character as memorable as anybody in fiction. President Franklin D. Roosevelt once invited him to have dinner at the White House with the King and Queen of England. Ford sent back word that he couldn't make it because his wife's garden club was meeting that day.

Ford was a collector of violins, McGuffey Readers and all sorts of early Americana. He was also a bird watcher, a folk dancer, a health-and-diet faddist who never permitted smoking in any of his factories or offices. Sometimes he ate carrots for days, and when he was specializing in a soybean diet, he ordered not only soybean soup and soybean bread but also soybean ice cream.

Henry tried to dominate everyone around him except his wife, Clara, a woman with a strong mind, who always had the last word.

She died in 1950, three years after her husband. They were married for 59 years, and during all that time were tenderly devoted companions. When Henry entered the door of Fair Lane, his estate in Dearborn, he would stand in the hallway and whistle. From upstairs or from her favorite chair on the sun porch, where both sat in the daytime with a pair of binoculars and an Audubon bird book beside them, his wife would whistle back to him. They spent their evenings alone together. She would read aloud to him such books as *The Yearling, Bambi* and *Gone With the Wind,* or they would both listen to "Amos 'n Andy" or "The Quiz Kids" on the radio. Her slightest whim was his command.

Henry gave Thomas Edison a mammoth testimonial dinner in 1929 on the golden jubilee of his electric light. It was attended by President Hoover and 500 other celebrities collected by Ford from all over the world at his expense. The cost of the dinner and the transporting and housing of the guests was said to have exceeded a million dollars. Ford later asked his personal artist, Irving R. Bacon, to paint a picture of the Edison dinner. It was 7 feet high and 17 feet wide, with 266 recognizable portraits of the guests; it took several years to complete.

From time to time Ford would drop in to suggest changes in the painting. "Take that woman out," he said one day, pointing at the wife of a Ford company official. "Mrs. Ford doesn't like her." Whenever he brought in a visitor to look at Bacon's work-in-progress, he would put his finger on the face of his wife and say, "There's the best-looking woman in the whole crowd." Various Ford executives who enjoyed Ford's approval when Bacon started the painting fell into disfavor before it was completed. He had them removed from the canvas, and new favorites inserted in their places.

At least one of the company's great decisions was made by Mrs. Ford. It took place in 1941 during the strike that arose when the CIO's United Automobile Workers were fighting for the right to organize the company's employes. Up to that time Henry had never recognized a union. Gate 4 of his giant River Rouge plant became famous as the UAW's bloodstained battleground. Finally, however, he was forced to permit a National Labor Relations Board election in the plant, and his workers voted for the CIO.

Charles Sorensen, Ford's longtime production chief, recalls in his memoirs, *My Forty Years with Ford*, that after the election Henry came to his office and said he would never sign an agreement with the CIO. "Close the plant," he said. "Let the union take it over if it wishes." The next morning Sorensen turned on his radio and heard that Ford not only had given in to the CIO, granting them a union shop, but had astounded the labor leaders by giving them additional concessions they had not asked: pay raises and a check-off system, whereby the company deducted union fees and assessments from the workers' paychecks and turned the money over to the union. A few weeks later Ford told Sorensen why he had suddenly changed his mind. "Mrs. Ford said there would be riots and bloodshed and she had seen enough of that," Ford said. "I'm sure now she was right."

An important character in the story of the Ford family, and one more subtle, more shaded with deep undertones than Henry, was his son, Edsel. A handsome, quiet man with a taste for fine things, Edsel was out of place in the Detroit of the Roaring Twenties. It was for him that in 1913 Henry started to build the stern and rather gloomy limestone house, Fair Lane, on 1369 acres adjoining the land where Clara and he had lived when they were first married. The mansion had a billiard room with the first indirect lighting seen in Detroit, a $30,000 organ, a bowling alley and an indoor swimming pool. And on Edsel's twenty-first birthday Henry gave him one million dollars in gold.

Ford executives say that Edsel, whom his father named president of the company at 26, was 30 years ahead of his time, not only in his ideas about automobile styling and engineering but in his theories of labor relations and the responsibilities of big business. Although Edsel never went to college—Henry was against higher education—he knew more about Cellini and Renoir than most art instructors. Clearly, a son like Edsel could never be understood by a father like Henry, and there were bound to be conflicts.

The differences between Edsel and Henry began to crop up in

the mid-twenties when it became apparent to everybody in the company except Henry that the Model T was finally losing its popularity. Henry had designed it for the bad roads of pre-World War I America, with emphasis on durability and economy rather than on comfort and looks. Now there were smooth highways with no mudholes, and the average motorist was willing to pay a few extra dollars for a more luxurious car. The Ford jokes of the vaudeville comedians were beginning to hurt. ("A Ford is like a bathtub. It's useful, but you don't want to be seen in it.")

In the higher circles of the Ford Motor Company, Henry was surrounded by yes-men who never disagreed with him. Only Edsel and a few desperate sales managers were brave enough to tell him that the Model T had to go. The elder Ford fought with his son. Finally, confronted with declining sales figures, he gave in. Then there were more clashes between the two Fords about the design of the new Model A. Edsel wanted a car with hydraulic brakes and a manually operated sliding gearshift, like the Chevrolet, which was beginning to creep up on the Ford in sales. Old Henry hated hydraulic brakes; he contended that their fluid would leak. Eventually, however, the elder Ford allowed a hand gearshift, but he stuck to mechanical brakes. After a long delay the Model A came out late in 1927. That was an extraordinary year for big front-page news stories, but in *Only Yesterday*, his history of the twenties, Frederick Lewis Allen rated the debut of the new Ford as "one of the great events of 1927."

From the standpoint of popular interest, no other car has enjoyed such a dramatic unveiling, because no automobile maker with Ford's reputation has ever made such a drastic change in his product. The new Tin Lizzie, still the lowest-priced car, now had not only such fixings as four-wheel brakes and a windshield wiper, but the buyer had his choice of several different colors! Tin Pan Alley celebrated the occasion with the smash song hit, "Henry Made a Lady Out of Lizzie."

After the friction with Edsel over the Model A, Henry Ford withdrew into semiretirement. He began to devote most of his time to his hobby of collecting Americana. He restored the Wayside Inn at South Sudbury, Massachusetts, and placed near it the red schoolhouse claimed to have been the one to which Mary was followed by her Little Lamb. He established the Edison Institute and Museum with its adjoining Greenfield Village, the tourist attraction near the Ford plant in Dearborn. The museum, later renamed after Ford, became a fascinating hodgepodge of old dresses, pots, lamps, sleighs, trolley cars, locomotives, buggies, printing presses, harnesses, furniture, plows and automobiles, including Ford's own "999," the racing car that broke speed records early in the century with Barney Oldfield behind the wheel. Years later, Ford said to Oldfield, "Well, Barney, you and I made each other." Oldfield replied, "Yes—and I did a much better job than you did."

Old Henry lived on until the spring of 1947, his 83rd year. On his last day he seemed to be in better health and spirits than he had enjoyed in a long time. He went for a drive through the Rouge plant and around the familiar sights in Dearborn. When he returned to his Fair Lane estate, he asked to stop at the powerhouse to see how Charles Voorhess, its superintendent, was getting on with the work on the electric turbines. Old Henry was very proud of Fair Lane's private power system: always independent, he wanted nothing from public utilities; he made his own electricity with water power from the River Rouge.

On this day, however, the Rouge was swollen by spring thaws and had overflowed its banks, flooding the turbines at the powerhouse and leaving Fair Lane without lights. Two motors had been brought in and attached to an auxiliary turbine, and while Old Henry was there, watching the work, the lights came on again. Ford looked at Voorhess and said with a grin, "You won't get sore, will you, if I tell Mrs. Ford I was the one who fixed the lights?" But the load was too much for the motors. That night they stopped and plunged Fair Lane into darkness.

Henry Ford, the miracle man of modern mechanical production, went out of the world as he had come into it 83 years before—by the light of a few candles and a kerosene lamp.

THE MICROBE SLAYER

By J. D. Ratcliff

A FEW YEARS AGO a restaurant in La Plata, Argentina, served hundreds of customers a salad dressing contaminated with the toxin that causes botulism, a deadly form of food poisoning. When 30 deaths resulted, terror seized the city. At once an appeal was flashed to a laboratory in Paris and, before the day was done, hundreds of glass vials of vaccine were winging across the Atlantic. This prompt action saved the lives of other stricken patients. On a sugar plantation in Madagascar, now the Malagasy Republic, an epidemic of bubonic plague broke out. A medical team from one of the 21 globe-circling substations of this same Paris laboratory was flown in and halted the epidemic.

Throughout the world countless millions of people are alive today because of the Pasteur Institute in Paris. Founded in 1888, when most medical discoveries were made on a hit-or-miss basis by lone workers in university laboratories, the Pasteur Institute ushered in the era of scientific medicine in which teams of trained men make planned attacks on killer diseases. In the past 75 years it has showered mankind with new drugs and vaccines.

Louis Pasteur was born at Dôle, France, on December 27, 1822. Until 1885 the little man with the scraggy goatee and a partially paralyzed leg was largely unknown to the nonscientific world. Others had seen and described microbes, but Pasteur was the first to grasp their vital importance for good and evil. He had written texts on fermentation that are still bibles for the wine, beer and vinegar industries. He had laid the foundation for germ-free surgery at a time when infection was the horror of operating rooms.

He had opened the way for pasteurized milk, which was to save millions of children from the ravages of tuberculosis.

Now Pasteur set himself another task. In his tiny laboratory on rue d'Ulm he pitted his talents against rabies—a disease so deadly that not one person in medical history had survived it. If the rabies virus were sufficiently weakened, Pasteur reasoned, it might be used as a protective vaccine, prodding the body to build defenses against the deadly full-strength virus.

At peril to his own life, he used a glass tube to suck saliva from the foaming mouths of rabid dogs, then injected this material into rabbits. When the disease began to rage in the rabbits, he extracted their spinal cords, chief target of the rabies virus. He hung the deadly cords up to dry, hoping this would weaken the virus to a point of impotency. Animal experiments proved his hunch correct; an emulsion made from the cords after 14 days of drying could no longer produce rabies in research animals. But it did protect them against the disease.

Would the emulsion afford the same protection for human beings? Pasteur had an opportunity to answer this fateful question on July 6, 1885. A nine-year-old boy, Joseph Meister, had been bitten 14 times by a rabid dog and was almost certainly doomed to die. Yet Pasteur knew that if he administered vaccine and it failed, his medical enemies might charge him with murder.

With anxious concern Pasteur shot vaccine made from 14-day rabbit cord into the stricken child. Next day the little boy got a stronger dose, from 13-day cord. On, on went the treatment. Finally the child got a dose from the cord of a rabbit that had died only the day before. As Pasteur had hoped, bodily resistance had built up to a point where even that ordinarily deadly injection caused no reaction. The child was safe.

The electrifying news spread. Scores of bitten people, seeking salvation, crowded into the tiny laboratory on rue d'Ulm. Among them were 19 Russian peasants bitten by a mad wolf about two weeks earlier. They knew but one word of French: "Pasteur." Because so much time had elapsed since they were exposed, Pasteur had slender hopes of saving them. Even so, he tried—and 16 survived!

Never before had public imagination been so captured by a research achievement. A worldwide movement got under way. Pasteur should have his own research institute. School children contributed coins. In Italy a Milan newspaper collected $1200 from readers. Czar Alexander III of Russia sent $20,000; the Emperor of Brazil and the Sultan of Turkey made contributions. The large brick building began to rise on rue Dutot—later to be renamed rue du Docteur Roux, after one of Pasteur's greatest disciples. At the dedication on November 14, 1888, attended by the President of France and other notables, Pasteur was so overcome by emotion that he dabbed at his tears while his son read his speech for him.

Though he was in frail health, Pasteur's head buzzed with plans. Since the world desperately needed trained researchers, his institute would become a training center. Since there were no firms to manufacture serums and vaccines, the institute would do it. Since disease knows no international boundaries, Pasteur Institute men would attack sickness anywhere.

Drawing on a declining fund of energy, Pasteur directed the work of his talented teammates. Albert Calmette would go to Saigon to start a vaccination campaign against rabies and smallpox. Alexandre Yersin would go to Hong Kong to battle bubonic plague. (He eventually identified the causative bacillus and developed a protective serum.) Pierre Roux would stay in Paris to devote his time to the most dreaded of childhood diseases—diphtheria.

Pasteur lived to see only the first of his institute's great triumphs. In 1894, a year before Pasteur's death, Roux was ready with a diphtheria antitoxin. At Children's Hospital he divided the diphtheria patients into two groups. One got the best treatment doctors could then provide—but no antitoxin. The other got his new treatment. Of 520 children conventionally treated, 60 percent died. Of the 488 receiving Roux's antitoxin only 25 percent perished. The door was now open for conquest of this awesome killer.

Over the years the Pasteur Institute has established a reputation as the world's most productive medical-research laboratory. One of its top achievements is BCG vaccine (for bacillus Calmette-Guérin, named after two Pasteur researchers), which prevents tuberculosis. More than 200 million people around the world have been given this vaccine, and it is largely credited with cutting short the TB epidemic that swept Europe after World War II. Pasteur researchers also produced the first antihistamine and the first synthetic curare—the muscle relaxant which stills contractions and makes organs lie quiet, thus simplifying abdominal surgery.

Throughout history, typhus has been a deadly companion of war; the disease, spread by lice, thrives in the overcrowding of uprooted populations and poor sanitation. In one of the great research breaks of our day, on the eve of World War II, Pasteur Institute's Dr. Paul Giroud discovered a typhus vaccine. During the war more than seven million doses were distributed by the International Red Cross to prisoner-of-war camps and other threatened areas. This contributed mightily to saving Europe from what might have been one of the great disasters of modern times.

While Dr. Jonas Salk and Dr. Albert Sabin were doing research on polio vaccine in the United States, a Pasteurian, Dr. Pierre Lépine, was working along parallel lines in Paris. All three found successful preventives, and millions of children the world over have received polio protection.

The Pasteur Institute has done a brilliant job of putting its findings to work in the field. Its chain of laboratories girdles the globe, from Martinique in the West Indies to Nouméa in the Pacific. Because of the work of mobile vaccination teams in former French West Africa—once a yellow-fever pesthole—there has not been a single case of yellow fever in that area since 1953.

The Pasteur Institute today is a far cry from the founder's tiny laboratory on rue d'Ulm. Nearly 2000 people work in its clutter of buildings in Paris and the suburb of Garches, another 2000 in its field stations. Pasteur insisted that his institute remain rigidly independent. Its annual budget of eight million dollars relies on no government subsidies, but supports itself from the sale of serums and vaccines, from donations and from foundation grants and endowment funds.

Big, busy, bustling as it is, there are still reminders of an earlier day. On the lawn at the institute stands a bronze statue of a little boy—Joseph Meister, who was the first to be saved from rabies and who lived out his life as an institute gatekeeper. Pasteur's apartment in his beloved institute is maintained exactly as it was at the time of his death. His instruments and laboratory notes are displayed in glass cases. Louis Pasteur has been called "a legend in the annals of humanity." So, too, is the institute he founded.

The only life worth living is the adventurous life. Of such a life the dominant characteristic is that it is unafraid. In the first place, it is unafraid of what other people think. Like Columbus, it dares not only to assert a belief but to live it in the face of contrary opinion. It does not adapt either its pace or its objectives to the pace and objectives of its neighbors. It is not afraid of dreaming dreams that have no practical meaning. It thinks its own thoughts, it reads its own books, it develops its own hobbies, it is governed by its own conscience. The herd may graze where it pleases or stampede when it pleases, but he who lives the adventurous life will remain unafraid when he finds himself alone. —*Raymond B. Fosdick*

When we encounter the rare individual whose conduct is inspired by a moral ideal, we cannot help noticing his aspect. Moral beauty is an exceptional and striking phenomenon— one never forgets it. This form of beauty is far more impressive than the beauty of nature. It gives to those who possess its divine gifts a strange, an inexplicable power. It increases the strength of the intellect. Much more than science, art and religious rites, moral beauty is the basis of civilization. —*Dr. Alexis Carrel*

THE F.D.R. LEGEND

By Hamilton Basso

WHEN THE historian of the future gets around to evaluating the character and influence of Franklin Delano Roosevelt, one of his conclusions certainly will be that within a few years of his death in 1945 a legend of glory had already begun to form about him.

A steady stream of books and reminiscences about him has appeared. His Secretary of Labor, Frances Perkins, wrote that she first met the future President when he was 28 years old and had just been elected to the New York state legislature. He seemed to her an ordinary, respectable young man with an artificially serious expression and little if any concern about social reform. He had the habit of throwing his head up and thrusting out his chin, which, in combination with his pince-nez and great height, gave him the unfortunate appearance of looking down his nose. Miss Perkins remembers an old-line politician, Tim Sullivan, saying to her, "Awful arrogant fellow, that Roosevelt." She also gives us a snapshot of Roosevelt arguing on the senate floor, his mouth pursed, his nostrils distended, saying, "No, no, I won't hear of it!"

Miss Perkins had gone to Albany to fight for a bill to establish a 54-hour week for women in industry in New York. She hoped Roosevelt would get behind the bill, but he did nothing to help. She took his indifference hard at the time, but, looking back in later years, she felt that his early lack of interest in social reform could be traced to "a youthful lack of humility, a streak of self-righteousness, and a deafness to the hopes, fears and aspirations which are the common lot."

Franklin D. Roosevelt was born January 30, 1882. His father was one of the leading members of the Hudson River gentry—a self-contained, comfortable, moneyed class. Young Roosevelt's playmates were the children of families in similar circumstances. Instead of being sent to school he was turned over to tutors. He was taken abroad several times, and enjoyed other vacations at the family summer place in Campobello, New Brunswick. It was not until he was 14, when he entered Groton, that he began to mingle with groups of boys his own age.

Roosevelt went to school, as author Alden Hatch has said, with a mind "like a jackdaw's nest, full of shiny bits of unrelated knowledge." But, says Mr. Hatch, touching on a point that Roosevelt's enemies often aimed at, "in all Franklin's miscellaneous collection of knowledge there was one significant blank: that was in relation to money." His sense of financial security was so strong that he never thought about it at all. At Groton, Roosevelt was interested in sports as well as in books, and went out for baseball, football, track and crew. His special love, and one that he never lost, was for boats. Even as President, Roosevelt was capable of almost childish vanity about his seamanship.

Roosevelt wanted to go to Annapolis, but his father persuaded him to go to Harvard instead. There he majored in government and history, joined all the right clubs and became editor of the Harvard *Crimson*. Graduating in 1904, he went to Columbia Law School. But here also, as at Groton and Harvard, Roosevelt was an indifferent student, and he did not graduate. He was admitted to the bar in 1907 by examination, but did not like practicing law any more than he had liked studying it.

So it would seem that F.D.R. went into politics largely because he did not know what else to do. In 1910 he was elected to the New York state senate, and in 1912, at the Democratic national convention, worked hard for Woodrow Wilson's nomination. When offered the post of Assistant Secretary of the Navy, he said, "I'd rather have that place than any other in public life."

One of his jobs was to listen to the grievances of state committeemen, and he gained a lasting insight into the workings of politics. "A little patronage, a lot of pleasure and public signs of friendship and prestige," he once told Frances Perkins, "—that's what makes a political leader secure with his people."

Roosevelt's attack of polio in 1921 was, in the opinion of nearly everyone who has written about him, the real educative process of his life. "The man emerged completely warmhearted, with humility of spirit and with a deeper philosophy," wrote Miss Perkins. "His viability—his power to grow in response to experience—was beginning to show."

Roosevelt went on to be governor of New York for two terms, but his health was whispered about as early as 1932. These rumors were silenced by Roosevelt's obvious and apparently inexhaustible vitality, but in 1944, after the passage of 12 years was reflected in thin hair, lost weight and a furrowed face, the stories revived. Roosevelt did not intend campaigning for a fourth term as President in 1944, but after reports showed that his opponent, Tom Dewey, was making a rather good campaign, he changed his mind. He also wanted to combat the whisperings about his health. "There has been this constant rumor that I'll not live if I am reelected," he announced one day at a Cabinet meeting. "Apparently 'Papa has to tell them.'" From electioneering he came back to Washington, having gained 12 pounds. "What'd you expect?" he asked. "These campaign trips get a little tougher, but I thrive on 'em!"

Roosevelt had a genuine affection for Winston Churchill. He felt confident that he would be able to get along with Stalin, too. But at the Teheran Conference in 1943, he found that the Marshal was not going to be as easy as he had expected. He had done everything Stalin had asked him to do—stayed at his embassy, gone to his dinners, met his generals and admirals—but Stalin remained correct, stiff and solemn. Roosevelt began to think he had made the long trip for nothing. "I had to cut through this icy surface," he explained.

On the way to a meeting one morning he drew Churchill aside. "Winston," he said, "I hope you won't be sore at me for what I am going to do." Churchill shifted his cigar and grunted.

A few minutes later in the conference room Roosevelt said, in a loud stage whisper, "Winston is cranky this morning. He got up on the wrong side of the bed." A vague smile passed over Stalin's face. Roosevelt pressed his advantage. He began to tease Churchill about his Britishness, about John Bull, about his cigars. Churchill reddened and scowled. The more he did so, the more Stalin smiled. "Finally," Roosevelt told Miss Perkins, "Stalin broke out into a deep, hearty guffaw. It was then that I called him 'Uncle Joe.' From that time on our relations were personal." That Stalin was finally won over by Roosevelt is not surprising.

Roosevelt's personal habits were simple to the point of bareness. As President he slept on a narrow, white iron bed with a thin, hard-looking mattress, a couple of pillows and an old gray shawl for a blanket. "Don't like those heavy things," he once explained. He wore a sweater to bed to keep his shoulders warm when he had a cold. A small wooden table, painted white, stood near the bed. On it were aspirin, nose drops, a glass of water, bits of paper with telephone numbers, a few books, a watch, an old prayer book, a package of cigarettes, an ashtray and a couple of telephones. In addition, the room contained a heavy, dark wardrobe (there were no closets in the White House), an old-fashioned rocker and an old bureau.

Roosevelt seems to have had a genuine religious feeling. He did not go to church as frequently as some people thought he should, but he read the Bible and the Book of Common Prayer a good deal, and knew many passages by heart. He went to church more often when he was away from Washington. "I can do almost everything in the 'goldfish bowl' of the President's life," he once told Miss Perkins, "but I'll be hanged if I can say my prayers in it. It bothers me to be looked at by all the tourists in Washington when I go to church."

Like Jefferson, Jackson, Lincoln, he was portrayed as a man of the people. They believed he was one of them and that he was for them. The Roosevelt legend rests solely on this. Its strength lies in its simplicity, and because of its simplicity it seems likely to endure.

JUNGLE PHILOSOPHER

By John Gunther

T HE VILLAGE of Lambaréné lies on the Ogowe River 40 miles south of the equator, in Gabon, formerly French Equatorial Africa. The area resembles the beginning of the world—clouds, river and forest melt into a landscape that seems unbelievably ancient. Most of the year the air is like steam coming out of a green mist. This is the setting of one of the most famous missionary enterprises of the world—the bush hospital of Dr. Albert Schweitzer.

Without a doubt Schweitzer is a great man—one of the greatest of this or any time. He has had four different careers—in philosophy, medicine, theology, music. He has written learned books on Bach, Jesus and the history of civilization, and is the world's foremost authority on the architecture of organs, as well as one of the most renowned living organists. Also Dr. Schweitzer knows a great deal—more than many men who have devoted their lives to these fields—about esthetics, tropical zoology, anthropology and agriculture; and he is an expert carpenter, mason, veterinarian, boatbuilder, dentist, draftsman, mechanic, pharmacist and gardener.

Born in Kaysersberg, Alsace, on January 14, 1875, Albert Schweitzer was a sickly child, in contrast to his later extraordinary robustness. Also—more strangely—he was slow to read and write, and was a poor scholar. Because of this, as he grew up, he *made* himself master subjects that were particularly difficult for him, like Hebrew. In music he was amazingly gifted. He composed a hymn when he was seven, began to play the organ at eight, when his legs were scarcely long enough to reach the pedals, and at nine substituted for the regular organist in a church service.

He studied philosophy at the University of Strasbourg, and a thesis on Kant brought him his first doctorate. He studied theology, and in 1900, when he was 25, became curate of St. Nicholas' Church in Strasbourg. He studied the theory of music and began his career as a concert organist. By the time he was 26 he had degrees as a doctor in philosophy, theology and music. Meanwhile a stream of books began to come from him and has never stopped. Then, at 30, he abruptly quit his three careers in order to become a doctor and go out to Lambaréné for the rest of his life as a medical missionary.

Why medicine? Because he was tired of talk and wanted action. Why Lambaréné? Because it was one of the most inaccessible and primitive spots in all Africa, one of the most dangerous, and one without a doctor. Relatives and friends tried to make him change his mind, but he told them he felt that he had to "give something in return" for the happiness he enjoyed. He was obeying literally the command of Jesus, "Whosoever would save his life shall lose it, and whosoever shall lose his life for My sake . . . shall save it."

Schweitzer worked at his medical studies from 1905 to 1912 and finally, aged 38, became an M.D. These years were the most difficult and fatiguing he ever spent. A medical education is a grueling enough process; yet he managed to continue teaching philosophy, kept on with his activity as curate of St. Nicholas' and started work on a scholarly edition of Bach's organ music, while giving organ concerts all the time!

He married in 1912. His wife, daughter of a noted Strasbourg historian, learned nursing in order to be able to help him in Africa. When they arrived in Lambaréné in 1913 they found conditions extremely unfavorable. Every inch of habitable land in the area had to be scraped out of the giant forest, which was thickly populated with beasts like pythons and gorillas. The rivers were heavy with crocodiles.

Albert Schweitzer built his hospital from scratch, practically with his bare hands. Once he had to move and rebuild the entire establishment because the old huts were too small to contain his increasing practice. African patients, suffering anything from leprosy to elephantiasis, were not always easy to handle. One of Schweitzer's biographies reports that they sometimes ate the ointment prescribed for skin afflictions, swallowed at one gulp a bottle of medicine supposed to last weeks or tried to poison other inmates. For one brief period, after the death of a patient who came too late for successful treatment, Schweitzer was suspected of being a leopard in disguise, who deliberately took lives.

My wife and I visited Dr. Schweitzer in 1954. We were met at the airport by Miss Emma Haussknecht, an Alsatian nurse who had been with Schweitzer since 1925. She was a sort of general manager of the whole establishment and served as the Doctor's interpreter from French or German into English. After we had been assigned quarters she led us up a dirt path, through bush and fruit trees, toward the new leper village that Schweitzer was building. Finally, near a clearing, the Doctor himself came forth. He looked like pictures of Buffalo Bill, with a powerful aquiline nose, dripping gray mustache and eyes that really fixed you. He was strongly built, and wore a sun helmet, an open white shirt, tattered pants and heavy black shoes.

Schweitzer led us to the leper village. Here the old Doctor immediately got to work, bossing a labor gang. He took a spade himself, then chanted a kind of tune to mark time for the digging: "*Allez-vous OPP! Allez-vous OPP-upp-OPP!! Hupp, upp, OPP!*"

Dr. Schweitzer's hospital startled some visitors because it looked like what it was—a native village. Patients came from miles around, often with their families. There were no paved walks or roads, no running water, no electricity except for the operating room, no X ray.

More animals seemed to be about than human beings. The hospital had about 150 goats, and there were all manner of other creatures, like parakeets and a baby mandrill. Near the dining hall was a wild pig in a cage and a monkey tethered to a tree. Four graceful antelopes stood in a rough wire pen; the Doctor fed them after dinner every night.

What appeared to be the main hospital ward was a long, one-story structure, cut into narrow, dark rooms, each of which opened on a court. The patients lay on wooden bunks covered with matting. Outside each door a small, smoky fire was burning; here the patient's family did the cooking. If a man had no family and was too sick to cook for himself, he became a serious problem. Most patients would not accept food from anybody not in their own tribe, in fear of being poisoned.

There was, so far as I could see, no mechanism at all for sterilizing bandages under pressure; water had to be boiled in kettles over open wood fires. For years drugs and bandages were in short supply. Every safety pin was precious. Things that we would take for granted in a hospital were objects of wonder, if they existed at all. I was told that Schweitzer did not like elaborate modern gadgets. For one thing they were difficult to maintain in a tropical climate. What point in having hot-water bags if they rotted in a week? For another, he wanted the Africans to feel comfortable, in circumstances that made them think they were at home.

We peered into the operating room one morning; it was startling to be able to look right in from the courtyard. On the table lay a naked patient, his abdomen streaming with mercurochrome. The doctor who performed the operation—a routine hernia— came in to lunch an hour later. He had not had time to wash up completely and, in his shirt sleeves, sat down with his arms still scarlet with mercurochrome.

Life at the hospital centered in a crowded open space near the dining hall. Africans came and went carrying produce in rude barrows. Women squatted on the ground, binding palm fronds together for roofing; others were busy at sewing machines on a veranda above, and still others ironed the wash with primitive irons containing wood coals. The Doctor strode back and forth amid this orderly animation, seeing that everybody worked. The bustle and clatter was that of a frontier camp.

The chief doctor at Lambaréné at the time of our visit (Schweitzer himself was then 79, and not so active in medical work) was Hungarian; another was one of the old man's nephews. The nurses, all Europeans, seemed as shy, as devout and as removed from external life as nuns.

At meals Schweitzer sat at the middle of a long table, with guests of honor opposite. Immediately before each meal he said a brief grace in French; immediately after dinner (no meal took more than half an hour) he announced a hymn in a booming voice, and hymnbooks were passed around. He marched to a tinny piano at one end of the room and played briefly but with great vigor and precision as the company sang. Then he returned to his place at the table, inspected a list of Bible passages, snapped open a Bible and read a few lines.

We found Schweitzer a most incisive, alert and authoritative conversationalist, but he seldom talked at meals. The explanation, and a perfectly good one, was that he was too tired. On leaving the dining hall he filled his pockets with odd bits of food, which he gave to the antelopes. Then—after curfew had descended on the rest of the camp—he worked till midnight or beyond, writing or answering his mail. He once startled the customs officers at Bordeaux when he boarded ship carrying some unanswered mail. It filled four potato sacks.

When he set out for Africa, Schweitzer thought he was giving up forever what was dearest to him—the arts and teaching. But he has always had a piano with him in Africa, and so has been able to keep up with his music. His organ recordings of Bach, made when he was on holiday in Europe after World War II, are a profound artistic success. He has lectured widely whenever he has returned to civilization, and has been honored by universities without number; moreover, by working at night he has managed to keep up a steady literary output. He was awarded the Nobel Peace Prize for 1952.

He has always had a shrewd sense of values, and a nice sardonic sense of humor. When he visited the United States for the first (and only) time in 1949, to attend the Goethe Festival in Aspen,

Colorado, he was much pleased by the attention he got from the reporters and news photographers. "Dear me!" he exclaimed. "You obviously think that I must be as important as a prizefighter!"

On our last night at the hospital we were invited to accompany Schweitzer to his quarters after dinner. He had a small bedroom and an adjoining office. Here was an amazing assortment of books, papers, supplies, tools—a saw was lying across a sheaf of manuscript—empty tins, piles of music and bits of carpentry. When he finished writing a book chapter, his habit was to loop a string through the pages and hang them behind his desk, "like a bag of pheasants." (Metal clips cannot be used in Lambaréné; they rust at once.)

Schweitzer led us to his celebrated piano, presented to him by the Paris Bach Society. It had organlike pedals and was lined with zinc to protect it against the incessant damp and against termites; it weighed three tons. It seemed magnificently out of tune. Schweitzer, my wife and I all sat on the small bench—indeed there was no other place to sit—and he played some Bach. He saw us off next day, but this brief nocturnal recital was the last touch, the authentic Schweitzer ceremony of farewell. It is this picture of him, sitting at that battered old wreck of a piano in the middle of the silent, creeping jungle, that I shall remember best.

Just do what you can. It's not enough merely to exist. It's not enough to say, "I'm earning enough to live and to support my family. I do my work well. I'm a good father. I'm a good husband." That's all very well. *But you must do something more.* Seek always to do some good, somewhere. Every man has to seek in his own way to make his own self more noble and to realize his own true worth. You must give some time to your fellowman. Even if it's a little thing, do something for those who have need of help, something for which you get no pay but the privilege of doing it. For remember, you don't live in a world all your own. *Your brothers are here, too.*

—*Dr. Albert Schweitzer*

A VISIT WITH GANDHI

By Louis Fischer

OHANDAS K. GANDHI ran a thin weekly magazine in English called *Harijan*. In 1946, when the British Cabinet Mission published its plan for giving India a national government, the real question was not: Will Indians accept the British scheme? It was: Will Gandhi accept it? For Gandhi was the biggest thing in India.

Gandhi indulged in "four days of searching examination" and then wrote a brief article for *Harijan* declaring that "in the circumstances the Cabinet members have devised the easiest and quickest method of ending British rule." Every newspaper in India reprinted this article. It was cabled to Washington for the perusal of high officials. Full excerpts appeared in the British press and elsewhere.

Immediately below Gandhi's analysis of England's history-making offer to liberate India, *Harijan* published a second article signed by the Mahatma, entitled "Mango Seed Kernel," in which he extolled its food value as "a fair substitute for cereals and fodder."

This issue of *Harijan* was characteristic of Gandhi. He was many-sided because he was interested in the life of the individual. In one article Gandhi defined independence for India; in another he urged a reduction in the sugar ration for candy making; in a third he treated the problem of crime; in a fourth he discussed the uses of the "ground nut," as they call the peanut in India. To Gandhi, the mahatma ("great-souled") saint, politics was not too big and peanuts were not too small.

I visited Gandhi for a week in a sizzling Indian village in the summer of 1942. A few years later I visited him again for six days. Perhaps the most astonishing thing about this extraordinary man was that he lived in public 24 hours of every day and seemed to thrive on it. His bed was a mattress placed on the stone terrace of Dr. Dinshah Mehta's Nature Cure Clinic in Poona. The terrace was open and level with the earth. Several disciples slept near the master. I was given a room inside with a good bed.

At four in the morning I could hear the Mahatma and his group reciting prayers. After prayers he usually drank orange or mango juice, then answered letters by hand. He was over 70 at the time and his handwriting was clear and firm. He saw and heard well, and hoped to live to be 125. Once a day Rajkumari Amrit Kaur, a Christian woman of an Indian prince's family who had renounced everything to serve Gandhi as chief English secretary, read the news to him from the mimeographed bulletins of a British telegraph agency. He never read newspapers or listened to the radio.

But India came to him in thousands of letters and hundreds of visitors. Every visit was timed by the Mahatma's nickel-plated dollar watch. It hung from a cord which held up his handspun cotton loincloth. He was extremely punctual, always immaculate, and he enjoyed everything he did, especially talking, walking, eating and sleeping.

I used to stroll with him in the morning at 5:30. Several mornings it drizzled. "Surely you are not going to walk in the rain," I suggested. "Oh, yes," he said briskly. "Come along. Don't be an old man."

Gandhi subsisted on raw and cooked vegetables, fruit, dates, milk puddings and paper-thin Indian pancakes. He never ate eggs, meat or fish, and took no coffee, tea or spirits. I marveled at his energy. He never went to bed before ten. On occasions when I passed him as he lay on the terrace ready for the night, he would tell me that if I prayed more I would sleep better.

I traveled with him by train from Poona to Bombay, a 3½-hour journey. Our party included about ten secretaries and devotees, and Gandhi's personal physician. We occupied a special third-class car furnished only with hard wooden benches. It rained torrents, and soon water began to drip from the roof. Gandhi wrote an article for *Harijan*. Then he talked to political leaders who had boarded the train for an interview. At all stations, despite the downpour, crowds assembled to see him. During one stop, several small boys, soaked to their brown skins, stood outside the window yelling, "Gandhiji! Gandhiji!" ("Ji" is a suffix of respect.)

One of Gandhi's aims was to wean the caste Hindu from his cruel mistreatment of the Untouchables. He compelled sacred Hindu temples, closed for hundreds of years to Untouchables, to open their doors to them. By birth, he was a caste Hindu, but he identified himself with the Untouchables so that other Hindus might do likewise.

Most Indians bowed low before Gandhi when they came into his presence. Often he banged them on the back with his fist and told them to stop. Then they squatted on the floor, and the interview began. Anyone in the house could enter and listen. Many times I came to the entrance of Gandhi's room (there was no door) to find ten or more pairs of sandals and shoes on the threshold. I would slip mine off and join the company on the straw mats. But normally the talking was confined to Gandhi and the person to whom he had granted an appointment. Congress Prime Ministers of Indian provinces came for his advice and instructions. Educators came to test their ideas on him. Whoever had a new scheme sought his blessing. While I was with him an Untouchable couple who were unhappy in married life brought him their tale of woe. He spent hours with them. Peasants and workingmen requested his help.

The core of Gandhi's religion was a faith in God, in himself as an instrument of God and in nonviolence as the way to God in heaven and to peace and happiness on earth. I asked him why he did not preach nonviolence to the West. "How can I," he replied, "when I have not even convinced India? I am a spent bullet."

He realized that the temper of the youth of his country was violent, impatient. If the British had refused to part with power peacefully, a fire would have swept the Indian subcontinent and burned up every vestige of foreign domination. Asia was tired of bearing the white man's burden. I found a mounting consciousness of the conflicts between the white and colored races.

Gandhi dedicated his life to the independence of his country. Yet he did not wish to achieve that goal through violence. During the civil disobedience campaign which Gandhi launched in 1942, the Socialists practiced sabotage, organized an underground and forcefully hampered the authorities. All these things were outlawed by Gandhi's code of nonviolence.

In talking to Gandhi one saw the entire world in the mirror of India. For him, a conversation with a high British official and the cultivation of peanuts had one goal: the welfare of 400,000,000 Indians. He was, I believe, the most loved and the most influential man in India. Hindus worship one God, but they also worship many gods and idols, and there are idols of Gandhi in some Hindu temples.

The East is so hungry, ragged and unhappy that it thinks with its stomach, sees with its nakedness and feels with its misery. The hundreds of millions stand in awe of the mighty but they give their heart only to those who renounce personal advantage and dedicate themselves to the general welfare. Gandhi was such a person. Many Indians might differ with him, but all respected his sincerity, wisdom and passion for truth.

Mohandas Karamchand (Mahatma) Gandhi was born on October 2, 1869, at Porbandar in western India. He lived to 78, an extremely old age in a country where, according to official statistics, the average age is 27. Even then, Gandhi did not die of natural causes. He was on his way to hold a prayer meeting in New Delhi when he was shot to death by a youthful Hindu extremist on January 30, 1948. Less than five months before, the Mahatma had won a great personal victory when India had been declared an independent nation by the British.

"The gates of Heaven are waiting to receive Gandhi," a hard-boiled Bombay financier once said to me. But Gandhi made them wait until he had made the earth more heavenly.

WILDERNESS TRAIL BLAZER

By Donald Culross Peattie

ANIEL BOONE, most famous scout of the American forests, became a legend before he reached middle age. From backwoods taverns to Lord Byron, who put him in a poem, Boone was celebrated as a mighty deerslayer and woodsman. With simple humility he believed that God had appointed him to lead this nation westward. If that was indeed Divine Will, no man ever obeyed it better.

But until he was 35 Boone was just one more hemmed-in farmer who plowed his Carolina fields and every year saw his debt sheet at the store grow longer. He was an unimpressive figure, of only medium height; his voice was soft, his manner unassuming. Yet his gray-blue eyes were remarkable for the look of aim and distance in them. For he had a vision of a rich land, a happy people, with prosperous flocks and splendid horses—the future Bluegrass State.

Kentucky, however, lay beyond a practically unexplored wilderness, in a part of America denied to Americans. George III had forbidden them to set foot in it, choosing to dispose of it for profit or to court favorites. Few men had ever been there and come back to tell of it. Those who had survived Indian attacks spoke of loam like black velvet, of clover meadows rolling away to the horizon, of elk and deer and beaver and buffalo past counting.

On a May morning in 1769, Boone set out determined to reach this forbidden Canaan—*Caintuck*, as the Indians called it, meaning "among the meadows." With him went his brother-in-law John Stuart, John Finley the scout, and three camp-keepers, joined later by Dan'l's brother Squire—seven immortal "Long Hunters," so called because they were long absent from home. Behind him Boone left a failing farm, his wife, Rebecca, a crop of barefoot children and all his cares. Ahead lay adventure, discovery, wealth perhaps, freedom certainly, and danger in every rustling leaf.

The way led over the Blue Ridge to the last outpost of the white man, the Watauga settlements in what is now the northeast corner of Tennessee. Then began a region of sharp tossing ridges, of rivers that howled in their deep gorges like wildcats, of trees so thick they could not fall but leaned dead in each other's arms, while vines stout as a man's leg bound up the timber in unbreakable cables. And the only way through was the Warriors' Path. This trail was the red man's secret, the white man's dread. To walk it unaware was death.

The Long Hunters set their feet upon the Warriors' Path, and the boughs of the forest closed behind them like the quiet springing of a trapdoor. Rebecca Boone didn't see her husband again for nearly two years. And when Dan'l returned he was empty-handed. The redskins had stolen his horses and every pelt gathered in a season's trapping. But in the wilderness he had learned how to walk as the Indians did, along fallen trees or over rocks or up streams, leaving no trace of his passing, and how to break his trail by swinging on the great ropes of wild grape. Often he left a campfire burning, then slipped into a canebrake to sleep securely.

He learned to make friends with his ruthless enemies. Instead of his "rifle gun," which he called "Ticklicker," he used caution and diplomacy. Once, surrounded as he slept, he saved his life by sitting up with a hearty laugh and shaking hands all around with the redskins so genially that they let him go. Again, pursued to the edge of a cliff, he jumped off into the top of a sugar maple, followed only by the admiring grunts of his enemies.

He had got out of Kentucky alive this time, but the Indians had warned him never to return. For Boone now knew too much; he knew the course of the Warriors' Path through Cumberland

Gap; he knew the bison herds, the springs and the salt licks.

To those in the settlements who heard Dan's tales, Kentucky gleamed like a promised land. When in 1750 the Boones—Quakers of Welsh and Scotch-Irish stock—had brought 16-year-old Daniel from his birthplace on a farm near Reading, Pennsylvania, a boy could kill more deer in those Carolina woods than he had strength to haul home. But now the game was almost gone, and however hard you worked you were never free of taxes and church tithes and lawyers and sheriffs. The land was burdened with debt, through the evil quit-rent system by which a man was never quit of paying rent even after he had bought his land. So in September of 1773 six families elected to head for *Caintuck*, and they chose Dan Boone for their guide.

This was the opening he had been looking for and he took his own family with him. On the Warriors' Path, however, Cherokees fell on the rear of the emigrant train, killed several men in their sleep and took Dan's 16-year-old son James alive and tortured him to death. That sent the horrified emigrants back to their settlements and safety. But the agony fixed Boone in his purpose: to "make a way in the wilderness," as the Bible has it.

Boone's next opportunity came when Colonel Richard Henderson offered the Cherokees $50,000 worth of trading goods for most of Kentucky and employed Boone to clear a trail there. On a March morning in 1775 Boone was waiting, with 30 picked axemen, at the Holston River in Tennessee, when a messenger galloped up with word from Henderson: the deal with the Cherokees was going through. Boone swung his axe for the first blow in the breaking of the Wilderness Road.

In one week Daniel and his men had pushed more than 100 miles, up to the Cumberland Gap. Beyond, the wilderness waited. Indians attacked; four men were killed; some turned back. But Boone and the stoutest of his men pressed on. Boggy spots must be bridged, fallen timbers lifted aside, enormous vines pulled down and canebrakes cleared lest they hide the lurking enemy. Yet in another week the weary axemen were gazing on the "pleasing and rapturous plains of Kentucky." The Wilderness Road was to be a highroad to America's future. In oxcart, on horseback, on foot, over it were to pour Carolinians, Virginians, Marylanders, bringing their slaves, driving their cattle, leading their horses, to found the Bluegrass State and make Boone's dream come true.

But in Boone's day Kentucky was a besieged frontier. There at the end of the trail, Dan founded Boonesborough, at a bend in the Kentucky River, in a meadow shaded by great elms and sycamores. For 20 years it was to be the shield and buckler of the pioneer, a haven of rest after the long hard trail, the fitting-out place for further settlement. So close was the breath of Indian danger that when Dan's 14-year-old daughter Jemima and two other girls crossed the river in a canoe one day, they were kidnaped by the Shawnees and taken far into the forest. But the girls stamped heel-marks as they were dragged along, broke the bushes, left scraps of petticoat. And Dan, with a number of companions hot beside him, read the signs as for two days he stole in pursuit.

Rescue was a ticklish business—at the first alarm the Indians might tomahawk their captives. But Ticklicker did not miss, and the other guns cracked in unison with it. A moment more and Jemima was in her father's arms.

A few months later Jemima, dashing out of the stockade at Boonesborough in the face of besieging Shawnee fire, helped to rescue her wounded father. For Boonesborough was now a battlefield of the Revolution: the British had armed the Shawnees and were offering bounties on American scalps. The tiny settlement looked to Dan as its protector; when he and 26 others were captured while on a saltmaking expedition, the settlers mourned their leader for dead.

Dan and his companions had been carried off to Shawnee villages in Ohio. Here Boone pretended a great love for his brothers the Shawnees, talked the Indians out of torturing or killing their prisoners, gave Chief Blackfish exaggerated ideas of an enormous force defending Boonesborough and got himself adopted into the tribe. Then he escaped and reached Boonesborough, not much ahead of a tomahawk flung at the stockade to announce another and fiercer siege.

Boone negotiated. For days he spun out the powwows with his new red "relatives." While still in the midst of truce talks, Blackfish attacked the whites. He tried firebrands, night assaults, sudden rushes, pretended retreats. Boonesborough held, but the settlement was hopelessly outnumbered. The women and girls, dressed as men, showed themselves above the stockade with bewildering frequency. Boonesborough ran out of water; it was almost out of ammunition. That night, surely, Blackfish would attack, for a violent storm arose, providing him with cover. But dawn disclosed empty woods, and the American flag—the first flown west of the mountains—waving in victory on the forest wind.

Though Boonesborough was saved, the Kentucky settlements were imperiled long after the Revolution's end. The Shawnees, once set on the warpath, were not easily recalled; and Dan lost another son to them, who died in his father's arms. Still Boone kept his head and used his wits; no other white man was held in such high regard by the Indians, and Dan was thus able to secure the release of many white prisoners.

Even when the tomahawk was at last buried, peace on the land brought little peace of mind to Daniel Boone. For he who had opened a green empire was left in poverty. Kentucky named a county in his honor—and immediately the sheriffs sold 10,000 acres of his land for taxes. For cutting the Wilderness Road he had been paid by Henderson in land; but Boone's claim to this now proved worthless, since Henderson had no legal right to purchase Kentucky from the Cherokees. Over the trail came a swarm of speculators, lawyers and sheriffs; waving legal papers, they took the very land under Daniel's cabin. Boone was further robbed, as he slept, of $50,000 entrusted to him by neighbors to purchase titles to property; and to pay this back he labored for 20 years. He worked as a surveyor, tried farming again, kept a store, trapped for otter and beaver, rounded up wild horses. Years after the Bluegrass State grew rich, Daniel and Rebecca Boone remained poorer than when they came to Kentucky.

So Dan, nearly 70, felt it was time to find a new frontier. His immense reputation preceded him into the little settlement of St. Louis in Spanish Missouri. There Spanish officials gave him title to 8500 acres of land in the Femme Osage district. No sooner was he settled than hundreds came pouring after him from Kentucky, sure of good pickings wherever Dan'l cabined. Better still, his sons and daughters and their mates and children all settled near him. Boone's children, grandchildren and great-grandchildren totaled almost 400, though he lived to know only about a hundred of the lot.

So the last years were good years. The Spanish authorities made *Señor* Boone syndic, or magistrate, of his district, and he held court under a great elm known as the Justice Tree. In the War of 1812 he volunteered, and was disgusted to be turned down because he was 78. At 80 he longed to get to the Rockies, and even talked of California. One after another the great exploring expeditions—Long's and Pike's and the Astorians—passed his way, young men, strong men, rolling back the frontier. Sometimes they recognized Boone as he watched them from the riverbank, cradling Ticklicker in his arm.

These last days he spent toting his grandchildren on his shoulders, playing with pet otter and beaver cubs, and carpentering. He carved seven mantelpieces for his son's house, and every now and then he'd build himself a coffin—though each time he would give it up to some needy corpse. Each time but the last. In 1820 he drew a peaceful final breath and was buried in a cherry casket of his own making, beside Rebecca, on a knoll looking westward through the trees.

But a quarter-century later Kentucky demanded him back. At the state capital, four white horses drew the remains in a black hearse to a grave where Kentuckians made flowery speeches. Then they weighted him down with a monument faced with Italian marble sculptured in scenes from the legend of his life.

The real Daniel Boone does not rest there. You find him in all things brave and free. He is in the running of a doe and the coming of the day. He is the wind in the bluegrass, the path like a shaft of light in the wilderness, the Road, the American way.

BULLDOG WARRIOR

Condensed from Winston Churchill

By Robert Lewis Taylor

THE LAST of the great statesmen, Winston Churchill, a man of multiple genius, will be fondly remembered as one of the most exasperating figures of history. Before moments of British crisis he has been so frequently right that his ability to foresee future events became a burden to his countrymen. His has been the voice of Britain's conscience, the court of last appeal in time of danger. Yet to the day of his retirement he remained impish, mischievous and remarkably boyish; even his appearance seemed to change little over the many years.

Churchill's must be considered the most notably independent spirit of modern times. He has attained immortality as statesman, orator, historian, biographer, wit, war correspondent and brandy drinker, and has established lesser records as artist, bricklayer, novelist, aviator, polo player, soldier and racehorse owner.

What causes a man of genius to rise above the ordinary and the merely talented? Those who have known Churchill best believe that his motive power comes from a blend of matchless energy, a combination of intelligence and memory, and the pushiest ambition since Alexander complained about the scarcity of worlds to conquer.

Winston Leonard Spencer Churchill was born on November 30, 1874, in the regal grandeur of Blenheim Palace, then owned by his grandfather, the seventh Duke of Marlborough. Churchill's mother, an American, was a glittering beauty, with a keen wit and a mischievous sense of humor. "I loved her dearly," he has written, "but at a distance. She always seemed to me a fairy princess." His father, Lord Randolph, was an immensely gifted man who enjoyed a vivid though brief career in Parliament.

As a boy Winston Churchill's appearance left no doubt of the smoldering fires within: he was small, red-haired, peppered with freckles; had a slightly pug nose and a mouth that plainly signaled competition. His eyes were blue and gazed out with unflinching calm and a touch of impatience on children and grownups alike.

Churchill's early school days have few counterparts in the annals of great men. He took an early stand against learning, which being sent to an expensive boarding school at Ascot did little to mend. From the start he was a frequent visitor to the "caning room," where the headmaster administered floggings. He disliked Latin, and steadily refused to learn it throughout his schooling. (Later, when he saw the value of a few high-sounding Latin phrases in political speeches, he sat down and, in true Churchillian fashion, memorized an entire dictionary of Latin quotations.)

In 1888, when the future Prime Minister entered Harrow, he was placed in the lowest division of the lowest form, or class. "He was not an easy boy to deal with," says a former master. "Of course he had always a brilliant brain, but he would only work when he chose to and for the masters he approved of." Over-endowed with energy, and hostile to education, he got into an unbelievable variety of mischief, and some of the boys found Churchill a nuisance. But all of them left with vivid impressions of "Carrot Top," as he was known at Harrow.

Churchill himself claims that "by being so long in the lowest form I gained an immense advantage over the cleverer boys. They all went on learning Latin and Greek and splendid things like that. But I was taught English. Mr. Somervell—a delightful man, to whom my debt is great—was charged with teaching the stupidest boys the most disregarded thing—namely, to write mere English. He knew how to do it. He taught it as no one else has ever taught it. As I remained in the Third Form three times as long as anyone else, I had three times as much of it. Thus I got into my bones the essential structure of the ordinary British sentence—which is a noble thing."

Churchill twice failed to pass the entrance examinations for the Military Academy of Sandhurst, and a Captain James who tutored him for the third, and finally successful, attempt was reputed to have remarked: "That lad couldn't have gone through Harrow; he must have gone under it." But once in the Academy, a change took place in Churchill. The old stubbornness, the bold and fearless spirit remained, but the mood of dissent began to fade. He was competent and quiet in the classrooms and spent most of his evenings in study. In a class of 150 he ranked eighth.

After Sandhurst Churchill joined the Fourth Hussars, a cavalry regiment which for splendor and good connections matched any in the army. Assigned to foreign service in India, the regiment immediately settled down to intensive polo practice. Churchill attacked the game with frenzied enthusiasm and displayed a natural genius for it. But the monotony of army life soon got on his nerves. Early in 1897, he persuaded his friend Sir Bindon Blood, who had just been sent to India's northern frontier to put down a rebellion among the Pathan tribe, to let him join the expedition as a correspondent. The *Daily Telegraph* agreed to take his dispatches at some $25 per column. His pieces were an instantaneous success in London, as was his book, *The Story of the Malakand Field Force*, into which he later collected them. The book netted Churchill the equivalent of two years' army pay.

When Churchill returned to England he had resolved to quit the army. The golden vistas of journalism offered more opportunity. The Boer War had no sooner broken out in the autumn of 1899 when he was offered an appointment to report this struggle for the *Morning Post*. He succeeded in upping his rate, as a veteran warrior-correspondent, to $1250 a month and all expenses, and gleefully took off for Africa.

When he reached the British outpost at Estcourt, Churchill found a friend from the Indian wars, a Captain Haldane, who was subsequently chosen to lead a reconnoitering party into hostile Boer country by means of an armored train. The assignment depressed him and he talked it over gloomily with Churchill. "Never mind," said the latter, "I'll go along with you. I consider it my duty to the *Morning Post*."

A few miles out from Estcourt the train was ambushed and two cars were overturned. Despite frantic efforts, only the engine and tender could be got clear of the wreckage, and the 40-odd wounded were loaded into them and started back. The rest of the party followed on foot, but the exhausted soldiers soon fell to the rear, and Churchill ran back to rally them just as Boer horsemen charged from the hills. He had left his revolver in the engine, and was almost immediately forced to throw up his hands by a rider who motioned him toward the Boer lines.

Churchill was taken to the Boer capital of Pretoria as a prisoner of war, but after a few weeks managed to escape. By good fortune he found a railroad, scrambled aboard a freight train, and eventually made his way to Portuguese East Africa, 300 miles away, the nearest neutral territory. The war had been going badly for the British, and Churchill's exploit had at last given them a victorious hero. When he boarded the steamer for Durban, the local British colony gave him a tremendous send-off. Churchill now reentered the army and continued his well-paying job with the *Morning Post* until the end of the war.

Upon returning to England he decided to stand for Parliament in the next election and won by a narrow margin. Thus in 1900, at the advanced age of 26, he began his life of public service. As Members of Parliament were then unpaid, Churchill's next step was to make some money. He therefore arranged a lecture tour in England and America. Churchill's American tour was rigorous; for more than five months he spoke every day except Sunday. But it netted him nearly $50,000 toward taking his fling at politics.

As a rule, fledgling members in the House of Commons sat by with deference while their elders showed them the ropes. Not so with Churchill. When he first came in, he immediately stepped up to the seat formerly occupied by his father, made himself comfortable, and on the fourth day Churchill made his first speech.

Psychiatrists have observed that a few people appear destined to envelop themselves in trouble. They are the destroyers of serenity, and the builders of the world. Churchill is one of these. He had not been seated a month before he began to defy the party leaders. He savagely attacked a proposed high military budget, advocated a soft peace for the Boers, and otherwise so outraged his fellow Conservatives that one day when he rose to make a speech they all got up and filed out noisily, pausing in the doorway to jeer at Churchill like schoolboys. In its way the episode, which had no parallel in the House of Commons before, brought him as much notoriety as his escape from the Boers.

Churchill finally switched his political affiliation altogether, moved over to the Liberal side of the House, and in the general elections of 1906 accepted an invitation to stand from a Liberal constituency in Manchester. He was elected, and since this election also removed the Tories from power, it established Winston Churchill, the Liberal, as a Cabinet Minister. His post—Undersecretary for the Colonies—was relatively unimposing, but in securing it at the age of 31, he continued the legend of the Boy Wonder.

During the years just prior to the First World War, Churchill became what one biographer described as "the most hated politician in the country." As Undersecretary for the Colonies, then as President of the Board of Trade, and later as Home Secretary, he championed many liberal measures. He fought through an antimilitary budget. Without doubt he was one of the hardest-working ministers ever to fill a Cabinet position, and in the light of history there can be no question that Churchill almost alone saved England's skin in the First World War.

He foresaw the early course of the war with uncanny accuracy. In 1911 Britain's military leaders believed that, if Germany attacked, the French Army was sufficiently strong to counterattack in 9 to 13 days, and then roll the Germans back. Churchill's analysis, a historic document which is still viewed as one of the world's classics of prophecy, predicted that the French would still be in full retreat on the 20th day, and could not attack until at least the 40th day. Three years later, the French were in full retreat on the 21st day, and the Battle of the Marne, generally conceded to mark the turning point of the war, began on the 41st day.

The English generals rejected Churchill's document as "silly" and "utterly amateur." But Prime Minister Asquith, well aware of England's danger, soon embarrassed them by asking Churchill if he would be interested in being First Lord of the Admiralty. "We have only the navy," said Asquith. "It is our only hope."

Churchill accepted eagerly. Ignoring seniority, he immediately embarked on a pugnacious reshuffling of the Admiralty that had high naval brass sulking in their tents. In his effort to build a supreme navy he made a great many changes, including a much-disputed shift from coal to oil fuel for the fleet. And he ordered 15-inch guns, instead of the usual 13.5-inch, for all new battleships. A heartrending cry arose from naval people, but Churchill bulled right ahead, and when war came his ships could outfire any the Germans had.

Then, in the early summer of 1914, he called off the usual navy maneuvers and announced instead—over a Cabinet veto and without the King's signature—a "practice mobilization" of the total naval reserve strength of the nation. His daring decision again displayed almost mystical foreknowledge. The unpopular mobilization, well under way when the assassination of the Austrian Archduke Ferdinand embroiled all Europe in conflict, was completed just three days before Britain's formal declaration of war. It was one of the few times on record when a defending navy had been even halfway prepared.

Perhaps never before had such a whirlwind of human energy been loosed upon a wartime government. Churchill set in motion the development of an air arm, and promoted a series of air attacks against German airship sheds and submarine bases. He blandly earmarked $350,000 for the production of 18 "landships," and may thus be described as the father of the tank. When 48 of these machines were sent into action in September 1916, the Germans threw down their guns and fled, and warfare underwent another lasting alteration.

Churchill's scheme for bringing the war to an early end, in 1915, was to send the Royal Navy through the Dardanelles, detach Turkey from the Central Powers, then win over the Balkan states and pave the way for a sweeping Russian victory in the East. It was his blueprint for smothering the war rapidly, a "backdoor" attack on the enemy, and he overrode all protests against it. The catastrophe, which got under way on March 18, 1915, was not long in taking form. While entering the Dardanelles, the assault group ran into a minefield and lost three battleships, causing the commanding admiral to break off the action. In London, Churchill assembled his "Admiralty War Group" and showed them a telegram instructing the admiral to renew the action. But further attack was disastrously delayed, the enemy was given time to increase its defenses, and the ensuing actions provided one of the goriest chapters in the ugly and unending history of war. The total British casualties reached 205,000, and as the sad and straggling remnants of the army and navy were evacuated, the public's wrath rose up in a terrible storm. As a result, Churchill was swiftly removed from his post.

Early in 1917 a Committee of Inquiry on the Dardanelles campaign decided that Churchill's basic plan had been sound and he was brought back into the Cabinet. He was awarded the United States Distinguished Service Medal by General Pershing for his part in equipping the American forces (the only Englishman so honored). Just after the Armistice he was made Secretary of State for War and Air. In the postwar reaction, however, he not only was swept out of office but failed of election to Parliament for the first time since 1900.

The most slavish of Churchill's followers seldom wax eloquent over his course as Chancellor of the Exchequer, an office he took in 1924 in Stanley Baldwin's Tory administration. (He had broken with the Liberals and had been returned to Parliament as a "Constitutionalist," a new party consisting of one member.) It was a time of economic decline, of restless and dissatisfied labor, of numerous strikes. Churchill moved swiftly to put down the strikes, and in general turned more sharply to the Right than most of his new Tory colleagues. The old cry was raised that he had gone too far. Even the Tories were suspicious of his weathervane convictions and impulsiveness. In a word, he was too much for nearly everybody. In the busy time since Sandhurst he had fought five wars, held nine Cabinet offices (an all-time British record), made 8000 public speeches, and seen himself, in quick order, the most popular and the most unpopular man in England.

During the interval between 1929 and 1939, sometimes described as his "out of step" period, Churchill occupied himself chiefly in writing. He had already published *The World Crisis* in four large volumes, which netted him over $100,000, and now settled down to an even more massive project, the monumental *Marlborough, His Life and Times*. His fees for magazine articles had grown to be among the highest ever paid, and his output was colossal. Such earnings, together with an inheritance of $150,000 from his mother on her death in 1921, considerably eased the burden of upper-class living for the Churchills.

From his literary earnings Churchill, in 1924, bought his estate, Chartwell. Not long after he bought the place, he watched for a while as some bricklayers patched it up, then got a trowel and some bricks and set to work himself on a crumbling outbuilding. When the head bricklayer advised him that bricklaying involved joining a union, Churchill practiced till he could lay two bricks a minute, then applied for membership. During a lull in his career Churchill had turned to painting. Characteristically, he provided himself with every known accessory of the guild, including a light-blue smock and a beret. He forged ahead rapidly and Paris was treated to an exhibition by an unknown artist named Charles Morin, which was the *nom de brush* Churchill had chosen. Churchill's skill as an artist can only be described as professional. "If that man were a painter by profession," Picasso once said, "he'd have no trouble in earning a good living."

Politically, Churchill was in an extraordinary situation in these years. He was still in Parliament, but without influence. Both Germany and Italy were on the march and, as he watched the growing menace of Hitler, he warned that England must arm. Churchill's one-man stand against the Fascists was perhaps his finest hour. In parliamentary and journalistic warnings, he lashed out at the Nazi threat to a nation afflicted by mass blindness.

All too late, Britain awoke to the fact that Churchill, again, had been right from the start. At any of a dozen points, experts say, Hitler could have been stopped without bloodshed. Churchill had pleaded for action in every case. Now the die was cast, and the juggernaut was rolling. On September 1, 1939, the Nazi war machine rolled with gleaming precision into Poland. On September 3, France and England declared war, and on that evening Churchill was called upon to resume his old post at the Admiralty, and the memorable message went out to all units of the fleet, by radio, blinker and signal flags—"Winston is back."

The public, too, welcomed him with a flood tide of approval, and during the formal announcement of war he walked into Parliament to a standing ovation from both sides of the House. Only the week before they had been denouncing him with gusto. But it was a bleak hour in English history. The nation was ill prepared for war. Churchill's stay of less than a year in the Admiralty was marked by little encouraging news, and the frequent U-boat sinkings severely tested British morale.

Years before, during one of his unfavored periods, Churchill had confided to a friend, "I would quit politics forever if it were not for the possibility that I might some day become Prime Minister." On May 10, 1940, in England's worst hour of the civilized era, his perseverance was rewarded. Norway had fallen, Chamberlain had at last stepped down, and King George sent for Churchill. The following Monday, Churchill produced the stirring address on "blood and toil, sweat and tears" that would be democracy's theme for the next five years.

Everybody who came into contact with Churchill during the war felt the strong stirring of courage that he stimulated. The effect was almost hypnotic. At the time of Dunkirk, not long after he took office, it was principally his urging that saved the Expeditionary Army. When the news came from Dunkirk of the necessity for quick evacuation, he sprang into action. On the evening of May 26, the first troops were taken off the beach at Dunkirk. The following day the word spread quickly, via radio and newspapers, that "Winnie needs boats," and shortly the famous, oddly assorted flotilla put out from the ports of England, providing one of the most gallant chapters in British military annals. But Churchill made no attempt to disguise the rescue as a victory. Instead, he painted England's position in dark colors, emphasizing the enormous sacrifices of equipment and supplies.

Europe was all but lost, Russia had signed a nonaggression pact with Germany the previous year, and America proclaimed her unshakable neutrality. Churchill called a meeting of his Cabinet, whose members joined in solemn council to hear his dread predictions. They had never found him in better spirits. "Well, gentlemen, we are alone," he told them. "For myself, I find it extremely exhilarating."

The burdens of leadership from May 1940 to July 1945 took a great toll and Churchill could not be dissuaded from foolish, unnecessary expenditures of his energies. When air-raid warnings sounded, he perversely waited until the bombs were actually falling before he left No. 10 Downing Street. He then strolled leisurely through the barrage to the stronger No. 10 Annex, some thousand yards away. Inspector Walter Thompson, his bodyguard, once sneaked up from behind, removed Churchill's hat and clapped on a regulation tin helmet. Churchill removed it without comment and tossed it into the bushes. No matter how heavy the bombing, he left the shelter before it was over, and nearly all well-wishers finally gave up trying to keep him underground. As one Whitehall worker said, "When the Premier was cooped up in an air raid shelter his blistering temper was far worse than the raid." He worked 16 and 18 hours a day and seemed never to tire. But by the spring of 1945 some of his household thought he showed signs of emotional wear.

The news of President Roosevelt's death provided undoubtedly his worst moment of the war. Thompson, suddenly summoned at three o'clock in the morning, went into the Prime Minister's bedroom to find him weeping and saying, "Terrible, terrible." A few minutes later, he added, "He was a great friend to us. He gave us immeasurable help at a time when we most needed it. I have lost a good, good friend."

On V-E Day, Churchill's and England's great day of the war, Churchill made a triumphant drive to the House of Commons from 10 Downing Street. By the time the procession reached Parliament Square, he had clambered up on top of the front seat of the open car and was standing bareheaded, grinning and making his sign of victory to the crowds. At one point he realized that he'd left his cigars behind. "Go back and get one," he yelled to Thompson. "They expect to see it."

When the Prime Minister finally strode in to face the legislators, he was given the greatest ovation in the history of the assembly. Members gave up all attempts to observe the rituals and leaped up on the benches, shouting and waving papers. Churchill stood at his accustomed place beside the dispatch box. Tears were running down his face and he was nodding his head, while he waited to exercise his priceless privilege of making the formal announcement of victory.

Two months later, when the British voted Churchill out of office, he was apparently unmoved by the abrupt rejection. He soon settled into the pattern of life that he led until the October 1951 election, which so dramatically reestablished him in 10 Downing Street.

Named a Knight of the Order of the Garter by Queen Elizabeth II in 1953, Sir Winston Leonard Spencer Churchill remained in office until 1955. Then, feeling the weight of his years, he turned over the office of Prime Minister to Anthony Eden and quietly withdrew from the political scene.

But in retirement he was far from forgotten. For England continued to cry Hail! to her man of heroic size, the last of the great statesmen, a giant among pygmies. In the words of Shakespeare: "When comes such another?"

PRINCE
OF STORYTELLERS

By Donald and Louise Peattie

ONCE upon a time there was a poor boy, son of a shoe-maker's widow, who went to seek a boon of the Prince of the Realm. Hopefully he sang and recited for His Highness, and when the Prince kindly asked him what boon he wanted, the bold lad said, "I want to write poetic dramas and act at the Royal Theater." The Prince looked at the gawky boy, all feet and hands, with a comical big nose and sad eyes, and gave a commonsense answer. "It is one thing to recite plays, another to write them. We advise you to learn a useful trade like cabinet-making."

But the boy, who had no common sense, only the very un-common kind called genius, went home, broke open his clay money-pig and, saying farewell to his mother and indifferent stepfather, set out to seek his fortune. He was sure that genera-tions yet unborn would honor the name of Hans Christian Andersen.

To swallow such a story, one would have to believe in fairy tales! Hans Christian was steeped in them. Some he had heard from his father, a man of mental gifts who had taken up a useful trade—and always regretted it. For solace the cobbler read aloud at bedtime from *The Arabian Nights*, while his son drank in every word. Often Hans Christian listened outside the spinning room of the poorhouse, and heard all the old wives' tales. In those days there were as many legends in Denmark as there were thatched roofs with storks on them. Among the legends of the town of Odense, where Andersen was born in 1805, was one about an elf-woman who danced her partners to death.

Now Andersen the shoemaker thought that his fortune was made when a fine young lady ordered a pair of scarlet silk slippers; when she heartlessly refused to pay for them bitterness filled that humble house. Out of that small tragedy blended with the old Odense legend, the cobbler's son was to write the now well-known story *The Red Shoes*. For the genius of Andersen is that in the magic of his fairy tales there is so much everyday truth.

Hans Christian's mother as a little girl had been sent out on the streets to beg. Instead, she hid under the city bridges, warming her naked feet in her hands, afraid to go home. The first love ever offered her was a seducer's; he vanished before her daughter was born. Her son, in his pity for her and his anger with the world, would one day write the angry story *She's No Good* and the pitiful tale of *The Little Match Girl*.

His pen was a wand which transformed, in time, every early grief, even his father's failing health. One day the boy stood admiring the frost ferns on the window and his father showed him a white, womanlike figure in the crystals. "That is the Snow Queen," said the cobbler. "Soon she will be coming for me." A few months later he was dead.

When the stepfather entered his story, and after the Prince told him to be a cabinetmaker, Hans Christian at 14 went to seek his fortune in Copenhagen. Here he rang the doorbells of all the notables. For a famous ballerina he tried to dance; she took him for a zany and had him turned out. In his threadbare best, with a hat that came down over his ears, he recited to a renowned playwright the tragedies he had written for puppets his father had carved for him; the writer was unimpressed. Now he had only seven pennies left.

And a boy's clear soprano. It happened to touch the heart of Professor Siboni, a teacher at the Conservatory of Music, who made up a purse to keep the lad while he studied singing. Hans Christian was in heaven. He was also within a few months of

puberty. Soon his boy's soprano was gone forever. But this hob-
bledehoy, by his puppylike ardors, his awkward brilliance,
speedily won new friends, even a princess, who gave him bits
of money for food and clothes—which he spent on books of
poetry and theater tickets.

Up in his attic he had a grand view of the gables and spires
and domes of the old city. He was old friends with the late-burning
streetlamps, and the lonely candle left by the bed of a sick child.
None of all this was lost upon the future author of tales like *The
Old Streetlamp* and *What the Moon Saw*.

But he could not see a big fact right under his own big nose:
his epics and tragedies and romances were rubbishy imitations.
Yet there were gleams of gold in the rubbish, and these caught
the eye of Jonas Collin, the director of the Royal Theater. This
kindly official obtained an educational fund for the young author.

Filled with hope, Hans Christian entered a school at Slagelse,
kept by one Simon Meisling, with whom he was also to live. An
unsuccessful poet, Meisling was roused to sadistic fury by Hans
Christian's gifts. So he set the great gawky youth down with the
ten-year-olds, and hurled algebra, geometry, and Greek and
Hebrew grammar at his bewildered head. And although Hans
Christian did passably well, Meisling reduced him to tears by
telling him he was failing. Yet the mean schoolmaster was careful
not to lose this unpaid baby-sitter. The neglected Meisling young
were quiet by the hour at the tall boy's bony knee while he told
them fairy stories—immortal classics taking their first shape.

When Meisling's cruel treatment of him came to light, Collin
brought the boy to Copenhagen to be tutored. Here, too, it was
the children with whom he felt at ease. He ate his dinner in turn
at the homes of six charitable friends, and in each the children
climbed on his knees and begged for stories—the adventures that
befell storks, a snowman, a Christmas tree and Ole Shut-Eye, the
Danish Sandman. He could tell a tale so vividly that you saw and
heard tin soldiers marching, or the coach horses galloping. And
he could cut out of paper the liveliest patterns; these are treasured

today in the Andersen Museum in Odense, the house where he was born.

But for the love of a woman the awkward, penniless fellow yearned in vain. The good Collin family became all the family he was ever to have, three generations of them. However, they felt it their duty to keep this dreamer's feet on the ground. They urged him to aim for some modest government post; they talked as he was to have the animals talk in his most famous tale. "'I tell you for your own good,' said the Hen to the Ugly Duckling, 'you should learn to lay eggs like me.'" In *The Ugly Duckling* Hans Christian Andersen with clear-eyed Danish irony told the story of his own life.

But understanding of himself came slowly. For years he wrote epic poems, romantic novels, tragic plays—all but forgotten today. He had successes but his many failures fell like blows on his heart. The first of his fairy stories were published in 1835, half carelessly, without expectation. But children read them and wanted more. So, dragged by their eager hands from the path to nowhere, he began seriously what we know as his great work. "Now I dip into my own bosom, find an idea for the older people—and tell it as if to the children, but remembering that father and mother are listening!" For 37 years, at almost every Christmastime, a new volume of Andersen's fairy tales appeared, piling up a treasure of fanciful truth, of sorrowful beauty, of humorous irony, such as never before was laid before wondering childhood.

For Andersen's tales are a poet's revelation of truth in the life about us all. So deeply did he look into the heart of things that he could see even in a broken bottle, a ball drifted into the gutter, some story with a lift and glint in it. All of us laugh at the sly joke of *The Emperor's New Clothes*—garments (said the rogues who persuaded the Emperor to order them) which, for all their splendor, would be invisible to those not clever and noble enough to perceive them. So the Emperor and his courtiers praised to the skies these fabrics displayed on the empty loom. Indeed, the Emperor paraded before all the city in these clothes which he would not admit he could not see, and everyone in the great crowd cried "Oh!" and "Ah!" in admiration. Except one innocent child who said, "But, Mother, he has nothing on!" That story makes its point afresh every time pretense founds a new cult.

Though he was famous now, he was more gentle of heart than ever. Meisling met him on the street and apologized for his earlier cruelty; Andersen forgave and comforted him. When the King sent for him—that same Prince who once had advised him to learn a useful trade—and hinted the poet might ask for royal favors, Andersen answered simply, "But I earn something myself."

What he had earned was the love of the wide world. So renowned had become his ungainly figure and sweet, homely face that his friends the children knew him at once and swarmed to him. He was translated into more languages than any book but the Bible. He was received at Europe's courts and decorated with her most glittering orders. The greatest writers of the day, from Dickens to Victor Hugo, welcomed him as one of their own, and among birds of such a feather he learned happily at last that "it doesn't matter if you are born in a duckyard, as long as you are hatched from a swan's egg."

Happiest of all was the day when he returned to the "duckyard" in triumph, nearly 50 years after he had left it. All Odense turned out in the great celebration for the shoemaker's son, the prince of fairy tale. The people sang him songs and cheered his name; a great feast was held for him. That night, the crowds with lighted torches gathered under his window and called him forth. What was then in his full heart—that big and tender heart so long lonely—is best recorded in his own words: "To God and man my thanks, my love!"

The Reverend Henry Ward Beecher, on a very cold day, stopped to buy a newspaper from a ragged youngster who stood shivering on a corner. "Poor little fellow," he said, "aren't you cold standing here?" The boy looked up with a smile and said, "I was, sir—before you passed."

THE INCOMPARABLE BEN FRANKLIN

By Bruce Bliven

OF THE famous heroes of America's past, most seem to inspire awe. Washington was so severely perfect that even those close to him were a little afraid of him. Those who came in contact with Jefferson were taken aback by his intellect. Lincoln had the common touch, yet his image is tinged with a majestic sadness. But there is one famous person, the most typical example of an American, of whom no one can think without a glow of personal warmth. Benjamin Franklin, printer and author, philosopher and statesman, scientist and inventor, was in some respects the greatest man this continent has produced. In any age he would have been extraordinary. Mirabeau, the French revolutionary leader, called him the philosopher who did most to extend the rights of man over the whole earth. "Antiquity would have raised altars to this mighty genius," he declared.

Yet so simple was Franklin's character, so charming his personality, so delightful his sense of humor that our affection for him has no reservations. His appearance commanded instant liking and respect. His glance was steady and kindly. He had big gray eyes set in a large face, a wide and humorous mouth and, as a young man, ample blond hair. Though the best-known portraits of him as an elder statesman belie it, he had in earlier years the build and energy of an athlete. Once in England, sailing on the Thames with friends, he jumped overboard and swam alongside the boat, performing fancy stunts on and under the water.

Franklin, born in Boston in 1706, was the 15th of 17 children of a poor candlemaker. Ben was to become the first self-made American, breaking the rigid class bonds inherited from England. He taught himself almost everything he knew, in science, philosophy, languages—Latin, French, German, Spanish and Italian. He had an intimate knowledge of the classics. Yet he had little more than a year of formal schooling; his father put him to work at ten. When he was 12 he was apprenticed to his brother James, a Boston printer. At 17 he was writing anonymous contributions to his brother's newspaper, slipping them under the office door at night. That same year, after friction with James, he left home and sought work, unsuccessfully, as a printer in New York. Hearing of a possible job in Philadelphia, he went there—much of the way on foot. Generations of American children have read how on arrival he spent almost his last coppers for three puffy rolls of bread, walked down the street eating one, the others tucked under his arms—and was laughed at by the girl who afterward became his wife. From then on, success piled on success. He got a job as a printer, soon went into business for himself, started a newspaper and later a magazine. By the age of 42 he had made a modest fortune and retired from business—only to spend 40 years more in the service of his country, including 25 years on two long tours of duty in England and one in France.

As statesman, Franklin was the first to think in terms of the nation rather than of separate colonies. Two decades before the Revolutionary War he invented the dual system of state governments united under a federal authority. During his years in London he presented the American case unceasingly, in conversations with important leaders, in letters and articles in British newspapers, in pamphlets. On a famous occasion he stood all day in the House of Commons, patiently and skillfully answering members' questions about American opposition to the hated Stamp Act. As a result, Parliament repealed the Act, and war was thereby postponed for a decade, giving the colonies badly needed time to prepare. Without Franklin, the Revolution might have dragged on years longer or ended in defeat. Sent to France in 1776, he persuaded the reluctant monarchy to send supplies secretly to General Washington, and finally to enter the war openly as an ally. After the British were beaten, Franklin prevented collapse of the Constitutional Convention. The small states wanted equal representation in Congress, the big ones wanted delegations based on population. Franklin engineered the compromise under which the Senate is based on the first plan and the House on the second. When the Constitution was finally written, Benjamin Franklin more than any other man was responsible for getting it ratified by the states.

Franklin was also a scientist and inventor of the first rank. Dr. Bernard Cohen, Harvard historian of science, says Franklin and Newton were the first two important scientific figures of the modern age. Everyone has heard how Franklin drew electricity from a cloud on a kite string, but few are aware that he wrote a book on electrical phenomena that was translated into several languages and widely acclaimed in Europe. He was the first to identify positive and negative electricity; we owe to him the words and concepts for battery, electric charge, condenser, conductor. His invention of the lightning rod removed a real terror from people's lives.

The Franklin stove, containing a hot-air radiator, is still in use to this day. So is his mechanical hand for lifting objects from a high shelf, and his kitchen stool that folds over into a stepladder. At 78 he invented that blessing of the elderly: bifocal spectacles. Mozart and Beethoven composed music for his "glass harmonica"—a series of glass hemispheres mounted on a rod and touched by the finger while revolving, to make music. (He was a skilled musician, performing on the harp, guitar and violin, and he wrote learnedly on problems of composing, especially on fitting music to words so that the latter are intelligible.) Franklin was the first to study the effect of water on a boat hull moving through it, and thereby became the father of hydrodynamics. He charted the Gulf Stream, and discovered that storms rotate while traveling forward. He proved that the thinner the air, the lower the temperature at which water will boil. He was the first to learn that dark-colored cloth retains heat; it took 100 years for Europeans to accept his advice and wear white clothing in the tropics.

In the midst of all his accomplishments, Franklin formed a club called the Junto, forerunner of the service clubs of today. In 1743 he organized the American Philosophical Society, the first scientific association of the country. "Philosophy" in those days embraced natural science; Franklin stipulated that among the members there must always be a botanist, chemist, mathematician, geographer and physician. For its first 50 years the Society was in practice a national academy of science, as well as the first national library and museum and the first patent office. Over the years, 95 of its members have won Nobel Prizes. Today it finances highly complicated projects in many aspects of science.

Ben's influence was so strong that 30 years after his death, the Franklin Institute was created to honor his memory. It still flourishes, specializing in something dear to Franklin's heart—interpreting science and technology for the layman. It has one of the world's finest science museums, conducts scores of research projects for the government and private industry, has a planetarium, computing center, huge library of scientific books and journals, a file of patents second only to that of the U.S. Patent Office, an observatory and many other projects. Its annual medals to outstanding scientists are highly valued; among the recipients have been Thomas Edison, Guglielmo Marconi, Orville Wright, Albert Einstein and Enrico Fermi.

Franklin started the first professional police force, the first volunteer fire company, the first fire insurance company, the school that became the University of Pennsylvania, the world-famous Pennsylvania Hospital. He was the sparkplug of the Abolitionist Society. He improved the postal service when he became Postmaster General, speeding up mail between New York and Philadelphia from once a week to three times a week in summer and from once a fortnight to once a week in winter. Mail went to England with unheard-of frequency—once a month. Through post roads were extended all the way from Canada to Florida.

In his time Franklin was perhaps the best-known writer of the English-speaking world. His *Autobiography*, though he never found time to finish it, is still one of the most widely read books of its kind. He wrote the first half of it in two weeks, in England and from memory, recording correctly names and dates of 40 and 50 years earlier. The magnificent English style was no accident. At 14, admiring the *Spectator* essays of Addison and Steele, he copied them out to get the rhythm, later tried to reproduce them from memory. To improve his vocabulary, he rewrote them in verse. In much of his writing he pretended to be someone else, and did it so well that often his readers were deceived. His first published work, at 17, purported to be the confessions of an elderly widow who had led a stormy life. It sounds genuine.

Working in London before the Revolution, he published a mock *Edict by the King of Prussia*, laying claim to the whole of Great Britain with exactly the same arguments by which the British King claimed the American colonies as his property. Another piece of propaganda that quickly ran around the world was his *Rules by Which a Great Empire May Be Reduced to a Small One*. The rules were precisely the injustices suffered by the colonies. Sometimes his humor was more effective than any angry speech could be. An overexcited Englishman denounced the colonials for planning bootleg whale and cod fisheries on the Great Lakes. Franklin agreed this was serious, even though the lakes were fresh water. "Cod, when attacked by their enemies, fly into any water where they can be safest. Whales pursue them wherever they fly. The grand leap of a whale up Niagara Falls is esteemed one of the finest spectacles in nature."

The first great publishing success in America was *Poor Richard's Almanack*, started by Franklin when he was 26. An almanac was at that time the only printed matter found in every American home. It contained all needed astronomical data, predicted the weather a year in advance, gave medical information and filled up the spaces with true sayings and bits of philosophy. Franklin's at once outdistanced all its rivals, selling 10,000 copies a year. He made "Poor Richard" Saunders, the supposed author, so real that he overshadowed Ben himself—and in the minds of many people, still does. Dozens of the sayings are still in use. Franklin never pretended he had invented all of them, but even those he borrowed he often sharpened by rewriting. Everyone knows "Early to bed and early to rise, makes a man healthy, wealthy and wise"; "Experience keeps a dear school, yet fools will learn in no other"; "He that goes a-borrowing goes a-sorrowing"; "Nothing is inevitable but death and taxes"; "Half a truth is often a great lie." Less familiar but equally wise are: "Now I have a sheep and a cow, everybody bids me good morrow"; "Approve not of him who commends all you say"; "Having been poor is no shame, but being ashamed of it is"; "Love your neighbor—yet don't pull down your hedge"; "It is ill manners to silence a fool and cruelty to let him go on."

Many of Poor Richard's sayings convey the message of self-reliance: "If you'd have it done, go; if not, send"; "God helps them that help themselves"; "It is hard for an empty sack to stand upright." In his will, Franklin left $5000 each to Philadelphia and to Boston, to be lent to young mechanics apprenticed in those cities. Typically, he did not make it too easy for them; each borrower was to pay five percent interest and ten percent of the principal each year. He wanted to help a man get on his feet—and stay there. These funds, greatly increased through compound interest, are still in existence today.

Franklin's long life was at least partly due to his intelligence about health. He was a great advocate of walking as the best exercise; he went everywhere he could on foot. Most people consumed huge quantities of food and drink; Ben urged moderation. The theory then was that night air was dangerous; he slept with his windows wide open. Once he and John Adams shared a room, and Adams was horrified to see Franklin throw open the windows at bedtime. When he protested, he got a lecture on the merits of fresh air so lengthy that he fell asleep before it was finished. For half a century, Ben poured out advice for successful living. Since he stuck to basic truths, nearly everything he said is valid today. He firmly believed that by conscious self-discipline one can improve one's character. "It is an art to be studied," he said, "like painting or music." When still a young man, he made a list of admirable qualities, resolving to improve himself in each. He would be sensible in eating and drinking, avoid idle chatter, be systematic in business, fulfill every task he undertook, avoid extravagance, eliminate idleness and waste motion, be sincere, treat others fairly, bear unfairness patiently, not let trifles upset him, and so on. He made "a little book, in which I allotted a page for each of the virtues. I determined to give a week's strict attention to each of them successively." Later he attributed whatever degree of success he achieved to this youthful routine.

Franklin preached the joy of work and practiced what he preached. As a young man he sometimes worked all night to finish a promised job on time. When he bought paper for his printing shop, he was not too proud to trundle it home himself in a wheelbarrow. On his first journey to Philadelphia, though he had paid his passage, he volunteered to help row the boat down the Delaware, and proved so useful that the boatmen didn't want to take his money. "Diligence is the mother of good luck," he wrote, "and God gives all things to industry."

As a boy Ben liked to argue belligerently. But he soon saw that people were rarely persuaded by a frontal attack. Taking his cue from Socrates, he learned to ask questions that, when answered honestly, would force an opponent to change his mind. "Quarreling," he remarked, "is like an insect bite which can infect you if you scratch it." In his old age he was able to say, "For these 50 years past, no one has ever heard a dogmatic expression escape me." When his work on electricity was attacked on religious grounds, Franklin declined to answer. "I concluded to let my papers shift for themselves, believing it was better to spend what time I could spare from public business in making new experiments than in disputing about those already made."

While Franklin was in London getting the Stamp Act repealed, word was spread in the colonies that he himself was the author of the outrageous tax. As usual, Ben did not bother to answer. "When truth and error have fair play, the former is always an over-match for the latter. I leave my [ideas] to take their chance in the world. If they are right, truth and experience will support them; if wrong, they ought to be refuted and rejected."

Franklin, with a wonderful gift for looking into the future, found it hard to understand those who could not see next year's oak in this year's acorn. In Paris he saw the first balloon ascent carrying people aloft. When a skeptic in the crowd asked what use a balloon could be, he promptly countered with the question, "What good is a newborn baby?" With his power to look ahead, he at once visualized the possibilities of air transport, including the rapid movement of troops in wartime. The British captured Canada from France in 1760. In the subsequent peace settlement, the English negotiators hesitated as to whether they should keep the vast unexplored northern wilderness or the rich, sugar-producing island of Guadeloupe in the West Indies. Many favored the latter; Franklin argued that Canada would ultimately prove the greater prize.

Throughout his long life Franklin had the deep humility of greatness. As a scientist he was very careful about crediting the discoveries of others, on occasion suppressing his own scientific papers if another investigator had paralleled his findings. He did more than anyone else to establish the first Pennsylvania library. But when in his old age he wrote the inscription for a new cornerstone, he struck his name off the list to be carved on it.

Franklin left his beloved France for the last time at 79. The people of Passy, where he had been living, clustered around the sedan chair in which illness forced him to travel, many of them weeping and imploring him to stay. Though he was suffering from a stone in the bladder, his spirit was unshakable. He afterward served as president of the Pennsylvania executive council, and as delegate to the Federal Constitutional Convention of 1787. At 82, he retired from public life. A few months later he received this letter: "If the united wishes of a free people, joined with the earnest prayers of every friend to science and humanity, could relieve the body from pain and infirmities, you could claim an exemption on this score. If to be venerated for benevolence, to be admired for talent, if to be esteemed for patriotism, if to be beloved for philanthropy, can gratify the human mind, you must have the pleasing consolation to know that you have not lived in vain. As long as I retain my memory you will be thought of with respect, veneration and affection by, dear Sir, your sincere friend and obedient humble servant, G. Washington."

The following year, 1790, Franklin died at 84, the most famous private citizen and the best-loved public figure in the world. His funeral was the largest ever seen, up to that time, for any person not in office. The entire French government went into mourning for three days, and Jefferson wanted the American government to do the same. Washington regretfully said no, not wishing to set a precedent that might later prove embarrassing.

Franklin's career is well summed up by one of his biographers, Carl Van Doren, who says he was not "one of those men who owe their greatness merely to the opportunities of their times. In any age, in any place, Franklin would have been great. Mind and will, talent and art, strength and ease, wit and grace met in him as if nature had been lavish and happy when he was shaped."

One of the best-known epitaphs ever written is the one Franklin composed for himself when still a young man: "The Body of B. Franklin, Printer, Like the Cover of an old Book, its Contents torn out, and stript of its Lettering and Gilding, lies here, Food for Worms. But the work shall not be wholly lost: for it will, as he believed, appear once more, in a new & more perfect Edition, corrected and amended by the Author."

None preaches better than the ant, and she says nothing.
                                                —*Benjamin Franklin*

One man with courage makes a majority.—*Andrew Jackson*

POET OF OUR LAND

By Max Eastman

E VERY GREAT people has its poet. Shakespeare, Goethe, Pushkin, Dante, Hugo, Li Po—these names float over their countries almost like the national flag. There are many who believe that, in America, it is Walt Whitman who occupies this unique place.

To me there is drama in this, for within my lifetime Walt Whitman died in a shabby little house in Camden, New Jersey, hardly known to the reading public at all and, where known, regarded for the most part as a disreputable and rather unclean character. He was, in fact, immaculate—so much so that all his friends mentioned it. He was, moreover, by comparison with most poets, a model of Christian virtue. He had no vices or bad habits. He never swore or smoked or gambled; he seldom took a drink. His chief dissipation was to ride on Broadway horse cars.

Whitman was born in 1819 near Huntington, Long Island, in a small gray-shingled cabin, but most of his boyhood was passed in Brooklyn, where his father built houses. By the time he was 20 he had learned the printer's trade, taught school and started a newspaper—writing and printing it himself and delivering it on horseback. For the next nine years he worked in the print shop, newsroom or editorial office of various New York and Long Island papers. During the last two of these years he was editor of the Brooklyn *Eagle*. While working on these papers he wrote a number of sentimental verses. But until he was 29 the idea never occurred to him, and certainly never to anybody else, that he might be a great poet.

Everybody around town knew Walter Whitman, and everybody liked him. He was big and strong, had a perfect build, and his face and head were as fine as nature ever produced. But the one thing he was famous for was a magnificently casual attitude toward work. Any afternoon he didn't knock off and go swimming, it was because he had spent the morning riding back and forth on Fulton Ferry, or up and down Manhattan on the Broadway car. One of his first employers remarked that "if the boy came down with fever and the ague, he would be too lazy to shake," and that reputation grew up with him. There is a fog around the question of why Whitman left the *Eagle*, and you can see his character looming pretty clearly through the fog. He was a Free-Soil Democrat; that is, he wanted slavery excluded from the new states. The owners of the paper wanted the states to decide. Less than a month after leaving the *Eagle*, he took a job on the New Orleans *Crescent*. His trip to New Orleans was the turning point in his life. It woke the emotional and imaginative giant slumbering within him. I think there are three reasons for this.

First, the journey over the Alleghenies and down America's great rivers astounded his eyes. He saw spread before him the vastness and incredible richness of the young republic. He fell in love with America. Second, he cast loose a little, in the freely languorous French atmosphere of New Orleans, from the stern mood of the reformer. Most important, he fell in love with a girl whom he could not, or would not, marry. Nothing is known of that love beyond the girl's heart-melting picture pasted in one of his notebooks, for Walt kept silent about the whole incident. But there is little doubt—in my mind, at least—that her touch was what finally broke open the fountains of immortal song that this strange, indolent, ardent, majestic and yet callow youth contained.

Walt came home from New Orleans, like Saul of Tarsus from the road to Damascus, a changed man. He had seen a vision—a vision of the American republic leading mankind into a new era of fearlessly free and equal, boldly scientific and yet richly poetic, joyfully expanding physical and spiritual life. He came back the poet and prophet of that sublime event.

Like Saul, he made a slight change in his name: he would be what his good friends called him—Walt. And he made a big change in his apparel. As the poet of democracy he peeled off his bow tie, unbuttoned his shirt to where the undershirt showed, and put on for good and all the everyday clothes of the ordinary workman or mechanic. The change was not quite so artificial as it sounds, for he was working as a carpenter for his father. But it was deeply meaningful to him. He believed he was making a corresponding change in poetry. Instead of turning pretty verses, he would say what he had to say straight out—the way American workmen do and the Bible does—and let the words sing their own song.

It was not his way of singing, however, that made Walt Whitman great. The greatness lay in the things he sang. A Song of Myself—a declaration of the divine and sovereign importance of the individual man, not to be found elsewhere in literature. A Song of Sympathy—a larger giving of the self than had ever been sung before. Walt kept working on his book of verse year after year, jotting down the lines on ferryboats, along the wharves, on horse cars or at Coney Island. He brought them home to the house on Myrtle Avenue and worked them up on a pine table in a little upstairs room. To signify democracy and the sacred worth of small and simple things, he called his book *Leaves of Grass*.

When Walt spoke of himself in the book, he spoke *for* the everyday working American. What he was trying to say was: "This is the way the American common man should talk. This is how he should stand."

And I or you, pocketless of a dime, may purchase the pick of
    the earth,
And to glance with an eye, or show a bean in its pod,
    confounds the learning of all times,
And there is no trade or employment but the young man
    following it may become a hero,
And there is no object so soft but it makes a hub for the
    wheel'd universe,
And I say to any man or woman, Let your soul stand cool
    and composed before a million universes.

Walt printed 800 copies of his book in a little print shop, seeing them through the press himself. Then he inserted an ad in the New York *Tribune*, sent review copies to critics and editors, and gift copies to a number of eminent Americans. To the bookstores in New York and Brooklyn he peddled them himself in a big canvas bag. Not a copy, so far as historical records show, was sold. A friend on the *Tribune* wrote a mildly favorable hack review. Other critics either ignored him or burned him up: "A heterogeneous mass of bombast, vulgarity and nonsense." . . . "He is as unacquainted with art as a hog with mathematics." . . . "We can conceive of no better reward than the lash." The verdict of the eminent Americans was little better. Wendell Phillips remarked that he found all kinds of leaves there except the fig. John Greenleaf Whittier threw the book out of the window.

Such was America's reception of her national poet. And then out of the clear sky, out of New England's icy silence, came a letter—a letter that is almost as famous now as the poems: "Dear sir, I am not blind to the worth of the wonderful gift of *Leaves of Grass*. I find it the most extraordinary piece of wit and wisdom that America has yet contributed. I greet you at the beginning of a great career." It was signed with the preeminent name of those times—Ralph Waldo Emerson.

Walt never doubted his own greatness from that day on. But his rise to the heights of fame was slow. The average American for whom he sang preferred the jingly tinkle of Poe's "The Bells" or "The Raven" to Walt's full-throated song.

The Civil War delayed Walt Whitman's climb to glory. Walt was no soldier. As he moved through the world, he loved it all, the good and the bad, instinctively. It is hard for those with a genius for love to take sides in a fight. Moreover Walt had dedicated himself to be the poet of the whole nation. He moved to Washington where the great military hospitals were, abandoned his writing and gave himself to the task of tending the wounded soldiers. Earning a meager livelihood in a paymaster's office, living in a small room, he visited the hospitals each day from noon till four o'clock and again from six to nine. He carried a big bag full of gifts for the soldiers—tobacco, paper and envelopes, oranges, gingersnaps. But his greatest gift to them was a mother's tenderness in the robust and powerful figure of a man.

Before each visit he walked a while in the sun and wind or under the stars. He drank only water and milk, avoided "fats and late suppers," in order to assure himself of a "pure, perfect, sweet, clean-blooded, robust body" through which the healing powers of nature could flow to the suffering soldiers.

Walt gave his good health in that service. He was himself like a wounded soldier when the war was done. He was at home in Brooklyn with his mother, recuperating a second time from "hospital malaria," when the shocking news of Lincoln's assassination came in 1865.

It was spring and the lilacs were in bloom in the yard of the little house where they lived. Brooklyn in those days was little more than a rural village, and he did not have to walk far to hear a hermit thrush singing as the evening star peered out in the twilight. He composed his noblest poem, twining the lilac, the star, the song of the bird and his grief into as sublime a tribute to a hero—and to life and death—as has ever been spoken. Swinburne described his poem "When Lilacs Last in the Dooryard Bloom'd" as "the most sweet and sonorous nocturne ever chanted in the church of the world." More perhaps than any of his other works, this poem has given Walt Whitman by gradual universal consent the name of America's poet.

After the war Walt got a clerical job in the Indian Bureau. He was working on a new edition of *Leaves of Grass* and kept the scribbled proof sheets in his desk. Secretary of the Interior Harlan, a preacher-politician from Iowa City, got an itch of curiosity one night and sneaked in and took a look at the book. It gave him a terrible shock there in the lamplight, and he won himself a place in history as a snooping prude by firing his immortal employe. Walt's Irish friend William O'Connor wrote a sizzling pamphlet about the incident, under the title of *The Good Gray Poet*.

In 1873 Walt's glorious physique gave out. He woke up one night and found he could not move his left arm or leg. He went calmly to sleep again and the next day waited quietly for his friends to come. Throughout the 20 years of decline and increasing confinement that followed, he never lost that calm. He never lost his patient, friendly humor. Friends and admirers, a tiny but increasing company, sent funds to help him. He followed the slowly growing fame of his book with anxious joy, as a parent follows the career of a well-trained child. Tributes came, once in a while—and visits—from those foresighted enough to encourage his belief that his book would live.

Walt would have been proudly delighted—and yet also, in his still depths, unsurprised—to know that 50 years after his death a British Prime Minister, reporting a great military victory to the House of Commons, would quote, like a text from the Bible, his noble admonition: "Now understand me well—It is provided in the essence of things that from any fruition of success, no matter what, shall come forth something to make a greater struggle necessary."

In the many years he taught philosophy at Harvard, George Santayana held his classes spellbound with the beauty of his speech. He was a walking lecturer, wandering about the room and using pauses in his stride to punctuate his speaking. Joseph Auslander, then at Harvard, told me of one beautiful spring morning, when in the course of his lecture Santayana went often to the window and looked out upon the disturbing yellow of a hedge of forsythia. Finally he paused for a long time, longer than ever before, while the class in the big lecture hall sat with pencils poised to take down his next words. At last he turned to the class and said: "Gentlemen, I very much fear that last sentence will never be completed. You see, I have an appointment with April." And then he walked out of the room. He never lectured regularly again.

—*Louis K. Anspacher*

THE FABULOUS QUEEN

By Don Wharton

C LEOPATRA is usually thought of as an Egyptian siren who killed herself for love of the Roman general Marc Antony. Little of this is true. Although Cleopatra was queen of the ancient kingdom, not a drop of Egyptian blood flowed in her veins. She was a Macedonian Greek; her Egyptian capital, Alexandria, was a Greek city, and her court language was Greek. Her dynasty had been founded by Ptolemy, a Macedonian general of Alexander the Great, who, after Alexander's death, seized Egypt and made himself king.

There is not a shred of evidence that connects Cleopatra with any man except Julius Caesar and, three years after his death, Marc Antony. These were not idle liaisons but unions approved by her priests and recognized in Egypt as marriages. The idea that she employed all her wiles to seduce these men is absurd. Yet the legend has persisted for 2000 years, chiefly because poets and playwrights, including Shakespeare, emphasized her physical charms and passions rather than her brains and courage. Her deeds, however, reveal her as a brilliant, resourceful woman who spent her life in a struggle to keep her country from being swallowed up by the Romans.

Born in 68 or 69 B.C., Cleopatra grew up amid palace intrigue and violence. Her father, Ptolemy XI, died when Cleopatra was 18, and she then became queen, ruling jointly with her ten-year-old brother, Ptolemy XII. Two years later the young Ptolemy, dominated by a trio of palace schemers, forced Cleopatra into exile in Syria. Showing the spirit that was to characterize her life,

she promptly raised an army and started to march back across the desert to fight for her throne. This was the Cleopatra whom Caesar met in the autumn of 48 B.C. He had come to Egypt in pursuit of the Roman general Pompey, his adversary in a struggle for political power—the kind of struggle that was to keep Rome in turmoil for almost a century.

What did Cleopatra look like? The only clues are a few coins stamped with her profile, and a bust dug from Roman ruins some 1800 years after her death. They show an aquiline nose, a beautifully formed mouth with finely chiseled lips. A number of ancient historians wrote of her "ravishing beauty," but they were not men who had actually seen her. Perhaps the most accurate description is by Plutarch, whose grandfather was told about Cleopatra by a physician acquainted with one of the royal cooks. Plutarch wrote that her actual beauty "was not in itself so remarkable that none could be compared to her."

All early writers agreed, however, on her "fascinating" conversation, her lovely voice, "her adroitness and subtlety in speech." She spoke six languages, was well acquainted with Greek history, literature and philosophy, was a shrewd negotiator and apparently a first-rate military planner. She also had an ability to dramatize herself. When summoned by Caesar to leave her troops and come to the palace he had taken over in Alexandria, Cleopatra slipped into the city at dusk, had herself tied up in a roll of carpet and, thus concealed, was carried to Caesar's apartment. Whether her clever scheme was to elude assassins in her brother's hire, or to impress Caesar, it was one of the most dramatic entrances of all time. Her courage and charm helped convince Caesar that it would be wise to restore her to her throne.

Possibly to impress Caesar with Egypt's wealth, Cleopatra the next spring organized a huge expedition up the Nile. For weeks she and Caesar floated along in an elaborate houseboat accompanied by 400 vessels carrying troops and supplies. Then, in June, Cleopatra gave birth to a son, Caesarion—Greek for "little Caesar." The infant, his father's only son, seems to have been the root of an ambitious plan for Caesar and Cleopatra to merge Rome and

Egypt into one vast empire to be ruled by them and their line. Promptly on the birth of the boy, Caesar left Alexandria and began military operations in Asia Minor and North Africa, mopping up all remaining opposition. Within a year he returned triumphantly to Rome—undisputed dictator. Cleopatra was there with Caesarion, established by Caesar in a magnificent villa.

As a queen with a royal court, Cleopatra began to exert her influence on Roman life. She brought coiners from Alexandria to improve the Roman mint, financiers to arrange Caesar's tax program. Her astronomers reformed the Roman calendar, creating the one on which our present system is based. Caesar had her statue placed in a new temple built to honor Venus, and he issued a coin on which Venus and Eros could be recognized as Cleopatra with Caesarion in her arms. His power seemed absolute. Then suddenly, 20 months after Cleopatra came to Rome, Julius Caesar was a corpse—murdered on the Ides of March. Was Cleopatra grief-stricken? No one knows. After a month she sailed back to Egypt. Historians have no facts about the next three years of her reign, except that in the power struggle that now plunged Rome into civil war the contestants sought her aid. Apparently her policy was one of cautious waiting to see who was to become Caesar's successor.

When Marc Antony emerged as the strong man of the East, he bade Cleopatra meet him at Tarsus, in Asia Minor. For a time she ignored his summons; then she set sail with a splendid fleet, carrying gold, slaves, horses and jewels. At Tarsus, instead of going ashore in a humble role, Cleopatra coolly waited at anchor. After she had deftly maneuvered Antony into becoming her guest, she confronted him with a dazzling spectacle: the galley's silver-tipped oars beating time to the music of flutes and harps, its ropes worked by beautiful slaves dressed as sea nymphs and graces, incense burners pouring out exotic perfumes. Reclining under a gold awning was Cleopatra garbed as Venus, fanned by young boys resembling cupids.

When the banquet was over, Cleopatra presented Antony with the gold plates, elaborate drinking vessels, couches and embroideries they had used. The next night she entertained Antony and his officers again, and lavished similar gifts on each guest. Her goal was not to gain Antony's affections but to impress upon him the wealth of Egypt, hence its power as an ally.

Three months later Antony came to Alexandria and spent the winter. He left in spring, six months before Cleopatra bore their twins, and did not see her again for nearly four years. Cleopatra meanwhile strengthened her country's defenses, built up her navy, amassed gold and supplies. When Antony, hoping to extend his power in the East, asked her to meet him in Syria, she came as a determined bargainer. She extracted an agreement whereby Egypt would be given all the vast areas the Pharaohs had possessed 1400 years before, but which were now Roman provinces: Antony also agreed to a legal marriage, and in celebration of this event coins were struck bearing their two heads. At that time Cleopatra began a new dating of her reign. Now 33, she set out with Antony to make war on the Persians, but at the Euphrates River she had to give up the campaign. She was pregnant again. The child arrived in the autumn, and that winter there came desperate appeals from Antony: his army had been cut to pieces, and the haggard remnants had barely escaped to the Syrian coast. Cleopatra, with money, supplies and weapons, sailed to his rescue.

The next year, 35 B.C., she had to use all her wiles to keep Antony—his mind clouded with prolonged drinking—from attempting another invasion of Persia. Realizing that their true enemy was Octavian, Caesar's nephew and legal heir who from Rome dominated the West, she urged Antony to concentrate on his overthrow. In 32 B.C. she precipitated war with Octavian by persuading Antony to take two steps: issue a writ divorcing his other wife, Octavia (Octavian's beautiful sister), and order troops to cross the Aegean Sea into Greece. Cleopatra was now at her peak, with vassal kings from the Middle East paying her court, the Athenians showering her with honors, hailing her as Aphrodite and erecting her statue in the Acropolis.

Then, at Actium on the west coast of Greece late in the afternoon of September 2, 31 B.C., everything crumbled. Historians have never agreed about this crucial battle: why Antony, with a superior army, let it become a naval engagement; or why Cleopatra, with the sea fight raging and the outcome still undecided, hoisted sail and made off downwind for Egypt with her 60 warships; or why Antony left his huge army behind, boarded her ship and sailed away with her.

At home, when news of the disaster spread, Cleopatra firmly put down all discontent. She tried to strengthen ties with neighboring countries. She also began transferring warships from the Mediterranean to the Red Sea—a stupendous project which involved dragging them across miles of desert.

When Octavian's troops arrived and Egypt's frontier forts fell to them, Cleopatra remained in Alexandria, prepared to bargain with Octavian or battle him. But when the invading army closed in, the queen's navy and cavalry deserted. Antony killed himself. Taken alive, Cleopatra was put under guard and warned that if she killed herself her children would be put to death.

Though Octavian promised to be merciful, Cleopatra assumed that her fate would be like that of hundreds of other royal captives who had been paraded in chains through the streets of Rome, then executed. Spirited and daring to the end, she pretended to abandon all thoughts of suicide. Securing permission to visit Antony's grave, she apparently made contact with faithful followers as her litter was carried through the streets. She returned to her quarters, bathed, dined and had her attendants dress her as Venus. Of what happened next we know only this: Roman officers breaking into her quarters found Cleopatra dead. According to legend, the queen had allowed herself to be stung by an asp smuggled to her in a basket of figs.

When Octavian's conquest of Egypt was celebrated in Rome, a statue of Cleopatra was dragged through the streets with an asp clinging to one arm. Her three children by Antony—Caesarion had been executed—were forced to march in the degrading procession. It was then that Roman poets, to court favor with the victor, began to spread the myth of a wicked and immoral Egyptian queen, the myth which continues to this day.

PIONEER OF FREEDOM

By Donald Culross Peattie

OVER 300 years ago there was born a man whose ideas were so modern that the world is just catching up with some of the best of them. He died 70 years before the birth of the United States of America, yet he was the first to propose it. And not only did he urge a union of the colonies, he even drew up a plan for a league of nations. Pennsylvania, most prosperous of all the original colonies, was founded upon this man's personal fortune and on his faith in the great democratic principles embodied in the Declaration of Independence and the Constitution, though he lived too soon to sign either. "William Penn," declares the historian John Fiske, "was by far the greatest among the founders of the American commonwealth."

Son of the old sea dog, Admiral Sir William Penn, young William was born in 1644 in the shadow of the Tower of London—

a gloomy shadow, symbol of tyranny. Men could be cast into prison there for nothing worse than their honest beliefs. And it was because of his own principles that this wealthy aristocrat, when only 24 years old, found himself a prisoner in the Tower. For he belonged to the persecuted Quaker faith. Yet in demanding freedom of speech and freedom of worship he did not speak merely as a member of the Society of Friends, but as the friend of the society of free men everywhere.

For his faith Penn had been expelled from Oxford and driven from home with blows by his father. Not this, nor even nine months of almost solitary confinement in the Tower, discouraged him; he went about the British Isles, Holland, France, Italy and Germany, attracting crowds of two and three thousand, most of them not even Quakers but simply men in search of their lost rights, men who heard in Penn's strong voice the trumpet call to freedom. One day in London, he and his followers found their meetinghouse locked against them by soldiers, and Penn led the assembly in prayer in the street. He was at once arrested and haled into Old Bailey court, charged with unlawful, seditious and riotous assembly.

He was brought before the bewigged and frowning magistrate, Sir Samuel Starling, Lord Mayor of London, and asked if he were guilty of the offense as charged. "The question," flung back young Penn, "is not whether I am guilty but whether the indictment is legal!" Above the hubbub which followed he proclaimed that a law denying the God-given right of a man to obey his conscience is not valid.

"Stop his mouth! Clap him in the bail-dock!" thundered the Lord Mayor. And, while the jury was instructed in so many words to bring in a verdict of guilty, Penn was forced into a cagelike room as if he had been a wild beast.

"You are Englishmen," he called to the jurors. "Mind your privilege. Don't give away your right!"

"Nor will we ever!" cried the foreman.

Quaking but resolved, 12 good men and true returned to pronounce Penn guilty of no crime. The angry judge threatened to have their noses cut off, and sent them back, without food or fire, till they should change their minds. But nothing broke their will. After five days the judge, beaten, clapped jurors and accused into Newgate prison for contempt of court. Penn's dying father paid the fine. The jurors sued the judge for illegal imprisonment, and won. Today a monument, on the site of the Old Bailey, commemorates "the great trial for liberty of conscience."

Five times did William Penn go to prison for his religious and political views. Each time he grew stronger. While he meditated and wrote some of his greatest books within prison walls, he became clearer about what he thought. His fame increased; he was a martyr dear not only to Quakers but to freedom-loving men everywhere.

Born to the world of nobility and high offices, widely traveled and a linguist, Penn moved at ease in the courts of Europe, talked like an equal to Peter the Great, enjoyed a glass of wine with Samuel Pepys, and was just as much at home under a thatched cottage roof. He had the ear, successively, of four British monarchs—Charles II, James II, William III and Queen Anne—and by his influence saved scores of people from imprisonment without cause and from unjust seizure of property. Indirectly he saved thousands more by the principles he championed.

Unlike many idealists, Penn was not too whitehanded to take part in local politics. He threw himself into the rough and tumble of elections, which were as dishonest and violent as in the worst-run city wards of today. He knew that you can't have good government without working for it. Only when his candidate was twice defeated by dishonest returns did Penn turn his thoughts toward what he called the "Holy Experiment"—the founding of a new society in America.

Penn had inherited a claim of $80,000, which his father had loaned to Charles II, and he now formally requested the King to discharge this with a land grant in the New World, where he and other Friends could find refuge. Delighted to get rid of an old debt and a new sect, the Merry Monarch gave Penn a charter to a lordly tract west of the Delaware River—almost all of what we call Pennsylvania, nearly equal in size to England, and but thinly inhabited by Indians, Swedes, Dutch and Englishmen, under no definite government.

That is how, one beautiful Indian summer morning in October 1682, the good ship *Welcome* glided into Delaware Bay. At the little settlement of New Castle (now in Delaware) Penn stepped ashore and received the delegation bringing him a "porringer of river-water, earth and a green twig." Thus symbolically did he take possession of earth and stream and woods—Penn's woods, or Pennsylvania.

The banks of the Schuylkill were flaming with autumn tints when Penn's barge landed on the site of his future capital. How well he selected the spot is proved by the fact that Philadelphia is today the fourth largest city in America. With the enthusiasm of a boy he planned the streets and named them—Broad, Chestnut, Spruce, Pine—for a tract covering 10,000 acres. Regarding him as a visionary, more practical people cut his plans down to 1200 acres, unable to foresee that within two centuries "Philly" would exceed Penn's wildest dreams. Every house, Penn decreed, should stand in a large yard of its own; every street should be broad and planted with trees.

Although Penn owned the king's grant outright, he honorably paid the previous settlers full value for their lands. More, he bought the land all over again from the Indians, going forth unarmed to meet the fiercely painted Susquehannocks, the slant-eyed Shawnees, the stately Leni-Lenape. For 70 years the Quakers and the Indians were to live in harmony—a record in the turbulent history of the American frontier.

Penn himself drew up a Frame of Government for his colony. Without reference to property or church membership, every free-man was given a vote. Absolute religious freedom was granted to all comers. In an age when English law enumerated 200 offenses for which hanging was the penalty, Penn reduced capital punishment to murder and high treason. Imprisonment for expression of opinion or for debt was abolished. There was to be no race discrimination.

Next Penn set up courts. In cases involving an Indian, the jury was to be composed half of red men. A witchcraft case came up, and old European superstition threatened to break out as it was soon to do in Massachusetts. But when the old woman confessed she was a witch, Penn informed her he knew of no law (unless it was gravity) to prevent her from riding through the air on a broomstick, and so he blew away the case with a gust of laughter.

Having established freedom of speech and freedom of worship, Penn worked hard to make possible freedom from want. He toiled ceaselessly to make his colony self-supporting, yet enriched with the best things of life. Industrious, skillful artisans and farmers brought over from the Rhineland helped to make Pennsylvania the most productive colonial state. Shipbuilding, lumbering, milling and fur trading all made swift progress.

In no colony was there a finer system of education. One of Penn's first cares was a schoolhouse, and the William Penn Charter School still exists today. Penn believed that the poor should receive their education free and that the well-to-do should pay for the schools. "It isn't *what* you leave your children," he insisted, "but *how* you leave them." Penn fixed his hopes for humanity upon the younger generation. He had 15 children of his own, eight by his first wife, seven by his second. With his children and grandchildren, he delighted to romp in a way that would have astounded those who knew him only as the grave Quaker or the polished courtier.

Near the present Tullytown, 20 miles north of Philadelphia by barge, Penn built his "beloved manor," Pennsbury, a two-and-a-half-story brick dwelling with fine chimneys and wood-paneled walls, set among gardens and shady avenues. Here Penn hoped to live out his life. But to protect his colony's interests at Court, he had to make lengthy stays in England. Penn never saw Pennsbury Manor after 1701, and his children allowed it to fall into ruins. Not until 1934 did the Pennsylvania Historical Commission begin its restoration. Archaeologists dug up from the soil fire-place tiles and hinges. Every detail of the house and all the plans had been preserved, so that in 1939 the commission opened the doors of a Pennsbury Manor restored perfectly, though at a cost of $200,000, or about ten times what it cost William Penn to build originally.

Penn's reputation is today achieving a rebirth. Yet his life seemed to end in failure. In England, financial and political difficulties multiplied; his estates were swept from him; for a time he had to go to debtors' prison. During one of his visits, because he had written the exiled James II an innocent letter, he was accused of treason and escaped prison only by hiding for two years.

It was under these discouraging circumstances that in 1693 Penn, who never despaired of humanity or its capacity for self-government, showed the ultimate flash of his genius. Entitled *An Essay Towards the Present and Future Peace of Europe*, this document was Penn's unheeded effort to bring to all the world freedom from fear. What he proposed, in simple and noble terms, was in effect a United States of Europe where every nation should agree to submit its disputes to a world court for hearings, and all nations would promptly unite to crush an aggressor. The world will have to make great strides to come abreast of this noble spirit which in 1718 stepped forth from earthly confines.

It is not the critic who counts; not the man who points out how the strong man stumbled, or where the doer of deeds could have done them better. The credit belongs to the man who is actually in the arena, whose face is marred by dust and sweat and blood; who strives valiantly; who errs and comes short again and again; who knows the great enthusiasms, the great devotions; who spends himself in a worthy cause; who, at the best, knows in the end the triumph of high achievement, and who, at the worst, if he fails, at least fails while daring greatly, so that his place shall never be with those timid souls who know neither victory or defeat.   —*Theodore Roosevelt*

HEAVENLY GENIUS

By Peter Farb

N O GREATER musical fiasco could be imagined than that which seemed in the making at Berlin's austere Academy of Song in March of 1829. A rambling work so unwieldy that it called for *two* sets of orchestras and choruses was in rehearsal. A Passion based on the Gospel of St. Matthew, it had caused little attention at its first performance, 100 years before.

Its composer was as little known as the music: Johann Sebastian Bach had lain in an unmarked grave for eight decades. And conducting this Passion was its unknown "discoverer," a 20-year-old Jew named Felix Mendelssohn, who would now stand before a combined orchestra and chorus for the first time. As a young boy, Mendelssohn had come across a manuscript of the Passion at his teacher's home and had fallen in love with it. The music had almost no other credentials.

Yet members of the Academy spread such favorable reports of the rehearsals that, for the public performance, every seat was taken. And from the first notes the listeners were swept up in a tide of religious emotion, for the *St. Matthew Passion* is perhaps the most deeply stirring music ever written. A cathedral hush greeted the lyric melodies, the moving solos of contemplation, the ringing hymns of exaltation. Not only did the audience hear and feel deeply; it also *saw.* For so great was the genius of this unknown Bach that he seemed able, with mere notes, to paint vivid stage scenery and create mood lighting. Each time Christ spoke, for instance, Bach had surrounded the words with a shimmering "halo of sound" played by the strings. As Christ was led away, sounds evoked a picture of footsteps dragging under the weight of the Cross.

So successful was the performance that it had to be repeated not once, but twice—to packed halls. Thanks to Mendelssohn, a sudden interest was kindled in Bach's music, and great composers fanned the enthusiasm. Chopin advised all pianists to study Bach closely. "This is the highest and best school," he said. "No one will ever create a more ideal one." Investigation revealed that many unpublished masterpieces by Bach had fortunately survived—sacred music, works for orchestra, string instruments and forerunners of the modern piano. Bach societies sprang up in Europe to search out and perform these neglected works.

Today Bach is entrenched in our hearts and lives. His musical settings for many Christian hymns can be heard any Sunday in churches around the globe—"O Sacred Head now wounded," "Jesu, Joy of man's desiring" and many others. For Bach, music was an act of worship, as if the notes, once out of range of human hearing, still ascended heavenward in a song of praise. "The sole object of all music," he advised his students, "should be the glory of God and pleasant recreation." On many of his scores he scribbled the dedication: "To God Alone the Glory."

Bach's inward nobility of spirit received rough packaging. His portraits show him to be thickset, with a stubborn jaw that thrusts out beyond a double chin. His nose is massive, his eyes squint—the expression is that of a man who has tasted the bitterness of life along with its glories. For into the piety and generations of musical craft that molded this master went huge doses of humanity. The man who praised God in his scores also jotted on them his household budget. Fervor flamed within him, but he was also constantly driven to find better-paying jobs to support his 20 children, 11 of whom died in childhood.

As a church organist and composer, Bach ground out thousands of compositions, much as a minister prepares a weekly sermon, and they were accepted by the parishioners just as routinely. Not one of his church works did he ever bother to have published; some of them, left in a church-school cupboard, were said to have been used by schoolboys to wrap their sandwiches. Bach would have been astonished to hear that 200 years after his death he would be a fixture of the concert stage, for he was roundly condemned by the two leading music critics of his day. The only large commission he ever received was to compose a set of pieces for the clavichord, the forerunner of the piano. These compositions were called the "Goldberg" Variations, and were used to quiet a Russian envoy who had trouble falling asleep.

Johann Sebastian Bach was born in 1685 in the town of Eisenach, in central Germany. For nearly two centuries his family had produced expert musicians—town organists and bandsmen. In fact, such was the family reputation that in his part of the country a musician was known as a "Bach." Orphaned at the age of ten, he went to live with an older brother who, jealous of his talent, denied to Sebastian a collection of advanced organ pieces. So, almost nightly for months, the boy climbed to the top shelf of the bookcase, helped himself to the scores, copied them out by moonlight, then returned them to their shelf at day-break. When his brother heard him playing these forbidden pieces, he took away the long-labored-over copies. The youngster was left only with permanently impaired eyesight.

When Sebastian was 15, he heard of good singing jobs available at Lüneburg, so he hiked the 200 miles to make his fortune. He stayed three years, singing in a choir, playing in an orchestra and spending endless hours at the organ and clavichord. In later years, when asked the secret of his keyboard brilliance, he said, "If you are equally industrious, you will be equally successful."

Bach became so expert that he was offered the important post of court organist at Weimar, where he spent nine years. Here he wrote his famous organ toccatas ("touch" pieces, because of the dexterity required to perform them) and complicated musical compositions called fugues. His renown spread so that once when, unannounced, he visited a village church and drew magnificent tones from the wretched organ, the amazed organist exclaimed, "This can only be an angel from heaven—or Bach himself!"

Bach was not happy in the court at Weimar, however, and in his next post—director of chamber music for the Duke of Cöthen—he had no access to a decent organ. So, when he was 38, he turned away from court life and applied for the recently vacated job of organist at St. Thomas' Church in Leipzig. His base salary was only a fourth of what he had been getting, and the job was degrading and tiresome. In addition to pouring out a continuous stream of music, he had to teach classes in Latin and music and also act as housemaster for noisy youngsters in the church school.

During his 27 years in Leipzig, Bach complained of "vexation, envy and persecution" at every step. Still, the pettiness of his life could not dry up his inspiration. In his first two decades there he wrote a body of religious music that has never been equaled: nearly 300 cantatas for every holy day in the church calendar, two oratorios, Masses and motets, the *St. John* and *St. Matthew* Passions, the monumental B-minor Mass.

But the years of writing out the notes, studying and playing all night what he had written during the day, ruined his already weakened eyes. He took hope in the visit to Leipzig of a famous English oculist, who performed two operations. Both were failures. Bach was left blind and in shattered health. During the time of his blindness, however, he wrote *The Art of the Fugue*, a work of breathtaking intricacy and skill.

Today much of Bach's music sounds strange to our ears at first. The music we are accustomed to—popular songs, folk music, even much of the classical music of the last century—is constructed like an arch, with pillars of chords in the bass holding up a single melody. Bach's music is contrapuntal: melody is piled on top of melody, and all of the melodies are sounded at the same time, crossing one another, blending their tone colors, making a veritable tapestry of sound. So perfect was the Bach craftsmanship that when, in an experiment not long ago, a player-piano roll of one of his compositions was reversed—so that the high notes became the bass and the low notes soared upward—the music sounded as melodious as before.

Play a recording of a Bach choral work or of one of his familiar organ works. The first time you hear it, pay attention to only the highest melody, the soprano. Now listen again, this time separating from the strands of melody the bass part. Next, concentrate on the middle voices alone. Soon much of the music you are used to—those pillars of chords—will sound almost dull. It is the genius of Bach that you can listen to him hundreds of times and continue to discover beauties previously unheard.

Suddenly, in July 1750, Bach's sight miraculously cleared. Almost immediately, however, he suffered a stroke. He died ten days later—but not before he had completed one of his most stirring works, an organ arrangement of the hymn of distress, "When in the hour of utmost need." There is no sound of suffering in this final composition, and at the last moment Bach changed the hymn's title to "Before Thy throne, O Lord, I come." He died as he had lived, praising God in his music. It was the ultimate personal offering of one who had heard the chords of a heavenly harmony.

I shall always believe that Cockey Roberts, a parrot who used to come regularly to my room when I was practicing, was really interested in my playing. If I had closed the door, he would knock sharply with his beak. I would keep very quiet, and he would knock again, a little harder. "Who is there?" I would call out. An angry voice would answer, "Cockey Roberts." "Who?" I would say, pretending not to understand, and that angry shrill little voice would come again: "Cockey Roberts! Cockey Roberts!"

Of course I had to let him in after that, and he would walk straight to the piano and perch on my foot for hours; the pedaling—and my pedaling is very strenuous—did not seem to disturb him in the least. He would sit on top of my foot, and from time to time he would say in a very loving and scratchy voice, "Oh Lord, how beautiful! How beautiful!"

Ah, it was touching.—*Ignace Jan Paderewski and Mary Lawton*

BOLD DISCOVERER

By Donald Culross Peattie

YOU CAN still see, in the cathedral of Pisa, the lamp that lit the spark in one of the greatest geniuses who ever lived. Someone, that day in 1581, had drawn the lamp aside to light it, then let it swing free on its chain. Quietly over the heads of the worshipers it swept in wide arcs that gradually grew shorter. And a 17-year-old boy forgot his prayers as he watched. Common sense would say that the pendulum would take longer to swing through a wide arc than a short one, but young Galileo Galilei perceived that it did not. He was exact about it: having no watch, he clocked the swings by his own pulse. And the beat of his heart told him that what he had felt in his bones was true.

Young Galileo had caught a fragment of the harmonies of the universe. Fired, he experimented at home with pendulums of many lengths and weights, hung from ceiling beams and the boughs of trees, till his family was exasperated. He invented a pendulum which could be made to synchronize with the human pulse and which registered its beat on a dial. So physicians, in days when watches were a rarity, could measure a patient's pulse exactly.

This boy, born in Pisa on February 15, 1564, was the son of Vincenzo Galilei, an impoverished nobleman with a marked gift for difficult mathematics and a great love of music. But as higher mathematics was of no use in running the linen shop which this nobleman was forced, to his shame, to keep, he refused to let his eldest son have anything to do with "the useless science." In music Vincenzo found comfort for his failures and his wife's violent rages. So he taught the boy to play the lute and organ.

From his mother young Galileo got a weakness for sarcasm and quick anger that was to bring him enemies. From his father the boy received the gift for mathematics. The Vallombrosian Fathers in a school near Florence gave the boy his primary education; he loved the life of scholarship. At 13, Galileo wrote home that he wished to enter holy orders. The elder Galilei, however, thought it was time the boy went to work. So into the linen shop went Galileo, where he failed dismally. Therefore, in 1581, when he was 17, his father sent him to the University of Pisa to study medicine instead.

Preparation for that profession then included the study of Aristotle's philosophy. Though he had been dead almost 2000 years, to question him was practically going contrary to the beliefs of the Church. The Church still insisted, moreover—as Ptolemy the Greek had taught more than a thousand years before—that the earth was the center of the universe, with a little moon and sun and some pinprick lights called stars revolving around it. Young Galileo, disgusted with this little universe and the little minds that upheld it, sought proofs instead of the set doctrines of the Church. Studying by himself, he discovered Archimedes, greatest of all Greek mathematicians and physicists. Presently the eager student invented a set of scales for analyzing metals by their weight, based on an application of Archimedes' theory. He worked out a simple method for determining the center of gravity in solids. His fame spread among scientists. In 1589, aided by influential men who had noted his gifts, the 25-year-old Galileo received a professorship in mathematics at the University of Pisa.

Once inside the academic walls, the young professor dared to refute Aristotle. Theorizing without experimenting, Aristotle had stated that the heavier the weight of a body, the faster it must fall. Some say that Galileo summoned the learned faculty to the foot of the famous Leaning Tower and from the top pushed a ten-pound weight and a one-pound weight together. Both hit the pavement at the same instant. The professors, however, preferred to believe their books rather than their eyesight. Nonetheless, Galileo experimented further with freely falling bodies and bodies rolling down an inclined plane. He proved that not only do all bodies fall faster in each interval of time but that the increase in velocity is uniform, no matter what their weight.

Galileo was fascinated by artillery fire. Gunners already knew they had to elevate their sights to hit a distant object, but they did it by guess. Galileo demonstrated that the path of a missile is a parabola, and built up a series of calculations that tell a gunner the elevation necessary to hit a target of known distance. Thus he founded the science of masses in motion—which we today call dynamics. In the basic laws he laid down, Galileo gave physics a new concept: inertia—the tendency of all matter to stay at rest, or, if in motion, to continue at the same rate in a straight line unless acted upon by an external force. We call this "Newton's first law" because the great Englishman gave it precise expression, but Galileo first explored its possibilities. First of all men, he saw that inertia applies to all bodies on earth or in the sky.

Before Galileo, the experimental method was almost unknown. Since the faculty of Pisa couldn't or wouldn't adopt it, they intrigued to get the young experimenter out. Unfortunately, he had covered with sarcasm the showy harbor-dredging engine of the reigning Duke of Tuscany's half brother. Worse still, Galileo had been right; the costly invention broke down. Allying themselves with this influential fumbler, the professors got Galileo's pay diminished. Resigning in disgust, he went back to the linen shop. Fortunately, Galileo's friends were as numerous as his enemies, and through them the republic of Venice summoned him in 1592 to teach at the University of Padua. The pay was good, and there was an atmosphere of intellectual freedom.

For the next 18 years Galileo designed fortifications, siege machinery and bridges. He invented the ancestor of the slide rule for calculating interest, extracting square and cube roots. To this was joined a quadrant for taking angles and getting divisions of the astronomical compass. His instrument was in such demand he had to hire assistants to help produce it. Many of these objects of exquisite workmanship are still in existence.

At Padua, Galileo's classes overflowed the largest hall. He had to lecture outdoors. Students flocked to him from as far off as Sweden and Scotland—among them the future great who were to carry their master's science to the ends of the earth, or to become protectors of science, like Archduke Ferdinand, future emperor of Germany. To them Galileo spoke of the universe and how nothing in it stands still, but all things (contrary to Aristotle), all atoms, all stars, have their motion. And how Pythagoras the Greek, who lived before Aristotle, had said that the earth, too, moves and that it is not the center of the universe but only one of the planets of one of the stars burning out there in the shoreless sea of blackness.

In 1609 a rumor reached Galileo that a Dutch spectacle-maker's assistant had accidentally discovered that by looking through two lenses, held a foot or so apart, things appeared larger. Although he had no model, Galileo made a telescope himself and took it to the top of the bell tower, the highest building in Venice.

Up to the very top after him puffed the Doge and the senators of Venice, in their velvets. And there, sure enough, they could see through Master Galileo's lenses the streets of Padua and people walking in them. The Senate voted Galileo an increased salary and a life professorship. He started making telescopes for sale.

To the instrument which he reserved for his own use he gave the loving name of "Old Discoverer." It made objects appear 33 times nearer. On that memorable night when Galileo swung Old Discoverer upon the heavens there leaped to his eye the grandest spectacle open to mortal sight—the vista of infinity, its utter darkness lit by endless suns. Where his naked eye had seen only a misty veil, the lenses turned the Milky Way into a band of stars, and other stars seen beyond those stars. On that night modern astronomy was born.

By day Galileo trained darkened lenses on the sun. He found its fiery surface swept by strange dark storms—sunspots we call them now—and from their apparent motion across the face of the sun he realized that it rotates on its axis, like the earth. If so, was the sun not also traveling on some incomprehensible track of its own? He swung his lenses on Jupiter, and discovered that the three bright stars on a line with Jupiter were not fixed stars, but were moving around it, moons to Jupiter. Later he found a fourth satellite of Jupiter, of the 12 we now know. Here was a revolving system in miniature—evidence, to one who could reason, of a planetary system too.

So Copernicus the Pole had been right when in 1543 he announced that the earth turns daily on its axis and the planets revolve around the sun. Giordano Bruno had been right when he taught the Copernican theory in the universities—right, though they burned him alive for it in Rome in 1600.

That was only ten years before Galileo swung Old Discoverer on the skies. No wonder that some of the professors refused to look at the skies through this telescope. Thousands did look, however, and were convinced—scientists, nobles, cardinals, Pope Paul himself. But jealous philosophers joined forces with ignorant fanatics in denouncing Galileo to the Inquisition, the church court which judged and punished acts against established beliefs. For the heavenly movements which his lenses and intellect revealed were, they said, contrary to Scripture.

The Inquisition forbade him to teach his doctrines about the solar system, and for 16 years he obeyed. Then in 1632 he ventured to publish his *Dialogues Concerning the Two Principal Systems*— the Ptolemaic versus the Copernican. In this the supporter of the Ptolemaic system, a character named "Simplicio," made out a weak and silly case. Whereupon Galileo's enemies persuaded Pope Urban that Simplicio was a caricature of himself.

The publisher of the *Dialogues* was told to stop the book's sale—though it had spread over Europe. Galileo was summoned to Rome. Now approaching 70, infirm with double hernia and palpitation of the heart, he faced the examining committee of cardinals. He was threatened with torture unless he recanted his scientific views. After four months in detention he yielded abjectly to the Vatican.

Legend says that no sooner had Galileo recanted his belief in the earth's movements than he muttered under his breath, "Nevertheless, it does move." The spirit if not the fact of the story holds good. He had to get down on his knees and read aloud and then sign a document which "confessed" that the Copernican theory was a gross falsehood, and he promised never again to preach it or speak of it, on pain of death. He was then condemned to imprisonment and his book was placed on the *Index* of forbidden works. There it remained, in spite of the efforts of great Catholic scientists to get it removed, until 1835.

By the intercession of the Duke of Tuscany, Galileo was released to become a permanent prisoner in his own house, where he was surrounded by spies. But though he was a prisoner, the great of the world crowded to his door, eager to say they had seen the now gnarled old features and the piercing blue eyes of the chained eagle.

At risk of his life Galileo smuggled out bits of the new manuscript on which he was working, to circulate in countries where thought and press were still free. He worked feverishly, for he realized he was losing his eyesight. That last book alone, *Dialogues Concerning Two New Sciences*, makes Galileo a titan, the founder of modern experimental physics. In it he took up the first principles of the flotation of bodies in water, and announced scientific principles of sound. He gave musicians experimental proof of the mathematical basis of pitch and overtones. To engineers he left his knowledge of stresses and strains. He perceived the gravitational pull of a great body on a small one.

The 78-year-old Galileo died in 1642—the year that Isaac Newton was born. Even dead, he inspired panic among his enemies. They persecuted his friends, tried to keep not only his works but even his bones hidden. Let us not judge them too harshly: they were only sharing in the superstitions of the age. Let us remember, rather, that Galileo was himself a deeply religious man. He believed that God reveals Himself every moment in the majesty of nature's laws. Science is the lens through which to see those laws, and science, Galileo declared, can only advance.

A LADY WHO
NEVER STOPPED

By Emma Bugbee

A S OUR PLANE from New York droned toward Washington that December afternoon, I sat studying the tall woman in the adjoining seat. Although I had known her for several years, I never ceased to be amazed at how much she could accomplish, even on the fly. When we first took off, she had been reading some reports. Then she chatted with other passengers who had come by to greet her. Now she was writing busily on some copy paper she had borrowed from me. She was Mrs. Franklin D. Roosevelt, the First Lady of the Land, and I was a newspaper reporter assigned to cover her activities.

When we landed at the chilly Washington airport I said good-bye, planning to take a taxi to a midtown hotel. "Emma, dear, I can't bear to think of you all alone in a hotel room tonight," she said suddenly. "Why don't you stay with me?"

So my night was spent not in a hotel room but in the Rose Suite of the White House, with President and Mrs. Roosevelt as my host and hostess at a week-before-Christmas dinner. The impulsive warmth and kindness of this sudden invitation were completely typical of Eleanor Roosevelt. She was the greatest and at the same time the humblest woman I have ever known.

When Mrs. Roosevelt entered the White House, she proved to be a totally new sort of First Lady. She dreaded the stiff social routine the White House imposed on Presidents' wives, and feared

it would stop the welfare activities she considered so important. "I shall not toe the mark," she declared, in a masterpiece of understatement.

She brought a breezy informality and bustle of activity to the White House. At the inaugural buffet, the President waited his turn to be served like anyone else, and Mrs. Roosevelt helped with the serving. She also horrified chief usher "Ike" Hoover by insisting immediately on operating the elevator herself. "That just isn't done, Mrs. Roosevelt," he protested. "It is now," she said, slipping in alone and closing the door.

During Mrs. Roosevelt's first day at the White House, a woman reporter whom I knew telephoned and asked for Mrs. Roosevelt's secretary, Malvina Thompson. "Miss Thompson isn't in," a voice replied. "May I help?"

"Who is this?" asked the reporter.

"Mrs. Roosevelt," was the reply.

The startled reporter protested that she didn't want to trouble the First Lady, but Mrs. Roosevelt insisted on personally getting her the information she wanted. "You may call me any time," she said.

She was the despair of the Secret Service, but she would not have a bodyguard. After President-elect Roosevelt narrowly escaped death at the hands of an assassin, who killed Mayor Cermak of Chicago, he urged her to accept protection. "Nobody's going to shoot me," she scoffed. "I'm not that important." The Secret Service insisted that she carry a revolver, which she grudgingly learned to shoot. However, she usually forgot to carry it.

Washington had never seen anything quite like her energy. She got up at dawn and went horseback riding before breakfast. She wrote a syndicated newspaper column and articles for magazines. She joined a union (the Newspaper Guild). She took voice lessons, spoke on the radio, lectured (giving the money earned to charity)—all in addition to the formal duties of a First Lady. She moved about so quickly that White House servants sometimes had to trot alongside her to get in a word about household plans.

But no matter how hectic her schedule, she always had time for little acts of thoughtfulness. She worried about *us*, for instance—the corps of newswomen who covered her activities. Once, when Ruby Black, correspondent for the United Press, fell ill, Mrs. Roosevelt immediately noticed her absence and asked me where she was. I explained.

"I wonder if Ruby and her family would take our house at Campobello for a vacation?" she said. They did, and Ruby returned reinvigorated.

Another time a small-town teacher who was bringing a boy crippled by polio to Washington wrote asking Mrs. Roosevelt's advice on what to see in the capital. Not only did Mrs. Roosevelt arrange a special tour of the city, but she put the boy up at the White House. Such episodes multiplied as the years went on. Her day didn't end when the sun went down. Late into the night, after everyone else in the White House was asleep, she would pore over her mail. She received bushels of it—in the first year more than 300,000 pieces. It increased as her activities broadened, as her visits to hospitals, schools, migrant-labor camps, industrial plants increased. A staff of secretaries helped with the official letters, but the personal ones she answered herself in a loose, flowing hand. Critical letters she answered as cheerfully and faithfully as admiring ones.

Strangers were invariably surprised when they met Mrs. Roosevelt face-to-face for the first time. "Why, she's so much better-looking than her pictures," they always said. What the pictures never conveyed was the soft coloring of her fair hair, her keen, friendly blue eyes, the warmth and patience of her personality. This patience prevailed even when people who disliked President Roosevelt attacked him through her. Once a man in the audience shouted, "Mrs. Roosevelt, do you think that being a cripple has affected your husband's mind?" There was a shocked silence at this cruel question. All eyes were on the First Lady.

"How could it be otherwise?" she replied. "One couldn't suffer as my husband has and fail to be affected. Suffering has made him more sensitive, more responsive to his fellowmen."

Mrs. Roosevelt had considerable influence on her husband, particularly by indirection. Because of the press of duties, F.D.R. saw mainly official, important people. She wanted him to meet all kinds, and so there was always a stream of guests in and out of the White House. She gave a garden party for the inmates of a girls' reform school; she invited actors, labor leaders, reporters, college professors.

She influenced her husband, too, by acting as a lively sounding board and a frank critic. Frequently, when faced with some thorny issue, F.D.R. would bring it up at dinner and provoke his wife into expressing her opinions. Once he baited her so sharply on a problem that she became furious and gave vent to her feelings heatedly, while he smilingly advanced contrary views. The next day she was thunderstruck to hear him blandly quoting her remarks to the British ambassador as *his* views.

Often her ideas outraged people, but Roosevelt did not try to restrain her. "Lady," he said, "this is a free country. Say what you think. If you get me in Dutch, I'll manage to get myself out. Anyway, the whole world knows I can't control you."

Within a week after her husband's death Eleanor Roosevelt left the White House; the last day was spent in saying farewell to saddened employes and friends. She invited the newspaperwomen to a final tea in the state dining room. "This is not a press conference," she said. "I just want to say good-bye." Later she added, "The story is over."

But the story was far from over. Indeed, a new and perhaps even more fulfilling chapter of her life was about to unfold. President Truman appointed her a delegate to the General Assembly of the United Nations, which first met in London in 1946. Within months she had proved herself a well-informed and vigorous debater, and both friend and foe came to recognize her abilities. When she walked through the General Assembly in Paris in 1948 after its passage of the Declaration of Human Rights, which she had patiently shepherded for three years, the entire body of hundreds of delegates rose and gave her a rousing ovation.

In this new job, she got about 1000 letters a week, most of

them from ordinary people or obscure organizations. Almost all asked for help. One might be a request to plead some cause before the U.N., the next an appeal to find a missing husband. They were usually answered late at night after a full day of work and one or more diplomatic functions in the evening. People all over the world who had problems and did not know to whom to appeal inevitably thought of Mrs. Roosevelt.

She held her U.N. post throughout President Truman's two terms, resigning when Dwight D. Eisenhower was elected in 1952. Thereafter, still thinking of the U.N. as her husband's greatest memorial and her own best hope for world peace, she worked for the American Association for the United Nations.

She also continued to write her column, "My Day," and to make radio and TV appearances. She was as vigorous as ever. She arose at 7 a.m. and usually was busy until after midnight. She gave up cold showers and calisthenics, but made her own bed, turning the mattress each day to get extra exercise. "I look like Methuselah," she said, "but I feel no older than my youngest friends."

After she passed the Biblical threescore and ten years, Mrs. Roosevelt circled the globe three times, interviewed Khrushchev in Russia, faced down a Communist mob in India, swam with Tito at his island hideaway.

"I think I have a good deal of my Uncle Theodore in me," she said on her 77th birthday, "because I could not, at any age, be content to take my place in a corner by the fireside and simply look on. Life was meant to be lived. One must never, for whatever reason, turn his back on life."

It was often suggested that she run for political office, but she always laughed off the idea. In the spring of 1962 some New Yorkers proposed her for governor. At a public luncheon she described this as "sheer idiocy for one of my age." She then bolted down a long stairway, too impatient to wait for the elevator. It was the last time I saw her.

Finally, her seemingly inexhaustible energy began to flag. She had developed anemia. But her spirit rebelled at the idea of ill health, and she obeyed her doctor's orders only occasionally. The New York State Democratic primary campaign of 1962 found her again electioneering, enlisted in the reform ranks against the "bosses." In late August she went on a sound truck to the far reaches of New York City's boroughs. She had a fever of 102, but made five short speeches. At one place a little Negro girl gave her an armful of flowers. "You see, I had to come," Mrs. Roosevelt said to a friend. "I was expected."

The next day she went to Hyde Park to rest. She thought she "must have picked up a bug." Actually, she was suffering from a rare type of bone-marrow tuberculosis, and her 78th birthday, on October 11, was spent in the hospital. Then, on November 7, she died. She was buried beside her husband in the rose garden at Hyde Park on a blustery autumn day. At her graveside were three Presidents of the United States. There were also people from all over the world, some from nations whose existence had never been dreamed of in her youth, but who now mourned her as their friend. "What other single human being has touched and transformed the existence of so many others?" asked Adlai Stevenson. "What better measure is there of the impact of anyone's life?"

Even as her life had ebbed painfully away there had been time for small kindnesses. A few days after Mrs. Roosevelt's death, a housewife in Tacoma, Washington, received a check for $10. The woman was the daughter of a hitchhiker Mrs. Roosevelt had once picked up. He had been out of work, and she had found him a job. Gratefully, he said that if he ever had a daughter he would name her for the First Lady. When the man did have a daughter, Mrs. Roosevelt asked to be the godmother. She saw the child only a few times.

The girl grew up, married and moved to Tacoma. Each birthday she received a $10 check from Mrs. Roosevelt. The last came on November 10. The signature was a feeble but legible "A.E. Roosevelt." It was mailed the day before she died.

"That was the kind of woman she was," the Tacoma housewife said. "She never forgot."

THE EPIC OF MICHELANGELO

By *Donald Culross Peattie*

WHAT went on behind the high board fence was a secret from the city of Florence. For months, and now years, passersby had been hearing the clank of steel on stone, the thwack of mallet on chisel. But, as all knew, that particular piece of marble had been ruined when an earlier sculptor, having blocked it out impracticably narrow and thin, had carved a deep triangular gash near the base. Though many artists eyed it, the mutilated block remained on the city's hands for decades, a giant unconquerable.

Then on a workaday Monday morning (September 13, 1501) young Michelangelo Buonarroti, chisel in hand, strode to meet it. For two and a half years he toiled. When the judges viewed what he had done, they awarded him 400 golden florins (worth about $2000) and his choice of a site for his work. Unblushingly, Michelangelo selected the most conspicuous place in Florence— before the great grim palace in the Square of the Nobles.

Forty men toiled four days with windlass and rollers to move the statue to the spot. Steady-eyed, David the giant-killer faces his enemy, Goliath. Every flaw of the original block has been turned into perfection. The excessive height and thinness became the compact body of a towering athlete; the gash at the base is the space between the stalwart legs. Every cord and sinew, every vein in the readied limbs is shaped with precision as if indeed a young fighter's blood coursed hotly there. "David," like all

Michelangelo's great works, is more than a statue; it is a living truth—as alive today as 450 years ago.

Michelagniolo di Ludovico Buonarroti Simoni was born in 1475 at Caprese, where the Tiber rises in central Italy. The infant was put out to nurse with a stonecutter's wife; he liked to jest, later, that he drew in his profession with his nurse's milk.

His mother died when he was six and not till he was past 60 would he again know a woman's tenderness. He grew up in a harsh male world, with selfish, mediocre brothers who sponged on him all his life, and a grasping, complaining father. At school the boy did poorly. He was always drawing pictures and he drew them on the walls at home, too. So he was beaten. As this did no good, he was beaten again, and harder. But the artist remained unbroken.

Eager to get financial profit out of the stubborn boy, Buonarroti senior sent him at 13 to the studio of the famous Ghirlandaio brothers in Florence. Here he had his only lessons in painting. One day, when several apprentices were studying a drawing of a female figure by Domenico Ghirlandaio, Michelangelo picked up a broader pencil and corrected it. Worse still, Domenico saw that the forward boy was right. So Michelangelo found himself ushered out of the shop (with the highest recommendations). He landed in the art factory of Bertoldo, the sculptor who was turning out imitation classical statuary for Lorenzo de' Medici, richest banker of Europe and unofficial dictator of Florence, called "The Magnificent" for his lavish spending and extravagant tastes.

Michelangelo was employed in roughing out blocks of marble in the Medici gardens. Every day the young shoulders grew stronger, the eye surer—so sure that when Lorenzo happened on a carving made by the boy from a piece of waste marble he took him into his palace, cloaked him in velvet, had him served with his sons. At that princely table, where poets and scholars clustered, readings took the place of chatter. Here the youth heard the great thoughts of Plato, the mighty lines of Dante. A second talent—poetry—was born in him; he was to become the author of 77 sonnets that seem in their sincerity hewn out of his very soul.

It was a soul great as some ancient prophet's, full of sublime visions and moral passion. Yet his human personality was pitifully faulty. Arrogant, touchy, harsh of tongue, the youth got his nose broken in a quarrel with an older apprentice. The disfigurement lasted for life and went deeper than his face. For he who worshiped beauty now thought himself repulsive. Of medium height, with overdeveloped shoulders, he may not have been a handsome young man, but the years were to make unforgettable the wrinkled face; the bitter, generous mouth; the hazel eyes filled with an almost Biblical sorrow and love.

In 1492 Lorenzo died and his son Piero could think of no better employment for Michelangelo than to summon him one winter morning to make an enormous snowman in the palace courtyard. Soon the young artist fled the city and drifted to Rome. There Michelangelo produced his first masterpiece—a Madonna holding the dead Christ on her lap. He overheard visitors ascribing the work to another artist, so he stole into St. Peter's at night and chiseled his name on it, leaving the "Pietà" the only signed Michelangelo in existence.

When Julius II succeeded to the Papacy he made grandiose plans for monuments and buildings that often had himself as center. Thus he hastened the razing of the old St. Peter's Church so that it might be he who laid the cornerstone of a new edifice. Michelangelo was in Florence at the time, but Julius, conceiving that history would expect of him the biggest tomb ever raised, sent for the artist with the biggest ideas.

So began his friendship with Michelangelo. It was as much a quarrel as a friendship. Michelangelo's plans for the tomb delighted Julius. It was to contain no less than 40 statues showing saints and prophets clustered about the Pope's bier. Off went Michelangelo to Carrara for marble, but when at last he came back to ask His Holiness to pay the freight costs, Pope Julius, now involved in an expensive war against Bologna, had him put out. Michelangelo dashed off a furious note to the Pope; then, appalled at his rashness, he fled to Tuscan territory, outside papal control. The Pope demanded that Florence arrest and return him. Cool Florentines instead persuaded the artist to meet Julius in Bologna, and, to safeguard him from seizure, conferred upon him the protective rank of ambassador. The pontiff, with Bologna defeated, was feeling merciful and Michelangelo, forgiven, followed the Pope back to Rome.

But someone had persuaded Julius that it is unlucky to have your tomb built while you live. More, the coming painter Raphael and his relative Bramante, architect of the new St. Peter's now being built, were jealous of Michelangelo. They persuaded Julius to require him to paint the ceiling of the Pope's private chapel, called the Sistine. "Painting isn't my art," protested the sculptor. "Let Raphael do it." But Julius insisted and for the next four years Michelangelo was practically a prisoner—first of the Pope, then of his own fever of inspiration.

Never was a more forbidding task set for any artist. The Sistine Chapel is a dark, narrow box of a place, higher than it is wide. The ceiling space is interrupted by dormerlike windows, which results in unconventional curves and angles. All this—10,000 square feet of it—was to be filled with pictures, and in fresco. The technique of fresco painting is to grind the colors up with water, not oil, and then lay them on wet plaster. As the plaster dries, the color is set forever in the lime. The artist must paint at top speed.

Up the ladders, into the scaffolding, went Michelangelo, to lie on his back and paint overhead. Working in a slavery of creation, he often forgot to eat or sleep; he drove away one assistant after another, and locked the door to all but an old servant—and Pope Julius. Julius didn't understand art, but he knew grandeur when he saw it. He knew also that life is short. "When, when will it be done?" he would storm.

Finally Julius said, "It's done, I tell you. Get down off that scaffolding or I'll have you thrown off." Quailing, for he *had* fallen off once, Michelangelo agreed to let in the world of art, fashion and priesthood.

There above them, as if *Genesis* were blazoned on the sky, was the story of Creation, of the Fall of Man, and the Deluge! God, with a commanding gesture, is seen dividing the Heavens. He breathes upon the dust, and lo, there is Adam, in His image, God's finger just quitting Adam's, while Man gazes with adoring eyes into his Maker's face. And Eve, under the shelter of the Almighty's arm, turns her gaze, in eagerness and fear, upon her lord and master. Prophets and sibyls fill the difficult spaces. There are 343 major figures in the ceiling, every one sublime; each has the power of sculpture in the painting.

The same Old Testament grandeur is expressed in the marble "Moses," a fragment of the never completed tomb of Pope Julius, so majestic that it lights the gloom of the church housing it. The Prophet's very toes are gripping Mount Sinai as the thunder and lightning of the Lord seem to play about him; he holds the tablets of the Law, and his eyes blaze with moral fury. Legend says that Michelangelo, when he finished this sculpture, struck it a last mallet-blow, and commanded: "Now—speak!"

But while Michelangelo was uttering through his art such ageless truths, the times he lived in were rank with religious dissension. Worldly extravagance had bankrupted not only the fiscal but the moral treasury of the Vatican. As a result, half of Europe rose in the Protestant revolution. Italy was invaded by French, German and Spanish armies and torn with civil war. Pope Clement, who was now in the Vatican, marched on Florence. In her peril, the city of artists called home her greatest son. For months Michelangelo toiled at fortifying hills and placing cannon.

Out of the bloodshed and fear of these times emerged Michelangelo's work of profoundest calm—the Medici tombs. To visit them—and the stream of visitors never ceases—you go to the chapel adjoining the church of San Lorenzo in Florence and enter a room, of Michelangelo's designing, that lays a finger on the pulses and stills the restless spirit. There, on opposite walls, are the two tombs, one for Lorenzo de' Medici, one for his brother Giuliano. Clad in light armor, his hand on the sword across his knees, young Giuliano gazes with unsatisfied desire at the years he did not live to enjoy. This figure is popularly called "The Active Life"; its opposite, "The Contemplative Life," shows a brooding Lorenzo, secretive hand at his mouth, a helmet shading eyes that are looking down lonely avenues to death.

And now yet another Pope (how fast they followed one another, how many Michelangelo outlived!) summoned the aging artist to one more exhausting task. The wall of the Sistine Chapel behind the altar remained to be decorated. So for seven years the sculptor painted again—"The Last Judgment."

Michelangelo was old now—older than his years, worn with struggle over colossal tasks. For a brief time he enjoyed a deep friendship with a noblewoman, Vittoria Colonna. To her, as to no one else, he poured out his dark and lofty thoughts. When death claimed her, he became almost a hermit in an obscure little house in Rome. He behaved like a penniless man, when in fact he supported his brothers and had a fortune in cash hidden in his studio. Secretly he gave sums of money to poor girls of virtuous character that they might make good marriages.

Yet, in his 70's Michelangelo embarked on a new career—as an architect. He was still a novice when he was appointed to complete St. Peter's, still a roofless shell nearly 50 years after its cornerstone was laid. Many builders had worked on it; the only thing all plans had in common was size, for this was to become the world's biggest church. The task took so long that Michelangelo had time in between to design other buildings all over Rome— churches, palaces, bridges, museums. His style came to dominate the Eternal City like a mighty anthem, its chords frozen into stone.

Some of Michelangelo's plans for St. Peter's were never carried out, but the great, double-shelled dome is all his, and it caps the magnificent church with glory, as it capped his life. Engineers said it couldn't be done, but slowly, tier on tier, the great stone bubble rose, magnificent in proportion, each tier creeping out in seeming defiance of gravity as it approached the center. "I am so old," he said, "that death drags at my mantle." But before he died at 89, Michelangelo Buonarroti saw his work almost completed—the biggest and most beautiful dome in the world. Filled with light, with organ thunder and the choir's rejoicing, a vast and airy climax of power, it holds—if anything on earth can hold—a last echo of this titan soul.

THE ELECTRIC THOMAS EDISON

By Charles Edison

SHUFFLING about his laboratory at Menlo Park, New Jersey, a shock of hair over one side of his forehead, sharp blue eyes sparkling, stains and chemical burns on his wrinkled clothing, Thomas Alva Edison never looked like a man whose inventions had revolutionized the world in less than his lifetime. Certainly he never acted like it. Once when a visiting dignitary asked him whether he had received many medals and awards, he said, "Oh, yes, Mom's got a couple of quarts of them up at the house." "Mom" was his wife, my mother.

Yet every day, to those of us who were close to him, he demonstrated what a giant among men he was. Great as were his contributions to mankind—he patented a record 1093 inventions in his lifetime—it is not for these I remember him, but for his matchless courage, his imagination and determination, his humility and wit. At times he was just plain mischievous.

Because of his tremendous work schedule, his home life was relatively restricted. But he did find time to go fishing, motoring and the like with the family and, when we children were young, to play parcheesi and romp on the floor with us. One thing I remember well is Independence Day at Glenmont, our three-story gabled home in West Orange, New Jersey, now a national monument. This was Father's favorite holiday. He might start by throwing a firecracker into a barrel at dawn, awakening us and the neighbors as well. Then we would shoot off fireworks in varying combinations all day. "Mom's not going to like it," he would say, "but let's put 20 together and see what happens."

Always Father encouraged our experimentation and exploration. He provided clocks and other gadgets to tinker with, and kidded, challenged and questioned us into doing things. He had me washing beakers in his chemical laboratory when I was six, and when I was ten he helped me get started building a full-sized car. It never had a body, but it did have a little two-cycle marine engine and a belt drive. It worked. We kids had a lot of fun with it. Several times my brother Theodore and I played "polo" on the lawn with croquet mallets and autos—and nobody but Mother and the gardener objected.

Father could and often did give orders, but he preferred to inspire people by his own example. This was one of the secrets of his success. For he was not, as many believe, a scientist who worked alone in a laboratory. Once he had marketed his first successful invention—a stock ticker and printer—for $40,000, he began employing chemists, mathematicians, machinists, anyone whose talents he thought might help him solve a knotty problem. Thus he married science to industry with the "team research" concept, which is standard today.

Father usually worked 18 or more hours a day. "Accomplishing something provides the only real satisfaction in life," he told us. His widely reported ability to get by with no more than four hours' sleep—plus an occasional catnap—was no exaggeration. "Sleep," he maintained, "is like a drug. Take too much at a time and it makes you dopey. You lose time, vitality and opportunities."

His successes are well known. In the phonograph, which he invented when he was 30, he captured sound on records; his incandescent bulb lighted the world. He invented the microphone, mimeograph, medical fluoroscope, the nickel-iron-alkaline storage battery and the movies. He made the inventions of others—the telephone, telegraph, typewriter—commercially practical. He conceived our entire electrical-distribution system.

It is sometimes asked, "Didn't he ever fail?" The answer is yes. Thomas Edison knew failure frequently. His first patent, when he was all but penniless, was for an electric vote-recorder which the legislators refused to buy. Once he had his entire fortune tied up in machinery for a magnetic separation process for low-grade iron ore—only to have it made obsolete and uneconomical by the opening of the rich Mesabi Range. But he never hesitated out of fear of failure. "Shucks," he told a discouraged co-worker during one trying series of experiments, "we haven't failed. We now know 1000 things that won't work, so we're that much closer to finding what will."

His attitude toward money (or lack of it) was similar. He considered it as a raw material, like metal, to be used rather than amassed, and so he kept plowing his funds into new projects. Several times he was all but bankrupt. But he refused to let dollar signs govern his actions.

One day at his ore-crushing mill Father became dissatisfied with the way a rock-crusher machine was working. "Give her another turn of speed," he ordered the operator.

"I dasn't," came the reply. "She'll break."

Father turned to the foreman. "How much did she cost, Ed?"

"Twenty-five thousand dollars."

"Have we got that much money in the bank? All right, go ahead and give her another notch."

The operator increased the power. And then once more. "She's poundin' somethin' awful," he warned. "She'll break our heads!"

"Let her out!" Father shouted. As the pounding became louder, they began to retreat. Suddenly there was a crash and pieces flew in all directions. The crusher was broken.

"Well," the foreman asked Father, "what did you learn from that, Mr. Edison?"

"Why," said Father with a smile, "that I can put on 40 percent more power than the builder said she could stand—all but that last notch. Now I can build one just as good and get more production out of it."

I especially recall a freezing December night in 1914, at a time when still unfruitful experiments on the nickel-iron-alkaline storage battery, to which Father had devoted much of ten years, had put him on a financial tightrope. Only profits from movie and record production were supporting the laboratory. On that December evening the cry of "Fire!" echoed through the plant. Spontaneous combustion had broken out in the film room. Within moments all the packing compounds, celluloid for records, film and other flammable goods had gone up with a whoosh. Fire companies from eight towns arrived, but the heat was so intense, and the water pressure so low, that the fire hoses had no effect.

When I couldn't find Father, I became concerned. Was he safe? With all his assets going up in smoke, would his spirit be broken? He was 67, no age to begin anew. Then I saw him in the plant yard, running toward me.

"Where's Mom?" he shouted. "Go get her! Tell her to get her friends! They'll never see a fire like this again!"

At 5:30 the next morning, with the fire barely under control, he called his employes together and announced, "We're rebuilding." One man was told to lease all the machine shops in the area. Another, to obtain a wrecking crane from the Erie Railroad Company. Then, almost as an afterthought he added, "Oh, by the way. Anybody know where we can get some money?"

Later on he explained, "You can always make capital out of disaster. We've just cleared out a bunch of old rubbish. We'll build bigger and better on the ruins." With that he rolled up his coat for a pillow, curled up on a table and immediately fell asleep.

His remarkable succession of inventions made him appear to possess almost magical powers, so that he was called "The Wizard of Menlo Park." The notion alternately amused and angered him.

"Wizard?" he would say. "Pshaw. It's plain hard work that does it." Or, his much quoted statement: "Genius is one percent inspiration and 99 percent perspiration."

After the death of his first wife, Father married the woman who became my mother, Mina Miller. In her he found a perfect complement. She was poised, gracious, self-sufficient; she willingly adjusted to Father's busy schedule. Theirs was a marriage that warmed all whom it touched. Father's diary, the only one he kept (covering nine days in 1885, before they were married), indicated how smitten he was by her. "Got to thinking of Mina and came near being run over by a streetcar," he confessed. When he proposed, it was in Morse code, which she had learned during their courtship.

Thomas Edison has sometimes been represented as uneducated. Actually he had only six months of formal schooling, but under his mother's tutelage in Port Huron, Michigan, he had read such classics as *The History of the Decline and Fall of the Roman Empire* at the age of eight or nine. After becoming a vendor and newsboy on the Grand Trunk Railroad, he spent whole days in the Detroit Free Library—which he read "from top to bottom." In our home he always had books and magazines, as well as half a dozen daily newspapers.

From childhood, this man who was to accomplish so much was almost totally deaf. He could hear only the loudest noises and shouts, but this did not bother him. People asked him why he didn't invent a hearing aid. Father always replied, "How much have you heard in the last 24 hours that you couldn't do without?" He followed this up with: "A man who has to shout can never tell a lie."

He enjoyed music, and if the arrangement emphasized the melody, he could "listen" by biting one end of a pencil and placing the other end against a phonograph cabinet. The vibrations and rhythm came through perfectly. The phonograph, incidentally, was his favorite of all his inventions.

Many tributes were paid Father, but two pleased him especially. One came on October 21, 1929, the golden anniversary of the incandescent lamp, when Henry Ford re-created Father's Menlo Park, New Jersey, laboratory to be a permanent shrine in Ford's vast exhibit of Americana at Greenfield Village in Dearborn, Michigan. The other outstanding salute came in 1928, when Father was awarded a special gold "Medal of the Congress of the United States" in recognition of his achievements.

He never retired. Nor did he have qualms about the onset of old age. At the age of 80 he entered a science completely new to him, botany. His goal: to find a native source of rubber. After testing and classifying 17,000 varieties of plants, he and his assistants succeeded in devising a method of extracting latex from goldenrod in substantial quantities.

At 83, hearing that Newark Airport was the busiest in the East, he dragged Mother down there to "see how a real airport works." When he saw his first helicopter, he beamed. "That's the way I always thought it should be done." And he started sketching improvements for the little-known whirlybird.

Finally, at 84, ill with uremic poisoning, he started to fail. Scores of reporters arrived to keep vigil. Hourly the news was relayed to them: "The light still burns." But at 3:24 a.m. on October 18, 1931, word came: "The light is out."

The final salute, on the day of his funeral, was to be the cutoff of all electric current in the nation for one minute. But this was deemed too costly and dangerous. Instead, only certain lights were dimmed. The wheels of progress were not stilled, even for a fraction of a minute.

Thomas Edison, I am sure, would have wanted it that way.

Perhaps the most valuable result of all education is the ability to make yourself do the thing you have to do, when it ought to be done, whether you like it or not; it is the first lesson that ought to be learned; and however early a man's training begins, it is probably the last lesson that he learns thoroughly.   —*Thomas Henry Huxley*

EVERYBODY'S SAINT

By Donald Culross Peattie

C LOSE TO eight centuries ago in a hill town of Italy was born
one of the greatest souls that ever dwelt in mortal flesh.
Today he is still your friend and mine, and the gospel he
preached is still as true as bird song. Where other saints overawe
us by superhuman holiness, Francis of Assisi is as purely human
as a beautiful child. They called him *Poverello* (Little Poor Man),
but he was so rich in things of the spirit that merchant princes felt
beggared in his presence.

Giovanni Bernardone, to give him his baptismal name, was
born in 1181 or 1182 at Assisi, in central Italy. His father, Pietro
Bernardone, a prosperous merchant, called him Francesco, or
Cecco for short. Cecco wasn't any fonder of school than most fun-
loving boys and was poorly educated even for the times. Since he
was destined for a commercial career, his father kept him all day
behind the counter, learning how to wring out profits. But at
nightfall he was the leader of the gayest blades of his age. His
purse was open to all his friends; without stint he poured them
wine. He bought bright clothes insatiably. Pietro Bernardone
shook his head, yet didn't cut off his Cecco's spending money. For
extravagance showed the bankers that he was so well-off he could
afford a spendthrift son.

When the other young men of Assisi marched off in 1203 to one
of those local wars so popular then, young Bernardone went
along. Early in the campaign he was captured. After a year he was
released, but fell sick nearly to death, recovered, enlisted again,
again fell sick and this time was left without zest for his old life.

Some new impulse had begun to run in his blood. One night as he was prancing through the streets, he stopped still as if stricken, listening for he knew not what. His companions frolicked past him. Outside the city, on a little hill, he fell to prayer.

The turning point of his life was near. Once as Francis rode abroad he was approached by a begging leper. If there was anything this fastidious young man could not stand, it was lepers. Averting his head, he reached into his purse. Then a white light dawned in his heart. For it was not alms that the poor wretch needed. More terrible than the disease must be the loneliness of this unloved fellow human. Leaping from his horse, Francis ran to the leper and kissed him. After that he forced himself to go constantly to the leper hospital. He was soon giving all his spending money to help support it.

One day in 1206, when Francis was 25, he was sent to the town of Foligno to sell merchandise at a fair. He haggled and bargained as he had been taught to do till he squeezed out the highest profit. Receiving an offer for his horse, he sold that, too, like a shrewd trader. On foot he set off for home, unaware that he had transacted the last business deal of his life.

For as he walked through the ripening vineyards a great revulsion against all kinds of money-getting seized him. From possessions, he decided, stemmed all the ugly bickering and soulless grime that dirtied the world. While pondering these thoughts he stopped by the chapel of San Damiano and knelt amid its ruins. Down there in the city prosperity was god. But God's house here on the peaceful hill was crumbling away. No one tended it but an old priest, poor as the doves settling to roost in the eaves. And it seemed to Francis that he heard Christ's voice saying, "Rebuild my church."

Men were to argue bitterly, in later times, whether Christ meant merely "restore this chapel" or "reform the Church." But in his simplicity Francis did not balance any metaphysics. He roused up the old priest of the chapel and offered him the money he had made at Foligno. Dumfounded by such manna, the priest was cautious enough to decline it. But he allowed this young eccentric to share his poor fare and lodging.

When Pietro Bernardone found out where his son was and what he intended to do with the money, he rushed to the chapel with the bishop in tow. Gently the bishop reminded Francis that the money was not his to give. So Francis restored it all, and for good measure stripped off the clothes bought with his father's money. Henceforth the world would be his only home, and all men his brothers. Never would property fetter his feet. In his self-denial there was no rigid religious discipline for the sake of personal salvation. He was only trying to set himself free to imitate the life of Christ. Yet not for him the life of a monk, aloof from God's created world. Better the life of a hermit, where he could see heaven and hear the birds at their morning songs, and breathe the blessed air of liberty.

So he set forth in rags to beg not for food or for money—but for stones, to rebuild San Damiano. If he was given money, he bought stones with it and carried them on his back to the ruined church. And now volunteers came to aid him. When he preached the word of God, he stood not on a pulpit but barefoot in the midst of his fellows, poorer even than they—their "Poor Cecco." He was interested not in the weakness of men but in their strength, not in the ugliness of life but in its beauty. From an overflowing heart he would burst into songs of praise.

His first disciple was a certain rich man who, to the rage of his heirs, sold all he had and gave to the poor. The next was an eminent doctor of laws, who gave up man's way of life for God's. The three founded the little community of "The Poor Brothers of Assisi." They lived by no set order of rules as practiced in a monastery. Their only rule was the one Christ gave the Apostles: Go forth and preach; cure the sick and cleanse the leper. Freely have you received—freely give. Provide neither gold nor silver for your journey, neither two coats, neither shoes nor yet staves.

Soon the number of Franciscans had grown to 12. Francis would not let them accept a comfortable house that was offered them. The Poor Brothers dwelt in huts near the leper hospital. For their daily bread they depended on what they could earn as day laborers or servants on farms, in vineyards or in cities. If there was no work, they must beg food. Though the others called him Father Francis, he had them call one another friar, or brother, according to a religious custom of the time. And all Franciscans have been friars but not monks ever since.

In little groups of two to four, the friars set forth into the world to preach. They did not keep their eyes fixed on a prayer book; often they lifted up their faces to heaven and sang. When they conversed it was likely to be of wayside flowers and lark song, of mountain views and pure springs. But their work lay in the cities, as Francis reminded them. There dwelt the souls who must be saved; there men groaned in slavery to property and class.

But once out of Assisi, where they were now understood, the Franciscans met ridicule and abuse. The crowds took them for vagabonds who masqueraded as holy men; the well-to-do suspected them of being dangerous radicals, and priests feared they were heretics. Many a time they were stoned and driven out of town. Bishops refused them permission to preach.

Francis, who never became an ordained priest, saw now that he could not go on without papal sanction, and set forth for Rome. Presented at the Vatican, he proved as irresistible as a child and as bold in insisting on what he wished. Pope Innocent III granted the Poor Brothers the right to preach and, if they prospered, he promised to show them further favors. At that Francis took a hasty departure; favors were what he did not want. With joyful hearts the Franciscans took to the road again. The fame of the *Poverello* now preceded him. He was frequently met by crowds waving green boughs and singing, and the bells of the churches opened their throats for joy.

Francis himself often felt the need to slip away into nature. He would seek a secluded grove or sit alone on a hill. Most of all he loved a tiny island, where none but the lapping waves might find him. Everything in nature was kin to him. He spoke of "Brother Hare" and "Sister Swallow," and meant it. He could not endure to see animals caged or carried away for slaughter, and would intercede for them; so he spared the lives of doves and lambs, rabbits and pheasants. According to legend, the animals of the field and the forest showed their gratitude by remaining with him and becoming his pets.

The tale goes that when he came to Gubbio he found that a ravenous wolf was keeping the citizens in terror. He sought out the beast and spoke to him in this wise: "Brother Wolf, you have killed men, who are made in the image of God. For this you deserve to be hanged like a criminal. But I would fain make peace with you. If you will forsake your evil appetites, I promise that the men of Gubbio will hunt you no more with dogs, but will set out food for you. And now you must give me your promise." And from that day the wolf became the pet of the very children of Gubbio and never again did harm.

On the night of Palm Sunday in 1212, as Francis and the Brothers were at prayer, they perceived a torch borne toward them swiftly through the wood by a young girl of 18 who threw herself at Francis' feet. He recognized the girl as Clara, the daughter of an Assisi noble. She longed to give herself to a life of religion, but she was being forced into a worldly marriage, and she entreated Francis to hide her. To do so was to involve himself in the crime of abduction, not to mention exposing himself and the Brothers to ruinous scandal. Yet he did not hesitate. He himself cut off her hair; by virtue of authority vested in him by the Pope, he received her into his Order. Then he found her a shelter with the Benedictines, and when Clara's sister, and presently other women and girls, joined her, there was founded the Poor Clares, sister Order to the Poor Brothers of Assisi.

But the world was marching on heavier feet than the saint's sandaled ones, and Francis now joined in the Fifth Crusade to Egypt to preach the Word to the Saracens. That Crusade had started off magnificently. The Duke of Austria, the King of Hungary, John of Brienne, the Knights Templars, the chivalry of Italy, the Venetian merchants with their ships, all were there, with a representative of the Pope as commander in chief. But jealousies arose; no soldier liked taking orders from a priest, and the chief objective of the papal commander in chief turned out to be a huge money settlement from the Sultan. The moral hollowness of the Crusade horrified Francis. The Venetians were there only for gain, the Templars to blood their swords, the common soldiers to get booty.

So, to the rage of the Crusaders, Francis urged that the Sultan's offer of peace, with return of the Holy Land to the Christians, be accepted. But the impatient papal commander gave the signal for attack on August 29, 1219, and the Christians were routed. Unarmed, barefooted, Francis led his little band of friars across the burning sands toward an enemy drunk with victory, who fell upon him with sticks and stones. He was led at last into the presence of Malik al-Kamil, Sultan of Egypt and Syria, Buckler of Allah and Defender of the Faith, a man more terrible than 50 wolves of Gubbio.

What was there about Francis that could tame the beast in animals or men? We only know that he preached three times to the rapt and respectful infidel monarch. Perhaps when the Sultan sent Francis back unharmed to the Christian camp it was with the hope that this pious hermit would make better Christians of the Crusaders. By permission of the Sultan, Francis was allowed to visit the Holy Sepulcher, Nazareth and Bethlehem—the only one of all the Fifth Crusaders to reach the goal. Was it at Bethlehem, I wonder, that Francis had his quaintest inspiration? For back in Gréccio, at Christmastide of 1223, he had a miniature manger built; he filled it with straw; he had woodcarvers make painted figures of the Holy Infant and Mother, of ox and ass, of shepherds and dark-skinned Orient kings. So Francis raised Christmas—till then only a special High Mass—to a festival of love, with worship of the Christ Child shining like a golden candle at its heart.

Meantime the number of the Poor Brothers was growing. Some of the converts clamored for a more practical way of life. Why must they tramp the roads and perform in city streets like entertainers? Why must they live in huts? Why must they accept no money for charitable purposes, and why must they not become ordained priests? Why could they not accept some Rule, some code of conduct and formal charter for their organization? Some of the friars insisted that Francis was too innocent to govern the Order alone.

The Church was worried, too. The Franciscans now had grown to 1200; tomorrow they might be 12,000. The only way to weed out the unworthy was to organize them, on well-tested monastic lines. Even Francis knew that something must be done; people were calling themselves Franciscans whom he had barely seen, whose hearts he could not read, whose actions he could not predict. There was nothing to do but ask the Pope to grant the Franciscans a Rule and to appoint an official adviser.

Then Francis let the Church organize his Order, while he himself withdrew. Taking Brother Pietro by the hand, Francis proclaimed him the Father of the Order. "My health will not let me take care of you as I should," he said. In truth he was weary. His body was worn out with ceaseless deprivation and poverty. A dread malady had seized him and strange sores had appeared on his hands and feet. They looked as though nails had been driven through the four extremities—the "stigmata," or marks of the Crucifixion, cried the awed Brothers.

Of his sufferings Francis never spoke. Instead, as he lay ill he composed a psalm. He called it his *Hymn to Creation* and he sang it blissfully over and over; the Brothers must learn it too and stand about his bed and sing it to him. This is how it has been translated by the English poet, Matthew Arnold:

O Most High Almighty, good Lord God, to Thee belong praise, glory, honor and all blessing!

Praised be my Lord God with all His creatures; and especially our brother the sun who brings us the day, and who brings us the light; fair is he, and shining with a very great splendor: O Lord, he signifieth to us Thee!

Praised be my Lord for our brother the wind, and for air and cloud, calms and all weather, by the which Thou upholdest life in all creatures.

Praised be my Lord for our sister water, who is very service-able unto us, and humble, and precious and clean.

Praised be my Lord for our brother fire, through whom Thou givest us light in the darkness; and he is bright and pleasant, and very mighty and strong.

Praised be my Lord for our mother the earth, the which doth sustain us and keep us, and bringeth forth divers fruits, and flowers of many colors, and grass.

Praise ye, and bless ye the Lord, and give thanks unto Him, and serve Him with great humility.

And there you have the secret of Francis of Assisi—the core of his soul, the center of his gospel. It is gratitude—gratitude for the gifts of life with all its sweet experience. Gratitude springs to any heart in moments of happiness; it welled from the heart of the saint even in agony.

On the third of October, 1226, in one of the old huts outside the leper hospital, death came at last to Francis and relieved him of his sufferings.

Faith is to believe what we do not see, and the reward of this faith is to see what we believe. —*St. Augustine*

When a man says he can get on without religion, it merely means he has a kind of religion he can get on without.
—*Harry Emerson Fosdick*

Prayer is a force as real as terrestrial gravity. As a physician, I have seen men, after all other therapy had failed, lifted out of disease and melancholy by the serene effort of prayer. Only in prayer do we achieve that complete and harmonious assembly of body, mind and spirit which gives the frail human its un-shakable strength. —*Dr. Alexis Carrel*

Who rises from prayer a better man, his prayer is answered.
—*George Meredith*

GREAT LIBERATOR

Adapted from Man of Glory: Simón Bolívar

By *Thomas Rourke*

H<small>E IS MUCH</small> more than the George Washington of South America. He is the Washington, the Patrick Henry, the Thomas Jefferson, the Abraham Lincoln. He initiated the revolution against Spain which gave five nations birth; he commanded the armies which won their freedom; he formulated the principles upon which the republics were founded, formed their governments and wrote their constitutions. Many North Americans have never heard of him, and almost none pronounce his name correctly—See-*moan* Bow-*lee*-var.

To millions of South Americans today, more than a century and a quarter after his death, Simón Bolívar is almost a deity. Far more than any figure in English or North American history, the Liberator exists in the consciousness of his people as a living entity. In remote pueblos of the Andes, in the deep jungles, around the campfires on the vast plains, illiterate Indians and peons repeat his words as though they were spoken yesterday. In South American cities, statesmen raise their hats at mention of his name.

On a summer afternoon in 1805 two men climbed Mount Aventine, one of the hills of Rome, and rested on the summit. One of them, a slight, handsome young man, lay on the ground, his eyes—deep-set, dark and brilliant—staring in fascination at the Eternal City spread out below. The other—older, ill-kempt, his long hair flying in the breeze—stood beside him, talking. From time to time he read from the tattered pages of Rousseau's *Emile*,

Tom Paine's *The Rights of Man*, works of Voltaire. He talked of the past glories of Rome, of the noble experiments in republican government that had been tried there.

Finally, as the sunset spread its glow about them, the young man rose to his knees and, "his eyes moist, his face flushed with a feverish animation," spoke these words: "I swear by the God of my fathers and by my native land that my hands shall never tire nor my soul rest until I have broken the chains which bind us to Spain!" All the rest of his life was devoted to the fulfillment of that oath.

Simón José Antonio de la Santísima Trinidad Bolívar y Palacio was a native of Caracas, Venezuela, the pampered and precocious youngest child of one of the wealthiest families of the country. His companion that day in Rome was Simón Rodríguez, his tutor from early youth. Bolívar was 23 at the time. At 16 he had been sent to Spain for the "education" then typical of his class. For three years his life was a wild round of luxury and dissipation in Madrid, Paris and London. A master swordsman, a fine dancer, a superb horseman and with plenty of money to throw around, he became known as the young Prince Bolívar. London tailors copied his clothes, Paris shops featured the "chapeau Bolívar."

But this phase of his life came to a sudden end; he met, loved and married María Teresa del Toro. She was a lovely, fragile creature, "not," Bolívar said afterward, "created for this world." In a few months she died in Venezuela of yellow fever. Torn by profound grief, Bolívar saw in the death of his wife a mystic sign. "It lifted me from the realm of worldly things and centered my thoughts upon the problems of my oppressed land."

He sought and found again the teacher of his early youth, Rodríguez. On long walking trips in Europe, Bolívar absorbed with newborn ardor the doctrines of his mentor. In 1804 he stood in the Cathedral of Notre Dame and saw Napoleon crown himself Emperor. "The act," he said, "appeared to me as the fulmination of hell. The crown which he placed upon his head was a relic of the Dark Ages." Soon after, on Mount Aventine, he spoke the words which dedicated his life and determined the destiny of half a continent.

Bolívar's resolve was one of magnificent presumption. The 23-year-old youth enjoyed no particular prestige in the land he proposed to liberate. His military experience was limited to a few years in the Venezuelan militia. Though Spain had shamelessly exploited and oppressed her colonies in the New World for three centuries, there had never been any organized movement for independence. In fact, when General Francisco Miranda of Venezuela, who had fought under Washington in the American Revolution, attempted to deliver the colony, he had met armed resistance from his countrymen. His small army was destroyed, he himself was forced to flee to England. When Bolívar landed in Venezuela, he began to work underground through a group of young aristocrats, fostering the idea of revolution among the people. Then, realizing his lack of military knowledge, he persuaded Miranda to return.

On July 3, 1811, Bolívar uttered the word "Liberty" for the first time that it was spoken publicly in the land, and demanded absolute independence from Spain. A tremendous wave of patriotic emotionalism swept Caracas, and a congress of patriots declared Venezuela free. The die was cast. Miranda tried to whip together an army from motley bands of peons and elegant young aristocrats who fancied themselves as officers. It was a discouraging task and in the end he failed. The veteran Spanish legions routed the Venezuelan volunteers and captured Caracas. Soon the First Republic was dead, Miranda was on a Spanish ship, bound for death in the prison at Cádiz, and Simón Bolívar was a penniless exile on the island of Curaçao, then belonging to England.

To anyone less inspired, there would have appeared not the faintest glimmer of hope. Everything he had owned—his great estates, vast herds of cattle, blocks of city property—was gone, confiscated by the Spaniards. He had to beg from strangers to keep himself alive. But after only a few weeks he escaped to the colony of New Granada (Colombia) where a garrison of patriot troops held a bit of seacoast. Here he was given command of 200 men—ragged, barefoot Negroes, Indians and half-castes.

In the first phase of the struggle Bolívar had learned a great deal about how war should be waged against the Spaniards. He had been in action, acquitted himself with distinction. Now, on a night in December 1812, he took the Spanish garrison at Tenerife by surprise, destroyed it and captured its arsenal. The next night he swooped down on Mompós and dispersed the Spanish forces. So it went for six days—six battles, six victories, six towns delivered. In two weeks he cleared the whole area of the enemy. At every village Bolívar was received with acclaim by the people, and hundreds of recruits flocked to his banner. Encouraged, he now proposed a drive on his native Caracas. It was a major undertaking. Between him and his goal were 6000 Spanish troops and 500 miles of mountain terrain.

In mid-May 1813, Bolívar set out with over 600 men. Burdened with arms and packs, the men fought their way across frigid plateaus and deep, rocky gorges and struggled through trackless and steaming jungles, bleeding from the thorns and swarming insects. The military actions of the campaign were of the same heroic character. Bolívar, then and always, used audacity, swiftness, surprise—avoiding frontal attacks, taking the enemy in the flank, breaking off segments and destroying them. The Spanish forces fell one by one before him, and his own troops increased with each victory until they became a true army with artillery, cavalry and medical corps. Within 90 days from the start of his march he fought and won six major battles and reconquered the whole western part of Venezuela. When he advanced upon Caracas the frightened Spanish commander surrendered without a fight.

The demonstration that greeted his entrance into Caracas was something out of the annals of ancient Rome. At the city portals Bolívar, bareheaded, handsome in white and blue uniform heavy with gold lace, and great Wellington boots, stepped into a chariot hung with laurel and palm. Twelve maidens dressed in white and garlanded with flowers took up a silken rope and slowly drew him through the streets. The crowds cheered with wild frenzy, cannon thundered and church bells clamored, and the petals of roses, oleander and camellias showered down from balconies. A hastily formed congress declared the land a republic once more and conferred upon Bolívar the title of Liberator—the only title he used throughout his life.

But soon the great ships of Spain came sailing across the Atlantic, and Spanish veterans of the Napoleonic Wars swarmed in from the coast cities. Bolívar had to face them with what means he could wring from a poor, unsettled, primitive land. For 14 years the battle raged, spreading across the whole face of the continent, encompassing finally an area as large as the whole of the United States. Over this vast field Bolívar led his meager armies, always outnumbered, ill clothed, ill fed, without enough arms. Cut off here, Bolívar would strike there. An army lost here, he would appear miraculously with another one there.

Once the Spaniards, with strong artillery and cavalry units, were camped for the night; their 3000 horses were in a rope corral. One of Bolívar's cavalry leaders tied the dried hides of steers to the tails of 50 of his own horses, and sent them flying into the Spanish herd. The enemy horses, crazed by the noise, stampeded among the sleeping Spanish troops and, in the darkness and confusion, the patriots came in with saber and lance. Although his armies were often defeated, Bolívar's confidence in ultimate triumph never wavered. Once, at a banquet given by his officers, he jumped up on the long table and strode the length of it, crying, "As I cross this table from one end to the other, I shall march from the Atlantic to the Pacific, from Panama to Cape Horn, until the last Spaniard is expelled!" Then, turning, he strode back. "And thus," he shouted, "I shall return, never having harmed a soul save those who oppose the completion of my sacred mission!" And he meant that, too; for it was almost exactly what he did.

Bolívar's greatest achievement—recognized by military men everywhere as among the greatest in history—was his march from Angostura, now Ciudad Bolívar, on the lower Orinoco River, across the whole continent and over the main range of the Andes. Along most of the route there isn't a road or a trail even today. His army comprised 1600 foot soldiers and 800 cavalry. Several hundred women accompanied them. All were lowland people who had never seen a mountain or felt the bite of cold. The first part of the journey was across burning plains and through suffocating jungles in full rainy season, the hottest time of the year. Two hundred and eighty miles of that, and then the plains along the Casanare River—endless, flooded, a leaden mirror under the constant rain.

Day after day for three weeks the columns wallowed slowly forward. Water up to their waists, they held their muskets and their bundles aloft while the mud sucked at their feet with every labored step. Then, at last, the Andes. The exhausted plains people looked upward in astonishment at the towering peaks, gleaming with an icy whiteness. To keep the enemy in ignorance of his whereabouts, Bolívar chose a seldom-used trail that crossed one of the highest passes. The rock faces rose almost perpendicularly. The army scrambled upward, clinging to the ledges, their hands and bare feet bleeding. They climbed for six days. Then they came out onto the bleak Páramo de Pisba, 13,000 feet above sea level. Three thousand human beings had begun the march. Bolívar led 1200 scarecrows down the western slopes of the Andes. Yet after only three days' rest he defeated an army of Spanish veterans. This battle was the turning point of the whole war.

After the march across the Andes, Bolívar's star rose higher; his armies and resources grew, while the power of the Spanish forces waned. Bolívar, holding that freedom was impossible for any South American country so long as Spain had one colony from which she could attack, moved from one territory to another, ignoring colonial boundaries, fighting the Spaniards wherever he found them. He won four resounding victories—each liberating a whole country, each as famous in South America as any of the great battles of history—Boyacá, Carabobo, Pichincha, Ayacucho.

The southern part of the continent—Chile and what is now Argentina—had already been delivered from the Spaniards by another great liberator, José de San Martín. So, when the Spanish commander at Callao, Peru, surrendered to Bolívar in January 1826, the last Spanish flag on the continent came down and all of South America was free. Bolívar had fought for 15 years, directed nearly 500 battles and liberated an area comprising the republics known today as Venezuela, Colombia, Ecuador, Bolivia and Peru.

Yet it was not only for his military achievements that Bolívar became as a god to his people. His words inspired them as well. He was one of the most articulate men of all time. When he died there were ten trunks full of his manuscripts. One collection of his writings, filling 32 large volumes, represents only a small part of the total. For each of the liberated countries he wrote a constitution and organized a government down to the last detail: called a congress, arranged finances, formed cabinets, named diplomatic representatives and outlined foreign and domestic policies.

His prophetic vision was clairvoyant as judged from subsequent history. He predicted the future course of every country in the western world for a hundred years to come. He urged the building of the Panama Canal, predicted the formation of a great union of South American republics to stand as a bulwark against the decadent philosophies of the old world. He even took steps to form such a union, and invited all the nations to send representatives to a congress in Panama. The congress actually met and it was a failure. Bolívar had foreseen that it would be. "But the seed will be planted," he said, "and some day it will bear fruit."

As a man, Bolívar had the personality, charm and physical attractiveness that mean so much in the popular leader. During campaigns, he shared all the hardships of his men; they called him "Old Iron Tail," and adored him. But he was also fond of music and dancing, and never missed the opportunity for a fiesta.

He had achieved everything that he had sworn to achieve; now he took steps to form a political union of all the new states under one strong central government, somewhat like the United States. But the forces of nationalism, and political factions jealous of their own power in individual countries, opposed him bitterly. Old friends, companions in battle, now faced him as political enemies. The countries which had stood as one against the Spaniards were now ready to war against each other. Desperately, Bolívar set out again on long journeys, hoping to bring unity. His old power held. Everywhere he was greeted enthusiastically. But he could not be everywhere at once. And no sooner had he left a country than the waves of dissension closed in again behind him. "I have plowed in the sea!" he cried in weariness and disillusion.

He did not advocate a pure democracy. The South American nations were not yet ready for that, he felt. "Their eyes are too recently come from the darkness of slavery to stand that holy, dazzling light." What he proposed for the various republics were governments modeled more on the English than the North American, with an elected lower house, a hereditary senate, and a president elected for life. At any time, of course, he could have become dictator and forced his government on all the countries he had freed. But he had a horror of dictatorship. When one group proposed that he crown himself emperor, he replied, "The title of Liberator is superior to any that human pride has conceived; it is unthinkable that I should degrade it."

The years of hardship were beginning to take their toll. He was ill and tired, an old man at 47. When finally in Bogotá he heard that dictatorial governments had been set up in Venezuela and Peru, Bolivia and Colombia, Bolívar knew it was the end. "I am about to die," he wrote. "My cycle is completed. God calls me." He was determined to go away to die, believing that his very presence in the republics he had created would cause more dissension. His friends begged him to stay and impose his will by arms. Thousands, they said, would rush to his side at his call. But he refused to use such means against his own countrymen.

When he rode out of Bogotá, the whole populace lined the streets, weeping as he passed. The foreign ministers, the government officials and hundreds of citizens rode with him to the outskirts of the city. There they dismounted and embraced him. He climbed into the saddle with a great effort and disappeared down the road toward the coast. After Bolívar boarded a frigate bound for Jamaica, his illness became worse, and the captain put in to the Colombian coast and landed him at Santa Marta. They carried him ashore in a litter—a little bundle of bones that had been the greatest man of South America. Penniless, almost alone, he died in Santa Marta on December 17, 1830. Around his neck he wore a medallion bearing the face of George Washington, which had been sent to him by Lafayette.

Once when the people of Caracas had proposed to erect a statue of him, Bolívar said, "Wait until after my death, that you may judge me without prejudice. Monuments should never be raised to a man in his lifetime; he may change, he may betray. You will never have to charge me with that; but wait, wait, I say again."

They have judged him fully now. Twelve years after his death a great fleet of war vessels crowded the harbor of Santa Marta. Besides the colors of all the nations he had liberated, the flags of England, France and Holland hung from their staffs at half-mast. The town was crowded with the representatives of foreign countries. To the slow boom of cannon and the roll of drums, the remains of Bolívar were placed on a barge and rowed out to a waiting vessel. Soon the whole fleet raised anchors, hoisted great sails and moved eastward. Thus the body of Bolívar came home. Caracas was draped in mourning and arches had been built over the streets. Under them rode a long procession of great men of many nations and behind, drawn by black-shrouded horses, came a huge catafalque hung with wreaths, garlanded with flowers and draped with black silk. The people stood in silence as the procession passed to the beat of slow music.

Bolívar had come at last to find the place he had sought in the hearts of his people and in history.

Courage is the first of human qualities because it is the quality which guarantees all the others. —*Winston Churchill*

The only conquests which are permanent, and leave no regrets, are our conquests over ourselves. —*Napoleon*

Liberty is always dangerous, but it is the safest thing we have. —*Harry Emerson Fosdick*

THE ASTONISHING WORLD OF PICASSO

By Malcolm Vaughan

A WOMAN is a woman according to history, but to Pablo Picasso, the most famous artist alive, a woman is something else again: a combination of lines, forms and colors. Picasso changes the combination to suit his moods and his result is seldom Eve-like. The woman may have elephant ears, crossed eyes, two noses, breasts where her neck and navel ought to be. In the name of art, Picasso has been transforming natural appearances for well over half a century. People who don't like unconventional art say he is spoofing the public, and the public itself often scoffs at his works. When his chief masterpiece, "Guernica," was first shown, many thought it looked like a jigsaw puzzle. But a multitude of artists now following in his footsteps believe Picasso is liberating art from age-old academic tradition. Pablo Picasso himself believes he is demonstrating that art and natural appearance are two different things.

Picasso can paint conventionally—can depict a ravishingly Eve-like Eve—when he wants to. But in his teens, after painting numerous realistic pictures, he began to feel he was merely imitating nature. Within a few years he evolved what few artists achieve: a unique style of his own. The pictures he painted in this period—heartfelt portrayals of human misery—were semi-naturalistic. And this was only the first of a lifelong procession of original styles, including the now-famous cubism, which he evolved while still in his 20's. He also became a remarkable sculptor, etcher, ceramist and graphic craftsman. His lasting fame seems assured if for no other reason than that he is one of the most varied artists who ever lived.

He was born in Málaga, Spain, the son of a poor art teacher. From the age of seven young Pablo was always drawing, and the boy's marvelous technique soon attracted attention. At 16 he won honorable mention at the Madrid Fine Arts Exhibition; at 17, the gold medal in a show at Málaga. So great was his father's faith in the boy's genius that he handed over his meager savings to enable his son Pablo, then 19, to go to Paris, the art center of the world. Picasso lived in want for the next ten years. At one time he shared a single bed with a writer, working at night while the writer slept, and sleeping all day while the writer worked. To keep from freezing one night, he had to burn all the drawings he'd made that year—drawings which today would sell for thousands of dollars.

Short and thickset, with glossy black hair and jet-black eyes— "the bold eyes of a bull"—young Picasso looked more like a day laborer than an artist. His blue overalls and pullover completed the impression. During his first five years in Paris he turned out a total of 200 oils—as much as some artists produce in a lifetime. Though some were exhibited, they rarely sold, even at prices of $10 to $20.

Years ago Picasso said he'd like to be rich and live like a poor man. The wish has come true. A millionaire today, he eats simple food, lives in "destitute grandeur." His Paris and south of France homes are topsy-turvy jumbles, piled with pictures, pottery, books, press clippings, interesting stones he has picked up, shells, gnarled roots. When he moves, the hodgepodge is carefully crated and carried to the new house, where the crates stand, unopened, in the midst of fresh accumulations.

Picasso's unconventional pictures of a transfigured world have influenced thousands of other artists. Whether they will appeal to future generations, only time, the great art critic, will tell. Meanwhile the astonishing Pablo Picasso has dominated modern art for half a century.

ROUGH-RIDING
PRESIDENT

Condensed from Time

D OWN A wilderness trail in the Adirondack Mountains a buckboard jolted through the night, skidding off ruts, the horses barely under control. The passenger sat tensed and hunched, eyes screwed up behind steel-rimmed spectacles, mouth clenched tight beneath his reddish mustache, his thoughts on the future. "Too fast?" the driver shouted. Theodore Roosevelt, Vice President of the United States and due before dawn to become President, rattled back like a Gatling gun: "Go ahead. . . . Go on. . . . Go on!"

It was September 14, 1901. Eight days before, in Buffalo, President William McKinley had been shot by Leon Czolgosz, an anarchist, and now was dying. Roosevelt had been summoned back from a mountain-climbing trip by wire: COME AT ONCE. Later that day in Buffalo he was to take the oath of office as 26th President of the United States.

Theodore Roosevelt was born in New York City on October 27; 1858. His father, a merchant banker of an old New York Dutch family, was a "Lincoln Republican"; his mother, Georgia-bred and loyal to the Confederacy. One of T.R.'s first memories was of cheering for the Union troops in the Civil War. When his mother disciplined him, he would cheer even louder.

"I was a sickly, delicate boy," Theodore wrote, "and suffered much from asthma." His arm muscles were so weak that he could not stand up to other youngsters. His father encouraged him:

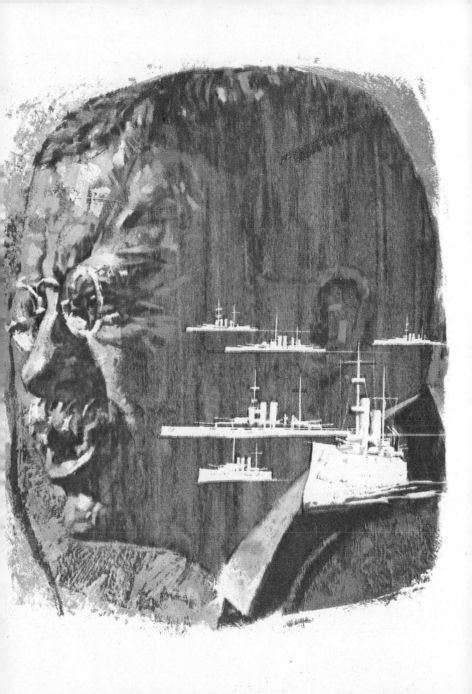

"You·have the mind but you must make your body. It is hard drudgery but I know you will do it." Theodore put up horizontal bars and a punching bag on the second floor of the house and set about to do just that.

After graduating from Harvard, where he became a college boxer and also made Phi Beta Kappa, the intense young man with high ideals joined Manhattan's 21st District Republican Club. He was elected and reelected to three unrestrained years in the New York state legislature. Then in 1884 his first wife, Alice, died in childbirth. On the very same day, his mother also died. Shocked by the double tragedy, Roosevelt headed west to seek peace in the silent spaces. There, in the Dakota Territory, T.R. ran two cattle ranches, rode the range beneath springtime stars and winter snow dust, got sworn in as a deputy sheriff and generally gathered in the feel of "the masterful, overbearing spirit of the West."

Recharged with energy, he headed back east, put in six years as Civil Service Commissioner in Washington, then two years as police board chairman of New York City, and in 1897 was appointed Assistant Secretary of the Navy.

Spanish reinforcements were pouring across the Atlantic to battle the Cuban patriots who were fighting for independence from Spain. But what was more serious, Germany and Japan were building fleets to challenge Great Britain and tilt the world balance of power. Roosevelt argued for war with Spain to kick the Spaniards out of Cuba and to get the United States into a strong position in world affairs.

On February 15, 1898, when the U.S. battleship *Maine* blew up and sank at Havana, the U.S. Navy was ready. T.R., with a fantastic display of leadership and gall, added the final touch to its readiness. One day Navy Secretary John D. Long took the afternoon off. Roosevelt, on his own powers as Acting Secretary, began sending out orders to concentrate U.S. warships, ammunition and supplies. He cabled Commodore George Dewey in the Pacific to prepare for action and to make sure the Spanish Asiatic squadron did not leave the Asiatic coast. Next day Long grumbled that T.R. had "gone at things like a bull in a china shop." But when war came, it was Roosevelt's early-warning order that made possible Dewey's great victory at Manila Bay.

Five days after the declaration of war, T.R. telegraphed a well-known outfitter in New York City for a lieutenant colonel's uniform. He also ordered "a couple of good, stout horses—not gunshy." Then he helped raise, train, lead and inspire the blue-shirted, slouch-hatted Rough Riders—the 1st U.S. Volunteer Cavalry. He was in the landing at Daiquirí in Cuba, the advance to Siboney, the heavy skirmish at Las Guásimas. Decked out in a sombrero and blue polka-dot handkerchief, T.R. caught the nation's imagination by leading the Rough Riders on his slamming, successful charge against the Spanish defenses outside Santiago.

Only 12 weeks after arriving home from war, Theodore Roosevelt was elected governor of New York, and for two years he was regarded by many as one of the best governors the state ever had. But he would not always coöperate with the state Republican machine. Boss Tom Platt wanted him out of New York State, and thought he knew just the place—the Vice Presidency of the United States.

At their national convention in the summer of 1900, the GOP, or the Grand Old Party, as the Republicans called themselves, nominated T.R. for Vice President, and the McKinley-Roosevelt ticket won in November. "Don't any of you realize," the national chairman and boss of the Republican party, Mark Hanna, said in private, "that there's only one life between this madman and the White House?" Then later, when McKinley was shot: "That damned cowboy is *in* the White House!"

Theodore Roosevelt was the youngest President the United States ever had—in office at 42, out at 50. He was also one of the most vigorous. "I do not like to see young Christians with shoulders that slope like a champagne bottle," said T.R., and he turned his White House years into a bully spectacle of romps and pillow fights with his sons, boxing matches with his aides, mass scrambles across Washington's Rock Creek Park with Cabinet members and foreign diplomats.

Roosevelt was also a wide-ranging intellectual, a great reader, an author of books. And he had the quality of decisive leadership. His very presence—the glint behind spectacles, the mustache, the teeth, the granite jaw, the Gatling-gun voice—rallied his countrymen behind him. Roosevelt understood power, believed in it, used it in a campaign to save his countrymen from "government by plutocracy or by mob." Two milestones: (1) first successful suit ordered by an American President to break up the control of a whole business by one big company and insure the right of free competition; (2) first time an American President acted as an arbitrator in a dispute between management and labor—in the anthracite coal strike—to safeguard the public welfare, including the rights of labor. But T.R. added: "I wish the labor people absolutely to understand that I set my face like flint against violence and lawlessness of any kind."

Abroad, Roosevelt used the symbol of U.S. armed forces to promote American self-interest in world peace and world order. Said T.R., one of the most successful peace-keepers of U.S. history: "I have always been fond of the West African proverb, 'Speak softly and carry a big stick; you will go far.'"

With a threat that he would use the U.S. fleet if necessary, Roosevelt effectively warned German Kaiser Wilhelm II away from Venezuela. He landed U.S. forces in Santo Domingo to forestall European attempts to "collect debts," saw that the debts got paid, then withdrew. He astonished the world by honoring the United States' Spanish-American War pledge to Cuba not to trespass upon her soil but to support Cuban independence. In one of the great decisions of his life Roosevelt sent the U.S.S. *Nashville* into the port of Colón in Panama to give support to a rebellion against Panama's colonial overlord, Colombia. His intention, of course, was to secure a canal zone in Panama, dig the canal and that way safeguard the defenses of both coasts of the United States.

In March 1905, Teddy Roosevelt was inaugurated President in his own right, while around him his ever-present ex-Rough Riders yip-yipped and bands blared the old Rough Riders' song, "There'll Be a Hot Time in the Old Town Tonight." But the nation's headlong progress kept getting ahead of T.R.'s promises of "a square deal all around," and he began to press harder against what he called "malefactors of great wealth." "A democracy can be such in fact," he wrote, "only if we are all of about the same size."

Time and again he brought lawsuits against big companies to break up their control of businesses. He maneuvered through Congress the United States' first Pure Food and Drug bill and the first law providing for federal inspection of slaughterhouses. Teddy Roosevelt was thus the great working pioneer of the new trend toward federal commissions to watch over key sectors of public welfare.

The miracle of T.R.'s second-term domestic struggles is that he won them while actually concentrating on foreign policy. At the time, world powers were in the mood for adventures. Secret treaties were being signed. So he began to move his ships and his diplomats, trying to head off history's first world war.

Across the Pacific, the Russo-Japanese War exploded in 1904. Teddy Roosevelt notified France and Germany not to combine against Japan, or the United States would "proceed to whatever length necessary." Later when Japan began to thrash Russia, T.R., determined to balance the power of Japan, moved in to mediate and to douse this world powder keg. In August 1905, aboard the U.S.S. *Mayflower* in Long Island Sound, off the Roosevelt summer place, Sagamore Hill, he met the representatives of Russia and Japan. These talks led to (1) the Treaty of Portsmouth, ending the Russo-Japanese war; (2) restoration of balance of power; (3) the 1906 Nobel Peace Prize for T.R.

Across the Atlantic, Germany's Kaiser Wilhelm II was already brewing a world war that then seemed destined to start over Morocco. At the Algeciras Conference in 1906, T.R. unexpectedly threw U.S. support against Germany, and the Kaiser backed down.

What Roosevelt did in 1907 was the greatest single act of his Presidency. He sent the U.S. fleet around the world, to show that from here on out the United States was part of the world, a great power, able to defend its interest and deter war anywhere. Around a shrinking globe threatened with war, the 16 U.S. battleships traveled, making goodwill stopovers. Such was the meaning of the gleaming white fleet that T.R.'s last significant act as President was to go down to Virginia to cheer the ships as they steamed into the port of Hampton Roads in a seven-mile line, belching black smoke, firing the Presidential salute.

After Teddy Roosevelt left the White House in March 1909, he was angered and then maddened by what he deemed to be the surrender of the Republican Party to its most conservative leaders by his successor, William Howard Taft. He challenged Taft at the 1912 Republican convention, and took a crushing defeat. He then launched his epic Bull Moose campaign and thereby split the GOP vote, handing the White House to Woodrow Wilson.

T.R. went off to explore the fabled River of Doubt (now called the Roosevelt River or Rio Teodoro) in Brazil—"my last chance to be a boy"—but was stricken with jungle fever; he returned to Sagamore Hill pallid, hollow-cheeked, 55 pounds lighter. When the United States entered the war in 1917, Roosevelt asked for permission to raise a division of volunteers and rush it over to the hard-pressed western front; 250,000 Americans, still drawn by T.R.'s magic, volunteered. President Wilson declined the offer. So, "beset by a sense of inadequacy," he had to watch his four sons, Theodore, Jr., Kermit, Archibald and Quentin, head off to war in his stead. Word came that his son Quentin, a pilot, aged 21, had been shot down over the trenches and killed. The stunned father wrote in tribute: "Only those are fit to live who do not fear to die."

Fiercely, never leaning back, the great man moved toward the close. His health grew poor. He was now blind in one eye and half deaf. And at five o'clock on the morning of January 6, 1919, T.R. died in bed. But even as he was dying, his country was throbbing with new vitality and hope. No American can forget his words: "The world has set its face hopefully toward our democracy, and, oh my fellow citizens, each one of you carries on your shoulders the burden of doing well for the sake of your own country and of seeing that the nation does well for the sake of mankind."

HAIL, CAESAR!

By Donald Culross Peattie

THE MEDITERRANEAN pirates little knew what a dangerous prize they had captured. This Roman youth, fair-skinned, dark-eyed, full-lipped, was clearly a noble, so they set his ransom at 20 talents (about $10,000). Julius Caesar laughed in their faces; he was worth 50, he told them, and promised that he would return to execute them every one! Ransomed, young Caesar was as good as his word. Guiding a naval expedition, he captured his captors, pocketed the 50 talents and watched the pirates hang.

This episode happened in 76 B.C., when Caius Julius Caesar was in his twenties, yet already a mature man. Educated at the great school at Rhodes, where the skills of speaking and writing were taught, he was one of the most widely cultivated men of his day, a brilliant conversationalist and superb orator. These talents and a relentless ambition drove Julius Caesar plunging into public life. He made a name for himself when on behalf of some Greek cities he prosecuted their Roman governor for corruption. Rome rubbed its eyes to see the master race called to account for exploiting the conquered, and Senator Cato, one of those who suspect everybody of being a subversive, marked him down for future investigation.

But this elegant aristocrat was a shrewd politician, and one office after another fell to him. To give the splendid entertainments befitting them, Caesar recklessly plunged into monstrous debts, which he paid off only by borrowing from a millionaire friend, Crassus. In the pursuit of power, he associated with the lowest as well as the highest. He became a fop and sensualist. He divorced his second wife, Pompeia, because "Caesar's wife must be above suspicion," and was not. Like a slow poison, the corruption of pagan Rome beclouded his brilliant promise.

And then, after dissipating many years, Caesar suddenly stripped off his vices like dirty garments. Accepting appointment as governor in western Spain, he there hardened himself to days and nights in the saddle. He shared with his legions all their fatigues and hungers. Of his body and will he forged implements of steel. Relentlessly through heat and dust, wind and snow, Caesar pressed after the brigands who infested this country he had come to govern. Chasing them, he reached the shores of the Atlantic, adding this area (now Portugal) to the Roman domain.

When he returned to Rome Caesar was unanimously elected a Consul of Rome. As an executive of the state, Caesar drafted a law to give free land to the veterans of foreign wars. Up to this time the discharged serviceman had found himself lucky if he so much as collected his back pay; and lands coming into the public domain were snapped up by the senatorial class for speculation.

The Senate blocked Caesar solidly. He took his bill to the Forum, that great market in the heart of Rome, and laid it before the *plebs*, or common people, asking them to vote on it. This procedure was allowed by the constitution, but Rome stared to see a Consul so stoop to the public. Caesar got the idol of the moment, Pompey the Great, to support him on the rostrum (the stone platform you can still see in the ruins of ancient Rome). The people roared approval, and Caesar strode back to the Senate to announce that the bill was now law.

Then, to keep the populace informed, Caesar ordered the Senate's doings to be reported daily on white wall spaces all over the city. He got a law passed obliging the governors of conquered provinces to account for their revenues. When his term of office ended in 59 B.C., the Senate promptly made him governor of Roman Gaul (now Mediterranean France), a distant province under constant threat by barbarian tribes.

Julius Caesar himself wrote the great chapter of his life that followed. His *Gallic Wars* is the most widely read of all military

classics, for boys and girls in many lands study it. But dusty Latin grammar obscures the excitements of the tale—the whizzing arrows, the hot pitch poured on the attackers from besieged walls, the wagon train surprised by cavalry in midstream, the screams of the wild Gallic women.

Caesar was the kind of commander soldiers idolize, forever thinking of rations and pay for the troops, always building up the pride of the outfit. He went to meet danger ahead of all the rest, sword flashing high and scarlet cloak fluttering in the wind of battle. Thus he first led his legions out to meet the Helvetians, who came pouring from their Swiss valleys. When he had beaten them, he mercifully supplied them with bread and grain for a year, and seed corn for their next crop, and sent them home.

A worse menace was at hand in the Germans, who had come swarming out of their forests into Alsace in eastern France. There Caesar destroyed them, and later, building the first bridge ever made over the Rhine (not far from Remagen), he carried the war into their country. The Belgians he conquered on the Marne, Meuse, Sambre and Somme. In two expeditions taken to punish the hostile Britons, he crossed the Channel and defeated the British king. For eight years he marched up and down, pacifying Gaul's turbulent peoples, turning them into staunch Roman subjects, bringing peace and unity to what is now all France and Belgium. So Gaul became a mighty bulwark that prolonged the life of the Roman Empire for 400 years of greatness. And the law, language, literature and architecture of France today all richly show the legacy from Caesar.

Caesar's great success brought consternation to the party called the Optimates, which represented aristocratic privilege. Pompey, their leader, was bitterly jealous of Caesar's new laurels. So, while the returning Caesar halted his victorious legions in the Po Valley north of Rome, the Senate "investigated" him, digging up old scandals, finally ordering him to disband his army and present himself in Rome for trial. Caesar knew that his legions would follow him anywhere. And no man saw so clearly that the once glorious republic was in decay; the Senate had seized the executive power, and Pompey was its tool. Caesar boldly crossed the Rubicon, the little stream that marked the northern boundary of Rome proper. He was now at war with the Senate.

Legions sent out to stop Caesar went over to him. As the swelling force marched on Rome, Pompey fled to his main army, in northern Greece. And there, on August 9, 48 B.C., the two military geniuses of the age matched wits at Pharsalus. By the end of the day Caesar was master of his world, Pompey a fugitive. Pompey fled to Egypt, to rouse it against Rome, and Caesar pursued him. But there the young King Ptolemy XII had Pompey murdered, presented the horrified Caesar with his head and was astounded that he had not thus won Caesar's favor. Ptolemy had driven his sister, Cleopatra, off the throne, though by their father's will the two were to rule together; the girl queen now welcomed Caesar as her champion.

According to tradition, she contrived to get into his presence by having herself rolled up in a costly carpet offered for sale to the Roman; when it was spread out, there stood the youthful Queen of Egypt (she was not Egyptian in blood but a Macedonian Greek), with a voice like seductive music, a body with a dancing girl's grace, a brilliant mind, a cold heart, hot blood, and a head for politics that she never lost even when making love. For her, and for Rome, Caesar conquered King Ptolemy. Cleopatra was restored to the throne under a Roman protectorate, and Caesar added the richest kingdom in the world to Rome's domain. Up the Nile, on an immortal journey, went these two, accompanied by 400 vessels filled with soldiers, servants, musicians, flowers, wines and viands.

Meanwhile the followers of Pompey regrouped their forces in Spain and North Africa. Caesar crossed North Africa to Tunisia to meet them, and there faced Cato's ten legions together with the King of Numidia's swift cavalry and 120 war elephants. Just before the battle of Thapsus an old enemy crept up on Caesar—epilepsy. He felt the approach of a seizure, yet calmly encouraged his weary troops and instructed his captains before unconsciousness overcame him. When he regained his senses, Cato's legions no longer existed; the King of Numidia was without a throne.

Caesar, accompanied by Cleopatra and their young son, Caesarion, returned to Rome in triumph. For four days the thronged city was a riot of spectacle, feasting, games, processions. The hot, bright air danced with standards and flung garlands. The earth shook to the tread of marchers bearing on high the glittering spoils of war, to the dragging steps of captives and the rumbling chariot wheels of the conqueror himself, erect and laurel-crowned. After him came his legions, scarred and sun-bronzed, swinging with tubas braying while all Rome shouted their glory. In arenas lit by torches at night, shaded by day with silken curtains, the populace cheered chariot races, sham naval battles, African hunts with 400 lions, Asiatic war dances, Grecian ballets.

And now the Senate outdid itself in servility to Caesar. It bestowed upon him for life the title his soldiers had long ago given him for love—*Imperator*. Caesar accepted this as a challenge to reform Rome's government, designed centuries earlier to fit a little city-state and now long outgrown by a vastly expanded domain.

Caesar began by cracking open that aristocratic club, the Senate, adding 300 members, mostly from the hitherto despised business and professional classes, together with representatives from conquered countries. He granted Roman citizenship to the freed sons of slaves and to the Gauls, planning to extend it to all freedmen of the entire Empire. He gave freedom of worship to the persecuted Jews.

He tried to stop the drift of disbanded soldiers and the unemployed toward congested Rome by settling 80,000 colonists in Seville, Arles, Corinth, Carthage. His great public works employed thousands in land clearance and beautification of the capital. He stopped the profiteering of tax collectors who were lining their pockets while looting business and agriculture in the provinces. The currency was stabilized by putting it back on the gold standard. He took the appointment of governors out of the realm of Senate patronage.

Even the calendar called for reform. The old Roman month

was a lunar one of 28 days, but extra days and even months were added at the will of the Roman consul in power. The Roman calendar had strayed so far out of line with the seasons that autumn was falling in July (a month renamed after the great Julius). Calling in a Greek astronomer from Alexandria, Caesar by his advice reformed the calendar into a solar year of 365 days, with leap year every fourth year.

But time, however he might mark it, was running out for Julius Caesar, for now drew near the Ides (the 15th) of March of 44 B.C. Shakespeare's great play, based upon the biography of Caesar in Plutarch's *Lives*, has the essential facts right but changes the meaning of the actions. The truth is that the conspirators, most of whom owed not only their fortunes but their very lives to Caesar, struck in defense not of the people's liberties but of the crumbling privileges of their own class.

The attack took place in the presence of the entire Senate. Casca, stealing up behind Caesar, struck the first blow, which glanced off his collarbone. Caesar spun round and struck back with his only weapon—a writing stylus. The conspirators closed in, raining 23 blows upon their victim. Cassius stabbed his dagger in Caesar's face and, through the blood pouring into his eyes, Caesar saw Brutus, who may have been his son, come upon him, to plunge a sword into his very loins. The words the murdered man cried out were his last, and they were in Greek: *Kai su teknon?* "Even thou, my child?" Then he fell dead, before the statue of his old foe, Pompey.

Now all beholders fled; though the conspirators, brandishing bloody weapons, shouted about "liberty," they roused not cheers but panic. Amid public grief wrought to high pitch by the funeral oration of Marc Antony, the bloody corpse was burned on a pyre in the Forum. But the good was not buried with Caesar's bones. He had brought to unhappy millions throughout the Mediterranean world the most just, merciful and intelligent rule they had ever known. He had conceived, and half achieved, a world of free men, all citizens in one great community. He had founded the Roman Empire, upon whose lasting stones grew up our western civilization.

HE CHARTED
THE COSMOS

By Joseph Phillips

THE creation of the atom bomb is probably the most significant event in modern history. It radically changed our concept of warfare and has become the foundation of our most hardheaded thinking about world strategy. Yet the man basically responsible for this was one who, for much of his life, was a leading pacifist, and whose ideas seemed to many visionary and unworldly. It was a letter from Albert Einstein to Franklin D. Roosevelt that started our development of the atomic bomb. And it was Einstein's "Special Theory of Relativity" that provided the basis for the development of atomic energy.

Throughout his life Albert Einstein was pursued by things he never wanted—publicity, fame, offers of money and power. He was surrounded by misunderstanding and controversy. Hundreds of scientists have devoted much of their careers to explaining, or trying to disprove, his discoveries. Although he believed in freedom of the individual and in democratic institutions, he was called both a "Bolshevik" and a "tool of Wall Street." Although he had an unshakable faith in God, he was assailed as an atheist.

Much to his astonishment as an objective physicist, he was offered as much as $25,000 to endorse products ranging from corn plasters to cars. His bust stands in libraries and universities throughout the world, and a monument has been erected to him in Germany. He was the only American citizen ever offered the presidency of another nation. All this came to a man who asked only for the solitude to think and work. "I am happy because I want nothing from anyone," he once said. "But I do get pleasure out of the appreciation of my fellow workers."

In 1933 when the Nazi government was coming to power in Germany, Einstein left his native land for the United States. There he joined the staff of the Institute for Advanced Study in Princeton, New Jersey. He was happy in Princeton, where he found the peace he had always wanted. Neighbors didn't consider it odd that he wore his hair long because he didn't want to bother with the barbershop, or that he dressed for comfort—unpressed slacks, loose pullover sweater, sometimes an old necktie in place of a belt.

From the time of his arrival at the Institute, Einstein received far more than professional appreciation. Scientists, habitually cautious of loose language, freely used "saintly," "noble," "lovable" in describing him. "Even when discussing theoretical physics," a mathematician said, "he radiates humor, warmth and kindliness." Yet after nearly a half-century of fame, Einstein remained a shadowy, remote figure to all but his friends and neighbors.

Each weekday morning at 10:30 he donned a shapeless black coat—and, in winter, a black knitted stocking cap, the kind worn by seamen—and left his frame house to stroll the mile and a half to the Institute. His long, untrained hair and raggedy mustache were white. His eyes, though they looked at you with patience and mild curiosity, were often tired and red-rimmed. He spoke in a low, soft voice, his words tinged with a German accent.

In his big, comfortable office with a relaxing view of a small woods, he would get down to work promptly on his Unified Field Theory, which absorbed him for more than three decades. The Theory connects the two great forces of our physical universe, gravitation and electromagnetism, and thus shows the relationship between all known physical phenomena.

He sat back in his chair, balanced a large pad on his knee and wrote in a small, neat script. When blocked by a problem he stayed with it, calm and serene, sometimes twirling a strand of hair around a finger. Each of his theories was the result of months and years of stubbornly pursuing what he called "idealized experiments." Pencil and paper were his scientific equipment; his mind was the laboratory. He wandered up wrong alleys, drew wrong conclusions. But he never gave up.

The answer was sure to be found, he felt, because "God is subtle, but never mischievous." Einstein believed in the simplicity and logical orderliness of nature. "It is a kind of faith that helped me through my whole life not to become hopeless in the great difficulties of investigation." When he weighed his own conclusions, he speculated: "Could this be the way God created the universe?" As a creative scientist he found a discovery as "beautiful" as it was "correct."

Like many great men, Einstein was humble and shy. When he walked into a Washington meeting concerning Palestine, every person in the room burst into applause. Taken aback, he whispered to a friend, "I think they ought to wait to see what I say." At a dinner in his honor, speaker after speaker spoke glowingly of his genius. Einstein squirmed. Finally he turned to author Fannie Hurst and abruptly brought her down to earth with, "You know, I never wear socks."

To an offer of a chance to become President of Israel, Einstein replied with his usual modesty that he felt unqualified for a role that involved human relations. He thought it better, he said, to continue his study of the physical world, of which he had "a little comprehension." Einstein never belonged wholeheartedly to any social group. He did not easily involve his heart with other people. It was not the result of his work, but rather the nature of the man. This aloofness could be noticed in his eyes in the earliest photographs taken of him as a child.

He was born on March 14, 1879, at Ulm, Germany, but spent his early years in Munich. His placid, shy nature soon set him apart from other children. He was so slow to learn to talk that his parents thought him abnormal. Teachers considered him a misfit. He had few friends and avoided games. His version of fun was to compose little religious hymns on the piano and hum them while walking alone.

By the time he was 12 he was pursuing an independent study of mathematics and science. He was, however, far from being well-rounded in his studies at school. Brilliant in mathematics and physics, he had no gift for languages. He wanted to continue his studies in Switzerland, but failed the entrance examination to the polytechnic college in Zurich. A year later he tried again and made the grade.

During the two years after graduation Einstein found and lost three teaching jobs, lived a hand-to-mouth existence and married Mileva Marec, also a science student, by whom he had two sons. In 1902, when he was 23, he landed a post as an examiner in the Bern patent office. The job wasn't too taxing and allowed him to concentrate on his own studies. He had set for himself the task of linking time and space, matter and energy. Sometimes he despaired, and on the very day before striking the correct results he told a fellow examiner, "I'm going to give it up."

At the age of 26, unknown in the scientific world, he submitted his "Special Theory of Relativity" to a physics journal. He expressed his theory in what is now the most famous equation of science: $E = mc^2$; roughly, that energy equals mass times the square of the speed of light. The equation demonstrated that if all the energy in a half-pound of any matter were released, the resulting power would equal the explosive force of seven million tons of TNT. Though it revolutionized man's idea of the universe, few physicists at the time realized its staggering importance. For years $E = mc^2$ was a lively topic for debate; then, with the explosion of the atomic bomb on Hiroshima, it became a grim reality.

Einstein provided more than the theoretical basis for the atomic bomb. In the late 1930's many scientists knew that the Nazis were going all out to develop atomic energy. The American scientists tried to interest our military leaders in a similar project, but made little impression. They appealed to Einstein to use his influence. One night in 1939 he drafted what was to be one of the most important letters in American history. "Recent work," he wrote to President Roosevelt, "leads me to expect that the element uranium may be turned into a new and important source of energy in the immediate future. . . . This new phenomenon would also lead to the construction of bombs." President Roosevelt immediately authorized the Manhattan Project to develop the atomic bomb, and the United States entered history's most fateful race for a military weapon.

Einstein continued to labor at the same pace that he maintained for 50 years. His Unified Field Theory was the result of 35 years of intense work. The heart of it consists of four equations that would take up but two lines on this page. In this series of equations he combined the physical laws that control the forces of light and energy with the mysterious force of gravitation that holds all material objects in its grip. Einstein believed his theory was "highly convincing," but didn't really know whether he was right or wrong.

Albert Einstein died at Princeton on April 18, 1955, at the age of 76, still seeking the answers to more secrets of time and space. The possibility of failure never disturbed him. He knew that man can never learn everything and that "the most beautiful thing we can experience is the mysterious."

The Princeton campus was quiet and beautiful in the falling snow, and the carol singers in the distance were an added touch to the Christmas Eve scene. I was walking my dog when I met the carolers going into the garden entrance of Dr. Albert Einstein's home. One of the boys started to sing, "O little town of Bethlehem, how still we see thee lie," and the others took it up. The front door opened suddenly and Dr. Einstein stood there a moment. Then he turned back into the house and reappeared with his violin. Without a word he started to play with the singers—each verse through the hymn. Without a word to break the spell, the young people turned away silently, and Dr. Einstein closed the door slowly on the snowy scene.

It was a Christmas Eve to remember.—*Evelyn Woods Ulyat*

INSPIRED JUSTICE

By Donald Culross Peattie

CHIEF JUSTICE John Marshall, the man who raised our Supreme Court from weakness to strength, from public contempt to awe, never had two months of legal training in his life. He was original, as only a genius dares be. He knew little about precedent and cared less. It is told that he was wont to say to his well-read associate, Justice Story, after concluding an argument in his office, "There, Brother Story, that's the law. Now you find the precedents." Yet he laid the cornerstone of America's legal structure.

John Marshall came of good yeoman stock in Virginia. He was a distant cousin to Thomas Jefferson, although the two men were politically on opposite sides. John was born in 1755 in a log cabin on what was then the Indian frontier. He was the oldest of 15 children. Hard work on a wilderness farm, with hunting for his chief diversion, made the boy self-reliant and brave.

His father, Thomas Marshall, had two ambitions for John. He wanted him to grow up idolizing his old friend George Washington as a model who could do no wrong. And he wanted him to be a lawyer. To start the boy right he gave him one of the first copies of Blackstone's *Commentaries* to come off the press in America. There is a suspicion that the future genius of the legal profession turned the pages of the great reference work languidly, then went fishing. Never at any time did he have much interest in law as an elaborate sort of chess game. John Marshall *made* more significant law than he ever read. The book that did influence the boy was Alexander Pope's *An Essay on Man*. Pope believed in "natural law"—a fundamental justice in the universe, which, since it is God-given, must be better than man-made law. This concept stayed with Marshall all his life.

When news of the Battle of Lexington blew into the Marshalls' backwoods, neither father nor son hesitated. They had been putting themselves through all the phases of rifle drill, their minds already made up about American independence. So, because he could drill other farm boys, John was made a lieutenant in the militia. He was 19, rawboned, powerful, clad in fringed purple hunting shirt and buckskin pants, with a "perfectly round" face, a low, strong brow, a shock of heavy black hair and deep-seated, flashing black eyes. He could outrun, outbox and outwrestle every one of his men.

Before long he entered the regular army, and two years later was promoted to captain. In the bitter defeats of Brandywine and Germantown he learned about the militia what Washington sadly knew when he said: "They come in, you can't tell how; go, you can't tell when; and act, you cannot tell where; they exhaust your stores, and leave you in a critical moment." The fault was not in a lack of brave militiamen but in the sovereign states to whom the militia belonged. The states could withdraw their militia at any time; they could even refuse to allow militia from another state to fight the enemy on their sacred soil. Each state would have let the young nation die rather than yield an inch of her own sovereignty.

In those days, and still more in the terrible winter at Valley Forge, young Marshall became a passionate believer in a strong federal government. "I became an American," he said of those times, "before I became a Virginian." He must have suffered equally with the rest at Valley Forge, but he had a quip for every hardship. His jokes were infectious, and he did not lose his popularity even when Washington appointed him to serve as a legal adviser on courts-martial. As a judge advocate, Marshall did something scarcely conceivable to "brass." He explained his decisions in writing, just as Supreme Court justices do now.

Later he actually settled down to study law at the College of

William and Mary, near the home of his beloved Mary Ambler. But six weeks after he had enrolled, Polly, as he always called her, and her family moved to Richmond. Unhesitatingly John followed her there, ending his education abruptly. Now he must earn a living. He had to apply to Jefferson, then governor, for a license to practice law. Jefferson must have perceived Marshall's native ability, for he signed the license.

For a long time no clients came. Marshall spent much of his time managing his father's farm. People who saw him riding through the streets with sacks of feed hanging from the saddle, or walking along eating cherries out of his hat, could be forgiven for not recognizing a future Chief Justice. One client who came was so upset by Marshall's casual dress that he took the case away—until he heard the young man handle a jury. For at that Marshall was an immediate success. Juries liked and trusted him.

The rural voters, when Marshall ran for office, had no objection to his appearing in shirt sleeves and suspenders, nor to his love of noisy horseshoe pitching, nor to his ability to down a tall julep before partaking of a huge barbecued steak.

He was easily elected to the House of Delegates at Richmond, and on the strength of his salary he married Polly. When the minister was paid, John had one guinea left in his pocket. Unworried, the blissful pair went to housekeeping in Richmond, in two rooms, one reserved for the law practice.

Marshall belonged to the unpopular Federalist party. One of the early political organizations in America, the Federalists wanted Virginia to stick to sound currency, to help creditors collect their debts, and to join the proposed new federation of the states, the United States of America. And no state was more doubtful of ratification than Virginia, where opposition—fearful that a federal government would turn into a despotism—was led by Patrick Henry, idol of the voters.

In the debate on ratification, Marshall and James Madison, "Father of the Constitution," bore the brunt of the fight in support of it. Marshall argued particularly for Article III, which defines the Supreme Court. In words whose importance was hardly noticed then, he promised Patrick Henry that the justices would have the power to wipe out laws which were unconstitutional. Marshall and Madison turned the tide of victory for the Union in the key state of Virginia.

Yet 12 years later the Supreme Court, whose vast powers Marshall had predicted, was weaker in actuality than it had been on paper. Of the three Chief Justices so far, one had gone doddery and two had resigned to take "better jobs"—with more pay and more honor. The Court neither inspired much respect nor had much power to enforce its will on the proud states. Often it met only to adjourn for lack of cases on the docket. When the first Capitol was designed, no one remembered to put in a room where the Court could sit!

Then in 1801, as his term was expiring, President Adams had suddenly to fill the vacancy of Chief Justice. The new administration, Jefferson's, was bringing with it a landslide of anti-Federalism, and the astute Adams wished to leave behind him in a key position one man who believed in a strong central government. John Marshall, who had been sent by Adams on a diplomatic mission to France in 1797, and then elected to Congress in 1799, had been persuaded some months before to serve as Secretary of State. Now President Adams nominated him for the position of Chief Justice.

Marshall was astounded and deeply gratified. True, the salary of Chief Justice was but a fraction of what he had been making as a highly successful lawyer. By this time he had a fine mansion in Richmond and a country estate to keep up; he had a thriving family with many needs. Yet he did not hesitate. Long must he have cherished the vision of what the Supreme Court might become; now it was in his hands to realize it.

So, at 45 years of age, John Marshall donned the robes of the highest appointive office in the land, amid a widespread lack of rejoicing. Thomas Jefferson, the man who believed that that government is best which governs least, now stood to take the oath of office before the new Chief Justice, John Marshall, unrelenting foe of states' rights, unshakable believer in a powerful central government. Courteously, smilingly, Marshall held out the Bible. Solemnly, Jefferson swore on it to uphold the Constitution. The country held its breath for the coming battle.

It was joined in Marshall's first important decision, *Marbury* v. *Madison*. Marbury, an insignificant Federalist henchman, had been promised a judgeship by the outgoing Federalists, who had rushed through many such commissions in order to pack the courts. James Madison, when he took office as Secretary of State, found Marbury's commission undelivered, and held it up. Marbury sued, asking the Court to issue a writ toward its recovery.

John Marshall saw and seized his opportunity. Marbury, the Chief Justice ruled, should by rights have had his commission, but the law allowing the Supreme Court to issue such a writ against Madison was unconstitutional, because it gave the Court more power than the Constitution specifies. This was a marvelously adept decision, for while denying the Court a small power, Marshall here and now armed it with a greater one—judicial review upon the constitutionality of any federal or state law.

It is this power to protect the constitutional rights of the citizen against the might of law itself which makes the Supreme Court the final bulwark of your liberties and mine. Although this authority of the Court to interpret the Constitution is not specifically designated anywhere in the great blueprint of our government, John Marshall deduced that it was implied there. And this inspired perception has been confirmed by a tribunal higher than the Court itself—the will of the people. For 150 years we have been content with what Marshall made of the Court. The states had ratified the Constitution with their fingers crossed. It was defenseless till Marshall rallied the Court behind it. It could never otherwise have survived destructive legislation passed against its letter and spirit.

If few had been present to hear the decision in *Marbury* v. *Madison*, the doors of the circuit court in Richmond were jammed with spectators, reporters, politicians, military men, ladies of fashion, to hear how the Chief Justice would conduct the trial of Aaron Burr for treason. Once rich, now bankrupt, once an outcast for killing Marshall's friend Alexander Hamilton in a duel, now the pet of society, Burr was an enigma. Was he indeed guilty—as so many people seemed to believe—of a treasonous scheme to carve a wilderness empire out of the Mississippi Valley, with himself as head of state?

It was in this case that the public first came to know Marshall's lofty serenity, which set the tone of the Supreme Court ever after. And when it came, the decision in this instance was, like most of Marshall's, constitutional to the core. For only God can judge treasonable men by what lies in their hearts; the Constitution requires, for conviction of treason, testimony of two witnesses to the same overt act committed against the United States. Thus instructed, the jury declared Burr not guilty. Whatever Burr deserved, countless innocent men were protected in future from wartime hysteria by this precedent.

After the Burr trial, the whole country began to realize that it had a titan on the bench. Lawyers respected, spectators delighted in, his dignified appearance there. But the Barbecue Club enjoyed equally the spectacle of the great Chief Justice down on his hands and knees, measuring horseshoe throws with a straw, then, if he had won, making the woods ring with triumphant shouts. He was good company, too, when he sat, swinging one dusty shoe above another, telling funny stories in a slow drawl. And always he was a man of his word, a man who believed in the sanctity of contract. It was in this firm faith that he decided the famous Dartmouth College case.

Back in 1769 a charter had been granted to the Reverend Eleazar Wheelock for a school to educate New Hampshire Indians under the guidance of the Congregational faith. There were no Indians at Dartmouth any more, but the college was thriving. Wheelock's son, who had been kicked out of the president's chair by the trustees, had gone to the state legislature and persuaded the lawmakers that the charter needed modernizing—to the extent of changing the name to Dartmouth *University*, installing him as president, seizing the buildings and removing all the professors and students loyal to the original *College*. Dartmouth *College* sued Dartmouth *University*, and hired as its lawyer, to argue before the Supreme Court, an alumnus named Daniel Webster.

The tense moment came in the closing speech for the plaintiff, the old College. "It is a small college," admitted Webster—and here, it is told, Webster had to pause to master his emotions and Marshall had to lean far forward on his silken sleeves of office to catch the words, husky with feeling—"but there are those who love it."

But Marshall's decision in favor of the college took no account of sentiment. The Constitution, he reminded lawmakers, forbids any legislature from passing laws in impairment of contract. And here Marshall nailed another principle: no contract would be worth writing if everybody could rush to a state legislature and lobby through special measures annulling it.

This, like the other Supreme Court decisions, was written and read by Marshall. Before his day each Justice had read his own decision, each one with perhaps a slightly different shade of meaning, till lawyers hardly knew what *had* been decided. Marshall stopped that. Now only one affirmative decision was given; if there was a dissent, that was read also.

While Court sat, all the Justices lived together, bachelor-style, in a boardinghouse. From this intimacy arose the tradition that the Justices call each other "Brother." In their fraternity, and over a glass of Madeira wine, many a momentous point was debated. But, to economize, the Justices resolved to cheer only dark days with wine. "Brother Story," Marshall would say wistfully, "step to the window and see if it's raining." Then if Story reported, "Brother Marshall, the sun is shining," the Chief Justice might cock his head and declare, "However, it is a presumptive fact that somewhere it is a rainy day. Brothers, let us drink."

Fond of good living though he was, Marshall cannot be called self-indulgent. A devoted husband and father, he could not, with ten children and an invalid wife, have been extravagant if he wished. Not on a justice's pay.

States' rights and Marshall's beloved Union clashed when the state of Maryland, urged on by selfish business interests, tried to tax to death a Baltimore branch of the Second Bank of the United States. The situation was politically tense, the courtroom crowded with the foes of a strong federal government, as Marshall entered it to pronounce on the fateful case of *McCulloch* v. *Maryland*. For this time it was a question not of the constitutionality of an act of Congress (passionate states'-righters didn't care how often Marshall slapped the federal government's wrist), but of the right of a state to do what she pleased within her borders, even to the extent of defying the federal government and destroying its branch bank. Marshall, in an opinion that is considered his greatest for logic and brilliance, crushed the arguments for state sovereignty, and once and for all made the Constitution what it claims to be, the supreme law of the land.

The crowning achievement of Marshall's career was the body blow which he dealt to the evils of monopoly, or exclusive business control, in the Steamboat Case, as laymen called *Gibbons* v. *Ogden*. Actually Gibbons and Ogden were but pawns. Robert Fulton and his rich backer, Robert Livingston, had lobbied through the New York legislature a monopoly of steam transportation in New York harbor; they had a similar stranglehold on the mouth of the Mississippi. They had won victories in the lower courts. In arguing the Steamboat Case, the legal giants of the age, with Webster for the antimonopolists, made the new courtroom in the Capitol ring for months. On the day the Chief Justice was to give his opinion the room was packed to the doors; hundreds waited outside.

The Constitution, Marshall pronounced, makes no distinction between vessels moved by steam and those moved by winds. The waters of New York harbor do not belong to the state of New York alone. If there was anything uppermost in the minds of the framers of the Constitution, Marshall declared, "it was to keep commercial intercourse among the states free from all restraints."

Free enterprise had won. Yet Marshall's age could hardly realize what a wall he had swept away. If one steamboat company had got a monopoly from the Supreme Court, one of the railroads so soon to come into existence might have had a stranglehold on all land transportation. The industrial age was then newborn; John Marshall undid the swaddling clothes that bound it and let it walk.

The last great phase of Marshall's life was his pioneering work in the law of the sea. At that time cases that involved shipping were tried in each country by admiralty courts, and foreign vessels had about the status of "prizes." Marshall, always at his best where there was no precedent, created by his maritime decisions a law that did not till then exist. Soon British courts were citing his shipping cases as authority. Marshall may be counted a founder of modern international law.

Now the old frame, though not the mind, wore out. The aged Chief Justice, in the days before anesthetics, endured a long major operation without flinching. He wanted to live, for his Court's sake, for his country's. But when Polly Marshall died, John loved life no longer, and in 1835 the hand that had preserved the Constitution and held open the door of free enterprise fell lifeless. The Liberty Bell, tolling for John Marshall's funeral, cracked then, to be silent for nearly a century thereafter. But he had left his Court so strong that it could for all time protect the liberties of the American people.

No horse gets anywhere until he is harnessed. No steam or gas ever drives anything until it is confined. No Niagara is ever turned into light and power until it is tunneled. No life ever grows great until it is focused, dedicated, disciplined.

—*Harry Emerson Fosdick*

The great use of life is to spend it for something that will outlast it.   —*William James*

THE MIDNIGHT RIDER

Condensed from Paul Revere and the World He Lived In

By Esther Forbes

IT WOULD BE a small world for the little boy Paul Revere in the Boston of the late 1730's: his mother's crowded kitchen and the good smells of herbs drying, a suet pudding bubbling on the hearth, ducks roasting, and the less alluring aroma of milk souring into cheese and of baby flannel drying. For Paul there was also the fascination of his father's shop. Paul Revere, Sr., a French immigrant known as Apollos Rivoire before his name was Americanized, was a silversmith.

Young Paul's education was good enough to enable him, later on, to write clear letters with no more bad grammar and spelling than many contemporary "gentlemen." But by 13 his formal schooling was over, for that was the age when apprenticeships began. By the apprentice system boys learned everything from law and medicine to soap-boiling and tinkering. They worked hours that would supposedly kill a modern boy. However hard the system sometimes was, the art, craft or trade was well served. No other method has turned out such good workmen. Young Paul Revere, learning in his father's shop, was to become America's finest silversmith.

Paul's father died in 1754; and now Paul, at 19, was nominally the head of the Revere household. It was his obvious duty to stand by his mother and provide for his brothers and sisters. Instead, in the spring of 1756 he enlisted to fight the French at Lake George, New York. At Fort William Henry, an English stronghold at the head of the lake, the camp was dirty; privies, slaughter pens, kitchens and graves were all mixed together. Hundreds of the men fell sick, and five to eight were buried daily. Neither the French nor the colonists felt strong enough to take the offensive. Both sat and died in their forts. And almost daily the Indians could sneak up and pick off a few of the troops.

In November, when food was scant, snow falling, men shivering in their light summer equipment, the Massachusetts troops were ordered on the long march home. They left many men in shallow graves about Lake George; and that winter Indian warriors as far away as Lake Michigan could wear at their belts the fair hair of boys who but a year before had been wearing it themselves about wharves and workshops. Paul Revere at least brought back his scalp with him to his smithy in Boston.

In 1757 the drums beat again, and troops marched to fight the French. But Paul Revere, now a master silversmith, stuck to his shop. At 22 he was a sturdily built young fellow, of medium height. He was courting a young lady named Sara Orne, whom he took rowing on the harbor and for picnics at Blue Hills in Milton. In August 1757 Sara and Paul were married. And on April 3 in the following spring, Sara was brought to bed of a daughter. As long as she lived, she never had a child in an odd year and never missed an even one.

By the summer of 1758 the end of the long French and Indian wars was in sight. In England, William Pitt, the elder, was showing his talent for picking out obscure officers and turning them into military geniuses. During his supremacy, Canada was won for

England, and the power of France was smashed. The victory over France ended America's dependence on England's protection. If she did not like the way the mother country restricted her trade, she would not now be too afraid of the French to say so.

On the first day of August 1764, "the greatest merchant in New England, Thomas Hancock, Esq., expired in the 62nd year of his age. He has left the Bulk of his Estate to his nephew Mr. John Hancock." At only 27, John Hancock was the wealthiest man in New England. One day, shortly after John Hancock came into his inheritance, two men were idly strolling Boston Common. Their talk was of the fortunes of the Whig party: in some way it must be strengthened to fight the taxes and customs England was determined to force upon her colonies *without representation*, which would be tyranny. The two men stopped before the great house of the Hancocks. These two were soon to be known as "that Brace of Adamses."

Samuel Adams was the mastermind of the Whig party. As astute a politician as even America has ever produced, he built up a strong political machine. He made it his practice to watch rising young men in Boston and to lure them into the Whig camp. His cousin, John Adams, was one of his recruits.

Sam Adams had an impressive piece of news for John Adams as they stopped before the Hancock house. "I have done a very good thing for our cause," he remarked, "by enlisting the master of that house and his fortune into it." Soon Sam Adams was bringing John Hancock to the Whig Clubs, in which Paul Revere was beginning to stand out as someone worth watching—a man capable of bridging the gap between the Revolutionary thinkers and the doers.

During the depression of 1765, England's Chancellor of the Exchequer, George Grenville, looked about for some form of taxation which would actually produce money, and put the Stamp Act through Parliament. As soon as the Stamp Act went into effect (which it never did), every legal document in the American colonies, every newspaper or commercial paper, would need a stamp;

costing from a ha'penny to 20 shillings. The colonies now in-augurated a joint Continental Congress, where all delegates agreed that "taxation without representation is tyranny."

Boston turned to rioting. The already notorious mobs of Boston's North End and South End pulled down fences, invaded the Stamp Collector's home, pelted Britain's Governor Thomas Hutchinson with stones and abuse—and finally completely looted his home. Now there emerged the mysterious Sons of Liberty. They frightened Britain's customs commissioners out of town and paralyzed all government but their own. At will they could summon thousands. How many of the genuine toughs of Boston were actually members we do not know, but we do know, from lists of the time, that Paul Revere was one of these secretly operating Sons of Liberty.

By the middle of 1768 the customs commissioners, who had taken refuge from mob rule on Castle Island in Boston Harbor, demanded that England send troops to protect them. When the English troops arrived, Boston settled down to make things as uncomfortable as possible for the soldiers. There were nightly tavern brawls. Redcoats were "accidentally" jostled off bridges and wharves into water. They were followed by small boys chanting "Bloody-backs" and "Lobsters for sale." On Monday night, March 5, 1770, more Redcoats than usual were out "driving the streets" in small packs. They pushed and cursed at civilians, who got in their way as much as possible and cursed back. By eight o'clock, a boy had been knocked down on King Street and was bawling that he was killed. A British officer was standing there as the crowd began to gather. It was too much for a solitary sentry who was stationed nearby. This sentry, Montgomery, had been enduring more than the usual amount of snowballs and provincial wit which was the fate of solitary sentries. Now he left his box and hit the boy. Instantly the crowd rushed him, yelling that the bloodthirsty British butcher was murdering the child.

Mysteriously, there was another crowd gathered in the neighborhood that night. The cry went up to kill all the "lobsters" they could find. This disciplined mob now joined the crowd around the sentry on King Street in front of the Old State House. The sentry, Montgomery, was by now hard-pressed by the crowd in King Street. "If you come near me," he panted, "I'll blow your brains out." An enormous mulatto loomed up over him. Crispus Attucks would have frightened any man. He was well over six feet, was part Indian, part Negro and part white. Attucks had a crowd of sailors at his heels and a stick in his hand. He poked at Montgomery and said he'd "have off one of his claws." The hard-pressed "lobster" did not fire, but he called in a loud voice, "Turn out Main Guard."

A corporal's guard stepped out of the main guardhouse, followed by Captain Preston, the officer for the day. The sentry joined the semicircle of level bayonets. Captain Preston ordered the soldiers to prime and load. Then the crowd made a sudden, blind rush at the soldiers. In the melee, no one knows who gave the order "Fire . . ."

Montgomery fired first at Crispus Attucks, who got two balls through the chest. British shots killed Sam Gray, a workman, and James Caldwell, a mate from a coasting vessel. Sam Maverick, a young apprentice, cried, "Fire away, you damned lobster-backs." The British bullets dropped him.

There is in the Boston Public Library a pen-and-ink diagram of the Boston Massacre which is said to have been prepared by Paul Revere. The handwriting on it certainly looks like his. There is more animation in the struggling figures than Paul Revere ever got into his more formal engravings. They suggest that he himself had stood in King Street that night and had actually seen the men dead and dying about him. Then Revere went to work on his more famous engraving of the Massacre. It was designed to be sold on the street. All of the prints that now exist are hand-colored, with emphasis on the scarlet of British uniforms and Yankee blood—a hair-raising Whiggish version of the "bloody work in King Street."

By this time Paul Revere was not only a silversmith and an engraver, but a merchant. And he was not yet, at 35, in his complete stride. Paul and Sara had been married for 13 years and the children were thickening about them. Six of their seven children were living and another was on the way. In those days, childbearing women quickly ran out of calcium, and a "tooth for every child" was an accepted law of nature. Hair fell out and bodies became misshapen. Sara was no longer the young girl who had caught Paul Revere's eye when he came back from the wars, but an old woman of 34.

Sara Orne Revere died on the third of May, 1773. In the custom of the time, her place at table, her pew in church, her half of the broad bed would be quickly filled. Rachel Walker was 27 at the time Paul Revere met her, a smart-looking girl, clever, capable, kindly. Their marriage brought years of mutual confidence, respect and love.

On the very day of the Boston Massacre, the far-off British Parliament had voted to abolish all the hated customs duties—except on one small item, tea. All that was left of British tyranny in America was that small tax. Even with the tax, tea was cheaper over here than in London. Merchants were importing it and people were drinking it. By November 1773, when three tea ships were hourly expected, Boston was in a ferment. The Sons of Liberty were back in full stride. One morning Boston was posted with the historic:

FRIENDS! BRETHREN! COUNTRYMEN!
That worst of Plagues, the detested tea shipped for this port by the East India Company is now arrived in the Harbour; the hour of destruction, or manly opposition to the machanitions of Tyranny, stares you in the Face; every Friend to his country, to Himself, and to Posterity, is now called upon to meet at Faneuil Hall, at nine o'clock this day, at which time the bells will ring to make united and successful resistance to this last, worst and most destructive measure. *Boston. Nov. 29, 1773.*

This meeting (in no way a legal town meeting) ordered the first of the tea ships, the *Dartmouth*, not to unload. Twenty-five hardy men were to watch that night to see that she obeyed.

Among them, armed with musket and bayonet, was Paul Revere.

Two more ships, the *Beaver* and the *Eleanor*, joined the *Dartmouth* at Griffin's Wharf. On board they had 342 chests of tea, valued at $90,000. Boston's mass meetings continued at Old South Meeting House, for Faneuil Hall was too small. By vote at these meetings, the tea ships were instructed to return to England. But Governor Hutchinson refused to permit them to leave.

On December 16, 1773, a dull and rainy day, 7000 people were gathered in Old South and crowded in the streets outside. It was quarter of six when word came of the British governor's final refusal to let the tea ships return to England. There were war whoops from the dark galleries, yells: "To Griffin Wharf!" and "Boston harbor a teapot tonight!" Shouts and running feet below. Men and boys with blankets and blackened faces. There were 50 to 100 "Indians," very meagerly disguised; Paul Revere was among them, although by going he risked liberty and life. At the wharf these men and boys silently divided into three groups and went aboard the ships. The tea chests were hoisted on deck, broken open, and the tea was thrown into the harbor.

Paul Revere was probably that night as tired and as pleased with himself as were all the others. But he did not get much sleep. That same day (for it was dawn when the men got home) an account of what had been done in Boston was drawn up by the Committee of Correspondence. It must go immediately to the Sons of Liberty in New York and Philadelphia. Paul Revere was chosen to do the riding. He was known as an excellent horseman as well as a discreet man. He started instantly. Sleep was always a thing he could do without. On the round trip to Philadelphia, Paul was gone but 11 days. His rate was about 63 miles a day, a good indication of his physical endurance. He brought back good news. The Sons of Liberty and the radical Whigs in both New York and Philadelphia would back Boston to the hilt.

On May 10, 1774, His Majesty's ship the *Lively* arrived in Boston with orders for her punishment. The port was to be completely closed to all sea-borne traffic until the town agreed to pay for the tea. Governor Hutchinson was to go to England to report, and during his absence General Thomas Gage was to be governor and keep order with British regiments. Soon Boston's streets echoed to the clumping of army boots and the rolling of drums. Gage brought in no fewer than 11 regiments. British frigates and other ships-of-war took up strategic stations. Not even ferries could cross to Charlestown.

Boston was angry and despairing. The First Continental Congress, in session at Philadelphia, agreed that if the British troops in Boston should take the offensive, the other colonies would help with armed force.

On December 7, 1774, Rachel Walker Revere bore her first child. It would be hard to leave "his dear girl," as Paul called her, only a week after her confinement. But the Sons of Liberty had discovered that General Gage intended to send soldiers from Boston by sea to Portsmouth, New Hampshire, to so strengthen Fort William and Mary that the local militia could not seize it. Someone must go immediately to warn of the plan. This was by far the most ticklish ride Revere had as yet undertaken—60 wintry miles at top speed through the snow.

The next afternoon, December 13, Paul Revere drew up before John Sullivan's door in Durham, New Hampshire, a few miles inland from Portsmouth. For over a year Sullivan had been drilling the local boys. He heard Revere's news, and sent for a handful of his young men. After dark they went down the river to Portsmouth Harbor, pushed their boat as close to Fort William and Mary as possible, waded ashore and demanded surrender. Captain Corcoran refused, fired three times, hit no one—and surrendered. He had only a few men and was completely surprised. For several hours the provincials waded back and forth, waist-deep in icy brine, carrying kegs of powder and small arms out from the fort. It was a tremendous haul. They got back to Durham, very frozen, very triumphant, and hid the stores in a pit under the pulpit of the meetinghouse. Nothing the Yankees had done thus far so enraged George III personally as this seizure of his fort and his stores. He demanded the punishment of every man concerned and the immediate confiscation of all rebel supplies.

In the winter of 1774-75 Paul Revere was one of a secret committee of 30 men formed to watch the movements of the British soldiers day and night. By the 15th of April he and his associates knew that something was up: that the British were planning a sortie, probably aimed at the powder and arms stored at Concord. Revere knew that John Hancock and Sam Adams were in Lexington, preparing to go to Philadelphia for the Second Continental Congress as representatives of Massachusetts. The British might well be after them, too. Early the next morning, a Sunday, Paul Revere rode out to Lexington to warn the two statesmen. They were living in concealment at the Clark parsonage close by Lexington Green. Revere may have ridden over to Concord also, for the town was warned that day.

Paul came back to Boston by way of Charlestown, where he hunted up William Conant, a prominent Son of Liberty. From here, over the broad mouth of the Charles, the spire of Old North Church was plainly visible. That evening Revere told Colonel Conant "that if the British went out by water we would show two lanterns in the North Church steeple—and if by land one as a signal, for we were apprehensive it would be difficult for us to cross the Charles or get over Boston Neck." He would himself attempt to reach Charlestown by boat, but it might be impossible. Watch, then, for the lanterns.

On Tuesday afternoon General Gage sent out a group of officers to block the roads leading toward Concord so no rebel messenger could ride through and warn the town. Of this, Paul Revere knew nothing. Of one precaution all Boston knew: the 64-gun frigate *Somerset* was moved into the very mouth of the Charles River, to guard the crossing to Charlestown. By dusk, boats were drawn up along the Common and troops were waiting to embark. It was clear that the British were going by sea.

At the house of Dr. Joseph Warren, a close friend of Paul's, plans were perfected. Robert Newman, sexton of Old North Church, would be notified and the lanterns hung. This he had agreed to do. The lanterns would give warning, but no details. Farther upstream the British boats would be ferrying over the troops. There was a chance Paul Revere could get past the *Somerset* to carry detailed information to Lexington. He was ready to take the chance. But first he sought out Robert Newman at the church. Newman took the lanterns and softly mounted the wooden stairs to the highest window of the belfry. To the north he could see the black hull of the *Somerset*, anchored in the Charles. Beyond was Charlestown, and there he knew men were waiting, watching for his signal. He lit the lanterns and hung them.

Meanwhile, with two friends, Paul Revere set out to cross the river in a rowboat. The *Somerset* blocked the shortest route, forcing them to keep rather well out to sea. Revere reached Charlestown undiscovered. At Colonel Conant's he found a group waiting for him. They had seen his signals. He told them "what was acting" and learned to his surprise that the roads toward Cambridge and on to Concord were already patrolled by British officers.

Paul Revere would need a good horse to slip through the cordon. He got one. John Larkin, one of Charlestown's wealthiest citizens, gave him the best horse in his stable. In the bright cold moonlight, Revere swung to the saddle. So away, down the moonlit road, goes Paul Revere and the Larkin horse, galloping into history, art, editorials, folklore, poetry.

"I had got almost over Charlestown Common towards Cambridge," Paul remembered, "when I saw two Officers on Horseback, standing under the shade of a Tree, in a narrow part of the road. One of them started his horse toward me and the other up the road, as I supposed to head me should I escape the first. I turned my horse short about, and rid upon a full gallop for Mistick Road." In this brief, slippery, cross-country race the heavier British charger was no match for the light-footed Yankee horse. Outdistancing his pursuer, Paul Revere followed the Mystic River into Medford. Here "I awaked the Captain of the minutemen: and after that I alarumed almost every house till I got to Lexington."

Bells rang, drums beat—"The regulars are out!" Women gathered children and silver, and fled to swamps. Men seized muskets and powder horns. Other men mounted and rode off to other towns to carry the warning—"The regulars are out." Close upon midnight, Revere came into Lexington. Captain John Parker had called out the local minutemen that afternoon when word first came that a handful of British officers were abroad. It does not seem to have been known in Lexington that a considerable force of the regulars was coming until Revere arrived. Paul went straight to the Clark parsonage and told his story to Hancock. It was not merely a patrol of British officers that was out this night, but probably "over a thousand light troops." He had seen them crossing the Charles at ten. They might be here any moment now. Revere once more mounted, to go to Concord and alarm the minutemen. Paul Revere says:

". . . about half way from Lexington to Concord, four officers rode up to me, with their pistols in their hands & said G—D d—m you stop, if you go an inch further you are a dead Man. I observed a wood at a small distance and made for that intending when I gained that to jump my Horse & run afoot, just as I reached it out started six officers, siesed my bridle, put their pistols to my Breast, ordered me to dismount, which I did. One of them, who appeared to have command there, and much of a Gentleman, asked where I came from; I told him. he asked what time I left it; I told him, he seemed much supprised, He said Sir may I crave your name? I answered my name is Revere. What said he Paul Revere? I answered yes; the others abused me much; but he told me not to be afraid, no one should hurt me. He said they were only after some Deserters they expected down the Road. I told them I knew better, I knew what they were after; that I had alarumed the country all the way up, and I should have 500 men there soon; one of them said they had 1500 coming."

The British officers formed a circle about Paul Revere and the little cavalcade "rid down towards Lexington, a pretty smart pace. The officer who led me said I was in a d—m—d critical situation.

I told him I was sensable of it. When we got within about half a mile of Lexington Meeting house we heard a gun fired. The Major asked me what that was for. I told him to alarum the country. The Major ordered us to a halt he asked me how far it was to Cambridge. He then asked the Sarjant, if his horse was tired, he said yes. He Ordered him to take my horse. I dismounted, the Sarjant mounted my horse, and they rode off down the road."

Revere made his way cross-lots back to Lexington. At the Clark parsonage John Hancock's clerk, John Lowell, asked Revere to go with him to Buckman's Tavern, where he was staying, and help him carry away a trunk containing Hancock's papers. He did not wish these treasonable documents to fall into British hands. Revere went. He crossed the Green, where in the unreal light of dawn some 50 or 60 men, farmers mostly and dressed as such, were forming ranks. Women and children and others stood at open doors and windows to gaze. Approaching were the orderly scarlet ranks of the grenadiers, the glitter of the just-risen sun glowing on pipeclayed baldrics, brass buttons, gold lace, steel bayonets. Paul Revere saw them coming from an upper window of Buckman's Tavern. But what would happen when this orderly flood of scarlet and steel met the frail lines on the Green was not his business. His was to rescue John Hancock's trunk.

With John Lowell he carried it through the militiamen, who were staring stonily at the approaching British, and to the Clark parsonage. The regulars, six companies under Major John Pitcairn, marched to 150 feet from the Green and came to a halt. Seventy-seven militiamen stood there, Captain Parker's words ringing in their ears: "Don't fire unless fired on, but if they mean to have a war let it begin here."

The evidence seems to be that it was one of the provincials, hidden behind a stone wall, who fired that first shot. The British immediately answered with a volley. In the brief exchange that followed, one British private was wounded, and eight of the provincials were killed and ten wounded. The militiamen were quickly routed and the British continued their march to Concord.

Unmolested, the British swept into the village like a scarlet tidal wave, and into the taverns as well. They had marched 15 miles without breakfast, and demanded food and drink. Colonel Francis Smith, the British commander, sent out small detachments to find what munitions they might. And he sent Captain Walter Laurie to North Bridge with orders to destroy it.

Word came to Colonel Smith that quite a number of the provincials had gathered on the far side of North Bridge. The colonel decided to take reinforcements to Captain Laurie. And slowly he walked off at the head of his men. Then from the direction of North Bridge a scattering of shots, followed by a volley.

In a little while Captain Laurie's men, with Colonel Smith's, returned to the Square. The provincials had won the skirmish at Concord Bridge. And one thing was noticeable: half of the British officers had been picked off. The militia were much better marksmen than their opponents. For some time Colonel Smith kept his men in the center of Concord. He could burn the town if attacked, and so was fairly safe.

Now in ever-widening circles the cry to arms spread over New England. Concord's bell was heard by Lincoln, Lincoln's by Carlisle, Carlisle's by Chelmsford. Thousands of men were hurrying toward Concord as fast as legs or horses would carry them. At noon, fearing the ever-increasing number of militiamen, Colonel Smith decided to march his men back by way of Lexington.

And then the slaughter began. No one opposed the British openly—in the honorable tradition of European warfare. From farmhouse windows, from behind stone walls and barns, an enemy they rarely saw fired and took a terrific toll. So the ever-decreasing column of redcoats ran a bloody gantlet. Colonel Smith was hit, Major Pitcairn unhorsed. For a long time the soldiers took this butchery very well. As their comrades fell, they closed up the ranks and went on. But at last panic seized them and they struggled into Lexington completely demoralized. It was not until after nightfall that these men got to Charlestown. All night long Gage's boats ferried what was left of his tired troops back to Boston.

The ferocious one-day skirmishes from Lexington to Concord,

from Concord back to Lexington to Charlestown, which have been abbreviated to "The Battle of Lexington," took place upon Wednesday. On Thursday, Paul Revere was in Cambridge. And there already ahead of him was Joseph Warren, who had got out of Boston by boat. Doctor Warren was president of the Boston Committee of Safety, most of whose members had by this time escaped Boston. In Cambridge they set up their headquarters. Paul Revere joined them, ready to serve in any way he might. Warren "engaged me as a messanger to do the outdoor work for the committee." He was to stand ready to ride at a moment's notice and "two of the colony horses" were turned over to him.

Thousands of minutemen were arriving from the surrounding countryside, anxious to finish off the redcoats, but without organization, camps, food, tents. While machinery was being evolved for their care and command, the dirty, ill-fed, unpaid men stuck it out and established the siege of Boston.

In May the Massachusetts provincial congress, which was establishing a makeshift civil government for the revolting colony, engaged Paul Revere to cut copper plates and print money. Except for the fact Paul Revere was paid for his services with his own "pasteboard" money, everything was going well for him. His family had now got out of Boston and joined him in Watertown. It was filled up with prominent Whigs, his best friends.

Early in June 1775 General Gage offered pardon to all rebels who would lay down their arms, except John Hancock and Sam Adams only. His proclamation was ridiculed and answered by earthworks thrown up on Breed's Hill or, as it was miscalled then as now, Bunker Hill, in Charlestown. It was believed that the British would certainly move against the earthworks. The next afternoon they crossed the river and engaged the provincial troops. As long as their munitions held out, the Americans were supreme. The redcoats suffered over 1100 casualties, almost one third of the troops engaged. But in the end the rebel powder gave out, and the Americans had to retreat.

This battle did much to hearten the Americans. It proved to

them that their men and methods were equal or superior to those of the British. And it permitted them to keep the British beleaguered in hungry and disease-ridden Boston. The siege dragged out into the winter, and by spring of 1776, the British finally gave up the long struggle and sailed out of Boston harbor.

The colonies' need for both gunpowder and cannon was desperate. So Paul Revere, the silversmith, who could learn a new trade as fast as most men turn around, now began to construct a gunpowder plant and to cast cannon. Most of the Massachusetts troops were now serving in Washington's army, far from home. Boston raised a regiment of militia for home defense, and Paul Revere was commissioned as a major.

Gloomy was the winter of 1777–78 for the half-starved citizens of Boston, and it was even blacker for Washington and the pitiful remnants of his Continental Army at Valley Forge. But with the spring came news to hearten all Americans. France was ready once more to go on with her old war with England. She would help the colonies with ships and men. On the 13th of March, Paul was ordered to "fire the Heavy Cannon on Castle Island when the French Frigate passes by the Castle Provided she Salutes the same."

One of the most tactful things the Frenchmen did was to bring sacks of silver money with them. The war was in its third year. Supplies were needed, and hard money. Now Revere could pay his men and pay himself.

All through the spring and summer of 1781, word came to Boston of the fighting to the south: the battles of Cowpens, of Guilford, of Eutaw Springs. October found Lord Cornwallis bottled up at Yorktown. On the 19th he surrendered.

So the six-and-a-half years of fighting were over. For the American colonies they had been lean years. Boston's population was far below its prewar figure. Her trade was ruined. By 1788 Paul Revere's stock in trade was largely hardware for shipbuilders. Much of this hardware was of local manufacture, and he soon decided to go into this work himself. But it was characteristic that he did not work only in simple iron castings. Any number of men could do that; Revere made his reputation as a foundryman in the extremely tricky art of bell-casting.

Paul Revere cast many bells for inland churches, but his primary interest as a manufacturer was in furnishing ships with "bolts, spikes, cogs, braces, pintles, sheaves, pumps, etc." Such ship gear had to be made from copper or brass and was largely imported. There were certain secrets about how the amalgam was made up (for pure copper would not serve). He went to work to discover for himself how it was done. Soon he could write that "no man but myself in the four New England States or Philadelphia or New York can melt Copper & draw it into Spikes."

The start of the American Navy, in 1795, was modest. Of six ships, the most famous was the *Constitution*, built so close to Revere's foundry that he could hear the shipwrights hammering. Paul Revere was determined to make the copper and brass for these ships himself.

He did furnish the metal for two of the frigates. His bill for the *Constitution* was for $3820.33. Some of the large copper bolts and sheaths he made for her were still in use a hundred years after. Paul Revere made things to last.

Letters of condolence are always hard to write. Early in 1800 Paul Revere, as one of the Past Grand Masters of the Masonic Grand Lodge in Boston, was asked to write to Mrs. Washington. The General had died on December 14, 1799. The letter follows the formalities of the day, but at the end is a burst of originality. "The Grand Lodge have subjoined an order that a *Golden Urn* be prepared as a deposit for a lock of hair, an *invaluable* relique of the Hero and Patriot. Should this favor be granted, Madam, it will be cherished as the most precious jewel in the cabinet of the Lodge." And so it was—and is. For it Paul Revere made an exquisite little urn, smaller than a pepper shaker, about the same shape, and all of gold. The top unfastens and, under glass, is the lock of hair.

In 1801 Paul Revere risked $25,000 of his own money, the United States Government lent him $10,000 and 19,000 pounds of copper, and he started out to set up a rolling mill. If he failed, he would be completely ruined.

Less than a year later he could write to our Secretary of the Navy, Robert Smith, "I have erected my Works & have Rolled Sheet Copper which is approved of by the best judges as being equal to the best Cold Rolled Copper." In 1803 the *Constitution* was dry-docked at Boston and recoppered with Revere copper, the first sheathing rolled in this country.

"Old Ironsides" was a wonderful ship. In all, she successfully fought the French, the Algerians and the English, and when she was old and doomed to be broken up, a 21-year-old Harvard boy wrote a poem about her and saved her. (The boy: Oliver Wendell Holmes. The poem, "Old Ironsides," starting with the bitter line "Ay, tear her tattered ensign down!" was published in the Boston *Advertiser* in 1830 and excited such public clamor that the ship was rebuilt and again put in service.)

Revere had had eight children by Sara and eight more by Rachel. Not one child seems to have disappointed the father in any way except by dying, which five of them did in infancy. His son Joseph Warren Revere, when he was 30, largely took over at the Revere bell foundry and copper mill. But Paul Revere retained his own deep interest in the work. There were, for instance, those years of close association with Robert Fulton, making the copper for the boilers of a curious contraption which might or might not work—a steamship. Much of its success would certainly depend upon its copper boilers.

Paul Revere now lived with his family in a house adjoining the rolling mill. From in front of his house started the slow, creaking wagons, carrying bells to churches and copper to shipyards. But the peace of his life was again interrupted. On June 18, 1812, war was declared between the United States and Great Britain. Paul Revere was 77. There still exists a small notebook with the names of 150 "Mechanics of the Town of Boston" who formally tendered their services to help build more forts in Boston Harbor. Paul Revere, already in his 80th year, was the first to sign—and is thought to have started the whole thing.

The end of this most shortsighted war came in February 1815.

The young republic had been trounced by her erstwhile mamma. But no one seemed to care. "Peace" was good enough. Paul Revere, the plain American, who in his own lesser way, along with the Adamses, Jeffersons, Washingtons and Hancocks, created the United States of America, would have been amazed at the debt he would owe in history to a little Portland boy whom he had never heard of. The boy's grandfather, General Peleg Wadsworth, he had known well in the days of the Revolution. When the general's grandchild, Henry Wadsworth Longfellow, grew up and wrote poems, he wrote one about the midnight ride of Paul Revere.

The generation which had organized the Revolutionary movement in Boston was mostly gone by 1816. Of the old leaders only John Adams and Paul Revere still lived. It was on a Sunday that Paul Revere died, May 10, 1818. In Boston's newspaper offices, journalists inked their pens. A prominent citizen and a very worthy man had died. They all knew "old Mr. Revere," something of his story and character. "Cool in thought, ardent in action," wrote the Boston *Intelligencer*. All agreed that his outstanding characteristics were his generosity and integrity. "Seldom has the tomb closed upon a life so honourable and useful."

That the tomb had also closed on one of America's most legendary heroes they could have had no idea, for the legend had not as yet risen up to swallow the actual man. They who had so recently seen the stocky, benevolent old gentleman walking the streets of Boston could hardly have guessed that he was destined forever to ride a foaming charger, his face enveloped in the blackness of a famous night, to become in time hardly a man at all— only a hurry of hoofs in a village street, a voice in the dark, a knock on a door, a disembodied spirit crying the alarm—an American patriot who, on a moonlit night in 1775, started out on a ride which, in a way, has never ended.

What on earth would a man do with himself if something did not stand in his way?
                                                        —*H. G. Wells*

BEETHOVEN THE INCREDIBLE

By George R. Marek

IN THE LAST years of his life the great composer Robert Schumann, beset with depression, was advised by his doctor to go for walks. He did go for a walk—every day the same walk. He walked to a statue of Ludwig van Beethoven.

In a sense, every composer since Beethoven has made such a pilgrimage. Certainly every composer who has since ventured to write a symphony must acknowledge his debt to that mighty architect of music in Vienna who, thinking, laboring, wrestling, sweating, shaping, smoothing, revising and then revising again, constructed an edifice so large that it has sheltered virtually all music down to our own times.

When Beethoven's First Symphony was performed, in 1800, he was not yet 30 years old. Full of ambitions, gay and not without vanity, he was attempting to capture the citadel of musical Vienna as a piano virtuoso. He felt in himself an enormous sense of power, but he was still conforming to convention, composing cheerful chamber music and appearing in the streets decently dressed, with a clean lace shirt. He attracted pupils and admirers from the best circles.

But soon alarming signs of deafness began to show themselves. At first Beethoven tried to hide the weakness. He began to avoid social gatherings. When he could no longer hide it—he was then 32—he retired to Heiligenstadt, a little suburb near Vienna.

Beethoven was always extreme in his reactions, both in joy and in despair. Now he poured out his misery in a long document called his "Testament":

> It was impossible for me to say to men, "Speak louder, shout, for I am deaf." How could I possibly admit an infirmity in the one sense which should have been more perfect in me than in others, a sense which I once possessed in highest perfection? What a humiliation when one stood beside me and heard a flute in the distance and I heard nothing. Such incidents brought me to the verge of despair—but little more and I would have put an end to my life.

Yet at this very time he composed the serenely lovely Second Symphony! It is cruel to say, but probably true, that Beethoven's deafness proved to be a blessing for music. Giving up his career as a virtuoso, hearing sounds only in his brain, shut off from the outer world, he constantly intensified and deepened his musical thought. But as he turned inward, his outward behavior became ever more contradictory. He would let no one touch his room, so that everything lay around in incredible disorder, papers strewn on chairs, ink spilled into the piano, remains of food on plates under the papers. He was so absentminded that he would forget to eat— once when inspiration was upon him he went into a restaurant, sat down and mused, forgot to order and finally called for his bill.

He constantly complained that he was not being properly recognized, that he had insufficient money to live on. In point of fact, he was enormously famous, enormously respected, and his financial rewards were greater than he pretended. (After his death, a considerable sum of money was found tucked away in a secret drawer in his desk.)

Beethoven refused to change his clothes—as a last resort his friends would steal in at night, take away his worn-out suits and replace them with new ones. He had a violent temper and was quite capable of throwing a dish of food, gravy and all, into a waiter's face.

In the summer of 1806 when he was a guest of his onetime patron, Prince Lichnowsky, the prince asked him to play for some of Napoleon's soldiers who were billeted in the castle. Beethoven refused. The prince jokingly threatened him with house arrest. Beethoven stormed out in a huff, walked through the night to the nearest town, there took a carriage for Vienna and, on reaching his lodgings, seized a bust of Lichnowsky and hurled it on the floor, smashing it to splinters.

Deafness made him increasingly suspicious. He would accuse his friends, his publishers and a theater manager of cheating him. The next day he would be sorry and apologize. Meanwhile, he promised one of his major works, the *Missa Solennis*, to six publishers and sold it to a seventh. He tried to fob off on the London Philharmonic an old composition as a new one.

He could also be considerate, tender and quietly kind: when one of his friends, the Baroness Ertmann, lost a child, Beethoven went to call on her, said nothing, but sat down at the piano and for a long time played music of consolation.

He read Plutarch and Shakespeare, but he could not master the multiplication tables. He was suffused with a genuine love of freedom; when in 1823 the debates about slavery were going on in England he used to follow the speeches in Parliament with the keenest interest. Yet he proved an absolute tyrant at home, particularly in the dispute over his nephew Karl. Beethoven hated his brother's widow, accusing her of loose morals, and managed to take the boy from her. At the age of 45 this man, so little versed in practical life, became the guardian of the child. The case was wrangled in lower and higher courts for years afterward. Beethoven suffocated Karl with his love, pumped him full of moral precepts, at the same time forgot to provide the boy with regular meals or winter clothes. Torn by the strife between uncle and mother, eventually the boy attempted suicide and finally disappeared into the anonymity of the Austrian army.

Beethoven also mistrusted and quarreled with his own servants. One of his friends presents us with this description:

There had been a quarrel which disturbed all the neighbors, and both servants had gone away. In the living room, behind a locked door, we heard the master singing parts of the fugue in the Credo—singing, howling, stamping. After we had been listening a long time to this almost awful scene, the door opened and Beethoven stood before us with distorted features calculated to excite fear. His first utterances were confused. Then with obvious restraint, he remarked, "Pretty doings, these! Everybody has run away and I haven't had anything to eat since yesternoon!"

Of all the hundreds of symphonies that have been composed, none can rival in popularity or emotional interest the nine great symphonic works that Beethoven wrote. Why? What is it that sets these symphonies apart? Do they have memorable melodies, good tunes? Does their profundity present to us a never-ending mystery which we must penetrate? Yes, but that isn't it. Is their orchestration particularly colorful and sensuous? Not particularly.

The reason, in my opinion, is this: Beethoven took music off the pedestal of formal beauty where Haydn and Mozart had left it and immersed it in the whirlpool of life. He roughened it up until it began to do what he expected it to do—to express problems, evoke emotions, move and struggle exuberantly. In his symphonies he set to music everybody's heartache and everybody's smile. Beethoven made music "human." That is why more people can respond at once to a Beethoven symphony than to any other.

Many composers have written fine symphonies, but Beethoven's remain in a class by themselves—as invaluable a part of our heritage as are Shakespeare's plays. The comparison is not farfetched. Like Shakespeare's, Beethoven's range was encompassing. Like him, he could be both gentle and angry, capable of childlike simplicity and maturest wisdom. Like him, he commands with equal skill tenderness and harshness; like him he has delightful humor; like him he loved nature; like him, and in spite of doubts, he believed in the victory of life.

Though our image of him is that of a brooding, dour, deaf, solitary man, the image is not altogether true. A man who knew

Beethoven in his later years described him as "an eagle looking at the sun." At other times he could be a swallow circling in the blue skies, or a wise owl observing the world with a winking eye. In spite of his unpredictable moods, his frightful table manners and his appearance (which was so wild that a child taken to see him thought he was Robinson Crusoe), Beethoven's friends remained utterly devoted to him.

His last sickness was made worse by his own carelessness and ignorance of the medical profession. In one month he swallowed 75 bottles of medicine. His bed was overrun with vermin, and one of the most welcome gifts that he received during this illness was a package of insect powder. To the very last he wanted to compose, and planned to work up some sketches he had for a tenth symphony. He died during a violent thunderstorm on March 26, 1827, at the age of 56. Such was the famous musical genius. Who can explain him?

When Toscanini was a director of La Scala, Milan, a certain quite untalented composer presented his manuscript in an opera competition in which Toscanini was a judge, asking that it be submitted especially for his opinion. The opera was rejected. Ten years later, the composer met Toscanini in New York City.

"Well, Maestro, it is a matter of the past," he said, "but I should like to know why you rejected my opera."

"I didn't like it," replied Toscanini.

"But I am sure, Maestro, that you never even read it. If you had read it, you could not have failed to like it."

"Don't talk nonsense," replied Toscanini, "I remember your manuscript perfectly; it's no good. Listen to this!" He sat down at the piano and played several passages from the opera he had rejected ten years before. "No, it's no good," he kept saying as he played. "It's beneath criticism!"

—*Ilya Ilf and Eugene Petrov*

MIGHTY TRAVELER

By Donald Culross Peattie

To MOST of us, Venice is as romantic as, to the Venetians of the Middle Ages, was China or Japan. Even if you get there it still seems like a dream. Those opalescent domes and palaces look fragile as blown glass, those carven arches fine as lace. Your gondola drifts under the Rialto Bridge which Shylock frequented, and past the palace called Desdemona's. And on one quiet little corner is a sign that says: "The House of Marco Polo." Marco Polo! With a start you realize that he was no fable but the greatest merchant of Venice who ever lived, the mightiest traveler the world has ever seen. In his tale of his marvelous travels we have our first eyewitness report on Asia.

Venice, in the 13th century, was a sailor's town and had heard many yarns, but those of Marco Polo, back from the ends of the earth, topped them all. He talked of a black rock he had seen dug up in China and set afire—a fuel that burned longer than wood. Venetians shouted with laughter; to them coal was fantastic. He told of another rock from which could be spun a wool that did not burn—and they held their sides. Asbestos was harder still to imagine. Nor would they believe him when he described a fountain in the Caucasus which flowed not with water but with oil.

In those days Venice was the greatest maritime trading power of the age. Long routes, extending over land and sea, led ultimately to the fabled city. From India the merchants of Venice obtained pearls, diamonds and sapphires. From Tartary (Siberia)

came the ermine on the Doges' robes, the sables for the wives of the merchant princes. And from Cathay (China) came spices, camphor and costly textiles. Yet no Venetian had ever seen the lands whence these riches came.

But there were two Venetian traders with stouter hearts than others. Their name was Polo, and they were the father and the uncle of Marco. While trading in southern Russia they found their return cut off by a local war. Since they could not go back, they boldly resolved to push forward—into the unknown Orient. Buying and selling, learning languages and markets, Nicolo and Maffeo Polo reached the great city of Bokhara, in the heart of central Asia, 3000 miles from home. For three years they trafficked there. One day there came to them officials of the great Kublai Khan, whose empire stretched from the Arctic Sea to the Indian Ocean, and from the shores of the Pacific to the borders of central Europe. The Khan had never met any western Europeans, and he was a man of the liveliest curiosity. Would the brothers Polo journey to his remote capital (Peking) in China?

For nine years the Polos were absent from Venice. And then one day these tanned, wind-bitten, deep-eyed travelers came home— but not to stay. Their friend Kublai Khan had sent with them a letter to the Pope, asking for 100 learned monks to convert the Mongols to Christianity and teach the arts and sciences of Europe. Never had the Church such a missionary opportunity! But it slipped through indifferent hands. Only two Dominican monks accepted the challenge and began the return journey with the brothers Polo, and at the first hint of danger the monks turned back.

Not so the youngest member of the party, Marco Polo, just 17. Surely no other boy ever embarked on such an adventure, or squared himself to such a geography lesson—24 years long. Born of a noble family, Marco had the youthful polish of his times and rank. But he also had a mind that blotted up facts, a lively curiosity and a memory that stored all he learned in orderly fashion.

From Marco's report of his travels, it must have been spring (of 1274) when he first saw the valley of the Oxus, lost in the heart of central Asia, for he says that all the countryside was enameled with wild crocuses, daffodils, snowdrops. Almost we can hear the camels squealing and the neighing and lowing from the dusty market, smell the spiced foods cooking, see the colorful costumes of Arabs, Persians, Turks, Tartars, Kurds, Mongols, Russians and Chinese—all bargaining in tongues like cymbals and twanging strings. Now, nearly 700 years after, Marco Polo's tales of all this are as fresh as that spring morning when the almond orchards were in bloom and the Hindu Kush mountains to the south twinkled their snows in the blue, arid sky.

But nature imposed her perils, too, and the Polos struggled through torrential rains, rivers in flood, sandstorms and avalanches. Up the giddy slopes of the Pamir Mountains they toiled, and over awesome gorges on swaying rope bridges. So high they climbed that even the birds ceased to fly, and now they saw great wild sheep "whose horns are a good six palms in length." These monstrously horned beasts were for centuries regarded as a myth—one more "marcopolo," or whopper. But modern scientists have secured specimens of this rare trophy, *Ovis poli*, which today you may see in museums.

Beyond the Pamir Mountains the Polos came to the Gobi Desert, where water may be poisonous with salt, where mirages tremble before doubting eyes, and where the bones of men and animals lie strewn along the way. From this wild lair, a century earlier, the fierce nomadic Mongols under Genghis Khan had overrun the greater part of Asia, and even reached Budapest.

Kublai, the grandson of Genghis, was no destroyer but a civilizer. Hearing of the Polos' slow approach, he dispatched an escort to sweeten the last month of their journey. And so, after almost four years on the way, the Polos, amid lavish celebration, entered the presence of the Khan before whom Asia trembled. Rather a slight man, Marco observed, with "large, fine black eyes, a good nose well set on and a fair countenance that flushes easily." The Khan stared back. "And who," he asked the elder Polo, "is this young gallant?" Proudly Nicolo Polo brought Marco forward. "He is my son, sire, and your servant."

From the beginning the Khan took a liking to the young man. He took him hunting on elephant-back, with falcons, and to his "stately pleasure dome" at Xanadu. For three years Marco was governor of the rich city of Yangchow; he was sent on missions to Burma, to the wilds of western China and the borders of Tibet and south to India. By now he had mastered four Oriental languages. His lively, colorful accounts of his missions, his memory for thousands of details enchanted the Khan, bored with the humdrum reports of his officials.

Marco saw and described a great and wondrous civilization, the stable and peace-loving China of the Middle Ages. How far ahead of Europe it was in some ways can be seen from the things Marco mentions as admirable and new to him: broad streets, paper money, police patrols at night, public carriages like a modern taxi fleet, bridges high enough to let masted vessels pass beneath, drains under the streets to carry off the gutter streams, roadsides beautified with double plantings, elevated superhighways.

For 17 years Marco served the Khan, while his father and uncle grew rich in trade. And then a great homesickness came over them—a longing for the tang of the Adriatic air, for the glittering dome of St. Mark's, for the haunting cry of the gondoliers and the sweet Italian speech. Again and again they asked for permission to depart; always it was refused. Suddenly their opportunity appeared. There came to the Khan a mission from a grandnephew, the ruler of far-off Persia, whose wife had just died. Her last wish had been that he should choose for his new bride a member of her own family at the court in China. A girl of 17 was selected—"very pretty and charming," says the observant Marco. And now the mission asked that the Polos, famous as travelers, be granted them as escort back to Persia. Reluctantly the Khan consented.

A dowry was bestowed upon the maiden, and on the Polos a great fortune in gold. Thirteen ships were fitted out. They set sail on a journey full of disasters, in which several ships and many of the company were lost. Three years later, one wintry day in 1295, there arrived at the door of the house of Polo on the San Crisostomo canal in Venice three strange-looking men in travel-stained, ragged garments. Their faces were not known; their tongues were clumsy with Italian words. The servants refused them entry. The three raised an outcry, and members of the Polo family issued from the house. But even the relatives shook their heads in doubt.

To convince all Venice, the Polos gave a banquet. For each course they appeared in a different costume, each surpassing the last in costly splendor. Finally they donned the tattered clothes in which they had arrived in the city. Before their amazed guests they ripped open the linings of these rags. Out tumbled a fortune in precious jewels—for it was thus that these merchant-travelers had carried their wealth through the perils that beset them.

The whole marvelous tale of their adventures might have died with the breath that told it, had it not been for the fortunes of war. Serving as "gentleman commander" on a galleon of Venice in one of her frequent clashes with Genoa, Marco was captured and, as luck would have it, put in a cell with a scribe. To pass the time, and to set the record straight, Marco dictated the volume we treasure as the *Book of Marco Polo*. Here for the first time a wondering Europe could hear the clangor of temple bells, smell the Mongol campfires of desert thorn and yak dung. Here could be read accounts of Japan, Korea, Indo-China, Burma, Java, the Andaman Islands, Siberia, Ethiopia, Madagascar. To many it remained all a "marcopolo"; before the great traveler died at 70, they asked him, since he was soon to face his Maker, to take back his lies. His answer was, "I never told the half of it."

Marco Polo never guessed that the world is round, but nearly 200 years later his report that a great ocean bounded Asia to the east suggested to Christopher Columbus that by sailing west across the Atlantic one might reach China. And so a volume of the *Book of Marco Polo* accompanied the discoverer of America on his momentous voyage. Still today the *Book* crooks a beckoning finger. True that a curtain has fallen between us and the China that Marco Polo loved. But his adventure—proof of the goodwill in the breast of man—gives us hope of a day when China and the West may meet again on a footing of peace, and exchange their gifts in friendship.

APOSTLE OF GOODWILL

By O. K. Armstrong

O N THE campus of Tuskegee Institute in Alabama stands a monument to Booker T. Washington, the great Negro educator who founded the school. Beneath his statue is this tribute: "He lifted the veil of ignorance from his people and pointed the way to progress through education and industry."

He it was who first raised the American Negroes from their knees and taught them that by their own efforts they could strike off their chains of economic slavery and win the respect and cooperation of their white neighbors. And no man knew better than Booker T. Washington how hard that was to do.

Booker was born April 5, 1856, in a one-room cabin on a plantation in Virginia. The boy's food was a piece of bread here, a scrap of meat there. His clothes were a shirt and pants. No Negro he had ever heard of could read or write. When he was nine, the Confederacy sank in defeat. But the lot of the Negro was little better than before. For emancipation carried with it responsibility, which in turn called for training. The shattered South was unable to cope with the schooling of its former slaves. So Booker's mother and her children migrated, most of the way on foot, to West Virginia. There Booker worked in coal mines, sawed wood and plowed fields. At night he attended an elementary school for colored children. When his teacher asked his name, Booker, aiming as high as he could, said it was Washington. And indeed he became the father of his people.

Hearing two miners talk about a Negro school at Hampton, Virginia, he set out at the age of 16, with a few dollars in his

pocket, to cover the 500 miles to the institution. When he arrived, a teacher told him to sweep the room. Characteristically, he swept it three times and dusted it four. He was forthwith accepted. To pay his board he worked as a janitor and waiter; to fit himself for a trade he studied bricklaying. Soon after graduation he was given a place on the faculty.

Down at Tuskegee, Alabama, a white merchant, George Campbell, and his friend Lewis Adams, a skilled Negro workman, conceived the idea of a training school for the black race. Through a friend in the state legislature, Campbell secured an appropriation of $2000 a year. When he wrote to Hampton Institute for a principal, Booker T. Washington was recommended. Arriving at Tuskegee, the eager young principal asked, "Where's the school?"

"There isn't any—yet," he was told. Undismayed, he declared he would build one. In the meantime he obtained permission to use a small Negro church. Then he went about making friends and inviting young Negroes to come to Tuskegee. What Washington saw in the Alabama countryside would have discouraged a man of less vision and determination. Most Negroes worked for a pittance. Their houses were shacks, their clothing coarse homespun, their food a diet of salt pork and beans. Disease was prevalent.

Professor Washington decided that cultural education without vocational training would be a waste of time. He named the school "Tuskegee Normal and Industrial Institute," and announced that every student would have to work with his or her hands. Opening day was July 4, 1881. Thirty persons came in, mostly from nearby cotton fields. The roof leaked so badly that on rainy days the pupils held umbrellas over their heads. Later, with $250 borrowed from a friend at Hampton, Washington made the first payment on an old plantation near town and laid the foundation for Porter Hall, their first building.

Booker Washington was forced to meet deep-seated prejudices. "Educate a Negro and he won't work!" was an oft-repeated saying among southern white people. Among Negro freedmen was the persistent belief that the one purpose of education was to prepare a person to live in leisure without hard work. A delegation of

Negroes protested against manual labor as a part of the Institute's program. Washington told them, "There is as much dignity in tilling a field as in writing a poem. And it is as important for your girls to know how to set a table and keep a house as it is to read Latin."

On one occasion, a spirited young teacher hired from a northern school, unused to the ways of the Deep South, angered a Tuskegee merchant. A mob quickly marched to the campus, demanding the "insolent" teacher. Washington faced them calmly. "We Negroes are handicapped by ignorance, therefore we may break the law. But you, our white friends, know the law, and therefore respect and obey it. We want to learn from you. Now, you wouldn't want to bring shame on Tuskegee by a lawless act, would you?" The mob dispersed.

Resolutely the Tuskegee schoolman took his crusade to the piney woods and the plantations, speaking at church meetings and visiting hundreds of homes to explain patiently how trained hands were needed with trained minds. "Our children must learn to do by doing," he would say. "We should not always look to the white race for leadership. Let us develop our own leaders."

Washington's sincerity won friends. Negroes began bringing gifts or volunteering their labor for the struggling school. White citizens of Tuskegee made donations. During the first five years, courses were established in bricklaying, carpentry, blacksmithing and farming for the boys, and cooking, sewing and housekeeping for the girls. It was Washington's pride that no youth was ever turned away for lack of money. Every student spent some hours in study and other hours in physical labor. They made the furniture for the buildings—tables, chairs, beds from pine trees, mattresses from cotton cloth stuffed with pine needles. Strict discipline was the rule, for Washington believed that education should develop character. Students were taught courtesy in manners and speech, and respect for the rights of others. "We cannot fail," the principal warned his teachers, "for then people would say that Negroes are not capable of self-education."

With courage, tact and patience, Washington used the Institute to draw into closer understanding and coöperation the people of both races. Once as he was passing the Varner mansion, Mrs. Varner, not knowing him by sight, called out to him to chop some wood. Professor Washington pulled off his coat, seized the axe, cut a pile of wood and carried it into the kitchen. A servant girl recognized him and told her mistress, "That was Professor Washington."

Early next morning Mrs. Varner entered his office and said, "I have come to apologize. I did not know it was you I put to work."

"It's entirely all right, madam," Washington responded. "I like to work, and I'm delighted to do favors for my friends." From that day, Mrs. Varner was the Institute's friend. She got wealthy acquaintances to give thousands of dollars for the school.

In the fall of 1895 the Cotton States and International Exposition was held in Atlanta. One pavilion was set aside for the products of Negro farmers. Professor Washington was invited to speak. Georgia's Governor Bullock introduced him to the several thousand people of both races in the exposition hall—probably the first time that an important white official had presented a Negro to a southern audience.

Not a person stirred as the tall, neatly dressed Negro eloquently explained his plan of education, pleading for understanding and coöperation. Turning to the distinguished white men on the platform, he said: "As we have proved our loyalty to you in nursing your children and watching by the sickbeds of your mothers and fathers, so in the future in our humble way we will stand by you with devotion, interlacing our industrial, commercial, civil and religious life with yours in a way that shall make the interests of both races one."

As the speech ended, Governor Bullock grasped the Negro's hand, while men and women stood cheering. The speech was printed in countless publications. President Cleveland sent a warm letter of congratulation. The occasion made Booker T. Washington a national figure, the recognized spokesman of his race in the United States.

A few years later in Chicago he addressed an audience of 16,000 people, in which sat President McKinley as the guest of honor. In countless communities of the South his were the first meetings ever to bring white and colored people together. He encouraged frank discussion of mutual problems. He told many a white audience, "You must understand the troubles of the man farthest down before you can help him." He also had the courage to come out and tell them, "The time to test a true gentleman is to observe him when he is in contact with individuals of a race less fortunate than his own."

With friendly persistence, he urged wealthy men and women "to invest in the future of the Negro race." One of the first he visited was Collis P. Huntington, noted railway magnate, who impatiently cut him off with, "Here is two dollars for your school." But the gentle black man persisted, and presently Huntington gave him a check for $50,000, and later enough additional money to build Huntington Hall. Shrewdly the principal would ask benefactors to underwrite various projects rather than give sums of money. Andrew Carnegie presented a library building. Later he gave $600,000 in one sum. Washington's faith in himself and his cause never wavered. If a new building was needed he would say, "Start the construction; I'll get the money."

By comradeship in toil, and with simple eloquence, he inspired his students. Teachers were required to send slothful workers to his office. Washington would reprimand them sternly; then, his face softening, he would say, "Come show me the trouble." Together they would go to the field or bench, and the professor would painstakingly demonstrate how the work should be done. In 1896 Washington talked the Alabama legislature into creating the Tuskegee Agricultural Experiment Station, "maintained for training colored students in scientific agriculture." He heard of the soil experiments of George Washington Carver, a former slave. "You are just the man to head our station," Booker Washington said. "Find out what can be raised from this southern clay." During nearly half a century, Professor Carver's experiments brought forth hundreds of new products, enriching American agriculture for people of all races.

Booker Washington carried the Institute out to the farms. He and Professor Carver would load a wagon with implements and drive around, giving demonstrations. Morris K. Jesup, New York philanthropist, donated a two-horse vehicle equipped to display all sorts of farming tools, and the Jesup wagon became famous as the "movable school." Far beyond the school he founded, Booker T. Washington advanced the progress of Negro education in America. He began by inducing Henry H. Rogers, Standard Oil executive, to help improve the schools of Macon County, of which Tuskegee is county seat. Rogers agreed to donate $600 per month for the first year. The results were so satisfactory that Rogers extended the aid to several counties.

Then the principal brought Julius Rosenwald to Alabama, drove him about the countryside and told him, "Every dollar invested in rural schools in the South will return many dollars in progress for the Negro race."

Mr. Rosenwald consented to finance a number of new schoolhouses in many separate areas. Washington insisted that colored people of each community raise money to provide the land for their school, and that county officials extend the school term. Thus he enlisted the active support of both white and Negro citizens. During its existence, the Rosenwald Fund made possible more than 5000 Negro rural schools in all the southern states. It helped provide for the education of nearly three quarters of a million colored children.

Honors came to Booker T. Washington from near and far. President Theodore Roosevelt found in the vigorous Negro a kindred spirit, and the two exponents of the strenuous life became fast friends. Washington's advice was constantly sought by business, educational and religious leaders. President Charles W. Eliot of Harvard, presenting to him the first degree awarded by that university to a Negro, called him "teacher, wise helper of his race, good servant of God and country."

Washington's constant traveling and speaking, added to his duties on the ever-expanding campus, literally wore out his great heart. His wife and associates begged him to take long rests, but he answered, "No—there is so much to do, and time is so short." In November 1915 he fell ill in New York, and arrived at his beloved school only a few hours before he died.

Today Tuskegee has a staff of 250 teachers, and a student enrollment of about 2500. There are 159 buildings and 5189 acres of campus and farms. Many similar industrial schools for Negroes have been founded by alumni of Tuskegee.

New honors signify the greatness of Booker T. Washington. The National Education Association included him in a list of ten who have contributed most to the development of education in America. A memorial fund was established to build an institute at his birthplace, and the U.S. Treasury issued special 50-cent coins to aid the project.

In May 1946, Booker Washington's likeness was placed in the American Hall of Fame at New York University. It reveals a brow furrowed by years of toil and responsibility, a mouth rich in humor yet determined. The lips seem still to be saying, "Each one should remember there is a chance for him, and the more difficulties he has to overcome, the greater can be his success."

Those deep words remind us to be conscious primarily not of our race but of our humanity. In the long climb upward of that common humanity, few have done more to help so many on their way than that man of goodwill, Booker T. Washington.

There are nine requisites for contented living: health enough to make work a pleasure; wealth enough to support your needs; strength enough to battle with difficulties and overcome them; grace enough to confess your sins and forsake them, patience enough to toil until some good is accomplished; charity enough to see some good in your neighbors; love enough to move you to be useful and helpful to others; faith enough to make real the things of God; hope enough to remove all anxious fears concerning the future.   —*Goethe*

NURSE CAVELL, THE LIFE-GIVER

By Jacqueline van Til

SHIVERING from anticipation as well as from the bitter December cold, I rang the doorbell of a brownstone house in a quiet Brussels suburb. This house, with the three adjoining ones, was a clinic and nursing school run by the Englishwoman Edith Cavell. I was a young Dutch girl from Hillegom, Holland, and had been accepted here as a student nurse. A maid showed me to a little room where the English nurse rose to greet me. The small study was as dark as a Rembrandt painting, so that her delicate white face and penetrating gray eyes stood out sharply against the gloomy background. Her navy-blue uniform, determined mouth and tightly coiled hair gave an impression of severity, but this was dispelled when she spoke to me warmly in French. After explaining what my duties would be, she said, "You must work very hard. To be a nurse is not easy, but it is worth the sacrifice."

The year was 1910, and the name of Edith Cavell was already well known in Belgium. She had earned a reputation for kindness and devotion to duty working in the squalor of the London slums. Hearing about her, Dr. Antoine Depage, a Belgian surgeon eager to raise his country's medical standards, brought her to Brussels, where scientific nursing was unknown. Nuns and untrained peasant girls staffed the few hospitals. There had never been a nursing school in Belgium until Edith Cavell opened this one.

Starting with four young students, she had built a trained staff of more than 50 nurses from Belgium and nearby countries. By the time I arrived she was also a director of several hospitals. She had done away with the drab, bulky clothes formerly worn by nurses. We wore bright-blue cotton dresses with white collars, aprons and caps. Where formerly nurses had been treated as servants, she demanded the highest respect for us from patients and doctors alike. In turn, she demanded from us absolute devotion to duty. We always addressed her as "Madame," using the word as a title in its literal French sense, "My Lady."

Every night at eight o'clock, after a long day's work in the clinic, we would gather in the classroom for lessons with Madame. She knew anatomy as well as a surgeon and illustrated her lectures on a large blackboard. But she gave us more than knowledge. Florence Nightingale was her inspiration, and always she held up the heroic nurse as an example to us. Once a new nurse saw a wasp in our classroom and went to kill it. "No," Madame said. "Turn it free. A nurse gives life; she does not take it."

She was quick, incisive and strict, for the task of turning a group of lighthearted girls of assorted nationalities into trained, efficient nurses called for rigorous discipline. We had one half-day a week off, and Madame would take away even this precious free time on the slightest provocation. Despite her serious exterior, Edith Cavell had a human side, too. Often after her lectures she would sit down at the piano in the classroom and play softly— usually hymns. Yet, though she seemed to love playing, she rarely smiled and never joined in the singing.

She was as fiercely protective of us as she was strict. Learning that a nurse had become a drug addict, she kept the fact from the hospital authorities until she had helped the girl break the habit. Another time she found that one of the student nurses had been slipping out at night and going to a cabaret. When the disobedient nurse was called in to the office, we all expected she would be dismissed immediately. But it didn't happen. "My child," Madame asked, "what will become of you if I dismiss you for such a reason? No other hospital would ever admit you." The student stayed, graduated and eventually became supervisor of a hospital.

I, too, had personal experience of Madame's protectiveness, when, in 1912, I was taken ill with an infection. "You'd better go to England to recuperate," Madame said. "You can stay with my family." At a beautiful home in Henley-on-Thames I visited her mother and two sisters, one married to a doctor, the other superintendent of a London hospital. From them I learned of the early life which had shaped Edith Cavell. She was born in 1865, the daughter of a clergyman, from whom she inherited her strong will and deep spiritual sense. From the time when she was a little girl and had nursed a sick dog back to health, Edith Cavell had shown an unusual concern for the suffering. It had seemed inevitable that she would devote her life to nursing.

I returned to the busy life of the clinic after my recovery, to find our school now was furnishing trained nurses for three hospitals, three private clinics, 24 public schools and 13 kindergartens in Brussels. However, this splendid progress was soon to be tragically disrupted when, in the summer of 1914, World War I was suddenly at our doorstep. Flags blossomed from windows. We waved gaily as soldiers marched off toward the front where the Germans were rolling across the Flemish plains. Quickly the excitement gave way to dread. The German nurses hurriedly left the clinic for home, then many of the girls from the neutral countries returned also. Madame accompanied them all to the station and bade them a sad good-bye.

Soon dazed peasants clogged the roads leading into Brussels, carrying their few belongings. In all the confusion Madame went tirelessly about her business, walking with her dog, Jack, through the streets to inspect her hospitals. Then one day an ominous reddish glow appeared on the horizon. Some other nurses and I rushed to the roof. Thick black smoke rolled toward us from the distance, and we could hear the rumble of cannon. As the sounds of war drew nearer, suddenly I found myself weeping. I felt a hand on my shoulder. "Your life is no longer yours alone, my dear," Madame said. "Now it belongs to your duty as a nurse."

On the afternoon of August 20 our janitress dashed into the clinic shouting, "*Les Boches* are here! *Les Boches* are here!" We all hurried to the street and watched sadly as the German troops goose-stepped past. Madame and the other English nurses were offered safe conduct to neutral Holland. They refused. Brussels was filling up with battle casualties, and her duty, Madame said, lay with the wounded and sick. Her deep religious faith helped to sustain Madame through these difficult days. Once when ten of our nurses set out for France to care for soldiers wounded in the fighting there, she accompanied them as far as devastated Turnhout. When it came time to leave the nurses, she knelt with them in the muddy road and led them in reciting the 23rd Psalm.

About this time we began to notice mysterious happenings in our clinic. One night a nurse whispered to me that there was a case in the ward we were not supposed to see. I tiptoed down and peered into the forbidden ward. From the darkness I heard a cheerful voice say in English, "Hello, nursie." Another nurse had seen Madame slipping out early in the mornings. Shadowy figures had been noticed coming and going after dark. Suddenly we realized: our clinic had become a haven for escaping Allied soldiers. I thought of the ominous red-and-black posters around the city warning against such activity.

Not until later did we learn the full import of the events taking place under our eyes. As the German army swept across Belgium into France, a schoolteacher, Louise Thuliez, searched the abandoned battlefields for lost and wounded Allied soldiers. She would hide them in a château in a deep forest. Hermann Capiau, an engineer, would provide them with forged identification papers and bring them to Nurse Cavell to be hidden and treated. Then, under cover of darkness, she would take them to guides who would smuggle them to the border of Holland for escape. It was a tiny but effective underground, and Philippe Baucq, an architect, was one of the leaders.

Soon the Germans became suspicious of our clinic. Once a German officer called to ask questions. Sister Wilkins, Madame's assistant, kept him engaged in conversation until three soldiers hiding in the rear could escape. Another time two German officers ransacked Madame's office. A few days later three Germans appeared. One whipped out a revolver and shoved several of us against a wall. When they left, they took Madame with them. Presently we received word that she was in ancient St. Gilles Prison. Almost all of the underground leaders had been rounded up; they would be placed on trial for their lives.

Days dragged by. We sent Madame flowers and got a note in return. Even in prison her thoughts were of us rather than herself. "I am happy to hear you are attending to your work," she wrote. "Remember, it is not enough to be good nurses; you should also be good Christian women." Finally Sister Wilkins was permitted to visit her. She found Madame pale and thin, in a small cell with a single, high, barred window. "I have done what was my duty," Madame told her old friend. "They must do with me what they will."

At her trial Edith Cavell would not lie. In a calm, clear voice she admitted that she had cared for, and helped to escape, over 200 English, French and Belgian soldiers. Her duty as a nurse was to save lives, she said. In a harsh voice the German judge barked out his verdict: "*Todesstrafe*"—death!

The father of one of the nurses came to the clinic and told us that Madame was to be executed the next morning. Three of us hastened to the prison. The Belgian warden was kind but there was nothing he could do. Panic-stricken, we hurried to the United States Embassy—perhaps the Americans, as influential neutrals, could help. The ambassador was ill, but his assistant, Hugh Gibson, said he would try to save Madame. With the Spanish ambassador, he drove off to the German ministry. We sat in the Embassy reception room, fearful, praying. When Gibson returned, his face gave us the dreaded answer: he had failed.

With heavy hearts we returned through the rainy night to our clinic. But sleep was impossible. About four in the morning several of us set out for the prison. The warden answered our knocks at the forbidding oak gates. If we waited outside, he told us, we might see Madame as she was taken to the rifle range. A short time later the ancient gates creaked open and two German military cars swept out. We peered anxiously through the clearing mist.

In the front car there was a flash of blue, dwarfed by gray-clad guards. That was all. Then the cars disappeared down the cobble-stone streets. Later in the day German soldiers tacked up notices: Nurse Cavell and Philippe Baucq had been executed.

After a few days we received a pathetic little bundle of her clothes and the sum of 50 francs—all that Edith Cavell had left from a lifetime given to humanity. With them was a letter to us: "I hope you will not forget the little talks we had each evening. I told you that voluntary sacrifices would make you happy; that the idea of duty before God and yourselves will give you support in the sad moments of life and in the face of death. I know that sometimes I have been harsh, but never have I been voluntarily unjust. I loved all of you more than you will ever know."

On the evening after the death sentence had been pronounced on Edith Cavell, the English chaplain at Brussels visited her in prison. She told him that she wished all her friends to know she willingly gave her life for her country.

"I have no fear nor shrinking. I have seen death so often that it is not strange to me. But, standing as I do in view of God and eternity, I realize that patriotism is not enough. I must have no hatred or bitterness towards anyone. They have all been very kind to me here."

The chaplain thus describes the rest of the tragedy:

"We partook of the Holy Communion together. At the close of the little service I began to repeat the words, 'Abide with me,' and she joined softly in the end. Then I said good-bye, and she smiled and said, 'We shall meet again.'"

Her eyes bandaged and her head covered by a black veil, she was brought out for execution. Until this moment she had walked bravely, but, realizing she was before the platoon of execution, she swayed and fell. The German officer in command of the firing drew from his belt his regulation wide-mouthed revolver, knelt down and, taking steady aim, fired.

—Ambroise Got

ALL THE WORLD'S
HIS STAGE

Condensed from Time

NEVER in the 400 years since their creator was born have Shakespeare's characters spoken to so many, or meant so much. Along the brooding battlements of Yugoslavia's 12th-century Lourijenac fortress, the ghost of Hamlet's father spurs his son's revenge; deep in Soviet Russia, at Tashkent, the jealous Moor strangles the blameless Desdemona. Halfway round the world, black-jeaned Australian troupers tour the outback by bus, with a crown and a sword or two as their props. Tribesmen in Southern Rhodesia play *Macbeth* costumed as Zulu warriors in animal tails and feathers.

In the theaters, tents and schoolrooms of every land, wherever the sun sets and curtains rise—in the kingliest English and in tender or rough translation—Shakespeare's people speak to man from mankind's heart. Nowhere do they seem more at home than at the three Stratfords—in England, Canada and the United States. England's Stratford-upon-Avon, at the age of 84 the oldest continuing Shakespeare stage, fills close to 391,000 ticket requests annually. Ontario's Stratford, started in 1953, has lured more than 2,000,000 theatergoers for a box-office gross of $7,000,000. Stratford, Connecticut, anticipated over 258,000 ticket queuers for 1964. To judge by the traffic rush to the Stratfords, today's audiences agree with critic Maurice Morgann, who wrote of Shakespeare in 1774: "It is safer to say that we are possessed by him than that we possess him."

Great gaps in our knowledge of Shakespeare's life have encouraged the strange game of pseudo-scholarship designed to show that Shakespeare did not really write the plays—that he was a front man for Sir Francis Bacon or Edward de Vere, 17th Earl of Oxford; or Christopher Marlowe; or Sir Walter Raleigh; or Queen Elizabeth; or even the Bard's wife, Anne Hathaway. Amateur cryptographers have thought they found hidden codes in Shakespeare's writing, pointing to the true authors. Underlying all this is a peculiar kind of snobbery—the notion that a man of simple origins and education could not have been so great a genius. These theories have been disproved in many ways, but the strongest evidence against them, apart from the historical record, is the plays themselves; the style is the man—the unmistakable code in which life and work meet.

Young Will had a far better family background, and probably far better schooling, than the anti-Shakespearean theorists usually admit. The Shakespeares were Warwickshire farmers, but Will's father, ambitious John, moved to Stratford and became a glover. He was one of the town's official ale-tasters, and donned the scarlet robes of high bailiff, or mayor, when Will was four. The boy presumably went to Stratford's King's School—no doubt unwillingly, since the schools of the day consisted of Latin drill, long hours (7 a.m. to 5 p.m., often longer in summer) and Spartan discipline.

Touring companies of actors played in Stratford. Attracted by their glamour, Shakespeare, while still in his 20's, left for London and joined an acting company. As actor and playwright, Will was a quick success. He wrote speedily—his editors noted that his manuscripts were scarcely ever blotted. Plots to Shakespeare were like pots to the magician Merlin: any borrowed tub, from Holinshed's *Chronicles* to Plutarch's *Lives*, would do to mix the magic in. Londoners worshiped him.

The city the temper of which Shakespeare had caught was in a ferment. After the Spanish Armada went down (1588), England ruled the waves, and the Elizabethan was agape at the wonder of himself: "What a piece of work is a man! How noble in reason! How infinite in faculty! In form and moving how express and admirable! In action how like an angel! In apprehension how like a god!" Dazzled by life, the Elizabethan was nonetheless on familiar terms with death. Plagues riddled London. The Elizabethans lived dangerously, and while they lived, they were asmile with daring. William Shakespeare held a magnifying glass to the spirit of his age, and set the Globe Theater blazing with his Muse of Fire.

Every age since has attempted to press Shakespeare into a contemporary mold. A history of changing Shakespearean fashions, as T. S. Eliot has pointed out, is a history of Western civilization. Orson Welles dressed his Caesar in Fascist-like uniform. Moscow has staged *Hamlet* as an army plot against the King. In New York a group staged an all-female *King Lear*. Some of the gimmick productions are offensive, but they do not necessarily violate the author's spirit. They are possible only because Shakespeare is timeless. He says everything. Protestants, Catholics and agnostics claim him. So do aristocrats and believers in democracy, optimists and pessimists.

What does Shakespeare say to an era that feels that the times are out of joint? He does not renounce the world or wallow in self-pity. He is the poet of this worldliness: he celebrates love, food, drink, music, friendship, conversation and the changing, changeless beauties of nature. Shakespeare's mature man distills his experiences into common sense and uncommon wisdom.

Yet man is also the "quintessence of dust," and "men must endure their going hence even as their coming hither." Shakespeare's tragic hero is called upon to face the unfaceable, to die with no hope of reward. As he meets his fate, the audience feels, "There, but for the grace of God, goes a better man than I." What links the audience movingly with the tragic hero is the quality that essentially separates them: nobility.

In the hands of lesser playwrights that nobility often rests on the splendor of the language, but beautiful lines alone may rest no further than the ear. Shakespeare speaks to the soul. He could do anything he wanted with language; the way he talks of a thing conjures up the thing itself. He packed worlds into single syllables. "To be or not to be" is man's largest question put in man's smallest and simplest words.

Shakespeare's breathtaking change of pace carries a man to the brink of eternity and then restores him to common humanity. On seeing Cordelia's body, the grief-stricken Lear cries, "Why should a dog, a horse, a rat have life and thou no breath at all?" In the extremity of human despair ("Thou'lt come no more"), he utters his towering, fivefold "Never, never, never, never, never!" Then the dam of his unbearable anguish breaks with the homely request, "Pray you, undo this button." No one but William Shakespeare would have dared to put those two lines together.

Shakespeare survives because the next to the last word can be said about him—but not the last word. His creations are as opaque as life's; his characters remain inexhaustibly baffling. Next to Jesus, Napoleon and Shakespeare himself, Hamlet has been written about more than has any other man. Yet all one knows for certain is that being Hamlet is Hamlet's tragedy—as being himself is every man's. Every age, and every man in his seven ages, finds a reflection in Shakespeare's universal mirror. The passion and the poetry echo in the corridors of the mind and, truer than "the infancy of truth," will go on echoing "to the last syllable of recorded time."

Harvey Breit, New York *Times* book reviewer, tells about a scholar who insisted that Shakespeare's plays were written by Queen Elizabeth. The eminent minister Dr. Hugh Black challenged him. "Surely," he scoffed, "you don't believe a woman could have composed such masterpieces." "You miss my point entirely," retorted the scholar. "It is my contention that Queen Elizabeth was a man."   —*Bennett Cerf*

CAVALIER OF THE WILD

By Donald Culross Peattie

ENÉ ROBERT CAVELIER, Sieur de La Salle, was 23 when he first saw the wild shores of New France (Canada) rising from the ocean foam. From his excellent family he inherited good looks, good manners and good health—practically all his worldly goods, except his bright sword blade of thin and nervous steel. With this he faced, without money or a patron, the American wilderness. That sword was to pass through the forest, two centuries ahead of our ancestors' axes that finally chopped a nation out of a wild continent.

In 1669, France had a toehold on the North American continent. Her missionaries and trappers were pushing west and south along the Great Lakes. But to consolidate her New World empire, France needed explorer-soldiers and forts. For the English, too, were dreaming of conquest beyond the Alleghenies, and already Spain's mailed hand was stretched in a gesture of claim from Mexico northward and eastward.

And so Courcelle, Governor at Quebec, sent the young adventurer La Salle with a party of priests and woodrangers to drive a wedge, made of the sword and the cross, between England and Spain. The party ran into Louis Joliet returning from the wilderness, carrying in his bronzed hand the first map of the Great Lakes. That meeting was crucial in La Salle's life and in American history, for it split La Salle's party in two. The priests, fired by missionary zeal, determined to go to the Mackinac country—known ground. But La Salle, eager for virgin empire, plunged southward into the great hardwood forests of what today we would call Ohio. His goal was nothing less than the legendary Father of Waters, and the erasure of Spain's faint claim to it.

During the next two years of wandering, even La Salle did not know precisely where he was. The Illinois prairies, perhaps, from his description. But wherever it may have been, the young explorer was being forged by wilderness travel into a blade of steel, an imperial weapon awaiting the hand of statecraft competent to employ it. And that hand belonged to Frontenac, new Governor of New France. La Salle told Frontenac what he had seen in the heart of the continent: forests to rebuild all the cities and navies of Europe; furs to overwhelm the Russian trade; loam black and deep; warlike tribes which could be stiffened into a wall against the English. And somewhere, beyond the prairie horizons, flowed a mighty river, a God-made highway through the wilderness. La Salle foresaw an empire of wheat, lumber, fur and cities. How great a prophet he was is seen in the names of the cities that sprang up on spots where he was the first to set foot: Buffalo, Louisville, Detroit, Milwaukee, Chicago, St. Louis, New Orleans, Galveston and Houston.

Guarding his secret schemes, La Salle journeyed to France, where he won an audience with Louis XIV. In the Grand Monarch he met another to match him in vision and determination. La Salle emerged from the audience room a titled nobleman and commandant of Fort Frontenac on Lake Ontario. Further, he had secured a monopoly of the entire fur trade of whatever areas he should explore.

The great fur merchants of Quebec were not merry at this; if La Salle were allowed to get into the Illinois country again, he would crack their fur monopoly and send prices tumbling. They tried by every means to prevent the expedition from departing. They persuaded La Salle's creditors to foreclose on his property. While he was building a vessel near the present site of Buffalo, Iroquois Indians were bribed to set it afire. His expedition was secretly "packed" with men hired to bring it to failure. But in 1679, when every trick had failed, the *Griffin* spread her sails on Lake Erie, the first European warship ever to plow the waters of the Great Lakes. With La Salle journeyed the Italian-born soldier Henri de Tonti, a brother-in-arms and lifelong friend who had lost a hand in battle and had it replaced by one made of metal. In his unsentimental way La Salle loved Tonti as no one else.

From Mackinac, last outpost of civilization, La Salle sent the *Griffin* back, laden with furs to pay his debts. This expedition, like all his others, had been financed by relatives, friends and merchants in Canada. But, like Columbus, La Salle was fated never to make a commercial success of any of his trips. The autumn leaves were scarlet and gold when La Salle, with four canoes filled to capacity, started south along the east shore of Lake Michigan. Fighting primeval forest and marsh, Tonti moved in a parallel land expedition. At the mouth of the St. Joseph River, La Salle built Fort Miami while he waited for Tonti and for the *Griffin*. Tonti came, but no *Griffin*. Ice gathered on the streams, and still the needed supplies and reinforcements did not arrive. Almost provisionless, La Salle and his men plunged into the wilderness, toward the Illinois River. Far off blazed the hunting fires of Indians, rounding the game up in circles of flame. But for La Salle and his men there was only cold, hunger, interminable portages and dreary marshes. A single false step might turn thin Indian hospitality to raging hostility. Indeed, the merchants of Quebec had sent Miami Indians to the Illinois, secretly urging them to kill the Frenchmen in their sleep. But La Salle had a genius with Indians. He was lavish with gifts and superb in oratory; he displayed no signs of pain or fatigue. By his talents and energy he turned the whole Illinois Indian confederation into a bulwark for France.

On the banks of the Illinois, La Salle built Fort Crèvecoeur, a second link in his chain of fortifications. But it needed resources. Leaving Tonti to garrison it, La Salle set out for Canada, only to learn that the *Griffin* had never been seen again, all its furs had been lost and his depot of furs at Fort Frontenac seized by creditors. A messenger soon arrived from Tonti: the men at Fort Crèvecoeur had deserted. On his heels, another came to say that the deserters had seized Fort Miami, burned it and carried off

La Salle's furs. Striking swiftly, La Salle ambushed the rascals as they tried to surprise Fort Frontenac, and handed them over to the stern justice of the Governor.

Back to the Illinois country went the unbreakable man, with new funds begged, borrowed and worried out of the government and Quebec notables. But he found Fort Crèvecoeur a shambles; corpses, charred and hacked, everywhere proclaimed an Iroquois victory. Tonti too was missing. In rage and grief, La Salle combed the forests for his comrade, vowing to find him if he had to burn down every Iroquois village. Finally, after he had almost abandoned hope, La Salle found Tonti at Mackinac; they embraced each other and once more the scheme of conquest blossomed.

Sheer glittering personal magnetism roused the beaten Illinois tribes to fresh loyalty. The dream of empire was raised again from the ashes. In December of 1681 La Salle plunged into the wilderness with his stout captains Tonti and La Forreste, 23 Frenchmen, a motley group of Indians, good old Father Zenobius Membré and Nika, the faithful Indian guide. The canoes, instruments, supplies and ammunition were mounted on sledges; they started down the frozen Illinois, a road of crystal into the frost-coated wilderness. When the ice gave way, the canoes were launched, and on February 6, 1682, the Mississippi caught them in its tawny current and bore them southward.

South they drifted, past the Missouri, past the Arkansas—the farthest south reached by Marquette and Joliet—the mighty river ever broadening, gloomy cypress lining its banks. On April 9 they met the smiling waters of the sea, and knew that they had come to the end of their voyage. Father Membré intoned *Te Deum*, guns roared, Indians whooped. La Salle set up a carved column, named the land Louisiana, claiming the whole of the Father of Waters for Louis the Great, King of France.

Knowing that a colony garrisoned by Frenchmen and cannon would be needed to peg this shadowy claim, La Salle returned to Quebec, planning to secure men and materials for such a garrison. But to his dismay he found that his friend Frontenac had fallen from power. The new Governor had already written to

Louis XIV, turning him against La Salle. To add the final crushing insult, the Governor had seized all La Salle's Canadian possessions.

Ruined, La Salle set sail for France. Gaining the King's ear, he in turn undid his enemies. By sheer grit and gall he raised another fortune for the colonial expedition to the mouth of the Father of Waters. Persuaded by La Salle's fervor, the Grand Monarch entrusted him with the founding of a French colony at the mouth of the Mississippi, the opening up of a trade line between the Great Lakes and the Gulf of Mexico, and the alliance or conquest of Indian tribes. Furthermore, he commissioned La Salle to make expeditions to the west to conquer New Mexico from the Spanish.

The great colonial-military expedition consisted of four ships, 100 "soldiers" (most of them professional beggars), some wretched mechanics and laborers, "gentlemen" whose only resource was the sword, faithful Father Membré, a number of orphan children and a bevy of husband-hunting girls. To these, add too many missionaries, most of them hopelessly ill-adapted for wilderness service.

La Salle's luck had turned. His faulty judgment caused the fleet to miss the mouth of the Mississippi by 400 miles. For the awful fact was that, though the explorer had taken the latitude at the mouth of the Mississippi, he had not known how to determine its longitude. So he coasted, lost, around the Texas dunes and lagoons. On a luckless day La Salle guessed that Matagorda Bay must be the west mouth of the Father of Waters and landed his colony. One ship was wrecked on the sandbars; the naval captain of the expedition, one Beaujeu, afraid of the strange coast, hoisted the flagship's anchor, leaving La Salle the little *Belle*, his only link with the world.

On this savage shore La Salle raised the valiant symbols of his dream—a fort, a chapel, a palisade with apertures for eight cannon (which had no ammunition but musket shot). Riddled with diseases picked up in the swamps of the West Indies on the way from France, the colony withered. Thirty died, and while La Salle was off on his first overland hunt for the Mississippi, the *Belle* was wrecked. The reserves of food, clothing and ammunition aboard her were nearly a total loss. La Salle, after forced marches and battles with the Indians, got back to camp months later with depleted numbers, the great river still rolling undiscovered somewhere beyond the endless horizon. The news that he soon learned was of the loss of the *Belle*, and it struck him down with brain fever.

But soon he was up and off again, striking out overland for Canada to bring help. Malcontents who stayed behind passed the time by fomenting trouble. Added to seething rebellion were discouragement and Indian hostility. After months, a sentinel heard La Salle's voice. But here were no troops from Canada; instead only eight straggling survivors of those who had set forth. On the dismal Twelfth Night of January 1687, the colony drank to a black future with cups of cold water. Even the stoutest must have seen that La Salle was utterly lost on a great unmapped continent, and that his sallies were as erratic and futile as it was tedious to remain in the fort and wait for the end.

Yet there was nothing to do but try again. This time La Salle decided to take the worst malcontents and villains. In the wilderness the conspirators killed La Salle's sleeping nephew and the Indian guide Nika, who died without the chance to strike a blow. Then the murderers lay in wait for La Salle himself, and from the tall Texas grass they shot him down. The blackest-hearted of them, swaggering, flung about his own shoulders La Salle's marvelous scarlet cloak with gold facings. The corpse of La Salle, stripped naked, was dragged into the bushes. Not even wilderness sod covered the body of the great man.

And so the Texas colony, La Salle's crowning dream and most heroic failure, was left to its fate. The Spanish, coming to destroy it, found only dismembered bodies and blackened ruins—horrible testimony that the Indians had been there before them. When, 14 years later, d'Iberville with a French fleet entered the mouth of the Mississippi to found New Orleans, a loyal Indian chief gave him a faded letter. It was addressed to Robert Cavelier, Sieur de La Salle, and told how Henri de Tonti had been all the way to the mouth of the fatal river, to look for his lost friend.

HER BOOK
BREWED A WAR

Condensed from Crusader in Crinoline

By Forrest Wilson

LATE IN November 1862, so the story goes, Abraham Lincoln received at the White House a diminutive, middle-aged lady. Clasping her tiny hand in his great knotted one, he exclaimed: "So this is the little lady who made this big war!"

The little lady was Harriet Beecher Stowe, author of *Uncle Tom's Cabin*. Publication of that novel ten years earlier had contributed largely to Lincoln's election as President. Contemporary statesmen and historians hailed it as the greatest single influence toward the abolition of slavery.

Born and raised in Connecticut, Harriet had lived for 18 years in Cincinnati, a station of the Underground Railroad. Here she had seen antislavery riots; she had helped runaway slaves and listened to their stories. Then in 1850 the Stowes moved to Brunswick, Maine, where Harriet's husband, Calvin Stowe, had been made a professor at Bowdoin College. But it was impossible to escape slavery, even in Maine. The newspapers were full of it. The United States Senate chamber was resounding with the impassioned Abolition speeches of Charles Sumner of Massachusetts. Harriet's brother, the already famous Reverend Henry Ward Beecher, was conducting his maddening "slave auctions" from the pulpit.

Harriet had written a number of short stories to eke out the ever inadequate Stowe income. Her deeply religious crusader spirit yearned to give to the world a picture of the brutality of slavery as she knew it. Show people slavery in the human terms of ravished girls, mothers bereaved by the auctioneer's hammer, families broken, masters debauched by arbitrary power—show them these pictures and they would tolerate slavery no longer. But to write on a political question went against a lifetime of training. A letter from her sister-in-law furnished the spark. "If I could use a pen as you can," wrote Mrs. Edward Beecher, "I would write something to make this whole nation feel what an accursed thing slavery is."

Harriet's children long remembered her reading the letter to them. She rose to her feet as if in an act of solemn consecration, the letter crumpled in one small, clenched hand. "I *will* write something," she said.

And so one day she sat down at her desk and began: "Late in the afternoon of a chilly day in February, two gentlemen were sitting alone over their wine in a well-furnished dining parlor in the town of P——, Kentucky."

The hairline of ink was starting on a long journey. Harriet did not know where it would end, but it ended at Gettysburg and Appomattox. Harriet had no preconception of the terrible power to be unleashed by *Uncle Tom's Cabin*. She regarded her story as a messenger of peace. "The Lord Himself wrote it," she said many times.

The scene in which Uncle Tom is flogged—written weeks before she had worked out a definite plan for her story—did, in fact, come to her in a vision during a communion service. As clearly as if she had been there, she saw an old slave being beaten to death by a white ruffian. After the benediction Harriet had walked home fighting back her tears. As though in a trance, she went to her bedroom and wrote out the vision as she had seen it. When she read it to the family, the children wept convulsively. And her husband told her, "Hattie, you must make up a story with this for the climax. The Lord intends it so."

Harriet planned the story as "three or four" sketches and offered it to Editor Bailey of the *National Era*, a small Washington

publication. He accepted it sight unseen, the price to be $300. Poor Harriet! Her "three or four" sketches became 40, and almost a year elapsed before she finally gathered all the threads of her tapestry together. Bailey did not raise the price as the story went on and on. In the *National Era* of June 5, 1851, on page one, appeared the first installment of the novel that would condition a whole generation of children—Harriet's son Fred among them—to march in the spirit of crusaders ten years later up to the cannon's mouth.

It all came out of her own life experience. Her only visit in the South had been a few days spent on the Kentucky plantation of a school chum, so Uncle Tom would have to be a slave there. But since the only people she met in Kentucky were nice people, she would have to have Uncle Tom sold by his kindly Kentucky master.

Uncle Tom was modeled after the Reverend Josiah Henson, Negro preacher and social worker who had bought his freedom and whom Harriet had met in Boston. In his youth, "Father" Henson had been permanently crippled by a flogging at the hands of a brutal Maryland master. Then there was the overseer her brother Charles had met on a New Orleans boat. Displaying a fist hard as an oak burl, he bragged that he "got that from knocking down niggers." So Harriet had her Simon Legree. The sinister name of the hairy, apelike master was sheer inspiration. Celeste was a small, mischievous Negro girl whom Harriet had tried vainly to Christianize in her Cincinnati Sunday-school class. Celeste became Topsy.

It is often brought forth as a modern discovery that the Southerner understands the Negro better than the Northerner, and knows better how to get along with him. Yet Harriet was writing this very thing in 1851 and 1852. She did not overlook the pleasant, patriarchal side of slavery, which was one thing that made her book so hard to answer. Some of the kindest and most upright characters in the novel were Southerners and slaveholders. And she made Simon Legree, the arch-villain of American literature, a Vermonter. Aunt Ophelia, St. Clare's New England cousin, could not bear to touch Topsy, but Little Eva's favorite perch was Uncle Tom's knee. It took a shrewd eye to note that point a century ago.

One of the miracles wrought by the story was the national furor it created while running as a serial in an obscure paper. Almost every community had at least one Abolitionist who subscribed to the *Era*, and his copy would be passed about from hand to hand until it was literally worn out. Letters began pouring in to the *Era* office. Each new character and incident was greeted with applause. And when in the fall Harriet failed to get her chapter to Washington in time for an edition, a storm of protest descended on the hapless publisher.

As she worked on and on, the end ever eluding her, the story more and more became Harriet's tyrant. Whatever she did, wherever she went, the specter of next week's installment stood forever at her elbow. She had to keep up her cooking and housework, and her boisterous family drove her frantic.

Another person was regarding the ever increasing length of the novel with dismay. John P. Jewett, head of a small Boston publishing house, had agreed to publish the serial in book form. He had foreseen a slender volume which could sell at a low price. By the end of October *Uncle Tom* was beginning to look like a two-volume novel; Jewett was appalled. He begged Harriet to terminate the story. She was writing on an unpopular subject, he said; two volumes might be fatal to the work's success.

Jewett could not have addressed a more receptive listener. A weary Harriet was ready to cry for mercy. The *Era* published the suggestion that since the story had already run to great length, Mrs. Stowe could finish it quickly in a few matter-of-fact paragraphs telling how everything turned out. The readers answered a thundering No. Editor Bailey hastened to reassure his subscribers, and Harriet wrote on.

The installment which appeared in the Christmas Day issue of the *Era* portrayed the death of Little Eva. When it was written, Harriet took to her bed for 48 hours, exhausted. It had been almost a personal bereavement. And what agonized letters she received from readers deploring the murder of the saintliest child in America by a heartless author for a literary effect! But the way ahead was now clear. Harriet had only to write to the scene of Uncle Tom's death, tie a few loose ends and be done.

In February Jewett made a final attempt to save some of his slender capital: he proposed to the Stowes that they put up half the cost of publishing, and share equally with him profits from its sale, if any. But the Stowes had no money at all, so Calvin declined in favor of a royalty of 10 percent on all sales. If Harriet had owned a half-interest in *Uncle Tom's Cabin*, the first year's sales in this country alone would have made her independently rich. Harriet, however, was well pleased with the contract. "I hope," she said, "it will make enough so I may have a silk dress."

The book, unheralded by advance publicity, was born in complete silence so far as the reviewers were concerned. But publication day, March 20, 1852, saw great excitement in the publisher's office. The first edition of 6000 copies was devoured immediately. Within the week Jewett had three power presses running 24 hours a day except Sunday, 100 bookbinders at work, and three mills running to supply the paper. Harriet's first royalty check for four months' sales was $10,300. On the first anniversary of the book's publication, Jewett announced the year's sales at 305,000 copies, "with demands heavy as ever."

Uncle Tom's Cabin was soon pirated by foreign publishers in a dozen countries and translated into a dozen languages. The downtrodden classes of Europe took the book to their hearts and read in it their own miseries. In London, New York and Boston, dramatizations of *Uncle Tom* were playing to hysterical audiences. Americans were singing Uncle Tom and Little Eva songs. A Rhode Island manufacturer advertised a card game called "Uncle Tom and Little Eva."

Surprisingly, the first attack on the veracity of the novel came from the North. Harriet had recognized that she could not pin the sin of slavery exclusively on the South, for there was plenty of Northern money invested in the cotton business, which lived by slavery. The spokesman for that money was the New York *Journal of Commerce*, which at the end of May fired the first big gun against *Uncle Tom's Cabin*. Editors throughout the country at once picked up the challenge, for and against Harriet, and a great newspaper debate began.

Heretofore, *Uncle Tom's Cabin* had been merely a controversial novel, circulating freely in the North and South and winning converts from both sections. Suddenly there was spontaneous suppression of the book in the South and it became dangerous to own a copy. Southern mothers began to hold Harriet up before their children as a wicked ogress. Her fan mail now included anonymous letters, threatening, scurrilous, branding her as a fomenter of slave rebellion.

Both sides were now aware that this was not just a novel, but a mine planted at the foundations of the republic, the fuse hissing. Harriet's propaganda had fired sectional hatreds that were not to subside until the hearts that beat so hotly with them had gone back to the dust.

Forty years later, Kirk Monroe, noted New York critic, estimated *Uncle Tom's* place in history: "The abolition of slavery was not, and could not be, accomplished by any one person. It was the result of united efforts. . . . But the greatest and most far-reaching of all these influences was *Uncle Tom's Cabin*."

Mark Twain one day went to call on Harriet Beecher Stowe of *Uncle Tom's Cabin* fame. Frequently careless about his dress, he was not aware on this occasion that he was minus a necktie. But on his return home, Mrs. Clemens pointedly called his attention to his social blunder. A little later Mrs. Stowe answered her door to find a messenger, who gave her a small package. Opening it, she found a black silk necktie inside and a brief note: "Here is a necktie. Take it out and look at it. I stayed half an hour this morning without this necktie. At the end of that time, will you kindly return it, as it is the only one I have. Mark Twain." —*Christian Science Monitor*

THE EVOLUTION
OF CHARLES DARWIN

By Donald Culross Peattie

WHEN His Britannic Majesty's brig *Beagle* set sail in 1831 for a surveying expedition around the world, no one dreamed that this was to be the most momentous voyage since Columbus. Nor had young Mr. Darwin, the ship's naturalist, the faintest inkling that he was about to discover a new continent of knowledge. Only 22 and fresh from Cambridge University, Charles Darwin was a retiring, sensitive, soft-spoken fellow who was almost constantly bedeviled by seasickness. But his keen mind was unflaggingly curious, and it had the trick of devising explanations for everything. He couldn't just accept a fact. He had to find out what caused it.

Darwin was as inquisitive as a dog's nose when he stepped ashore on the uninhabited Galápagos Islands, hundreds of miles off the coast of South America, in the loneliest doldrums of the Pacific. Here was a living museum of past geologic time, where giant lizards which ought to have been extinct long ago mingled with huge land tortoises, and enormous gaudy crabs crawled among the bellowing sea lions. So unaccustomed to man were the animals of this Eden that a hawk allowed itself to be knocked off a tree with a stick, and ground doves settled trustingly on the explorers' shoulders.

But the amazing fact that Darwin discovered about this isolated archipelago was that each island, seemingly identical in climate and soil to the others, had its own peculiar fauna. For instance, there was a group of finches that were obviously all related to each other and to similar birds on the South American mainland; yet no two of the islands had quite the same species.

What was true of the finches, Darwin found, was as true of the ground doves, the lizards, the tortoises, the insects and snails. But why should Nature without rhyme or reason create separate species of closely related forms for nearby islands? It wasn't logical. Yet to doubt, in those days, that the million or so species of living plants and animals had been in the world from the first day of Creation was to defy the authority not only of Genesis but also of leading scientists.

Darwin's diary records the first dawning of his great challenge. "One might fancy," he wrote, "that one species had been modified for different ends. On these small, barren, rocky islands we seem to be brought nearer to the mystery of mysteries, the first appearance of new beings on earth."

For five years the *Beagle* voyaged—to Tahiti, New Zealand, Tasmania, Australia, Ascension Island, the Cape Verde Islands and the Azores. And everywhere island life raised for Darwin the same puzzling question, and suggested the same incredible answer.

When Darwin returned to England, never to leave it again, he was a moderately famous young man—by reason of his fascinating letters and splendid collections. In time he became known for his work on the origin of coral atolls and his studies of marine life. But only one or two friends were let in on the secret of his theory. It was contained in a little pocket notebook wherein he patiently set down all the evidence that seemed to bear on his notion. He visited plant and animal breeders, endlessly studying their records. He bought pigeons—all sorts that he could procure—and raised, studied and dissected them. Though domestic pigeons are all descended from the common European rock dove, Darwin found that pouters, fantails, carriers and tumblers so differed from one another, as the result of centuries of selection by fanciers, that a zoologist would, if he came on them in the wild, classify them as separate varieties. The same was true, Darwin saw, of dogs and of various strains of wheat. So, perhaps, evolution had not only taken place on isolated islands, ages past; it seemed to be going on right before his eyes.

For 20 years Darwin patiently worked on his theory, with no thought of fame or little of publication. To a friend he at length confided: "At last, gleams of light have come, and I am almost convinced (quite contrary to the opinion I started out with) that species are not (it is like confessing a murder) immutable." But murder will out, and one morning at the breakfast table he opened a letter which outlined to him a theory so like his own that the faraway writer might have peeped into the 231 pages of Darwin's own unpublished manuscript. Out in the East Indies, Alfred Russel Wallace, a well-known zoological collector, had fallen ill and in the strange luminosity of fever had perceived with a flash of intuition how Nature has enriched the world.

"There is no limit," wrote Wallace, "of variability to a species, as formerly supposed. The life of wild animals is a struggle for existence. The abundance or rarity of a species depends upon its more or less perfect adaptation to the conditions of existence. Useful variations will tend to increase, useless or hurtful variations to diminish. Superior varieties will ultimately extirpate the original species. There is a tendency in Nature to progression, by minute steps."

"Struggle for existence," "adaptation to conditions," "tendency to progression by minute steps"—these were Darwin's very words! Excited by this confirmation of his discovery, Darwin was also deeply disturbed by the problem it posed in the ethics of science. How could he now publish his own findings without seeming to have stolen the distant scientist's ideas? A wise solution was found—both men agreed to publish jointly the new theory of evolution by natural selection, at the next meeting of the learned Linnaean Society. The argument presented that historic night in 1858 runs like this:

First fact: Living creatures reproduce in geometric ratio (by multiplication).

Second fact: Yet the numbers of individuals in any species tend to remain, in the long run, more or less constant.

Deduction from these two facts: Competition between individuals and between species keeps their numbers down. This is the struggle for existence.

Third fact: All creatures tend to vary noticeably. No two individuals are exactly alike and some are distinctly unlike within the same species. Though not all such variations are inheritable, experimental breeding shows that some are.

Deduction from these facts: Since there is a struggle for existence and not all individuals are alike, some of the variations will survive because those differences give them a slight edge of superiority. Inferior variants will be eliminated. This is natural selection.

Result: Continuing from generation to generation, natural selection tends to pile up enough small differences to amount to a major difference. And that is evolution.

After the meeting there was a polite buzz in the Linnaean Society. If Wallace and Darwin were right, then the lifework of many an older man was outmoded. On the other hand, the hitherto mysterious fossils of extinct animals and plants began to offer a picture of continuing creation more astounding even than the literal Biblical explanation. Next year Darwin brought out *The Origin of Species*. The first edition sold out on the day of publication. Now indeed the storm of controversy arose. The man was mad! The man was a genius! The man was creating scientific anarchy!

The liberal forces in the churches had long been seething beneath the tight-clamped lid of unquestionable authority. With publication of the *Origin*, discussion boiled over. Angrily cried the Victorian fundamentalists, if you do not accept Gospel truth literally, you open the floodgates of disbelief and wash away all moral standards. Stuff! cried the exhilarated thinkers. Here is a new freedom to worship God's truth graven on the geologic tablets!

That's how Bishop Samuel Wilberforce came to accept the challenge of a debate at Oxford against Darwin's fiery young champion, the biologist Thomas Huxley. The great hall was jammed. Ladies waved their handkerchiefs at handsome, smooth-spoken Bishop Wilberforce. Many clergymen were there, stalwart in the defense of public morals. Scientists had gathered to see "Soapy Sam," as they called the Bishop, knocked out of the ring.

Wilberforce's science, in which he had hastily been coached, would have been perfectly sound 20 years earlier. But he didn't rely on that alone; he dealt in ridicule. As a final crushing blow he turned to Huxley. "Is the gentleman," he asked, "related by his grandfather's or grandmother's side to an ape?"

Springing to his feet, young Huxley retorted: "I would far rather be descended from a monkey on both my parents' sides than from a man who uses his brilliant talents for arousing religious prejudice in discussions of subjects about which he knows nothing." A roar of rage went up from the clergy, yells of delight from the Oxford students. The day was Huxley's—and Darwin's.

All this time Darwin was living a recluse life at his country home in Kent. He would as soon have died, he said, as to have taken part in the Oxford debate. Darwin had reason for choosing quiet domestic exile. He was plagued by poor health. The least excitement could make him ill. Peace and quiet were necessary to his work. And work poured from his study and laboratory every year. *The Descent of Man* traced the family tree of the human animal, and set off fresh explosions of wrath from the churches. Undismayed, Darwin wrote *The Expression of Emotions in Men and Animals*, tracing our most cherished human traits back to the brutes. Just when his critics were shuddering in dread of another "ungodly attack" upon the divinity of man, he would baffle them with a study on the way in which orchids are fertilized, or the method by which primroses prevent inbreeding.

In vain was Darwin's life scrutinized for the moral weakness that his enemies were sure must underlie his free thinking. All they could discover was a gentle old fellow who passed his days amid flowers and with children—his two greatest delights. Never by any word of his was God denied, nor the soul of man.

Among scientists, no man was ever better loved. When he entered a scientific meeting in his later years, the entire audience would rise and cheer. It was hard to believe that this quiet man had been the center of the bitterest philosophical battle of the century.

Actually he had taken small interest in the fight. Like a hardworking gardener, he spaded up, year after year, great chunks of fertile thought, and paid scant attention to the squabbling of the birds that followed him up and down the rows of his orderly work.

Toward scientific criticism, though, Darwin lent an attentive ear, for he was ready to drop the most cherished theory at any moment in favor of a better. And that criticism has been searching. It has objected that natural selection can destroy but not create, and does not explain the initial variations on which it acts. The significant work of Mendel on inheritance, which helps answer these questions, was not publicized till after Darwin's death. Genetics as a science was unborn in his day. The mutation theory—*i.e.*, evolution by sudden and major jumps ("sports") instead of by little steps—had not yet been worked out by De Vries. But the later findings have not put Darwin in the discard; on the contrary, they support and complete his picture of evolution. For evolution has long since ceased to be a theory and is accepted as a fact by almost all scientists.

Darwin was not the first discoverer of evolution, any more than Columbus was the first to discover America, but he was the first to establish its facts unshakably. The impulse that his discovery made has spread far beyond the realm of biology. Astronomers now speak of the evolution of the stars; physicists find evolution in all material things. History is now viewed in the light of evolution, and sociologists recognize the evolution of society. Nothing stays what it was—not the sun, nor man's concept of God, nor the sovereignty of nations.

The life of Charles Darwin, born on the same day (February 12, 1809) as Abraham Lincoln, tranquilly ended on April 19, 1882—a life uneventful save for its great intellectual adventure. He had asked to be buried at his country home, but the British nation claimed his body. His coffin was carried to Westminster Abbey by pallbearers who included Huxley, Wallace and James Russell Lowell, and placed in a vault beside Sir Isaac Newton. So rests in honored peace one of the finest type of *Homo sapiens* ever developed in the forward march of civilization.

CONQUEROR OF THE SEAS

Condensed from the book

By Stefan Zweig

Translated by Eden and Cedar Paul

T HE QUEST for spices began it. From the days when the Romans first acquired a taste for the pungent seasonings of the East, the Western World had found it impossible to get on without them. Far into the Middle Ages the food of Europe was unspeakably insipid: fruits that now seem commonplace were unknown, there were no tomatoes or corn, there was no tea or coffee. Even at the tables of the rich there was nothing to relieve the sameness of the food unless spices could be had.

These were obtainable only from the Indies, and the trade routes thither and back were so long and perilous—so beset by robber bands—that by the time the spices reached Europe they had become excessively valuable. Ginger and cinnamon, for instance, were weighed out upon apothecaries' scales; peppercorns were counted out one by one and were worth their weight in silver.

The boldness that inspired the voyages of Columbus, Dias, John Cabot and the other great explorers of their era was above all the outcome of a yearning to discover new, unhampered trade routes to the Spice Islands of the East. And after Vasco da Gama, rounding the southern tip of Africa in 1498, had reached India by sea, the competition for trade and empire in the Orient grew frenzied. In 1505 the Portuguese sent a fleet to establish trading posts in the Indies, and with it went Ferdinand Magellan, a young Portuguese soldier of 24. From this and subsequent expeditions, which reached Malacca (near modern Singapore, gateway to the Spice Islands), Magellan returned with experience, and a Malay slave bought in Malacca. This slave, whom he named Enrique, was to play an amazing role in Magellan's later career.

Magellan's mind was now opened to far horizons, and he dreamed of reaching the Spice Islands by sailing west, as Columbus had dreamed before him. Other adventurers—including Amerigo Vespucci, Cortés and Cabot—had searched the coast of America for a passage to the Indies, and it seems probable that Magellan was inspired (and as the event proved, deceived) by a certain secret map based on Vespucci's observations—a map which indicated a hidden strait behind Cabo Santa María in Uruguay.

At any rate, where other explorers had said modestly, "I hope to find a strait," Magellan declared with certitude, "I know where to find it." And on the strength of his certainty he sought from King Manuel I of Portugal a fleet to explore this new route to the East. When the King refused his backing for so hazardous a gamble, Magellan offered his services to Portugal's great rival for the spice trade, Spain. At the Spanish court his bold assertion that he alone knew the position of the secret *paso* made a deep impression. King Charles, eager to steal a march on his Portuguese rival, granted the desired commission, and powerful Spanish bankers undertook to provide a fleet of five ships.

At this point King Manuel instructed his ambassador in Spain to smash the enterprise. Quarrels, delays and riots therefore hampered every detail of Magellan's labors. Crews were obtained with great difficulty. But among the haphazard company of adventurers there chanced to be a youthful Italian, Antonio Pigafetta, who went because he wanted to behold the "magnificent and dread things of the ocean." To him posterity is indebted, for he kept a most careful diary of this epoch-making voyage.

Magellan's fleet sailed from Sanlúcar, Spain, on September 20, 1519. Most of the 265 men aboard the ships were bidding their homeland eternal farewell. Before the start, Magellan had ordered that every evening the four other ships were to steer close to the flagship, the *Trinidad*, and receive orders for the night watches. By these daily contacts, discipline was to be maintained.

The captains had expected to be invited on board the flagship and consulted on the course. Instead, Magellan did not ask their opinions. They had to follow the flag by day, the beacon by night, with the dumb obedience of dogs. So when Magellan, instead of sailing southwest for Brazil as expected, steered southward along the coast of Africa, Juan de Cartagena, captain of the *San Antonio*, bluntly asked why the course had been changed. It is probable that Magellan changed the route in the hope of catching a favorable trade wind. However, his reply was merely that no one was entitled to demand explanations from him. This increased Cartagena's hostility to a point where, one night, the *San Antonio* failed to steer close to the flagship for orders. It was plain to everyone in the fleet that Juan de Cartagena did not acknowledge the unrestricted supremacy of the Portuguese commander.

For several days Magellan kept his own counsel. Then, as if capitulating, he summoned the four captains to a council on the flagship. Juan de Cartagena came with the others and, angered by Magellan's refusal to explain the new course, publicly refused obedience. Magellan immediately commanded his master-at-arms to arrest the mutineer.

The fleet, with Magellan's cousin Mesquita now in command of the *San Antonio*, sailed onward without incident and on December 13, after an 11 weeks' voyage, entered the bay of Rio de Janeiro. To the weary crew, this bay must have seemed a paradise. The natives emerged from their huts on the edge of the forest to welcome the soldiers in armor, showing much curiosity but no suspicion.

After 13 days of rest and reprovisioning, Magellan resumed his journey southward along the coast of Brazil, and on January 10, 1520, he reached Cabo Santa María. Beyond it the sailors saw a small hill rising out of an immense plain and called it Montevidi— today Montevideo. The huge inlet they entered is, in reality, the estuary of the Río de la Plata, but of this Magellan had no inkling.

He spent a fortnight exploring it, and bitter indeed was his disappointment when he found only the mouth of a gigantic river.

Magellan knew that none of the captains must guess his disappointment. Confidently, he sailed onward along a coast that became increasingly desolate. Magellan examined every bay, with hopes that rose and died again and again. Farther and farther south sailed the fleet; shorter grew the days, longer the nights. Snow whitened the sails; hurricanes shattered the spars. Half a year had passed, antarctic winter was at hand, and Magellan seemed no nearer his goal. On March 31, 1520, another indentation appeared. It was a closed bay. Still, Magellan entered. It was a sheltered place, and the water seemed well stocked with fish, so he gave orders to anchor. He had decided to winter in this Port San Julián, this unknown and uninhabited bay.

Cooped up here and put on short rations, the crews began to grumble, while the tension between Magellan and the Spanish captains increased until it flared out in open revolt. Under cover of darkness the mutineer Cartagena, with two other Spanish captains and 30 armed men, boarded and seized the *San Antonio*, killing an officer. Magellan decided upon heroic measures. He sent his thoroughly trustworthy master-at-arms, Espinosa, with five men, to the *Victoria*, carrying a letter to its mutinous commander, Luis de Mendoza.

The mutineers on board this well-armed ship had no suspicions when they saw the tiny boat approaching. How could six men attack a ship manned by 60? In a leisurely way Espinosa climbed on board, and handed to Captain Mendoza Magellan's letter summoning him to the flagship. Mendoza read the message and laughed at the obviousness of the trap. But this laugh ended with a hideous gurgle, for the master-at-arms stabbed him in the throat.

Magellan had no difficulty in arresting the two mutinous captains who survived—Juan de Cartagena and Gaspar Quesada. Gaspar Quesada was condemned to death. Juan de Cartagena, the real leader of the mutiny, and a priest who tried to foment a second mutiny, were no less guilty than Quesada had been. But Magellan decided to maroon them. When the fleet set sail once more, the two men were to be left on shore, furnished with a supply of food and wine. God Almighty would decide whether they should die there.

Port San Julián brought the Spaniards nothing but disaster. As soon as the winter was over, the captain-general sent the little *Santiago*, the most mobile ship in the fleet, to explore outside the bay. The vessel was destroyed in a storm, although the crew got safely to land, and Magellan promptly sent a boat to rescue the shipwrecked men.

At last, on August 24, 1520, Magellan gave orders to leave unlucky San Julián, giving a last glance to the two poor wretches he had marooned. One of his ships had been sunk, two of his captains had been killed, almost a year had passed since the beginning of the voyage—a year in which nothing had been gained, nothing discovered, nothing done.

These must have been the gloomiest days in Magellan's life. He tried to sail forward, but was stormbound off the barren coast for two more tedious months. Yet, without knowing it, he was near his goal. On October 21, 1520, he sighted white cliffs rising above a strangely indented shore, and soon entered a deep bay with black waters. No sign of human life, no vegetation; naught but the howling of the wind. The men looked dubiously at the inlet, black as Hades, encircled by mountains. But Magellan, obsessed by his idea of a hidden strait, insisted upon exploring this remarkable bay. The *San Antonio* and the *Concepción* reluctantly obeyed his order to sail as far westward as they could, but to return and report in five days.

No sooner had the fleet been divided than the waters of the bay were lashed by a storm and Magellan's ship was all but dashed on the rocks. But it was for the *San Antonio* and the *Concepción* that he felt the gravest anxiety. The hurricane must have overtaken them in the narrows; save for a miracle, they must be dashed to pieces. On the fourth day of agonized waiting, a sail was sighted. God be praised, one ship is saved! No, both ships, both the *San Antonio* and the *Concepción* are coming back, safe and sound. Their captains brought Magellan yearned-for tidings. The ships, driven west, were about to be wrecked upon the rocks which faced them when, at the last moment, a channel opened ahead! Though they had not found the western outlet, they were confident that it was a strait. Better news could not have reached the sorely tried Magellan. Let there be no more hesitation. Then, with steady courage, forward into the labyrinth which he then called Todos los Santos, but which posterity was to name the Strait of Magellan.

When at last the strait opened to show the broad ocean, tears of joy, we are told, ran down into his black beard. Magellan now summoned the captains to report on stores. They had achieved their first aim. Were they willing to go on to find the Spice Islands? He could not deny that the shortage of provisions entailed serious danger. Still, he himself was undismayed. The fleet would go on. However, Magellan ordered the captains to conceal from their crews the grave shortage of supplies. The *San Antonio*, sent to explore a long fork in the passage, failed to return at the appointed time. Magellan spent several days in a fruitless search for her, and at last summoned an astrologer to cast a horoscope. This astrologer announced the message of the stars, which happened, on this occasion, to speak the truth. The *San Antonio*, he said, had deserted and set sail for Spain.

Once more Magellan was faced with a terrible decision. On board the *San Antonio* was the major share of the provisions. To continue now would be practically suicidal. Yet such was his decision. On November 28, 1520, the three remaining ships set sail northwestward into an unknown ocean. Somewhere beyond the horizon must lie the Spice Islands, the islands of wealth; farther on still must be China and Hindustan; and beyond them, in the vast distance, must be the homeland, Spain. With a salvo of artillery, three lonely little ships respectfully greeted the unfamiliar seas.

The first crossing of this hitherto nameless ocean is one of the deathless deeds of mankind. Magellan was journeying into the void. His men were exhausted. Hunger and privation lay behind them, hunger and privation lay threateningly before. Their clothing was threadbare, the sails rotten, the rigging frayed. Many must have envied the comrades who had deserted. Yet they sailed on and still there came no land. Long since, thought Magellan, he must have got beyond Japan. Actually he had not yet crossed a third of the vast ocean which, because it was so peaceful, he called the Pacific. On January 24, 1521, they sighted an island (St. Paul) and here provisioned. Then again they were launched on the vastness of the waters. No less than 19 men, about one tenth of those still left with the expedition, died in torment on this dreadful journey across the Pacific.

At length on March 6, 1521, there was a cry from the masthead: "Land-ho!" It was time. Two or three days more in the void, and probably no record of this heroic exploit would have come down to us. But here was an island! Hardly had the fleet entered the bay when little painted boats, with sails made of palm leaves stitched together, put off from shore. Nimble as monkeys, the nude children of nature scrambled on board, and so foreign to their thoughts were the conventions of civilized life that they began to appropriate every object that was not nailed down. Even the *Trinidad's* skiff was paddled off in triumph to the shore. Magellan decided to teach the thieving islanders a lesson, and landed 40 armed seamen, who burned the natives' huts and took away whatever they could find—fowls, fish and fruit.

This plunder raid saved the Spaniards from destruction. Three days' rest, fresh fruit, meat and water quickly restored most of the crew to health. With renewed courage the westward voyage was resumed. When, a week later, another and yet another island were sighted, Magellan knew that they were saved. He had found a completely unknown group of islands, the Philippines, thus securing for Emperor Charles a new province, which was destined to remain under the rule of the Spanish Crown longer than any of the regions discovered by Columbus, Cortés or Pizarro.

On March 28, the fleet reached Mazzava, a tiny islet of the Philippine group, and here Magellan had one of the most remarkable experiences of his life. As the three large foreign ships drew near, the friendly inhabitants flocked to the beach, and Magellan sent his slave Enrique ashore as emissary, rightly supposing that the natives would have more confidence in a brown-skinned man than in the bearded whites.

Now came the wonder. When the chattering islanders surrounded Enrique, the Malay slave was dumfounded, for he understood much of what they were saying. It was a good many years since he had last heard a word of his native speech. By this amazing occurrence, Magellan knew that he had reached his goal. He was back among the speakers of Malay. What learned men had dreamed, now was certain. The earth was round, for a man had rounded it.

A week in Mazzava was the happiest part of Magellan's journey. Calambu, the king of the island, received him with hospitality, providing abundant food and drink. It remained now only to go forward to the Spice Islands and fulfill his commission. Yet he did not wish to leave the Philippine archipelago without having made of it a permanent asset for Spain, and it would not suffice that he had visited and annexed one little island. So he asked Calambu which was the largest of the neighboring islands, and was told that it was Zebu (Cebu). Thither Magellan now sailed, "for thus," writes the trusty Pigafetta, "his unlucky fate willed that it should be."

Magellan's first sight of Cebu showed him that here was a place of considerable importance. In the harbor lay junks from foreign ports together with quantities of native vessels. To disclose himself as the lord of thunder and lightning, Magellan signaled the fleet to fire an artillery salute, which caused the islanders to flee in all directions. Thereupon Magellan hastened to send Enrique ashore as interpreter, to inform the ruler of the island that the thunder was not a sign of enmity but a mark of honor for the mighty Rajah of Cebu. The admiral, declared Enrique, was prepared to show His Majesty various costly goods and to enter into trade with him. Humabon, Rajah of Cebu, invited Magellan's envoys to a banquet, and stated that he was ready to enter into a perpetual treaty of peace with the newcomers. Magellan, on his side, did his utmost to promote amity, and relations became so cordial that the Rajah and most of his followers spontaneously expressed a desire to become Christians.

One Sunday, therefore, April 14, 1521, the Spaniards celebrated their greatest triumph. In the marketplace a large cross was set up before which the Rajah and 50 others knelt, all of whom were baptized with great ceremony. The news spread far and wide. Next day there came from neighboring islands many more chieftains to be initiated into these magical ceremonies. Within a few days almost all the chiefs had sworn alliance with Spain, and had been sprinkled with the waters of baptism.

Magellan had succeeded in everything, as if angels had lighted his path. But now came strange tragedy. On a tiny isle called Mactan, close to Cebu, there ruled a rajah named Silapulapu who had always resisted the Rajah of Cebu. Since the arrival of the Spaniards, he had been doing what he could to prevent the other chieftains from supplying the strangers with food. This refusal of supplies seemed to Magellan an excellent reason for a demonstration. The Rajah of Cebu should observe the power of the lord of thunder and lightning. For the first time in his career, we find Magellan lacking in foresight. The Rajah of Cebu offered to send 1000 warriors against Mactan, but Magellan refused. He was concerned in demonstrating the prestige of Spain, in proving that natives armed with lances and krises could not even wound a Spanish soldier in steel harness. Therefore he took with him no more than 60 men, and requested the Rajah to watch the contest from a boat.

Disastrously for Magellan, however, the puny prince of Mactan had a powerful ally in the structure of the shore. The boats could not cross a coral reef, so a landing party of 40 men, led by Magellan himself, was compelled to wade ashore, deprived of support from the arquebuses and crossbows in the boats. A great number of natives, shouting defiantly, were waiting on shore. Pigafetta, who was one of the attacking party and was himself wounded by an arrow, describes the battle that followed:

When the islanders realized that our fire from the boats did not reach them, they rushed upon us, assailing us with arrows, javelins and lances so that we were scarcely able to defend ourselves.

When they became aware that, though our bodies were protected by armor, our legs were exposed, they aimed chiefly at these. The captain's right foot was wounded by a poisoned arrow, whereupon he issued orders for a slow retreat. But nearly all our men fled headlong, so that no more than six or eight of us stayed with him, who, having been lame for years, could not withdraw quickly. Recognizing the captain, the islanders aimed chiefly at him, and twice the helmet was struck from his head. He fought on until a heavy blow upon the left leg caused him to fall forward on his face in the water. Then the islanders threw themselves upon him, with spears and scimitars, and ran him through until they killed him.

The Spaniards lost no more than eight men in this trifling skirmish, but the fall of their leader made the reverse catastrophic. The myth of invulnerability was broken. Had not the Rajah of Cebu looked on while Silapulapu, one of the most insignificant of the princes, had vanquished the white god?

But it was a senseless insult to Enrique, Magellan's slave, which caused the ultimate tragedy. The faithful Enrique had fought by his leader's side to the last moment. He was brought back wounded to the ship, and lay motionless, wrapped in his mat. Thereupon Duarte Barbosa, who jointly with João Serrão had been elected to the leadership, was foolish enough to tell the poor devil not to fancy that a dog could play the idler after his master's death. If he did not promptly go ashore to aid the exchange of goods by interpreting, he should have a sound drubbing. Enrique made no sign at the moment, but his fierce Malay pride was outraged. Obediently he betook himself to the market, but there he plotted with the Rajah of Cebu. Then, four days after Magellan's death, Enrique brought agreeable news to the captains. The Rajah, he said, had many jewels to send to the King of Spain. Would Captains Barbosa and Serrão come ashore to receive them?

Serrão and Barbosa walked heedlessly into the trap. In all, 29 Spaniards went ashore, and among them were the most experienced leaders and pilots. (Pigafetta, fortunately, was still suffering from his wound and remained on board.) Ceremoniously received, they were escorted to a palm-leaf hut where a feast had been prepared. Suddenly the men on the ships heard shouts and screams: the crafty Rajah of Cebu was finishing off his guests. João Carvalho, who had now succeeded to the command, issued orders to train the guns on the town. One broadside thundered after another. Then the ships put about and hurriedly sailed away.

Of the 265 seamen who had signed on in Seville, there were left no more than 115, so that the three ships were undermanned. Better, then, to sacrifice one of the three. The leaky *Concepción* was unloaded and fired. The remaining two ships set forth side by side: the *Trinidad* and the *Victoria*. How sorely this reduced fleet missed its real leader was now shown by the uncertain course. Instead of steering for the Moluccas, to which they were quite close, they wandered about for six months. At length, they came upon the Moluccas—the Spice Islands—and on November 8, 1521, they landed on Tidore. The inhabitants were very friendly. Everything the Spaniards could wish was provided in abundance. Frenziedly they bought spices, giving their muskets, their cloaks, their belts in exchange; for now they were going home, to become rich men by the sale of these easily secured treasures.

The ships were loaded and provisioned. But as the sails were set, the rotten old *Trinidad* groaned and her seams opened. The *Victoria* could not wait longer. It was decided that 51 of the remaining mariners would have to stay in the Spice Islands until the *Trinidad* could be repaired.

The voyage of the battered *Victoria* round the second half of the globe, after 30 long months had been spent upon the first half of the journey, was one of the most heroic deeds in the history of navigation. She had been amply provisioned for five months, but no salt had been obtainable, and under the burning sun of the tropics her large store of pickled pork became putrid. To escape the odor the crew threw the whole stock overboard.

So famine again sailed with them as they crossed the Indian Ocean. The *Victoria* was loaded to bursting with vast quantities of spices. But who, with parched lips and empty stomach, can chew peppercorns, endure the nip of cinnamon or swallow nutmeg instead of bread? Day after day, one withered corpse after another was flung overboard. More than a score of her crew had died when, on July 9, 1522, after six months voyaging, the *Victoria* anchored off Santiago in the Cape Verde Islands, having rounded the Cape of Good Hope and sailed up the east coast of Africa.

Here was a Portuguese harbor in a Portuguese colony. To go ashore meant to put themselves into the enemy's hands. But hunger left no choice, and the commander, Sebastian del Cano, sent men ashore, instructing them to pretend that their ship came from America. The *Victoria's* boat returned from shore laden with provisions, and then was sent for one more load. But suddenly del Cano perceived that some ships in the harbor were preparing to put off. He realized that his ruse had been discovered. Leaving his comrades to their fate ashore, del Cano hastily heaved anchor and set sail.

Brief and risky as had been the stay in the Cape Verde Islands, it was here that Pigafetta, the industrious chronicler, observed another wonder, a phenomenon which he was the first man in the world to notice. The men who had gone ashore for supplies had returned with the astounding news that it was Thursday on shore, although on board ship it was unquestionably Wednesday. Pigafetta had kept his diary with the utmost precision for three years. Could he possibly have missed a day? He asked Alvo, the pilot, who had also kept a record of the days in the ship's log, and Alvo was equally sure that it was Wednesday. Steering persistently westward, in some unexplained way the circumnavigators must have dropped a day out of the calendar, and Pigafetta's report of this strange phenomenon later mystified the European world. No man till then had suspected that one who counters the earth on its rolling course will gain a day.

Not yet, however, had the *Victoria* reached home. With groaning timbers, slowly and wearily, exerting her last energies, she

continued the final stage of the voyage. Of the 66 souls on board
when she sailed from the Spice Islands, only a handful were left
and these had to work desperately at the pumps. When, on September 4, 1522, they sighted Cape St. Vincent, at the southwest
corner of Portugal, "they were feebler than men have ever been
before." Two days more and they sailed into the mouth of the
Guadalquivir—whence they had sailed three years before. Next
morning the *Victoria* sailed upriver to Seville. Seville! "Fire the
bombards!" shouted del Cano. A salute resounded across the
river. With the iron mouths of these guns, three years before, they
had bidden farewell to Spain; with the same cannon they had
solemnly greeted the Strait of Magellan, and had again greeted the
unknown Pacific. With these big guns they had saluted the newly
discovered archipelago of the Philippines. But never did the iron
voices sound so loud and so jubilant as now when they announced:
"We have returned. We have done what no one ever did before us.
We are the first circumnavigators of the world."

Huge crowds assembled on the riverfront of Seville. With profound emotion the citizens scrutinized the 18 survivors as they
left the *Victoria;* saw how they stumbled from weakness; how
sickly and exhausted were these heroes, each of them aged by a
decade in three years of hardship. They were offered food, but
first of all, to discharge a vow they had taken when in the utmost
need, they marched barefoot in penitent procession to church.
Solemnly they thanked the Almighty for their deliverance, and
murmured prayers for the leader who had fallen at Mactan and for
the more than 200 lost comrades.

News of their return spread like wildfire across Europe. Since
the voyage of Columbus no event had so stirred the contemporary world. Geographical doubts had been put to rest forever.
Since a ship had set sail from the port of Seville, and, sailing continually westward, had returned to the port of Seville, it had been
proved that the earth was a globe surrounded by continuous
ocean. Under the flag of Spain, Columbus had begun the work of
modern discovery, and under the same flag Magellan had com-

pleted it. Thirty years had taught more about the place of man's habitation than had thousands of years before.

Even the bankers who had equipped the fleet had good reason to be pleased. The 520 quintals (about 26 tons) of spices brought back as freight by the *Victoria* were worth 45,000 ducats, or $675,000—a gratifying profit. The cargo of this one bottom more than repaid the loss of the other four—the loss of over 200 men not figuring in the accounts. Only about a dozen persons in the whole world were seized with panic when the news came that one of Magellan's armada had got home safely. They were the mutinous officers who had deserted with the *San Antonio* and had got back to Seville more than a year before. They had described their rebellion as a patriotic act, and had made no mention of any *paso*. They spoke only of a "bay" which had been reached, and declared that Magellan intended to hand over the fleet to the Portuguese. Fortunately for these deserters, del Cano, the surviving commander, had been their accomplice in the mutiny at Port San Julián. Thanks to his aid now, they escaped punishment.

On del Cano was heaped much of the acclaim that should have gone to Magellan. In fact the very achievement for which Magellan sacrificed his life proved of little advantage to anybody. So many of the ships that subsequently attempted to sail through the Strait of Magellan came to grief, that navigators for decades avoided this perilous passage and preferred to get their goods into the Pacific or out of it by the laborious land route across the Isthmus of Panama. Many, of course, continued to use the older route around the Cape of Good Hope.

Within a generation the strait was almost forgotten. Fifty-eight years after its discovery Drake used it for a surprise attack on the Spanish colonies on the west coast of South America. But since then only a few whalers and other rare ships have traversed the route which Magellan had expected to become the main channel of intercourse between Europe and the South Seas. Yet history can never forget the first navigator of the strait—the man who, in discovering the true dimensions of our globe, demonstrated also the heights which human courage can attain.

A GENTLEMAN OF VIRGINIA

Condensed from Robert E. Lee

By *Robert W. Winston*

O N APRIL 18, 1861, after the Civil War had already begun, Robert E. Lee, West Point graduate and recently appointed colonel of the First Cavalry, was informed that President Lincoln wished him to take command of the Union Army. Lee was not a person of national importance, though he had fought in the Mexican War and had been superintendent of West Point. Thus far he had commanded a regiment but not in the field. In Texas he had been engaged in chasing Indians and Mexican bandits, duties well performed but bringing no fame. In truth when he had arrived at his home in Arlington, Virginia, on March 1, 1861, the occurrence was so inconsequential that no mention of it was made in the Richmond papers.

Although he disapproved of slavery, believing it "a moral and a political evil to any country, but a greater evil to the white than the black race," Lee declined Lincoln's offer. "I do not believe in secession, nor that there is a sufficient cause for revolution," he declared. "But if Virginia secedes I will follow my native state with my sword and if need be with my life." On April 20, following the thorny path of duty, he resigned his commission in the United States Army. Meanwhile Virginia had seceded and its governor inquired whether Colonel Lee would accept the position of Major General of the Virginia forces.

But when the Confederate War Department took charge of

affairs at Richmond, Lee was entrusted with no command whatsoever. He was retained in the office of President Jefferson Davis as a mere staff officer, and as he contemplated his career since he resigned from the army his heart must have sunk within him. In the struggle he seemed doomed to play a subordinate part. His wife and daughters were refugees. His home in Arlington had become a Union hospital. The family heirlooms were disappearing. All three of his sons were in the army. Almost in a moment his day had been turned into night.

Yet within a year, because of disasters in the West and the lack of confidence in President Davis as a military leader, Lee was chosen commander in chief of all the armies of the Confederate states. He knew the odds against the South were overwhelming. If there were no foreign aid, the United States, an organized government of 20-odd million people, would surely overcome an unorganized Confederacy of nine million, embarrassed by slaves and without the funds to finance a great war. "Lay aside your pencil," said General Lee one day to his subordinate. "Do not make any figures, figures are all against us."

But the people of the South soon discovered that in Lee they had found a man who would "take more desperate chances and take them quicker than any other general, Confederate or Federal." When, in the spring of 1862, McClellan invaded and attempted to take possession of Virginia, Lee, in seven days, with a poorly equipped army of 87,000 men, routed the well-supplied Union forces of more than 100,000, and completely frustrated McClellan's campaign, undertaken after six months of preparation at an enormous expense of men and money. Lee now became a magnet drawing together a group of fiery leaders whom he soon bound to himself with ties of affection stronger than steel. In after days General Henry Wise, one of Lee's officers, exclaimed, "Ah, General Lee, these men are not fighting for the Confederacy; they are fighting for you."

At Fredericksburg, another victory for Lee, the Union troops were mowed down by the thousands. "It is well war is so terrible or we would grow too fond of it," Lee exclaimed as he gazed upon the ghastly spectacle. After the battle of Fredericksburg the South looked upon Lee as invincible. Around the camp-fires the soldiers discussed their beloved chief. Women almost worshiped him, little children were his friends. In all the army he had no peer.

Lee not only directed the greater movements of his troops but inspected minor details, encouraging his men, stimulating their pride, supplying their needs as far as he could, sharing their privations. They were members of his household and he was their father; when he rode up to headquarters he came with no display or fanfare—as if he had been the head of a plantation riding over his fields. He appeared to have no mighty secrets, he assumed no airs of superior authority.

One night around the campfires, a brigadier general asked Lee why he did not wear the full insignia of his office, but contented himself with the stars of a colonel. Lee replied that he cared little for display. In a pole tent, without trappings or adornments, he dwelt among his men. A slouch hat and a suit of plain gray cloth constituted his apparel. Yet Lee was an aristocrat to his fingertips. One day at Valley Mountain he noticed a scion of an old Virginia family in one of the companies, and wrote his wife that he was "pained to see a young man of education and standing, serving in the ranks." But he was unwilling to invoke the rule of caste in behalf of his own son. Bobby Lee, Jr., served his apprenticeship as a powder monkey in Stonewall Jackson's Brigade and was so grimy with stains that his own father did not recognize him.

In the field as at home General Lee had a childlike confidence in an overruling God. Again and again, during the dark winter of 1863–64, he repeated, "Our times are in Thy hands." Indeed, the wits said of him that he cared more for Bibles than for bullets. The religious aspect of Lee's army was a striking feature. "It was no unusual scene, as the gloaming gathered, to see a group of soldiers quietly collect beneath the dusky shadows of the forest trees, whence soon arose the notes of a familiar hymn, while some youthful chaplain, in earnest tones, would tell his holy mission. And presently, by the waning light of pine torches, the weird figures of the soldiers would be seen reverently moving to the night's repose."

Lee's chivalry was illustrated when he sent to Jefferson Davis a captured letter that had been written by a Union soldier. The letter described the demoralization of the Union Army because of McClellan's retreat. "I would suggest," wrote Lee to Davis, "that no publicity be given the name of the writer, as it would injure him without materially benefiting us."

At Gettysburg he passed a wounded Federal who, seeing him, raised himself up and shouted in defiance: "Hurrah for the Union!" The soldier later reported: "The general heard me, looked, stopped his horse, dismounted, and came towards me. I confess that I at first thought he meant to kill me. But as he came up he looked down at me with such a sad expression upon his face that all fear left me, and I wondered what he was about. He extended his hand to me, and grasping mine firmly and looking right into my eyes, said: 'My son, I hope you will soon be well.'"

After the decisive Confederate victory at Chancellorsville, Lee gave first attention to the wounded of both sides. While he was thus engaged a note was brought from Stonewall Jackson congratulating him upon his victory. "Say to General Jackson," he replied, "that the victory is his and the congratulations are due to him." But after the disaster at Gettysburg, when General Wilcox came forward and lamented the state of his brigade, Lee took him by the hand. "Never mind, General," he said. "All this has been my fault; it is I that have lost this fight and you must help me out of it in the best way you can."

As the war progressed and the resources of the South became exhausted, the endurance and fortitude of Lee's army were remarkable. The troops were insufficiently clothed and nourished. At one time Lee wrote the authorities that in one brigade there were only 50 men with serviceable shoes and thousands were barefoot. Fuel was scarce. When the mercury was at zero, wood was selling for five dollars a stick. Sherman's march had cut off supplies from Georgia, and the Army of Northern Virginia, living from hand to mouth, was often without meat for days. Inevitable calamity was impending. In these distressing circumstances, while Lee was retreating before the vastly superior strength of Grant's forces, there was neither fear nor confusion. All men turned to Lee as their savior. If he had been marching to victory he could not have been more honored. Whenever he appeared, a hundred tattered hats were waved and cheers rent the air. But finally, after Appomattox, Lee's staff agreed the situation was so desperate that peace negotiations should be opened. The Mc-Lean house at Appomattox was selected as the place where the formal surrender would occur. Silently and deferentially the respective officers arranged themselves around the historic room. General Grant had come in such haste that he had not changed his clothes. He wore an old blouse, army jacket, and had on no sword—a plight which he explained as a desire to avoid delay. General Lee was attired in his best—sword and sash, embroidered belt, boots and gold spurs—because that suit was now all he possessed.

The two great captains conversed of things remote, of Mexican War days, of life on the frontier. Grant became so much interested he almost forgot the matter in hand. At this moment the booming of guns was heard. The Union troops were celebrating their victory. Grant ordered them to desist. He was sad and depressed and did not feel like rejoicing over so gallant a foe. Every request that an honorable man could grant was conceded. Lee's officers were allowed to retain their side arms, rations were issued to his hungry troops and they were permitted to take home their horses and mules. The short and concise document of surrender provided that the officers and men should not be molested, so long as they kept their parole. The tattered battle flags were furled. The Farewell Address, restrained but tender, was read. The drama ended.

In behalf of Virginia, and on the altar of conscience, Lee had sacrificed all—the command of the United States Army, followed by certain victory, wealth, fame, perhaps the Presidency. Now, with no home and no business or profession, he was a paroled prisoner of war, deprived of a citizen's right to vote or hold office. But his courage and integrity remained uncompromising. When some Richmond bankers arranged without his knowledge to have him elected as president of one of the great New York life-insurance companies, with a salary ample if not princely, the General quietly declined the position. He would not undertake a complicated business of which he was ignorant, nor would he permit his name to be used to draw patronage. But when he was asked to become president of a broken-down college, Lee's only misgivings were as to his competence to fill the trust.

During the war he had invoked divine approval. Now that the final issue had been decided adversely he would not deny that God had spoken. Southern leaders all about were hesitating. Some were defiant. A Confederate colony had been organized in Canada, another in Mexico. But Lee applied to President Andrew Johnson for a pardon, and when this became known in the South the irreconcilables stood aghast. "You are disgraced," exclaimed the impulsive General Wise to a soldier who had taken the oath of allegiance to the United States. "Why, General Lee told me to take it," the soldier replied. "Ah, that makes a difference. What General Lee says is right." In a short time following Lee's example, applications for pardon poured in on the President and were liberally granted.

Under Lee's administration Washington College (now Washington and Lee University), at Lexington, Virginia, became perhaps the most widely attended Southern institution of learning. Though he taught no classes, he listened to the oral examinations and was present in chapel at 7:45 each day. He sought to know the faces and the names of all the students. In the army he had been a father to his men; in the college he would be a father to their sons. He had long since given up his social drinking, declaring he stood more in dread of intoxicating liquors than of bullets, and now he urged total abstinence upon his students as the best safeguard to morals and health.

Lee Cottage became the center of a dignified, informal hospitality. When the college board passed resolutions to donate the dwelling to him, Lee suggested that the college was in no condition to make gratuities and that neither he nor his family would consent to become a burden upon it. Every day he visited Traveler, the gray horse who had been with him through most of the war. Frequently the General would ride him to the blacksmith shop to be shod. And before the glowing forge, Traveler, remembering the days of action no doubt, would snort and rear. "You must be patient with Traveler," the General would urge, caressing his old companion. "He has been through a great deal and is somewhat nervous."

Old age may be considered a test of character. How does one live his last days, how does he bear the ills that come with advancing years? Lee never lost heart. The future beckoned to him, the past guided. He was fond of an expression of Marcus Aurelius, "Misfortune nobly borne is good fortune." Washington College grew and diffused a wholesome learning, softening the hardships of the hour, while General Lee became the great peacemaker, the ideal college president. Strong, sensible and level-headed, a gentleman of the old school yet alert and practical, he was the finest flower of the Old South as he became the prophet of the New.

Shortly after the close of the Civil War, a Negro entered a fashionable church in Richmond, Virginia, one Sunday morning at the beginning of a communion service. When the time came, he walked down the aisle and knelt at the altar. A rustle of shock and anger swept through the congregation. A distinguished layman immediately stood up, stepped forward to the altar and knelt beside his colored brother. Captured by his spirit, the congregation followed.

The layman who set the example: Robert E. Lee.

—*Billy Graham*

THE WESTWARD VOYAGER

By Llewelyn Powys

O F THE EARLY life of Henry Hudson, explorer of Hudson Bay, Hudson Strait and the Hudson River, nothing is known. It is, however, a mistake to think he was a Dutchman, although the Dutch called him "Hendrik." He signed his name plain Henry and was unable either to read or write the language of his Amsterdam employers.

His first appearance in history occurs when, in 1607, he and his crew of ten men and a boy took holy communion in Bishopsgate, England, before setting out in their ship, the *Hopewell*, to sail straight across the North Pole to the far-fabled land of Cathay. This voyage, organized by a trading company called the Muscovy Company, turned out to be a failure. Hudson found it impossible to break through the ice barrier between Greenland and Spitzbergen and returned to London. The next year the Muscovy Company again employed him on the same quest. This time he tried to find a navigable strait through Novaya Zemlya, north of Russia, into the Kara Sea of the Arctic Ocean and from there, after rounding the legendary Cape of Tabin, to reach the wealth of the East through a warm sea perfumed with "incense-bearing trees."

This voyage was also unsuccessful, but although he never sighted the legendary cape, at least two of his sailors had a glimpse of something even more remarkable. Standing on deck just after an arctic storm, they caught sight of a mermaid. It is not the first time men have enjoyed such a privilege. The Dutch caught such a being near Borneo and kept her alive for nearly a week in a large vat. "From time to time she uttered little cries like those of a mouse. She would not eat, though she was offered fish, lobsters, etc."

Henry Hudson was at pains to state the exact appearance of this girl-fish. "She came close to the ship, looking earnestly on the men" and then was turned over by a wave and disappeared from sight. "From the navill upwards her backe and breasts were like a woman's, her skin very white, and long hair hanging down behinde; in her going down they saw her tayle, which was like the tayle of a porpoise and speckled like a macrell."

However arrested the London merchants may have been by this tale, they were profoundly discouraged by Hudson's second failure and soon he found himself out of a job. The Dutch, however, had heard of his exploits, and in their employ he set out again, sailed across the Atlantic in the *Half Moon*, and, on September 2, 1609, sighted the gleaming flats of Sandy Hook. As the sailors entered New York harbor "their nostrils inhaled a sweet smell." Indians came out in canoes carrying gifts of oysters and berries. On every side magnificent forests came down to the water's edge.

Hudson sailed the *Half Moon* as far up the river as Albany, and left the ship to see the Indians in their own homes. "I went on shore with an old man of a tribe consisting of 40 men and 17 women; these I saw there in a house well constructed of oak bark, and circular in shape, with an arched roof. On our coming some food was served in wide-made wooden bowls. Likewise a fat dog was killed, and skinned in a great haste with shells. They supposed that I would remain with them for the night, but I returned to the ship. The natives are a very good people, for when they saw that I would not remain, they supposed that I was afraid of their bows, and taking their arrows, they broke them in pieces, and threw them into the fire."

At Albany, Hudson, finding shallow water, turned back. Now came an unfortunate incident. One afternoon when the *Half Moon* was at anchor, surrounded by canoes, an Indian climbed onto the rudder, and through a window stole a shirt and a cutlass. The shirt belonged to an evil-minded English sailor from the slums of London, called Robert Juet. Better had the native stolen from a man-eating animal than from this ancient dockwalloper. The alarm was given, and the Dutch mate shot at the thief and killed him. All was confusion, with a general stampede of the Indians overboard. That night the *Half Moon* sailed as far down-river as possible. Next day a hundred or more natives were seen collecting on a certain point of land to shout across at the *Half Moon*, when Juet "shot a falcon at them, and killed two." Two days later they were "clear of the inlet," and with free hearts sailed away. Possibly the captain was unable to prevent this display of savagery. We know that he had already suffered from the insubordination of his crew.

Hudson's last voyage had the backing of the Prince of Wales and London merchants, and in 1610 the "Barke *Discovery*" set sail for Cathay. From the first there was an ugly underswell of discontent among the crew. Robert Juet indulged in mutinous talk and advised two sailors to keep their muskets loaded in their cabins for what "hee supposed would bee manslaughter, and prove bloodie to some."

At last they entered Hudson Strait. It took five weeks to sail through, owing to the great masses of ice. At one time the men refused to go on, but Hudson showed them his charts and persuaded them to continue. On and on they sailed, collecting fresh water from pools in passing icebergs. When they reached the entrance of the great bay, Hudson undoubtedly thought that the most difficult part of the voyage was over and that he had discovered the long-desired passage. But much time was wasted in sailing to and fro, and by November 1 the *Discovery* was frozen in at the southern end of James Bay. The gunner died, the men got scurvy, the food ran short. On shore they could see nothing but mud flats and snow-hooded rocks.

At first they lived on ptarmigans, or white partridges, and in the early spring on migrating birds on their way to nesting grounds in the Far North. Later on, so famished were the men that they wandered into the woods, up over the hills and down into the valleys searching like foxes for "all things that had any show of substance in them how vile soever." They ate moss and frogs "than the which the powder of a post be much better." At last the ice melted sufficiently for them to free the ship. Their only hope was to head north from James Bay to Cape Digges, where the year before they had seen wild fowl breeding. Hudson divided the last scraps of bread with his own hands and "hee wept when hee gave it unto them."

Presently they became shut in the bay by ice and on a certain Saturday night Juet led a mutiny. Three men leaped on Hudson, pinioned his arms and forced him, his son and the sick sailors into the ship's small boat. The mutineers had every intention of keeping the ship's carpenter with them, but when this honest sailor saw what had happened, he would have none of it. He went off to get his carpenter's chest and iron pot, swearing lustily that "as for himself he would not stay in the ship" but would choose rather to commit himself to God's mercy and "for the love of the master go down into the shallop, than with such villaines to accept of likelier hopes."

The mutineers now cut the small boat free and sailed away, the shallop growing smaller and smaller till Henry Hudson became a mote, a nothing, lost on the waters of the great northern mediterranean which he had discovered. It was the last glimpse we have of him. His end is clouded in mystery.

Man with his burning soul
Has but an hour of breath
To build a ship of Truth
In which his soul may sail . . .
For death takes toll
Of beauty, courage, youth,
Of all but Truth.

—*John Masefield*

THE WIDOW OF WINDSOR

Condensed from The Edwardian Era

By *André Maurois*

VICTORIA was at once the Queen of England, Empress of India, and a simple, painstaking grandmother, worrying about the illnesses of the living, mindful of the anniversaries of the dead. In her eyes the kingdoms of Europe were simply her family estates. Related to the royal houses of Germany, Greece, Romania, Sweden, Denmark, Norway and Belgium, she found little difference between her personal connections with monarchs and the relations of Great Britain with foreign powers. In 1899, at the age of 80, she was still first and foremost a woman, and the history of her time was fused in her mind with her own life. When France and England seemed on the verge of war over the question of Siam just when the Queen happened to be at Nice, she wrote to her Prime Minister: "I hope a crisis may be averted on national grounds, and also . . . personally it would be very awkward if complications arose with a country in which I am now residing."

She identified herself with her subjects. She protested, full of wrath, when a Chancellor of the Exchequer demanded a stiffer duty on *"her* people's" beer. By *"her* people" she meant chiefly the middle classes. They had grown up alongside her, for it was during her reign that industrial England had conquered the world's markets. Neither the working classes nor agricultural laborers came within her ken. Distributing warm petticoats to old women who took her hand and called down the divine blessing on her at

Balmoral was "very touching"; but of the hapless wretches living in the hovels of London she had only a vague picture in her mind. She was surprised by the election of the first Labor members to the House of Commons and invited them to Windsor Castle to be presented to her, which, as she noted in her journal, "gratified them very much."

The virtues and tastes of the middle classes were her own, and she referred to the aristocracy with a touch of scorn as "the upper classes." She occasionally compared the English nobility to that of France on the eve of the Revolution, and believed that the love of pleasure among that class would bring it to ruin. In 1900 a young American lady, describing London to her family, wrote: "Queen Victoria is not in society." Perfectly true. Society resented the retired life of the "Widow of Windsor." The Court had ceased to be the center of fashionable life. Victoria's ideas of the fine arts were those of the British middle class. For a time she refused to listen to Wagner's music. "Quite incomprehensible!" she declared. And when it was remarked that this was "the music of the future," she retorted: "I'm bored with the future altogether, and I don't want to hear any more about it."

She gave never a thought to the impression she made. At church, disliking long services, she would sometimes scandalize the clergyman by lifting her fan to indicate that his sermon was going to be too long. On one occasion someone mentioned the opinion held of Her Majesty by a new ambassador who had just been presented to her. "Dear me!" she said. "I did not give a thought to that. It is so beside the question. What really signifies is what I think of him."

That utter assurance made her unaffectedly natural. Very small and very stout, she had the look of a little mushroom, von Angeli the artist was quoted as saying, but she retained a remarkable dignity. Her slightly protruding blue eyes were still youthful, her gestures still charming, even in old age. Her voice was pretty, her laughter frank. She did not pretend to wit, nor even to wide culture, but her common sense amounted to genius. "I always thought," said Lord Salisbury, "that when I knew what the Queen thought, I knew pretty certainly what view her subjects would take, especially the middle class."

Punctual to a pitch of mania, the Queen liked her days to be regulated, unbroken and full. At half past nine every morning she went out in her open pony carriage, which she drove herself. A lady-in-waiting walked alongside to tell her about happenings in the house; petty details interested her no less than affairs of state. If a young lady-in-waiting had been to Portsmouth the day before, the Queen had to know whether she had come back, and whether the sea had been rough. She drew up at cottage doors to ask news of invalids. And if she had the good fortune to meet an organ-grinder, she stopped her carriage and talked to the little Italian, showing anxiety for the health of his monkey. She busied herself with everything: the promotion of bandmasters, a phonograph record of a speech she wished to send to the Queen of Ethiopia, a telegram to the Chinese statesman and general Li Hung Chang.

The number of documents which she had to sign with her own hand was formidable. She demanded the continual attendance of her secretaries. Sir Arthur Bigge, her private secretary, had to obtain her special authorization to go from Windsor to London. If the Queen's emissary had not brought back Sir Arthur at the exact moment when she required him, he would find a note on his desk: "The Queen wishes to know why Sir Arthur was not in his office."

Born in 1819 and ascending the throne as a young girl of 18, Victoria ruled longest of all European sovereigns. During her reign France had known two dynasties and a republic, Spain three monarchs, Italy four kings. When, in 1897, she celebrated her Diamond Jubilee, her 60th anniversary as Queen, it was compared to a challenge flung by England to the other nations of the world. They might well envy her, for England was a world in herself. British and native troops had been ordered home from all the dominions and colonies. The Jubilee procession was like a Roman triumph. The Queen noted in her journal: "No one ever, I believe, has met such an ovation as was given to me."

That day of June 1897, a day of diamonds, cheering and tears of happiness, had been the apex of her reign, perhaps the peak of

British power. Within three years of the glorious Jubilee procession, two small republics of farming folk at the southern end of the African continent were holding in check the most powerful empire of the globe. At the outset of the Boer war, the crowds in London had laughed at the unequal match. But throughout 1900 the news was bad, and nobody suffered more than the 81-year-old Queen. She seemed utterly tireless, writing to generals and soldiers, bidding farewell to regiments leaving for the front, visiting the wounded in hospitals. Nobody had wanted this war less than she. But in Germany and France the newspapers attacked her in the most unfair way.

When, after a visit to Ireland, she landed from her yacht *Alberta* on December 18, observers were struck by the great change in her from the previous year. She was no longer the small, plump lady, almost pretty, who had driven through London on Jubilee Day. Her only malady was old age and the extreme fatigue of that sad year. Her son, the Prince of Wales, was urgently summoned. Another son, the Duke of Connaught, happened to be in Germany and handed the telegram announcement that the Queen was dying to his nephew, Emperor William II. "I pointed out to him," said Prince von Bülow, the German Chancellor, "that it would be well to wait and see what course her illness took. The Emperor replied, with some impatience, that it was a question of his beloved grandmother's life, that he was absolutely determined to see her once again."

Relations between the two countries had not been cordial since the Kaiser's famous telegram to the Boer President, Kruger, congratulating him on the repulse of an English raid. But January 22, 1901, saw the German Emperor and the Prince of Wales walking together on English ground. For the first time in his life the Kaiser was popular in England. He wrote back to the Empress telling her that people in London wept with joy on the night when it was known that he was with his grandmother. She had been one of the few beings who had genuinely loved him.

All England went into mourning when she died at her residence on the Isle of Wight. It was impossible to buy a single piece of black cloth in London. For the funeral, battleships and cruisers lay moored in double column along the route of the yacht *Alberta* with the Queen's remains on board. The ships' bands played Chopin's Funeral March. Their guns boomed out. A proud scene: those eight long miles of sea thronged with vessels-of-war; the marines bowing their heads over their rifles reversed; the red flashes from the mouths of guns; and between the salvos, those bursts of melancholy, exalted music.

When the new monarch, her son, came aboard the royal yacht, he found the flag at half-mast, and asked the commander what this meant.

"The Queen is dead, sir," answered the officer.

"But the King is alive," replied Edward VII, and had the standard hoisted. The curtain was falling on a century of history.

The Kaiser stayed a few days after the burial. It was certain that by the time of his departure the wholeheartedness of his grief had reconquered the English, a race of sentimentalists. But the Germans, on their side, fumed because he had seen fit to confer the Order of the Black Eagle on Field Marshal Lord Roberts, the conqueror of the Boers. Personally the Emperor remained under the charm of England long after his homecoming.

The life of the capital resumed its course. A young officer named Winston Churchill, lunching with one of the elder statesmen, Sir William Harcourt, asked him: "What will happen now?"

"My dear Winston," answered Sir William, "the experience of a long life has convinced me that nothing ever happens."

And really, for 60 years past, nothing had happened. The Queen had reigned, signed, loved, grown old. The Empire had become stronger, more united. England's wealth had waxed greater and greater. Her population had doubled. Then, in a few months, everything altered. January 1901: the Queen was dead, a new pilot took the tiller, African farmers were defying the Empire. Every English family was receiving its letters from men at the front: "no sign of any end, far from it." Here was a whole country asking in surprised anxiety what young Winston Churchill had asked— "What will happen now?"

VOICE OF LIBERTY

By Donald and Louise Peattie

E VERY American knows seven words that Patrick Henry spoke; few could tell you what he did to give us liberty. Yet of the patriots who struck for freedom, Henry was the spearhead. He began by demanding for the colonists the rights of Englishmen. Many would have been content with a safe dependency on the mother country. Not Henry. He was all American; he was born in Virginia in 1736, with his back to the sea and his face toward the frontier and the future. He "grew up with the country," reaching maturity just as our nation reached it. He was homespun—the first of our "backwoods" leaders, of the fiercely independent, nonconformist breed of the Scotch.

Like many another great man, he was unsuccessful at everything he tried, till his genius was identified. He set up a store and failed. He married at 18 a bride who brought him a small sandy plantation. Unlucky at farming, he went back to storekeeping, only to fail again. At 23, he found himself with four children, a mountain of debts and no special training. But he had a brilliant memory, a logical mind, quick wits, slow angers. He was stubborn in debate yet courteous in address. He could always understand what the common man was thinking and could rouse him.

Toward what career did these gifts point? The answer flashed on the young man's mind. But how, without leisure and money, could he study for the law? He borrowed a standard work on the legal profession and a digest of the Virginia laws. In six weeks he had stowed these under his shock of red hair. Then, in his ill-fitting country clothes, he went to the colonial capital of Williamsburg and presented himself to the learned examiners for the bar. They soon detected how scant was his knowledge. But where basic justice was concerned he was infallible, a "born" lawyer. Shaking their heads, the examiners signed his application.

Returning to his hometown to practice, young Mr. Henry in three years tried over a thousand suits, most of which he won. Then came the great "Parson's Cause." The Church of England clergy in Virginia were generally paid in tobacco. Now they wanted the amount of it adjusted to the varying price of the leaf; they were, as we would say, playing the market. A test case was tried in Hanover County courthouse, and the judge, young Patrick's own father, had already decided in favor of the clergy; all the jury was asked to do was to fix the amount due. Self-satisfied parsons crowded the benches to watch the fun. An hour later they fled the court with buzzing ears and burning cheeks.

For the greatest jury lawyer of his time had flayed them alive, denouncing the clergy laws as an encroachment on the rights of Virginia freemen by the British Crown. The jury awarded the claimant one penny, and Henry left the courtroom on the shoulders of the crowd. Elected next year to the House of Burgesses (lower house of the Virginia colonial legislature), Henry had been in his seat only nine days when the first copies of the Stamp Act of 1765 arrived from Parliament. This required all legal documents in the colonies, as well as newspapers and pamphlets, to carry an expensive stamp—the revenue to help pay for maintaining British soldiers to protect the Indian frontiers. But to tax freemen without their consent, cried Henry, violated the Magna Charta. In a series of thundering resolutions he asserted that a free people cannot be governed by laws not of their making, and that the Virginia Assembly was independent of Parliament and Crown.

Young Thomas Jefferson, leaning in the doorway, was fascinated by the deadly drum of Henry's oratory. And a delegate named George Washington, who was known to have said that no one would catch *him* talking of such a wild notion as "independency," must have sat bolt upright to hear Patrick Henry shout:

"Caesar had his Brutus, Charles the First his Cromwell, and George the Third—" He paused, for he was a master of timing.

"Treason, treason!" came from many parts of the House.

"—may profit by their example," he ended slyly. And then shot the parting bolt: "If this be treason, make the most of it!"

In a storm the House passed Henry's resolutions. Copies were rushed to patriots all the way from Charleston to Boston, kindling a wild fire of hope. And a year later Parliament repealed the Stamp Act. When next the legislature met, Henry led every fight, and none so bitter as that over the hated Townshend Acts. The first of these had suspended the colonial legislature of New York for failure to comply with the Quartering Act, by which British troops were quartered at the colonies' expense. The second and third raised revenue by an import duty, levied without consent, on glass, lead, paper, paint and tea. Even in England, Pitt and Burke assailed this injustice. In Virginia so fiery were Henry and his followers that the governor dismissed the Assembly.

Out stalked "the forward men," as they called themselves. They marched down the broad street of staid, aristocratic Williamsburg to the Raleigh Tavern, called for a bowl of punch, locked the doors and went into a session as unauthorized as it was history-making. There Thomas Jefferson, Richard Henry Lee, Francis Lightfoot Lee, Dabney Carr, Peyton Randolph clinked glasses with Patrick Henry, pledging themselves to refuse taxation. So they flung defiance at Parliament. Brave words were those, uplifting as the new flag soon to be flung out onto the winds of the world. For the forward men were seeing into a future, and none was so farsighted as Henry. "It was to him," states Jefferson, "we were indebted for the unanimity that prevailed amongst us."

And it was unanimity that the colonies must achieve; for if they acted together they might frighten Parliament and King into a more reasonable attitude. So they called a Continental Congress to meet at Philadelphia in 1774. Most of the forward men, including Henry, were delegates, as well as such conservative members as George Washington. "These gentlemen from Virginia," wrote

John Adams in his diary, "appear to be the most spirited and consistent of any."

Patrick Henry opened the Congress, calling upon the delegates to forget that they represented sections and to vote as patriots. "I am not a Virginian, but an American," he cried. The Congress presented to Britain a statement that, Pitt told the House of Lords, "for solidity of reasoning and wisdom of conclusion," showed that "all attempts to impose servitude upon such men must be fatal." Most delegates went home satisfied, but Patrick Henry believed that Britain would take no heed and the colonies must fight.

Clashes between the British troops and the Boston crowds soon proved how right he was. On a March day in 1775, the Second Virginia Convention met in Richmond to get away from the royal governor, British warships and the Tories of tidewater Williamsburg. Richmond was a raw new town then, and the largest place the delegates could find to meet in was St. John's Church—though it looks small enough to our eyes and was smaller still when Patrick Henry rose to speak.

The church must have been hushed with expectancy, as now it is hushed with the quiet of a shrine. The country had the choice of war or peace. If it chose war, it could match veteran troops with only ill-armed amateurs, and confront the greatest of navies with fishing smacks. If the delegates chose peace, their property and their necks would be safe. No wonder if many that day were hesitant, cautious. As Patrick Henry began to speak, he did not sound too sure of himself. But he always began haltingly, timidly, in a low voice, as if abashed at his own opinions. Slowly he let his voice rise, till the wooden walls of the church thrummed with it.

> Gentlemen may cry "Peace, peace!" But there is no peace! Is life so dear, or peace so sweet, as to be purchased at the price of chains and slavery? Forbid it, Almighty God! I know not what course others may take, but as for me *give me liberty or give me death!*

Fired by Patrick Henry's words, the delegates authorized the training of troops. News came that Lord Dunmore, the royal governor, had seized the colony's store of gunpowder at Williamsburg. Rousing the militia of his hometown, Patrick Henry at its head marched on the capital. The frightened Dunmore sent payment for the powder and fled to a warship. Next day he declared "a certain Patrick Henry" to be an outlaw.

That outlaw was by now off to Philadelphia to attend the Second Continental Congress, which elected George Washington commander in chief. On Henry's return, he took the foremost part in drafting a constitution for Virginia, and was elected the commonwealth's first governor. When, after seven terrible years of struggle, victory came, the problems of the states were appalling and their debts mountain high. There had been plenty to cry for war, but few were in a hurry to pay for it. The most suicidal thing any politician could do was to propose to redeem the public word and pay off the veterans. Yet Henry forced Virginia to tax herself more heavily than Great Britain had ever tried to tax her. And he was five times elected governor.

But now this man feared in a strong central government the death of states' rights and individual liberties. When the Constitutional Convention was called, in 1787, to form a union out of the toothless confederation of states, Henry refused to attend as a delegate. When the Constitution was sent to the states for ratification, Patrick Henry opposed it bitterly. Yet when Virginia and the other states ratified the Constitution, Henry manfully announced his acceptance of it. Nonetheless, he became the center of opposition to federal power, as Washington became the tower of federal strength. Not one day would Patrick Henry serve under the new government, though Washington offered him the posts of Secretary of State and Chief Justice.

Patrick Henry was still battling for your liberties and mine. To him, as to Jefferson and others, there appeared a gaping hole in the Constitution. And into that chasm were slipping, he warned, the very principles for which the Revolutionary soldier had fought and died: freedom of speech and assembly, freedom from imprisonment without trial, the right to bear arms, to a trial by jury, to criticize government and officers, and liberty of religious conscience. The people had no check upon the all-embracing powers a centralized government might someday assume. On this subject Henry never ceased to talk until at last popular opinion forced through the first ten amendments to the Constitution. It is of these, the Bill of Rights, that the average American thinks when he speaks of the Constitution in glowing terms.

Less than 60 years of age, Henry was now an old man, broken by three decades of tremendous exertions. Wishing for nothing so much as the pleasures of country life, he withdrew to his country home, Red Hill, where there were green lawns and grandchildren tumbling on them.

Another man of the times, older and even greater than Patrick Henry, had also retired to his farm and his family life, where he might have rested content in the knowledge that no man ever did more for his country. But Washington could not rest. For he saw that country torn with disunion. One party was crying for war with England, the other for war with France. The champions of states' rights had passed resolutions which declared that any state had the power to nullify acts of the federal government. Both state and federal elections were approaching, and the young country was torn from within. The center of disaffection was Virginia. And as Patrick Henry went, so went Virginia. The master of Mount Vernon dipped his quill in ink, to cover page after page of eloquent pleading.

> . . . At such a crisis, when measures are systematically pursued which must eventually dissolve the union, ought characters who are best able to rescue their country remain at home? I hope that you will come forward at the ensuing elections. Your weight of character and influence in the House of Representatives [of Virginia] would be a bulwark against such dangerous sentiments as are delivered there at present. I conceive it to be of immense importance at this crisis that you should be there.
>
> Your most Obt and very
humble Servt
Geo. Washington

And Patrick Henry lifted his eyes from the page as if he had heard a battle trumpet. Just as we know today that the nations must unite for peace, so Henry knew that no right of a single state was as precious as the right of the United States to exist indivisible. Announcing that he would support the Federalist John Marshall for a seat in Congress, Henry himself ran for the Virginia Assembly. Sick and infirm though he was, he journeyed 20 miles to Charlotte, the county seat, to speak.

News that Patrick Henry had come back into the arena swept the state; crowds were waiting to meet him as he came out on the steps of the tavern on that March day in 1799. He seemed bowed with years; his careworn face was pale. His voice began haltingly. The union he had denounced so tellingly as an agreement holding danger to liberty, he must save, lest disunion snatch all our liberties.

But never had Patrick Henry stood so tall as when he straightened his bent form, like an old soldier. His voice, unleashed, lashed out in all its former power. No state, he warned, has the right to pass upon the validity of federal laws. No part can be greater than the whole.

"If I am asked what is to be done when a people feel themselves intolerably oppressed, my answer is ready: Overturn the government. But wait at least until some infringement is made upon your rights and which cannot otherwise be redressed. For if ever you recur to another change," he cried in words that Americans today may heed as they did then, "you may bid adieu forever to representative government."

When he had finished, Henry literally fell into the arms of the cheering crowd, and was carried exhausted to a couch in the tavern. "The sun," said a famous teacher who stood beside him, "has set in all its glory."

Next month Henry was elected, and Marshall too. But before the Assembly sat again there died George Washington, the man of the stainless sword, and Patrick Henry, the man of the sword-like tongue.

THE PEACE
THAT LIES WITHIN

By Max Eastman

BUDDHISM has had more followers than any other religion in history. They number 400 million or more today. And images of Buddha are as familiar as any object of art in the world. But how many Americans know who Buddha was, or what he had to say about life's problems?

Artists and sculptors have made Buddha plump; he seems too well fed and self-satisfied for a Holy Man. We expect the saints to agonize in their search for the inner light. So did Buddha's friends and those to whom he first preached. Indeed, the idea of spiritual enlightenment through suffering gained prominence in India some 500 years before Christ, when Buddha lived.

In that age it was not unusual for young men, harassed and puzzled by the evil in the world, to wind up their affairs, say farewell to their families and their friends and "go forth"—or, as we would say, "walk out." They lived in the woods, their only possession a wooden bowl with which, from time to time, they begged for a bite to eat. Their idea was that self-denial and severe bodily discipline would bring on a moment of sublime insight in which the secret of the universe would become suddenly clear.

The first revolutionary thing about Buddha—or rather Gotama, or Gautama, for that was his clan name—was that he tried this and decided it was foolish. Tradition tells us he was a prince in a small kingdom and was 29 years old, married and the father of a baby son. He walked out at midnight without a word to anybody. It was anguish to him—he stood a moment by his sleeping wife and child but turned away. His will was of iron; from being a prince of this world he became the prince of ascetics, and his fame spread "like the sound of a great gong hung up in the sky."

He had five companions, but they were so impressed by his superior gift of application that they mostly just sat around and watched him. One day after six years of rigid self-denial, when he had reduced himself to a faltering skeleton, he was attacked by violent pains and fell in a dead faint. When he came to, he decided that in order to crack the secrets of the universe you have to adopt a "middle way" between ascetic self-denial and sensual indulgence. In the religious culture of India this was revolutionary. Gotama was denounced as a renegade by his five cronies and he had to continue his search for the ultimate wisdom all alone.

Gotama's middle way was, from the viewpoint of American morals and dietetics, heroic. His chastity was absolute. His one big meal, taken at noon, consisted of curry and rice, and after that nothing solid, perhaps a little gruel for supper. He thrived on this, and became not only a healthy saint but a champion of intellectual endurance besides. It is said of Socrates that he stood thinking in a portico all of one night. A similar experience is reported of Gotama—except that he had the forethought to sit.

Gotama sat under a certain pipal, or sacred fig, tree afterward called the Tree of Enlightenment and Wisdom—Bo Tree in Singhalese. That tree has been replanted from its own seeds throughout the ages; you can still see it at Buddh Gaya. Gotama had

made up his mind that he would never get up until he received
spiritual enlightenment. Toward the small hours he fell into a
trance in which he beheld with a kind of radiant clarity the whole
intricate chain of causes and effects which regulates this misery
called life. And he beheld with the same clarity the path of deliverance into bliss:

These mystic experiences are, as a rule, irresistibly convincing
to those who undergo them. Gotama had no hesitation in pro-
claiming himself not only Buddha, "The Enlightened One," but
also Tathàgata, "The Perfect One." He went straight back to the
five hermits who had denounced him, and who were still starving
themselves in a deer park at Benares. They saw him coming.
"Let's show no respect to this renegade," they said, "this convert
to self-indulgence." But as the illumined Gotama came nearer
they rushed out to meet him, calling him "Brother."

He answered—it is hard to believe without a glimmer of triumph in his eye: "O monks, address not Tathàgata as 'Brother.'
Tathàgata is the holy and supreme Buddha."

Then Gotama, the Buddha, preached a sermon—probably
with one exception the most momentous sermon ever preached.
Like the Sermon on the Mount, it presented in concise outline a
new way of life. The two ways of life are surprisingly similar, although the beliefs they rest on are wide apart. Buddha's sermon
was pessimistic. It began with the assumption that life as we com-
monly live it consists mostly of suffering. East Indians find it natural to regard life as an affliction, possibly because they have
been so beset by poverty and disease. Perhaps if we believed as
they do in the monotonously recurring cycle of reincarnation, or
rebirth, we should not find the adventure of life so exciting.

Buddha's discovery under the Bo Tree was that the cause of
human suffering is ignorance. We are always craving satisfaction
for something we call self. But there is no self. We must abandon
this delusion and the ignorant cravings that go with it. And he
specified: "craving for the gratification of the passions, craving
for a future life, craving for success in this life." We must learn
through liberation of our minds from superstition, through the

strict discipline of our wills and through love, to interflow with
the world and be a humble and unhankering part of it. In this lies
peace and perfect happiness.

He called this ideal state "nirvana." It is the state of mind portrayed in the images of Buddha—a sublime and yet not supernatural peace. Not a peace that passeth understanding—a peace
that results from understanding.

Buddha now was wholly preoccupied with the effort to find
for mortal men a way out of their misery into a godlike state of
being. His eightfold path of salvation has none of the simple,
unaffected eloquence of the Beatitudes, but it might well be re-
spoken in that form. For "blessedness and how to reach it" was the
central theme of all his sermons:

> Blessed are they who *know*, and whose knowledge is free from
> delusion and superstition.
> Blessed are they who speak what they know in a kindly,
> open and truthful manner.
> Blessed are they whose conduct is peaceful, honest and pure.
> Blessed are they who earn their livelihood in a way that
> brings hurt or danger to no living thing.
> Blessed are the tranquil, who have cast out ill will, pride,
> self-righteousness, and put in their place love, pity and sympathy.
> Blessed are ye when ye direct your best efforts to self-
> training and self-control.
> Blessed beyond measure, when ye are by this means un-
> wrapped from the limitations of selfhood.
> And blessed, finally, are they who find rapture in contemplat-
> ing what is deeply and really true about this world and our
> life in it.

Although Buddha was silent about God, he believed in a
moral order such as only a just and all-powerful deity could or-
dain. He believed that every good act brings a reward, every evil
act retribution. No matter what you do with mind or body, you
cannot escape the moral law. Moreover, in substituting a rapt
contemplation of Reality for those priestly rites and sacrifices

which he rejected, Buddha took some steps at least in the direction of private prayer. His trance of contemplation is not prayer, but it is a thing often prayed for: resignation.

Another cause of the success of Buddha's religion is its disarming tolerance. There is no Buddhist dogma and, so far as we know, no follower of Buddha ever persecuted a heretic. Indeed, the most amazing thing about Buddha—when you look back to him over centuries filled with the wars and rages of fanatics—is his quiet appeal to each man's reason and experience. Not only must we work out our own salvation, according to Buddha, but we must think out our own creed.

"Do not believe anything because the written testimony of some ancient wise man is shown to you," he said. "Do not believe anything on the authority either of teachers or priests. Whatever accords with your own experience and after thorough investigation agrees with your reason, and is conducive to your own welfare and to that of all other living things, *that* accept as truth and live accordingly."

These words lend a modern, a Western significance to the sublime, contemplative repose of those sacred yet robust images of Gotama, the Buddha. He had things to say that no man or woman, after 2500 years of hustling and agitated chattering around the fountain of knowledge, can afford to ignore.

Greater perhaps than his wisdom was the example he set of what we in the West can only call Christlike living. For 45 years, until he died at the age of 80, this genius of will and intellect wandered about in the valley of the Ganges, rising at dawn, walking 15 to 20 miles a day, and generously teaching all men, without recompense and without distinction of class or caste, the way to happiness which he had found. He was no agitator and was never molested, either by the priesthood he opposed or by any ruler. He became so famous and so loved that throngs of people would come out as he approached a town, and spread flowers in his path. His real and triumphant aim was to define accurately and teach a noble and happy way of living and dying in this present world.

HE LIGHTED
THE DARK CONTINENT

By O. K. Armstrong

IN THE HEART of southern Africa, well over 100 years ago, a young Scottish missionary-doctor camped among the savages of a village. He made friends with the chieftain, gave medicines to the tribe and preached about a God who was the Father of all men. One night he heard sobbing outside his hut. It was a young girl who had fled from the village in terror because she was about to be sold to a neighboring chief. A huge man with a gun emerged from the shadows to take her back. Calling upon a native helper to strip off the beads the girl wore, the missionary gave them and other presents to the man and sent him away.

Such experiences made up the daily life of one of the world's great missionaries, David Livingstone. Through 33 years of toil and travel, fighting constantly against tropical diseases, exposed at all times to savage men and wild beasts, Dr. Livingstone carried the light of Christian civilization to the world's most backward area.

When he entered Africa in 1840, the entire central portion was a blank on the map. Largely because of his efforts it became a charted land, open to peaceful settlement and trade. And crowning his whole work was a ceaseless crusade against slavery, voodoo superstition and illiteracy.

David Livingstone was born on March 19, 1813, in Lanarkshire, Scotland. As a lad he worked in a spinning mill 12 hours a day. Later he studied for the ministry at Edinburgh University.

He was a handsome, well-built youth, but he was shy and ill at ease in public. On his first attempt to preach, words failed him. "Friends, I have forgotten all I had to say," he gasped. In shame he stepped from the pulpit.

At that moment of discouragement Robert Moffat, visiting Edinburgh after establishing a mission at Kuruman in South Africa, advised David not to give up. Perhaps he could be a doctor instead of a preacher. Livingstone decided to be both—and a foreign missionary besides. When the years of medical study were done, he was sent to Africa.

Livingstone soon developed a burning compassion for the black people of Africa. The traffic in slaves shocked and sickened him, and he vowed he would devote his life to stamping out the evil. He watched the fears and suspicions of the black Africans melt when he applied his healing medicines and tried to teach them better ways of living. He saw their joy at learning. They called him "The Good One." He noted how well the converts at Moffat's Kuruman mission worked among their own people. His plan was to establish a mission point, select native converts to lead it, then go on to new tribes and unexplored fields.

Every step forward carried the hardy crusader into exciting and dangerous adventure. Leading his caravan, fearlessly greeting tribesmen who never before had seen a white man, he would bargain cloth, beads and implements for their friendship, then set about treating the sick with his medicines. Accepted as a friend, he would work among them for weeks or months.

On Sabbath mornings he would gather the people about him and preach to them. With stubborn determination he practiced his gospel messages in the various difficult dialects. The wondering savages may not have understood his words at first, but they knew he was the Good One and that the God he talked about must be good, too.

Time and again Livingstone's life was saved by what he believed to be divine intervention. At Mabotsa an enraged lion attacked and mauled him, breaking his left arm. A young convert—whom Livingstone had chosen as his first native superintendent of

schools—engaged the lion, drawing the beast away until it was brought down. Never again was Livingstone able to lift that arm above his shoulder without pain.

The hardy preacher's endurance and scorn of danger became legendary. He came upon the Bakaa tribe just after their warriors had murdered an Arab trader and all his porters. Livingstone ate with the chieftain and gave him gifts, then calmly lay down in his hut and fell asleep. Next day he wrote in his journal that he had more than ordinary pleasure in telling these murderers how to be cleansed of sin.

Livingstone's work as a doctor was vitally important to his preaching. He demonstrated daily the use of quinine in treating malaria. During the first five years of his work he himself had 31 attacks of fever. Without quinine he could not have lived. With it he revived whole families and tribes.

Livingstone's feats of exploration rank with the greatest. Exploring one third of the huge continent—from the Cape almost to the equator and from the Atlantic to the Indian Ocean—he opened up a vaster unknown area of the earth's surface than any other single man. He charted all the regions he visited and sent precise reports to the Royal Geographical Society in London. He was the first European to find the great Lake Ngami. He came upon some magnificent falls, more than twice as high as Niagara. "Victoria Falls," Livingstone named them, in honor of his Queen.

After the Moffats returned to Africa Livingstone married Robert's daughter, Mary. Born in Africa, she was used to the hardships and dangers of the jungle and desert. Cheerfully she shared the perils of her husband's work, nursed him through numerous illnesses.

At Kolobeng the Livingstones built their only real home. Here in the course of six years four children were born. When repeated sickness threatened the lives of Mary and the children, Livingstone took them to Cape Town and sent them back to England, promising to see them in a few years. Returning to Kolobeng, he found that the Boers had raided his station, stolen his furniture, burned many books, closed the school and terrified his convert-helpers.

Here was warning that the South African authorities wanted no more of his agitation against the slave traffic.

Livingstone answered fearlessly. He denounced slavery at every turn, wrote fervent letters asking the British government to help stop the trade. Spurred by his mission, he accomplished the incredible feat of exploring a trail to the west coast and back again to the interior in four years.

Then he made his first visit home to England, to see his family and to write the first of several books, *Missionary Travels*. Livingstone was astonished to find himself a noted man. The Prince Consort granted him an interview; scientists summoned him for discussions. Her Majesty's government authorized an expedition for further exploration and gave Livingstone civil authority to deal with the African tribes. In March 1858 he sailed with Mrs. Livingstone and their youngest son, Oswell.

For the next six years Livingstone was an explorer rather than a missionary. In a steam launch he and his party explored the Zambesi and other waterways of eastern and central Africa. They discovered Lake Nyasa, established mission points, schools and trade routes. Livingstone sent Mary to Kuruman, where another daughter was born; a whole year went by before he heard the news. Soon after mother, baby daughter and son rejoined the exploring party, Mary contracted a fatal fever. In sorrow Livingstone lingered near his wife's grave for days. He sent his son and daughter back to England. In 1864 he completed his expedition. Now, as he visited tribes he had worked among years before, he could see results from his labor. Churches he had founded were thriving, children were going to school, sanitation practices were taking root.

The graying crusader had long hoped to discover the sources of the Nile so that European trade might come from the north to the interior of Africa. So, early in 1866, after another visit to his homeland, he undertook a dangerous task—exploration of the watershed between Lake Nyasa and Lake Tanganyika. From the time Livingstone left on this memorable expedition, only one white man saw him alive. He met with every possible discouragement. He was ill much of the time. Unfriendly tribesmen stole his supplies. Many of his helpers deserted. Incessant rains and tsetse flies made travel almost impossible. In 1869, desperately ill with pneumonia, Livingstone was borne on a litter to Ujiji on Lake Tanganyika—a two-month trek.

For more than two years no word of the missionary-explorer reached Britain. "Where is Livingstone?" was asked everywhere. Two relief expeditions were sent out, but both of them failed, cut down by tropical diseases.

James Gordon Bennett, Jr., manager of the New York *Herald*, sensed the journalistic possibilities in the story of this missionary "lost" in the heart of Africa. He told Henry M. Stanley, his star reporter, to find Livingstone, no matter how long and costly the search might be.

Stanley reached Zanzibar, assembled a party that numbered 192 and started westward in February 1871. He had only rumors of Livingstone's possible whereabouts. Soon many of his caravan mutinied. Two of the leaders tried to kill him. Heavy rains bogged the trails. Malaria and dysentery wore him down. Yet for nine months, with courage worthy of the man he sought, Stanley pushed into the interior.

On November 10 the people of Ujiji rushed to Livingstone to tell him the exciting news: a white man had arrived! Livingstone, emaciated but erect, stood before his tent, peering in astonishment at the big caravan headed by a tall white man flanked by a porter carrying the Stars and Stripes. The people parted to form a living avenue, down which Stanley stalked to one of the most dramatic meetings of all time.

"Dr. Livingstone, I presume!"

Stanley came just in time. For two years Livingstone had been without medicine of any kind. Gratefully he accepted the new clothes and supplies, eagerly read letters and heard news of the outside world.

But, for all of Stanley's pleading, Livingstone refused to return with him to England. "I still have much work to do!" he said. So Stanley turned back, carrying with him material for dispatches that made David Livingstone the most talked-of man of his day.

With a new caravan and supplies, the courageous preacher marched on, searching for the headwaters of the Nile. But now his strength again was ebbing. Stubbornly he continued, carried in a litter. At an Ilala village one evening he was too exhausted to talk. Gently his helpers laid him on his cot. Just before dawn they found his lifeless form kneeling by the rude bed, his head resting upon clasped hands.

"The Good One is gone!" The words sounded from hut to hut, from village to village. Thousands of his converts came to pay their last respects. They knew that in far-off England the friends of the white doctor would want to bury him, so with loving hands they embalmed the body, but removed his heart, to place it reverently in their own soil where it belonged.

Then began the longest funeral march in history. Chanting gospel hymns the Good One had taught them, the procession of mourners started their nine-month trek to the coast. From Zanzibar a British vessel brought the body to England. On April 18, 1874, David Livingstone was laid to rest in honor in Westminster Abbey.

Publicly acclaiming the late missionary for his crusade against African slavery, Queen Victoria announced early in 1880 that treaties had been signed with the Sultan of Zanzibar and other sovereigns, prohibiting the traffic by land or sea. And through the years since the passing of the Good One, the people among whom Dr. Livingstone carried the light of faith and freedom steadily followed the trail he blazed. Their great progress is his living monument.

A missionary in Africa, translating the Gospel of St. John into Songhai, couldn't find a word to express "believe." He took his problem to a native Christian. The dark man thought a few minutes and then suggested, "Doesn't it mean to 'hear in my heart'?"   —*Sunday School World*

SAM HOUSTON'S MAGNIFICENT LAST STAND

Condensed from Profiles in Courage

By *John F. Kennedy*

T HE FIRST rays of dawn were streaking into the Senate chamber of 1854 as one final speaker rose. Weary Senators, slumped in their chairs after the all-night session, muttered, "Vote, vote!" in the hope of discouraging further oratory on a bill already certain of passage. But Senator Sam Houston of Texas, whose straggling volunteers had routed the entire Mexican army at San Jacinto and established the independence of Texas, was not easily discouraged by overwhelming odds. At his bold words his colleagues shook off their stupor and sat upright and attentive. Standing erect, his chin thrust forward, picturesque if not eccentric in his military cloak and panther-skin waistcoat, Sam Houston, the "magnificent barbarian," spoke out with homely eloquence, begging his colleagues not to plunge the nation into new agitations over the slavery issue:

> This [bill] is an eminently perilous measure. If it is a boon offered to propitiate the South, I, as a Southern man, repudiate it. I adjure you to regard the contract once made to harmonize and preserve this Union. If this repeal takes place, I will have seen the commencement of the agitation; but the youngest child now born, I am apprehensive, will not live to witness its termination. Maintain the Missouri Compromise! Stir not up agitation! Give us peace!

The bill on which bitter debate now closed was the Kansas-Nebraska Bill, the new "unity" device of the Democratic Party and the latest concession to the South. It repealed the principle of the Missouri Compromise of 1820, which admitted into the Union at the same time one slave state and one free, and it reopened the slavery-extension issue by permitting the residents of that vast territory from Iowa to the Rockies to decide the question for themselves. For Democrats and Southerners this bill had become "must" legislation.

Sam Houston was a Democrat of long standing and a Southerner by birth, residence, loyalty and philosophy. But Sam Houston was also Sam Houston, one of the most independent and forceful individuals ever to enter the Senate chamber. He looked upon the Missouri Compromise as a solemn and sacred compact between North and South. He must have known that not a single other Southern Democrat would join him. Still, on that stormy dawn in 1854 he cast his lonely vote against the bill. "It was," Houston was later to remark, "the most unpopular vote I ever gave [but] the wisest and most patriotic."

Certainly it was the most unpopular. Texas, with 58,000 valuable slaves and with an overwhelmingly Democratic population consisting largely of citizens from other Southern states, identified her interests with those Houston had attacked. Now she cried for Houston's scalp as one who had "betrayed his state in the Senate" and "deserted the South."

This was not Senator Houston's first offense. He had attacked those who threatened to secede, describing himself as a Southerner for whom the Union was his "guiding star." He had called on men from every quarter "to sacrifice their differences upon the common altar of their country's good, and stand firm to the Union regardless of all personal consequences." Now, by a vote of 77 to 3, the Texas legislature condemned the stand of him who was once the state's most glorious hero. The Dallas *Herald* demanded that Houston resign his seat, and it was loudly whispered about the Senate that this was to be the last term for the colorful general.

Sam Houston's rugged individualism was nothing more than the expression of the frontier life he had always known. When still a boy, he had run away from his Tennessee home and been adopted by the Cherokee Indians. An infantry officer under Andrew Jackson in 1814, he had had his right arm shredded by bullets when he alone had dashed into enemy lines at the battle of Horseshoe Bend, his men cowering in the hills behind him. He was a rapidly rising success in Tennessee as prosecuting attorney, Congressman and finally Governor at 34.

His sudden resignation as Governor at the height of his popularity is shrouded in mystery: apparently he discovered a few days after his marriage that his beautiful young bride had been forced to accept his hand by an ambitious father, when in truth she loved another. His spirit shattered, he abandoned civilization for exile with the Cherokees.

Several years later, when Houston's balance and purpose had been restored, General Andrew Jackson sent him to Texas. His military exploits there became as much a part of American folklore as Valley Forge and Gettysburg. He had been acclaimed the first president of the Independent Republic of Texas, and when Texas was admitted to the Union he became, at the age of 52, one of the state's first two Senators. But neither adventure, adulation nor a happy second marriage banished his melancholy, more evident than ever in 1856 as his first political defeat threatened.

Sam Houston had already made several tours of Texas denouncing with equal vigor "the mad fanaticism of the North" and "the mad ambition of the South." Now he announced himself a candidate for Governor in the state's 1857 election. He would not run as a Democrat, or as the candidate of any faction— or even resign from the Senate. He would run as Sam Houston, to "regenerate the politics of the state."

It was the first real political battle solidly Democratic Texas had ever known. Frequently peeling off his shirt during the hot summer campaign, he harangued audiences in every corner of Texas with his great fund of abusive epithets and withering sarcasm. Well over six feet tall, still straight as an arrow, he stood with his penetrating eyes flashing scorn for his opponents and derision for their policies.

But his votes on Kansas and other Southern measures could not be explained away to an angry constituency, and Texas handed Sam Houston the first trouncing of his political career. Encouraged that the margin of his defeat was no greater than three to two, he returned to Washington unshaken in his beliefs. But soon thereafter Senator Sam Houston was unceremoniously replaced by the Texas legislature with a more militant spokesman for the South.

He was not able to retire from political battle. Returning to his ranch in Texas, the doughty ex-Senator found that the Governor who had defeated him in 1857 was threatening to lead the state into secession. So, in the fall of 1859, the aging warrior again ran as an independent candidate for Governor, relying in his campaign speech "upon the Constitution and the Union. In politics I am an old fogy, because I cling devotedly to those primitive principles upon which our government was founded."

It was a bitter campaign. But, strangely enough, the appeal of the issues he raised, his personal following among his old comrades and a surge of sentimental feeling toward him all combined to help elect Houston Governor, in the first setback for Southern extremists in a decade.

The wounds of his election were not easily healed, however; and as sentiment grew overwhelmingly in favor of secession during the heated Presidential campaign of 1860, Governor Houston could only implore his impatient constituents to wait and see what Lincoln's attitude would be, if he was elected. But angry sentiment was in the air, and violence. Houston's speech in Waco denouncing the secession was answered by the explosion of a keg of powder behind the hotel in which he slept.

When Lincoln was elected President, the Lone Star flag was immediately hoisted throughout Texas. Governor Houston was shoved aside as a secession convention was called. The convention leaders could not be stopped, but their headlong rush into secession was momentarily disturbed by the surprise appearance of the Governor they hated but feared. On the day the ordinance of secession was to be adopted, Sam Houston sat on the platform, grimly silent, his presence renewing the courage of those few friends of the Union who remained in the hall. "To those who tell of his wonderful charge up the hill at San Jacinto," said the historian Wharton, "I say it took a thousand times more courage when he stalked into the secession convention at Austin and alone defied and awed them."

The ordinance was adopted and submitted to the people for their approval at the polls. Immediately Houston took the stump in a one-man campaign to keep Texas in the Union. Ugly crowds, stones and denunciation as a traitor met him as in characteristic fashion he confounded his enemies with powerful sarcasm. At Belton, an armed thug suddenly arose and started toward him. Houston, looking him in the eye, put his hands on his own pistols: "Ladies and gentlemen, keep your seats. It is nothing but a fice [mongrel] barking at the lion in his den."

Now 68 years old, but still an impressively straight figure with massive white hair, Old Sam closed his tour in Galveston before a jeering mob. "Some of you laugh to scorn the idea of bloodshed as the result of secession," he cried, "but let me tell you what is coming. You may, after the sacrifice of countless millions of treasure and hundreds of thousands of precious lives, as a bare possibility, win Southern independence, if God be not against you. But I doubt it. The North is determined to preserve this Union."

His prophecy was unheeded. On March 2, the anniversary of Houston's birthday, the special convention reassembled at Austin. By a thumping vote it declared Texas a part of the Southern Confederacy, and decreed that all state officers take the new oath of allegiance on March 14. On that day, as an eyewitness described it, the convention hall was "crowded . . . electrified with fiery radiations, of men burning with the anticipation of revengeful battle." At the appointed hour, the convention clerk was instructed to call the roll of state officials. Silence settled over the audience, and every eye peered anxiously for a glimpse of the old hero.

"Sam Houston!" There was no response. "Sam Houston! Sam Houston!" The contemptuous voices began again. The office of Governor of Texas, Confederate States of America, was declared to be officially vacant, and Lieutenant Governor Edward Clarke stepped up to take the oath. As the convention stripped him of office, the hero of San Jacinto was in another part of the capitol scrawling out, with a broken heart, his last message as Governor:

> Fellow Citizens, in the name of your rights and liberty, I refuse to take this oath. But I love Texas too well to bring civil strife and bloodshed upon her. I shall make no endeavor to maintain my authority as Chief Executive. . . . I am stricken down because I will not yield those principles which I have fought for. The severest pang is that the blow comes in the name of the state of Texas.

Years before, rebuked by a Dixie paper for a Senate vote, Sam Houston had replied: "I know neither North nor South; I know only the Union." Now, at the end, this indomitable and fiercely ambitious Southerner cast aside a lifetime of political fortune, fame and devotion from his people, steadfastly sacrificing for principle all he had ever won or wanted.

When Sam Houston was running for Governor of Texas, he stopped at an old farmer's house for the night. After talking with the farmer and getting his promise of support, he was shown to his room by a long, lanky boy. Houston sized the boy up and thought he saw in him another prospective supporter, so he said, "Young man, you look old enough to vote; how old are you?"

The youth replied, "I was 21 las' gone April, but I didn't bow my head when dad ast the blessin', so he sot me back two years, he did, an' I can't vote." —*R. P. Littlejohn*

HE KNEW THE WORLD WAS ROUND

By George Kent

Based on Admiral of the Ocean Sea *by Samuel Eliot Morison*

In 1939–40 Dr. Samuel Eliot Morison, Harvard professor of history, headed an expedition which retraced Columbus' voyages in two small sailing vessels of approximately the same size as those used by the discoverer. His Admiral of the Ocean Sea *is a biography of the complex, fascinating man who inspired this scientific adventure. It won the Pulitzer Prize.*

CHRISTOPHER COLUMBUS was a tall, good-looking, hawk-nosed wool carder, map maker, book salesman, sugar buyer and sailor. He had high cheekbones, a long face, blue eyes, freckles and red hair, and a nice smile—but no sense of humor. He was a good talker who bragged, a decent man who was also frequently a rogue. His discovery of America was the most important single feat of courage in history.

Some of the things we take for granted about Columbus are false—for example, the myth that he alone believed the earth was round. Everybody of intelligence believed it! The schools and universities taught it. There was even a globe, not too different from those you see today, to be had for a price. Furthermore, contrary to the pictures painted of him in his day, Columbus never shot the sun with an astrolabe. He sailed by dead reckoning, and was good enough at it to hit a harbor on the nose.

Columbus' sail to the west was a great gamble, but it was not taken entirely in the dark. European ports were full of stories of men who had made either all or part of such a voyage. The Queen of Sheba reportedly had gone west, past Spain, and out into the sea as far as Japan. Seven Portuguese bishops, it was rumored, had fled persecution to an island which they called Antilla. And, of course, Leif Ericson had led Norsemen to a safe landing in what is now New England.

There was also a map, drawn by an Italian doctor and astronomer named Toscanelli, which was considered a sound and reliable job and which showed Japan to be about where America really is. Curious tree trunks, and also sea grapes, that could not have grown in Africa were picked up at sea. Such evidence made it pretty clear that there was land out yonder for a brave sailor to come and get. But nobody did much about it of which a record has been kept—nobody, that is, until Columbus had his idea.

Christopher Columbus was born in Genoa in 1451, eldest son of an easygoing weaver and tavern keeper. Of what he did between birth and the age of 25, little is known beyond the fact that he carded wool, sat at a loom and went to sea. Since Genoa was a great seafaring city-state, its harbor crowded with ships, a bright young man had an obvious opportunity to learn the arts of sailing and chart making.

There are records of a number of Columbus' cruises, including one to Iceland, but his luckiest voyage was that which beached him in Portugal. He was a sailor on a ship which a French task force attacked and sank. Although wounded, Columbus jumped overboard and swam ashore at Lagos, later ending up in Lisbon. It was the year 1476. Lisbon was a good place for a man with a dream of seafaring adventure, for it was the port where the wildest proposals for exploration received backing. It was also a place to learn mathematics and astronomy, shipbuilding and rigging—the knowledge a master mariner needed. Columbus and his brother Bartholomew set up a map-making shop and did well. Columbus married the daughter of a wealthy family, and she was all for his settling down to become a solid, stay-at-home member of the community.

But Columbus clung to his idea—the challenging, gnawing notion that he could reach the Orient by sailing west. It worried him and wouldn't let him rest. That was the difference between Columbus and most of his contemporaries. He was convinced. He knew. He wanted to go. But he was forced to wait a long time before anyone would give him the ships. Meanwhile he talked of his idea to anyone who would listen.

John II, King of Portugal, was interested and referred Columbus' idea to his committee of experts; they turned it down. But the King kept Columbus on the string until Bartolomeu Dias, a Portuguese, sailed around the Cape of Good Hope and so opened the eastern way to the treasure places of the Orient. Thereafter, John II was no longer interested in the western route.

When Columbus' wife died, he spent most of his savings giving her a noble funeral, and then went to Spain. King Ferdinand and Queen Isabella were fighting a costly war with the Moors. They therefore listened to Columbus' proposal with only half an ear. However, the Queen liked Columbus immediately and put him on a pension—as a sort of deposit—while her own committee of experts went into the matter.

The pension wasn't much, but it kept Columbus from falling apart, until after a year or two it was cut off. For three and a half years he eked out a living by selling books and drawing maps, waiting for Spain's war with the Moors to end. His red hair turned silver and he got arthritis; his cape and his shoes became so full of holes that he couldn't go out on rainy days. But he kept on waiting and talking, talking always of his dream.

In 1491, finally discouraged with Spain, he decided to try his luck in France. On the way he stopped at a monastery near the seaport of Palos de la Frontera, and got talking with his old friend the prior, who—always impressed with Columbus' story—arranged another audience with the Queen. Although Isabella's experts had previously disapproved of Columbus' proposal, the

Queen heard him out and said she liked the idea. She did think, however, that his price for the discovery was a little high: Columbus required the Queen to make him Admiral of the Ocean Sea and viceroy of all the lands he discovered, and to give him ten percent of all trade during his Admiralty. When Isabella balked at the terms, he said thanks for listening, got on his mule and started again for France. After six years of waiting, he was in no mood for haggling.

Meanwhile, Luis de Santangel, keeper of the privy purse, said to Isabella, in effect: "Any money you lack, I'll supply personally. What can you lose? And think what you might gain—thousands of converts, glory for Spain and gold." The Queen forthwith sent messengers out to bring Columbus back.

Columbus' first voyage cost Isabella and Santangel about $12,000, and Columbus borrowed his share of the money, about $2000. Compared with the total cost of this great voyage which gave Spain two continents, the price of $24 paid by the Dutch for Manhattan Island seems exorbitant. Columbus' three ships—*Pinta*, *Niña* and *Santa María*—were stout little vessels which in good weather averaged six to seven knots and could be rowed by means of long sweeps when the wind died. Each contained a cabin for the master, but the crew slept on deck. Once a day a fire was lighted in an open firebox amidships, and a hot meal, smelling heavily of garlic, was cooked for the two watches. Time was kept by means of half-hour glasses which were turned regularly by deck boys.

In the three ships were probably 87 men, including three doctors, a chief steward, an interpreter and a man sent by the Queen to keep track of gold and precious stones taken on board. Music was provided mostly by the deck boys, who sang little songs every time they turned the glasses or served a meal. At night the crew got together and sang a hymn, usually "Salve Regina." Contrary to most stories, they were not convicts, although three had had a brush with the law by helping a murderer escape from prison. Most of them were nice hometown boys who had learned the art of sailing by going to sea whenever the opportunity offered.

Columbus' expertness in navigation has aroused the admiration of all who came after him. The Portuguese, in their attempts to find a waterway to the Orient, had started far to the north, and so had got caught in the brawling westerlies. But Columbus started well to the south and thus caught the good east winds which pushed him straight across the ocean. It took him exactly 33 days to make a landfall. When he struck the seaweed-choked Sargasso Sea, his fellow captains besought him to turn aside to look for islands. But Columbus refused to listen, and kept riding westward. He did turn southwest once, but only to follow a flight of birds which he judged correctly were heading for land. Had he not made this switch he might have made a landing somewhere in the Florida Keys.

When the crew, which never before had been out of sight of land for so long a period, became rebellious, Columbus called them together on October 10 and said, "If we don't hit land in three days, I'll turn back." What made him so sure was the flight of birds and the sight of berry branches in the water.

On October 12 they landed on San Salvador (now Watlings Island in the Bahamas), which Columbus called by that name. There he knelt and thanked God and with great formality took possession in the name of the Catholic monarchs, Ferdinand and Isabella. The ceremony was watched attentively by the natives, who were naked and simple and friendly.

"They are so ingenuous and free with all they have," wrote Columbus, "that no one would believe it who has not seen it; of anything that they possess they never say nay; on the contrary they invited you to share it and show as much love as if their hearts went with it, and they are content with whatever trifle be given them." These people have been identified as the Tainos, a race which has long since disappeared. Columbus later told Her Majesty he thought they would make good slaves because they were gentle and intelligent.

Of the first days on shore, Dr. Morison writes, in his biography of Columbus:

So ended 48 hours of the most wonderful experience that perhaps any seamen have ever had. Other discoveries have been more spectacular than that of this small flat sandy island. But it was there that the ocean for the first time "loosed the chains of things" as Seneca had prophesied, gave up the secret that had baffled Europeans since they began to inquire what lay beyond the western horizon's rim. San Salvador, rising from the sea at the end of a 33-day westward sail, was a clean break with past experience. Every tree, every plant that the Spaniards saw was strange to them, and the natives were not only strange but completely unexpected, speaking an unknown tongue and resembling no race of which even the most educated explorers had read in the tales of travelers from Herodotus to Marco Polo. Never again may mortal man hope to recapture the amazement, the wonder of those October days in 1492.

From San Salvador, Columbus sailed south, discovering other islands, including Cuba, where men smoked cigars by placing one end in a nostril and inhaling deeply. He finally landed in Hispaniola—the island on which Haiti and the Dominican Republic are now situated. Here he ran the *Santa María* aground so badly that she could not be floated again. The Indians seemed friendly, so Columbus decided to leave about 40 men in a place he called La Navidad, on the island's north coast. It was the last he saw of them, and the presumption is that all 40 were murdered by the natives, whom they had treated very badly. Columbus headed north, caught the westerlies and at length arrived back in Spain.

The discoverer's account of his journey created a sensation. His parade through the streets of Spanish cities, with his souvenirs of gold, parrots, and Indians he had shanghaied in the New World, was the highest moment of his career. But when he knelt before King Ferdinand and Queen Isabella and they bade him sit beside them, his cup ran over. All that they had contracted to give him, they gave, and insisted that he get ready to start again, this time with priests and soldiers and artisans, to consolidate and extend his discoveries. Columbus' second voyage, in 1493, was his undoing in a way, because it revealed the serious mistake he had made in leaving the 40 men behind. It also made clear that he could not cope with insubordination, that he was alternately too gentle and too brutal with his men.

On his third voyage, five years later, he sighted South America for the first time. In Hispaniola, in 1500, a judge who was sent out from Spain found Columbus guilty of several crimes, including severity and injustice, and returned him to Spain in irons. The Queen, outraged on hearing of it, speedily freed him. However, when Columbus demanded the one-tenth share he had been promised, Their Catholic Majesties proved stubborn. The western realm of Spain was yielding ever greater wealth, and to give him the amount agreed upon would have made him unbelievably rich.

Finally, in 1502, he was given four ships, and his fourth and final voyage began. On this one he steered along the coast of Central America, but because of his preoccupation with finding a passage to the Pacific, he missed two things—the pearl fisheries off the Honduran shore and one of the world's richest gold mines. Moreover, his men mutinied and came within a hair of killing him. Bedridden with arthritis, with his ships rotted, he was forced to wait at Jamaica for a rescue party.

Meanwhile his good friend Isabella had died and Ferdinand ignored his requests for funds to pay off his crew. Still racked with arthritis, he went to see the King. Ferdinand offered him a dukedom in place of his title and privileges as Admiral of the Ocean Sea. Columbus refused. He believed he had touched the East Indies. To the end he thought the palace of the Great Khan of Cathay (China) was somewhere in Costa Rica. He wanted not wealth alone, but to find the passage that would lead him to the places Marco Polo mentioned—where there were all the delights, comforts and luxuries of civilization.

This, in brief, is the story of the man who gave Spain control of more territory than its rulers had ever imagined, and whose discovery turned the eyes of Europe westward. Columbus died unmourned in his 55th year. But his heroic figure looms ever grander through the successive centuries.

OUR UNKNOWN
EX-PRESIDENT

Condensed from the book

By Eugene Lyons

JUST BEFORE America entered World War II, the personal stock of ex-President Herbert Hoover was at an all-time low. With war fever mounting, he was staunchly noninterventionist. With the Roosevelt administration reaping credit for war-boom prosperity, he continued to battle the New Deal philosophy. Worst of all, in defiance of official opinion, he demanded that we feed starving children in France, Greece and other Hitler-held countries. He seemed on the "wrong" side of every issue, the center of the bitterest prejudices of the moment.

Yet, in 1947, the 15th year after he went directly from the White House to the doghouse, Herbert Hoover at 74 again enjoyed immense popular esteem and an influence in public affairs second to no other private citizen. Not since his first year as President had his views weighed so heavily. His "fan mail," which averaged a dozen or so letters a day from 1933 to 1946, now ran between 500 and 1000 a day—an almost mathematical measure of his renewed popularity.

The tone of the press had suddenly turned deferential. Even those who disliked Hoover's conservative ideas were impressed by his moral stature. In asserting that he was wrong they no longer implied that he was wicked. Except in the Communist propaganda, slander had given way to respectful disagreement.

The spiral of the ex-President's new popularity was touched off when President Harry S. Truman asked him to make a world survey of food stocks and relief measures in the spring of 1946. Accompanied by his own experts, Hoover girdled the globe and then, without a breathing spell, made a swing through Latin America. The gallantry of such an undertaking by an aging man somehow bridged three decades. It helped restore Hoover to his role as the most effective instrument of America's idealistic conscience and charitable impulses—in *Newsweek's* phrase, "the symbol of hope and sympathy" for a distressed world.

Anyone who attains the Presidency of the United States might reasonably be presumed to possess great political talents. Yet the one thing on which Hoover's friends and enemies seem to agree is that he was "no politician." There is no implication that he was deficient in grasp of political trends. Where he fell short was in dexterity—in maneuvering people, playing on crowd emotions, selling himself to the masses. He had no gift at all for that back-slapping, glad-handing, first-name familiarity one expects from the politician.

Few occupants of the White House curtained their private lives from public scrutiny as stubbornly as the Hoovers. Mrs. Hoover, who died in 1944, was a gracious, handsome, highly intelligent woman. The Hoover sons, Herbert, Jr., and Allan, are attractive, capable men who have become independently successful. The Hoover grandchildren who swarmed over the President were as cute as any youngsters born to the White House. Yet the private life of President Franklin D. Roosevelt's dog, a Scottie named Fala, received more press, screen and radio attention than the private lives of the whole Hoover clan combined.

Herbert, Jr., was attending Harvard Business School while his father was President. One summer he decided to get himself a job. He did, with the Baltimore Electric Company—under the assumed name of Watson. The secret leaked out, as secrets will, but the incident is typical of the family's attitude. When Herbert, Jr., was offered a post obviously too big for him, he turned it down indignantly. "My father's name is not for sale," he explained to a friend in describing the offer.

Men rarely outgrow their childhoods. Herbert Hoover's deepest faults and steepest virtues alike are related to his Quaker background. He was born on August 10, 1874, in a one-story cottage not far from his father's blacksmith shop in the Friends' settlement of West Branch, Iowa. Among the birthplaces of Presidents, only Lincoln's log cabin was a shade more humble. The Hoovers dressed in Quaker gray, used the plain speech filled with "thees" and "thys." Their days and years centered around the meetinghouse. To them life was real and earnest, and "doing good" its main purpose. In the Quaker view, man is born good, though the world may corrupt him.

Herbert Clark was only six when his father died; but before his mother passed away he was nearly nine, so that her sweetness and humility remained with him forever. In the three years of her widowhood Huldah Hoover supported her three children by taking in sewing, but her real vocation was preaching. Quakers throughout Iowa came to know her soft, unstudied eloquence. When he was a little over ten, the orphaned Hoover went to Oregon to live with an uncle, Dr. Henry John Minthorn, and spent six years among the pioneers of the Northwest. It was there that a visiting mining engineer fired the boy's interest in geology and gave the decisive bent to his life.

In the summer of 1891 he entered the newly opened Stanford University at Palo Alto, California, a member of its very first class. He paid his way by working as secretary to a professor, as agent of a laundry service, at other chores. He became a campus leader and made friendships that endure to this day. Above all, it was there that he met Lou Henry, the tall, good-looking, studious girl who was to share his life.

His first job after graduation was as a common laborer in a mine in Nevada City, at $2.00 a day. The experience stood him in good stead in judging mines and miners. Over in San Francisco a leading engineer, Louis Janin, reigned in the profession. Hoover went to him "cold." There was no job but he got one anyhow, for Janin was a connoisseur of ability. One year later Janin was asked by a London firm to recommend a director for its properties in Western Australia, where a gold rush was under way. The request was explicit: an engineer with "the strength of a man of 25 and the experience of a man of 75." The 23-year-old Hoover could scarcely believe his employer had picked him. But he signed up, at $7500 a year, and was off on an adventure that put him among the most celebrated and successful practical mining engineers of his generation.

Marriage waited another two years, until Lou Henry had gotten her engineering degree. A long trek of exploration in the heart of China was their honeymoon. Together they weathered a thousand trials and dangers, including the siege of Tientsin in the Boxer riots. The hundreds of Chinese and foreign lives they saved at the risk of their own made a saga of courage among old China hands. Hoover was in simple truth the Great Engineer. He climbed rapidly in his profession until his enterprises stretched around the globe. Meanwhile the seed planted by his mother flourished in his heart. He looked on his amazing success as only a prelude to the vocation of service. When the time was ripe, he stepped into it like one returning home.

When World War I broke out in 1914, some 200,000 Americans—tourists and permanent residents—were stranded in Europe. The banks ceased to honor American checks. Ships were scarce. Frontiers were closed. It was a tangled situation touched by panic. Then Ambassador Walter Hines Page in London asked Hoover to take hold of the whole mess.

This Hoover did quietly, without ballyhoo, and so expertly that only a few realized they were witnessing a miracle of efficiency. Somehow he found the staff, the transportation. Together with ten others whom he drew into the gamble, he induced an American bank in London to cash any kind of paper for stranded Americans—on the personal pledge of himself and his associates to make good the losses. Before the exodus was completed, $1,500,000 had been cashed. And his faith was vindicated: only $400 was lost in the gigantic transaction.

Hoover was winding up his European enterprises preparatory to going home when Ambassador Page invited him to organize relief for seven million Belgians facing almost certain starvation. It was not an easy decision. Though well-off, he was far from the goal he had set for himself as the measure of independence. With his associates he controlled a substantial part of the world's lead and zinc. At the start of a mechanized world war, these metals were suddenly worth their weight in gold.

There was never any doubt that he would answer the challenge of human misery. The real question was whether to retain business interests or to renounce private ambitions entirely. For three days he wrestled with the decision. Quaker-fashion, he and Mrs. Hoover prayed for guidance. On the fourth morning when he came down for breakfast, he seemed unusually serene. "Well, let fortune go to hell," Hoover remarked, as casually as if he were canceling a weekend vacation. His decision was destined to affect the lives of hundreds of millions of human beings. From that moment the story of Hoover became the stuff of world history. Never had a great business career been so abruptly renounced and a greater career of social service launched. "You can take the business," he announced simply to his associates. He was through with mining and moneymaking.

Since then, Hoover has not kept a dollar in remuneration from any source for his own use. From the first hour of the Belgian job to the last of his missions, he has paid his expenses out of his own pocket. His salary as Secretary of Commerce and then as President he distributed in full to raise the incomes of aides who needed it or to pay for expert personnel not provided by Congress. Money from writing or speaking went to private and public charities.

The Belgian relief effort was an entirely new kind of undertaking for Hoover, but it succeeded supremely under almost impossible conditions. Vast sums and mountains of goods were dispensed, at an overhead cost of seven eighths of one percent; normally charity projects are lucky if they keep overhead under 20 percent. It was the greatest relief undertaking in human history; greater ones came later, also under Hoover's management.

Hoover became Food Administrator for President Wilson during the war; "to hooverize" became a new verb in the dictionary. If it is true that food won that war, then he must rank with Pershing among the architects of victory. After the Armistice he became Director General of Relief and virtual economic dictator of all Europe; for three years he fed and clothed ten million children in Central and Eastern Europe. Then famine-stricken Soviet Russia absorbed his attention. All in all, in the decade 1914–1924, Hoover raised and distributed over five billion dollars—34 million tons of supplies—under war and chaotic postwar conditions. Every dollar, every pound was accounted for, without a single scandal, without taint of profiteering or waste.

The legend that he used food as a political weapon is dear to the hearts of Communists. But I have before me the resolution of the Council of People's Commissars, signed at the Kremlin on July 10, 1923. It thanks the Americans, and specifically Herbert Hoover, through "whose entirely unselfish efforts . . . millions of people of all ages were saved from death."

So far as he could do so without giving offense, Hoover evaded all honors. But grateful peoples in a dozen countries named streets and squares for him and raised statues to him. Messages of thanks signed by the great and the humble poured in on him—bearing a total of nearly four million signatures.

To friends of Hoover—there are hundreds of them, scholars, journalists, businessmen, diplomats—he was "the Chief" long before he became President. He never built a personal political machine; very few of his intimates are politicians. But they form a kind of loose fraternity. Because of their intense loyalty to Hoover, they are loyal to one another.

Herbert Hoover assumed the Presidency with an ambitious plan of social betterment in mind. The White House Conferences on Child Health and Protection, on Home Building and Housing, the President's Research Committee on Social Trends, his specific proposals for reform in every department of American life are indications of a program that was thwarted by events.

It was a tragic Presidency, and never so tragic as in its last four months, between the November election and the March inauguration of Roosevelt. To grasp the picture it must be recalled that the depression had been arrested and recovery started by the middle of 1932. "The change for the better in the last half of 1932 is beyond dispute," the Democratic New York *Times* wrote editorially on June 16, 1934. "That this evident revival of confidence was suddenly reversed in February 1933 is equally true." The new confidence was obliterated by the result of the election. Business was paralyzed; bank withdrawals skyrocketed; stock prices, which had risen from a low of 34 in July to 56 in September, tobogganed again. The panic which Hoover had warded off for three years was "around the corner."

The decline touched off by Hoover's defeat reached the panic point with the bank closings at the moment his successor took over. Whatever may be said about the preceding years, surely the final debacle had more to do with the incoming than the outgoing administration. But full blame for that, too, was loaded on Hoover by the busy mythmakers. Perhaps the most striking example of how Hoover was made the scapegoat of every new trouble is provided by the famous Bonus March made by dissatisfied World War I veterans in July 1932. In the folklore of our time it is firmly fixed that Hoover's federal "cossacks" shot down and killed veterans. That statement can still be found in Communist assaults on Hoover. But there is not a shadow of truth in it. Two veterans had been killed and several wounded in clashes between the local police force and rioters *before* U.S. troops came to the scene; it was that, in fact, which led to the calling of the troops. But—and I quote from a letter to me by General Patrick J. Hurley, then Secretary of War—"Not one single shot was fired nor was any person seriously injured after the arrival of United States troops. Law and order were restored in Washington."

Fate has been generous to our 31st President in allowing him to live long enough to see his own reinstatement in the public's good graces. Despite this, he remains the "unknown ex-President," so many facets of his personality are still hidden from the public. It is not generally known, for example, that Hoover's passion for research and knowledge is as deep as his passion for fishing, which is saying a good deal. His *Principles of Mining*, published in 1909, ranks high in the literature of that field. While working huge properties in China, he found time to write a paper on Chinese mathematics. For five years he and Mrs. Hoover worked on a translation of *De Re Metallica* by Agricola, dating back to 1556. Where generations of Latin scholars had failed to render this classic into English because of their lack of technical knowledge, the Hoovers succeeded.

The magnificent Hoover Library on War, Revolution, and Peace, pride of Stanford University, is also an expression of his liking for exact knowledge. In the midst of his vast labors during World War I, Hoover began to gather vital war documents which otherwise would have been lost to posterity. This collection he has kept up ever since. Priceless records of the Russian Revolution and civil wars—three carloads were transported with Lenin's help—are at Palo Alto, along with such invaluable finds as the archives of the Kaiser's General Staff, documentary materials on the underground resistance movements, valuable archive materials of the suppressed Baltic republics.

There are people who practice sin in secret—but Hoover has reversed the process. He is one of the rare few who practice virtue in secret. He goes to extraordinary lengths to hide his benevolences, especially from those who benefit through them. He will wangle a job, a loan or some other help for distressed individuals. Only years later, if ever, do they discover who was behind it.

The hallmark of Hoover's personality, however, is his limitless concern for children. Every one of his associates sooner or later remarked on this. Two of them confided that they had seen the Chief weeping. The incidents were more than 20 years apart, but they both involved Hoover's extreme sensibility to the sufferings of children.

The first incident was after the First World War, when a campaign for child famine relief was under way. Some 30 urchins called on Hoover, each clutching pennies in hot, not overly clean palms: their contribution to the fund. Hoover began to talk to them, but suddenly tears came to his eyes and he walked away to hide them. The second incident was in his New York suite, during the Second World War. My informant was present when a visitor was describing in detail the ordeal of little children in Nazified countries. Hoover suddenly walked to the window and turned his back on the room. The others looked away in embarrassment when his shoulders began to shake with sobbing.

There has been incomparably more work than play in Hoover's life, from childhood up. His favorite recreations have been of the meditative brand, particularly fishing and camping with a few loved friends. His capacity for work and his bodily stamina are legendary. During critical periods in the White House, most of his staff literally collapsed under the Hoover regimen—a typical day began at six a.m. and did not wind up until close to midnight.

In a letter home by Frank E. Mason, one of Hoover's companions on the 1946 world jaunt, I found this passage: "Several members of the crew were indisposed and even our medico, Dr. Rey, spent the day in bed. Through it all, the Chief goes imperturbably on, writing his talks with a pencil, and handing them over to Hugo Meier to be copied. He has stood up under the terrific pace in a miraculous manner."

Hoover's memory is close to phenomenal. He is an omnivorous reader—everything from economic and sociological works to mysteries. He can devour a large volume in one sitting and retain what he has read well enough to pass a test on it. In Shanghai during the 1946 visit, top American military officers spread out maps on the floor and explained the complex Chinese military picture. Drawing on his experience of nearly half a century before,

Hoover was able to contribute exhaustive details about local topography in out-of-the-way regions. The officers were awe-struck by that feat of memory.

Most revealing of his personality, however, are the stories his intimates tell that express his inborn humility, his flight from the limelight. One of his keenest annoyances as President was the constant presence of guards, reporters and cameramen when he went to Quaker meeting. One Sunday he escaped surveillance.

At breakfast Mrs. Hoover announced to their guests, Mr. and Mrs. Rickard, that she had heard of a tiny meetinghouse some-where near Baltimore. Like conspirators the Hoovers and the Rickards stole out of the White House and drove to this little prayer room. There were only a dozen or so worshipers. No one paid any attention to the new arrivals, as is the Quaker way. After long silent meditation, the Washington group headed for home. The President confided that it was one of his truly happy days.

Herbert Hoover's life has been long and variegated beyond most human experiences. It has run the gamut from Lincolnesque poverty to riches, from common manual labor to the Presidency, from global business to global benevolence. But in the variety there is a discernible pattern. Strands from one period continually show up in the design of other periods.

When he was visiting Oslo in 1938, a farmer journeyed a long distance especially to see him. The Norwegian brought with him a boy's jacket. He had kept the child's garment for nearly 20 years, he explained to the American visitor, as a memento of Hoover re-lief, and had come to thank him personally.

Hoover's arrival in Brussels in 1946 brought cheering thou-sands into the streets, among them many who owed their survival 30-odd years before to his work. In Belgrade, a member of Tito's cabinet, Foreign Minister Simich, declared at a public reception, "If it were not for Hoover relief in Serbia 30 years ago, I wouldn't be here tonight."

In Warsaw a woman physician in the course of a conference blurted out that she owed her life to Hoover: she had been one of the millions of East European children fed by his organization. Then she turned to the Communist officials at the conference table. "Own up," she said, "that but for Mr. Hoover's food you, too, wouldn't be here." They solemnly acknowledged the fact.

Some weeks later, in Shanghai, two socially prominent Chinese women asked separately to pay their respects to the former American President. Amazingly, each told the same story: she had been taken in by the Hoovers during the Boxer riots in 1900 when the lives of less fortunate children were being snuffed out.

Even at 70 years, the thought of retirement never entered Hoover's mind. Continuing public service, works of benevolence, historical writings kept a battery of secretaries and researchers busy. The monumental two-year study of government operations by the first Hoover Commission was completed in 1949. Some 70 percent of its recommendations, with a saving of an estimated two billion dollars a year, were adopted in the following years. In late 1953 Congress set up another such Commission and Hoover, though now pushing 80, again consented to head it. In 20 months of grueling labor, he organized and supervised some 20 task forces and himself wrote most of the reports—the most comprehensive analysis of the executive branch of government ever achieved.

During these twilight years the former President published three volumes of *Memoirs*, a four-volume history of American benevolence abroad beginning with the Belgian Relief, and other books, of which *The Ordeal of Woodrow Wilson* drew the largest popular readership. The Boys' Clubs of America, the Hoover Library in Palo Alto, fund-raising for medical education and other good causes absorbed much of his energies, yet he continued to speak and write extensively on public affairs. Not until Hoover passed 85 did age begin to take its toll of his robust constitution.

Yes, there is a pattern in the diversity of the Hoover career, and its distinctive design is mercy. Neither the ravages of time nor the malice of political propaganda has sufficed to blur it. The soft-voiced woman preacher of the Friends' settlement in West Branch, Iowa, though she died early, did not live in vain.

MAID OF ORLÉANS

By Louise Redfield Peattie

To MOST of us, Joan of Arc is a legend, the heroic idyll of a shepherdess who heard supernatural voices and by them was led to save a nation. But the idyll is only the shadow of the truth. There was nothing supernatural about Joan. She was a real girl, a peasant earthy as the sweet soil of France. Nor was that country yet a nation when she carried into battle her banner sown with its immortal lilies of France.

It is half a thousand years ago since Joan of Arc died in the flames at Rouen. Why, then, need we remember her today? Because hers is the age-old, terrible story of good warring with evil, a war which goes on in every century. Each of us who wages his part in this struggle will fight the better for knowing the Maid of Orléans. Joan died condemned a heretic and sinner. She lives forever a saint, conqueror of the forces of evil that killed her, a symbol of truth and courage.

When Joan was born in 1412, in the village of Domrémy in Lorraine, France was in fragments and bloody turmoil. The Hundred Years' War between France and England had been going on for some 75 years. The crown of France was claimed by England. Much of France was ruled by the Duke of Burgundy, ally of the English; the rest was loyal to the Dauphin Charles, heir to the throne of France but not yet crowned.

Of this turmoil Joan learned as a child, for past her rough dwelling ran the old Roman road that crossed the River Meuse, and down it would come bands of armed men marching, or wandering friars who lingered to tell tales of murder and pillage and to lament that the weak Dauphin would not prove himself King indeed and so make of the leaderless land a united nation.

By the age of 12, Joan was a sturdy, dark-haired and devout girl, of whom nothing remarkable had been reported. Then one day in her father's garden a great brightness spread all about her and a voice spoke to her. Terrified, she fell to her knees. With the voice came shining wings and a face of glory, and presently she knew that this was the Archangel Michael, patron of the Dauphin and beloved by all France. He was not alone, she was later to say, but "attended by heavenly angels. He told me that St. Catherine and St. Margaret would come to me, and that I must follow their counsel, for it was at our Lord's command."

For the next four or five years, the saints spoke to her often. Then, when she was 16, the archangel announced that it was God's will that she succor the Dauphin and raise the siege of Orléans. The voice "told me to go to Vaucouleurs, to Robert de Baudricourt, captain of the town, who would give me men to go with me." Revealing nothing to her parents, Joan went to Vaucouleurs, about ten miles from Domrémy. Twice she appeared before Baudricourt, telling him that she was divinely appointed to lead the Dauphin to Reims to be crowned King. Twice she was bluntly turned away. Undaunted, Joan came again. This time Sir Robert was convinced by her unearthly assurance. She was given a horse and the bodyguard she required; she was provided with the man's clothing she asked for; she had her hair cut short round her head. "Go forward boldly!" she heard her voices say.

Her hoofbeats clattered away from all that was familiar; she was riding now into destiny, by night, through enemy-haunted country. Halting before Chinon, where the Dauphin was, Joan sent word to the castle of her coming. The Dauphin Charles was a weak-willed, uncertain young fellow. He let her come but, to trick her, hid in modest clothes among the crowd. Into the magnificent hall lit by torches and packed with courtiers strode Joan and, going directly to the Dauphin, knelt at his feet. Charles pointed to a courtier. "That is the King," he said.

"In God's name, noble Prince, it is you and none other." And

she told him that she had been sent by God to help him and his kingdom and to see him anointed in the cathedral at Reims.

While all the court stared, Charles spoke privately to her at length, and whatever she answered made his face radiant. Yet still he wavered, fearing that she might be a tool of evil powers. He had her cross-questioned by learned clerics at Poitiers. The solemn conclusion was that there was nothing but good in this country girl. All this delay made Joan impatient. To the dawdling Charles she said with strange prevision, "I shall last a year and but a little longer; we must think to do good work in that year."

So Charles gathered an army. He gave Joan a suit of armor of polished steel. She sent word to a chapel dedicated to St. Catherine to look behind the altar and find a sword buried there. It was brought to her covered with rust but soon flashed in her hand. She had a white banner made, fringed with silk and sown with lilies, on it a painting of the Lord, an angel at each side, and the words *Jesus Maria*. So, banner in hand, she stood before the soldiery—"Daughter of God," as the Archangel Michael called her.

Orléans, a key point in the English campaign to open up the Loire River valley, for six months or more had lain under siege. The English had built a dozen bastions surrounding the town. The defenses of one such bastion consisted of a great stone wall some 30 feet high, set with strong towers. Reaching this bastion, Joan dictated a letter, had it tied to an arrow and shot over the wall.

"The King of Heaven sends you word and warning by me, Joan the Maid, to abandon your forts and depart into your own country, or I will raise such a war cry against you as shall be remembered forever."

Medieval warfare was a business of hand-to-hand combat with lance and sword, mace and battle-axe, and into such a melee it was that Joan rode to raise the siege. She and her companions stormed one redoubt successfully, and two days later attacked the key fortress. As she was about to climb a ladder against this redoubt, an arrow came whistling from a crossbow and struck her above the breast. She was carried from the field; with her own hands she pulled the arrow out. It was sunset; the trumpets were sounding retreat, but she rallied. Soon the soldiers saw her banner flash once more, heard her cry, "The day is yours—enter!" and beheld her dash toward the rampart and climb it. The bastion fell and Orléans was saved.

Joan passed through the streets to the sound of bells. She had her wound dressed and partook of food—five slices of bread dipped in wine and water. So ended the brief few days in which a girl of 17 re-created the morale of the French army and changed the course of the Hundred Years' War.

Charles, though obsessed with Joan's dream of his crowning, dillydallied. "Noble Dauphin," she implored, "hold no more so many and such long councils, but come as quickly as you can to Reims and take the crown." For she saw that only thus would the cause of a united France be established and England's claim be thwarted. The road to Reims led through towns strongly held by the foe, but Joan was dauntless. Her standard ever fluttered where the fighting was thickest. Throughout this Loire campaign, she bade the ranks: "Go bravely; all will go well." Yet in her courage there lurked a shadow, for she confided to a friend from her home village, "I fear nothing but treachery."

But all was triumph at the time. Reims excitedly made haste to receive the Dauphin. And on the fine summer morning of July 17, 1429, Charles rode to his crowning in splendid procession. Beside his throne in the cathedral stood Joan. It had been less than five months since she left Domrémy to obey her voices.

Charles VII, crowned at last, felt less need of Joan now. He would not heed her entreaties to march straight on to Paris, but listened to advisers jealous of the Maid. However, his laggard campaign at last got under way again, and Joan led the French forces in the capture of town after town. But an assault on a Paris fort failed and Joan was wounded in the thigh by an arrow.

In Easter week of 1430 Joan's voices gave her the bitter warning that she was to be taken prisoner by the enemy. Still she rode dauntlessly in the fore of the fray, until in a struggle at the drawbridge of Compiègne she was caught between the English and the Burgundians. Hands seized her horse, her person. Joan the Maid was captive. The man she had made King of France seems not to have dared lift a finger to help her. Instead, she was clapped into the castle of a Burgundian noble. There she learned of negotiations to sell her to the English, and in a frenzy to escape she flung herself from the lofty castle tower. She was not killed. Contrite, she prayed for forgiveness. Meanwhile, a trap was being set for her by letters to the Duke of Burgundy from the clerics of the pro-Burgundy University of Paris. It snapped fast upon her when a fat sum passed into the hand of her keeper, who thereupon released her to the Bishop of Beauvais.

This high dignitary, Pierre Cauchon, was in the pay of the English. He was a crafty and ambitious man, and Joan's trial for heresy promised to favor his interests—and those of the English, who wished to show clean hands in the business. So it was to be a religious, not a political, trial at Rouen, and Cauchon picked his ecclesiastical judges with skill. No one was appointed to defend Joan; not one witness was called in her behalf. Because of Cauchon's power, no man dared risk his life by speaking up for her.

So this illiterate peasant girl of 19 stands alone, abandoned, before the massed array of her learned and priestly judges, and speaks for herself. Every question, every answer was recorded; we hear her voice down the centuries. "You say that you are my judge; consider well what you do, for in truth I am sent from God, and you put yourself in great peril."

Under the inquisition, she related freely the story of her brief, strange career. She would admit to no heresy. Always she held that what she had done was by the Lord's will. They showed her the instruments of torture and she did not waver. "Truly, if you were to have me torn limb from limb, I would say nothing else." They threatened her with burning, and she answered, "Were I to see the fire, I would still say all that I have said." ("Superb response!" scribbled the recording clerk in the margin.)

Back and forth they hounded her, and not once was she shaken from the conviction that ruled her life. "I have a good master—that is, our Lord—to Whom I look, and to none other."

But Cauchon would not let her steadfast replies to the judges' questions decide her fate. Instead, he had her testimony reduced to 12 impersonal and distorted articles, and presented these as a basis for the judges' debate. And those eminent men of God, all subservient to the bishop, gave him the verdict he wanted.

So, on a fair day late in May, the wan young boyish figure in black was led forth, blinking at the bright sunlight, to hear sentence passed upon her. It was in the cemetery of the lovely church of St. Ouen amid a multitude of Rouen's citizens and jeering English soldiery. The patient prisoner was read a long sermon, and then exhorted to recant. Steadfastly she refused. Eyewitnesses became confused in their reports of just what happened next. Certainly a document was produced and read to the girl who "knew not A from B." Afterward they said to her, "Sign it, or you will burn." With a strange smile, she made her mark upon it. Now Joan thought she was safe. Trusting the Church she loved, she said, "You churchmen, take me to your prison, and let me be no longer in the hands of the English."

Bitter it must have been to be led back to the same dark cell and heavy chains. Upon promise that she would be allowed to hear Mass, she agreed to put on a woman's dress for it, for the matter of wearing a man's clothing was a grievous sin against her. But while she slept, her guards took the dress away. All morning she begged them for it, since she knew that to appear again in male attire would be considered a relapse into sin. But her pleas were in vain, and she was obliged to go from her cell in her boy's clothing.

On that "sin" they convicted her as a relapsed heretic, the most dire sentence that could be pronounced. Doubly to seal her fate, Cauchon queried if she had heard her voices again. Joan told him they had reproached her for signing whatever she had signed. "All that I then said and revoked, I said from fear of the fire." ("Fatal answer!" noted the clerk on his margin.)

Yet still her courage held. "By God's grace, I shall be in Paradise tonight," she said, and asked for communion. Strangely, this last request Cauchon granted. Did the bishop know his victim to be innocent? She, at least, knew his guilt. "Bishop, I die through you!" she flung at him.

Robed, her head shaven, she was led into Rouen's market square on the morning of May 30, 1431. Crowds covered every cobblestone and rooftop. After Cauchon read the sentence, a paper miter was placed on her head; inscribed in large letters were the words: *Heretic, Relapsed Sinner, Apostate, Idolator*. She begged for a cross; an English archer made one of twigs, which she put in her bosom. Another man ran to the nearby church for a crucifix.

This she kissed, then climbed to the high stake, her eyes fixed on the crucifix held before her. The flames, mounting, concealed her; only her voice came to the silent crowd, in prayer, in moans, in a final piercing cry of agony and love: "Jesus!" They say an Englishman ran through the crowd crying, "We are lost! We have burned a saint!"

Some 25 years after her martyrdom, Charles VII took steps to rehabilitate through the Church her reputation that it had destroyed. With due ceremony, the Church to which Joan was ever faithful and which had condemned her, proclaimed her innocent. Finally, in 1920, at St. Peter's in Rome, it canonized her. But there were those, 500 years earlier, who had known that there moved among them a living saint. And that completes the miracle.

There came into Sam Clemens' early life one of those seemingly trivial incidents which, viewed in retrospect, assume pivotal proportions. He was on his way home from the printing office when he saw flying along the pavement a leaf from a book. He caught it and examined it. It was a leaf from some history of Joan of Arc.

He had never heard of the subject before. He had never read any history. Now, however, there rose in him a deep compassion for the gentle Maid of Orléans. It was an interest that would grow steadily and culminate at last in the *Personal Recollections of Joan of Arc*, the loveliest story ever told of the martyred girl. From the moment when that fluttering leaf was blown into his hands, his career as one of the world's mentally elect was assured.   —*Albert Bigelow Paine*

HE'D RATHER
BE RIGHT

Condensed from Profiles in Courage

By John F. Kennedy

A s OUR story begins in 1803, Washington was no more than a raw country village. In the unfinished Capitol sat the Senate of the United States, already vastly different from the body originally planned by the makers of the Constitution in 1787. The founding fathers could not have foreseen service in the Senate as providing an opportunity for "political courage," whereby men would endanger their careers by resisting the will of the voters. For their idea of the Senate, in contrast to the House, was of a body which, like the British House of Lords, would not be subject to constituent pressures. Local matters, said Alexander Hamilton, were to be forgotten on the Senate floor; there were to be no questions as to "how will such a measure affect my constituents and . . . my reelection."

But, as it must to all lawmaking bodies, politics came to the U.S. Senate. Before long the local prejudices intensified, particularly as the Federalists of New England and the Jeffersonians of Virginia split along local as well as party lines. It was a time of change—in the Senate, in the concept of our government, in the growth of the two-party system. Men who were flexible, men who could move with the changing currents of public opinion—these were the men for such times. But young John Quincy Adams of Massachusetts was not such a man.

Few if any Americans have been born with the advantages of

John Quincy Adams: a famous name; a brilliant father who labored unceasingly to develop his son's natural talents; and an extraordinary mother. Indeed, he was born with everything to make for a happy and successful life, except those qualities that bring peace of mind. In spite of a life of extraordinary achievement, he was bothered constantly by a sense of inadequacy. He held more important offices and took part in more important events than anyone else in the history of our nation. He figured, in one capacity or another, in the American Revolution, the War of 1812 and the prelude to the Civil War. Yet at age 70, having distinguished himself as a brilliant Secretary of State, an independent President and an eloquent member of Congress, he was to record somberly, "I can scarcely recollect a single instance of success in anything that I ever undertook."

As a child in a tightly knit Puritan family, John Quincy had been taught by his mother to try to live up to his famous father, the last Federalist President of the United States; and as a Senator, when colleagues and friends deserted him on every side, it was to his father that he turned for support. Throughout his career, his guiding star was the principle of Puritan statesmanship the elder Adams had laid down many years before: "The magistrate is the servant not of his own desires, not even of the people, but of his God." It was therefore natural that John Quincy, returning to Boston after diplomatic service abroad upon his father's defeat for President by Thomas Jefferson in 1800, should become active in the affairs of his father's party. He admired the Federalists as the founders of the Constitution, the champions of naval power and a barrier against French Revolutionary influences.

Elected to the Senate in 1803, he promptly aroused a storm by becoming the only Federalist to support Jefferson's treaty for the purchase of the Louisiana Territory. With a vision of an America stretched to its continental limits, he regarded Jefferson's remarkable feat as far more important than the outraged astonishment of his Federalist colleagues. Concerned with maintaining the leadership of New England, they feared westward expansion would diminish the political and economic influence of the commercial Northeast, lower the value of eastern lands in which they were financially interested and provide the Jeffersonians with a permanent majority in Congress.

"Curse on the stripling, how he apes his sire!" wrote Theodore Lyman, a prominent Federalist. But there was only one Federalist whose opinion young John Quincy valued above his own—John Adams. Anxiously he sought his father's views; and the reassurances he received made up for all the abuse from the party. "I do not disapprove of your conduct," John Adams wrote his son, "though I know it will be very unpopular in the northern states. . . . I think you have been right!"

Despite the bitter opposition which the younger Adams aroused, however, it was not until 1807 that the split between party and Senator could no longer be repaired. The final break concerned this nation's foreign policy. As our relations with Great Britain worsened, our ships were seized, our cargoes taken and thousands of our seamen forced into the King's navy. With undisguised contempt for the Federalist merchants who advocated pacifying Great Britain, Adams in 1806 had introduced a series of resolutions condemning British aggression and requesting the President to demand restoration of the seized vessels. The Federalists had solidly opposed his measures, as they did an Adams-supported bill limiting British imports.

Finally, in the summer of 1807, the American frigate *Chesapeake* was fired upon by the British man-of-war *Leopard*. Several of the American crew were injured or captured; a few were killed. The incensed Adams was convinced that, party or no party, the time for forceful action had come. When Jefferson called upon Congress to strike back by enacting an embargo shutting off all further international trade—a measure apparently ruinous to Massachusetts, the leading commercial state in the nation—it was John Quincy Adams who rose on the Senate floor in support of the President's message, and who presented both the Embargo Bill and a bill of his own, barring British vessels from American waters. "This measure will cost you and me our seats," Adams remarked to a colleague as they completed their work.

His words were prophetic. As the Embargo Bill, with his help, became law, a storm of protest arose in Massachusetts. The embargo completely idled the shipbuilding industry, destroyed the shipping trade and tied up the fishing vessels; stagnation, bankruptcy and migration from the territory became common. The Federalist leaders insisted the embargo was an attempt by Jefferson to ruin New England prosperity and to provoke England to war. Talk of New England seceding was in the air. But, however great their hatred for Jefferson and his embargo, Massachusetts citizens were even more bitter over the "desertion" of their Senator to the ranks of the enemy. "A party scavenger!" snorted the Northampton *Hampshire Gazette*. Adams' own social circles in Boston—the rich, the cultivated and the influential—all turned against him. "He walks into State Street at the usual hour," wrote a leading Federalist, "but seems totally unknown."

John Quincy Adams was alone—but not quite. For when the unmerciful abuse from his home state was heaped upon him, John Quincy again turned to his father and poured out his feelings. His father replied, "My advice to you is steadily to pursue the course you are in, because I think it the path of justice." Once again the Adamses stood together, in a fight where John Quincy sided with the President who had defeated his father!

The Massachusetts legislature convened at the end of May 1808 with, as the Governor wrote Jefferson, but one "principal object—the destruction of John Quincy Adams." As soon as both houses had organized, the legislature immediately elected Adams' successor—nine months prior to the expiration of his term. (Until the passage of the 17th Amendment in 1913, U.S. Senators were elected by state legislatures.) And as its next order of business, the legislature passed resolutions instructing its Senators to urge repeal of the Embargo Act. Only one course was open to Adams— he resigned his Senate seat. "But," he wrote, "far from regretting any one of those acts for which I have suffered, I would do them over again, were they now to be done at the hazard of ten times as much slander."

Hated by the Federalists and suspected by the Jeffersonians, John Quincy Adams returned to private life. His star was soon to rise again; but he never forgot this incident or abandoned his courage of conscience. Soon after his retirement from the White House in 1829, Adams was asked by the voters of the Plymouth District to represent them in Congress. He agreed to run, but specified that if elected he would pursue a course in Congress completely independent of the party and people who supported him. On this basis Adams was elected by an overwhelming vote, and served in the House until his death, devoting himself to the struggle against slavery.

To be returned on this independent basis to the Congress from which he had departed in such disgrace 22 years earlier was a deeply moving experience for the courageous ex-Senator. "No election or appointment conferred upon me ever gave me so much pleasure," he recorded with pride in his diary. And none more triumphantly confirmed the ideal of public service he had set down in that same journal long before he had even entered the Senate: "I feel strong temptation to plunge into political controversy, but . . . a politician in this country must be the man of a party. I would fain be the man of my whole country."

One day when John Quincy Adams was 80 years of age a friend met him on the streets of Boston. "How is John Quincy Adams?" this friend asked gaily. The old man's eyes began to twinkle, and then he spoke slowly: "John Quincy Adams himself is very well, thank you. But the house he lives in is sadly dilapidated. It is tottering on its foundations. The walls are badly shattered, and the roof is worn. The building trembles with every wind, and I think John Quincy Adams will have to move out before very long. But he himself is very well." And with a wave of his hand the old man walked on.

—James G. Gilkey

EXPLORER
OF THE UNIVERSE

By Robert Strother

EARLY on Christmas Day in 1642 a premature and woefully weak baby boy was born in a stone farmhouse in Lincolnshire, England. The two midwives at the delivery sadly predicted that the tiny infant would not live through the day. And so the baby lived 84 years, and the "poor little weak head" that had to be supported by a special leather collar early in life proved to contain one of the finest scientific brains the world has ever known. Its owner, knighted and heaped with honors, made a fortune. His name was Isaac Newton.

There was nothing in the ancestry of this frail child to indicate genius. His father was a ne'er-do-well who died at the age of 37, a few weeks before Newton was born. His mother was undistinguished in any way from her farm neighbors in the village of Woolsthorpe. Geneticists in later years attempted in vain to trace Isaac Newton's ancestry beyond three generations and found no clue to his gifts.

These gifts were slow in appearing. As a schoolboy, Newton was often at or near the bottom of his class—until the day he licked a larger boy in a fistfight. This boy ranked higher scholastically than he, and Newton decided to complete his triumph by proving himself the superior student. Noting his increased studiousness, an uncle suggested that he be given a higher education, and obtained young Isaac's admission to Trinity College, Cambridge, at 18.

The Great Plague of 1665–66 broke out the year Newton graduated from Cambridge, and had a remarkable effect on his career. In one ghastly three-month period, one tenth of London's population died. Cambridge University was closed, and Newton, at 23, returned to Woolsthorpe to "meditate." These meditations during 18 months on his mother's farm laid the groundwork for all his subsequent achievements. As a boy Newton had been regarded as a "woolgatherer." The true character of this "absent-mindedness" became apparent during his enforced stay in the country. Plainly, the young man had an almost terrifying power of concentration, which he could bring to bear on the most complex problems for hours on end. And linked with this was another great gift—an intuitive sense for penetrating to the heart of a problem without lost motion.

From remotest times, wise men had believed that the sun, stars and planets possessed special heavenly qualities quite unlike anything on earth. To suppose otherwise was unthinkable—until Newton came along. It may have been, as Voltaire later declared, that the sight of a falling apple caused Newton to ask himself if the force that drew the apple to the earth might not also be the force that kept the moon in her orbit. This idea seemed to Newton more likely than the accepted theory of Descartes that the moon and planets were carried around their orbits by "vortexes" in an unseen, unfelt and unprovable substance called "ether." He went to work on the problem and, although his results were not published until 20 years later, he had worked out the laws of both motion and universal gravitation by the time he was 24. He also invented a new mathematical system to prove his theories: calculus.

During this 18-month period, Newton plunged into an amazing variety of other studies. He discovered the laws of the tides. By a series of brilliant experiments with prisms bought for a few pennies at a country fair, he proved that white light is composed of all the colors in the spectrum, and that each color bends in its own characteristic degree when passed through a prism. He ground lenses and mirrors and made a new kind of telescope. In his old age, when praised for his great contributions to man's understanding of the universe, he remarked: "I had no special sagacity—only the power of patient thought." He made his discoveries, he said, "by keeping a subject constantly before me until the first dawnings open little by little into the full light."

Newton said nothing about any of his Woolsthorpe discoveries at the time. This habit of keeping his own counsel was to involve him in angry arguments later on. In 1667 he returned to Cambridge as a fellow at Trinity. Isaac Barrow, professor of mathematics, considered him "a man of quite exceptional ability and singular skill." When Barrow resigned his professorship in 1669, he arranged for Newton, then 26, to succeed him, a position Newton was to hold for 32 years. Not long after his appointment, The Royal Society of London for Improving Natural Knowledge saw Newton's new reflecting telescope and immediately elected him a member. Surprised at the Society's enthusiasm, Newton sent in an account of the experiments with light that had led to his invention.

The paper touched off a storm—not because the experiments were not accurate and the conclusions drawn from them indisputable, but because his findings did not square with certain theories then held. So many voices were raised in complaint that Newton finally exclaimed in disgust, "I see a man must either resolve to put out nothing new or become a slave to defend it." From that time on he was more reluctant than ever to make his discoveries known.

Newton had begun to develop calculus while an undergraduate, but he had not described his method to anyone but Barrow. Some years later Gottfried Wilhelm von Leibnitz, the great German mathematician, came up with much the same system. Leibnitz at first conceded that he and Newton were working on a similar system simultaneously. When the issue was drawn, his supporters said that Newton had borrowed from Leibnitz.

To prove this point, Jean Bernoulli, a famous Swiss mathematician, published two problems and challenged anyone to solve them within a year. Leibnitz solved one, and was at work on the other as the year drew to a close. When Newton heard of the problems he promptly solved both in less than 24 hours. He sent his answers to the Royal Society. When the Society published them without disclosing the author, Bernoulli saw them and ruefully commented, "The lion is known by his claw." The test proved beyond doubt that Newton had indeed invented calculus. He could not have solved the problems otherwise.

Publication of the *Principia*, the greatest of Newton's works, was due largely to chance. Brilliant young Edmund Halley, who was later to become Astronomer Royal, was baffled in his attempt to compute the orbits of the planets. Going to Newton for help, he learned to his astonishment that Newton had already computed the orbits. But search of Newton's cluttered desk did not at once disclose the calculations—so Isaac Newton quickly did them all over again.

Halley, meanwhile, realized the great value of the unpublished research so carelessly stuffed into the pigeonholes of Newton's desk, and offered to publish the work at his own expense. Newton agreed, and thus the *Principia*, which was to be hailed as the greatest scientific book ever printed, came into being. Not until our own day when Albert Einstein came forward with his Theory of Relativity was a single scientific treatise to have such impact on the development of human thought. Newton spelled out the mechanics of our universe; Einstein unlocked the atom and established the identity of energy and matter.

In the *Principia*, Newton refined and clarified all that he had discovered about the movements of the planets and their satellites. During the months it took him to prepare the book, he would often sit motionless for hours, then dash to his desk and write for hours more without even bothering to pull up a chair. His secretary reported that he seldom went to bed before two o'clock— sometimes not until five or six—and often forgot to eat. Newton gave the book a sort of subtitle: "The Frame of the System of the World." Even mathematicians found it difficult to read, not only because the problems dealt with are complex but because Newton purposely made it difficult—so that he wouldn't be bothered by "little smatterers in mathematics." Written in Latin, the universal language of science at that time, the *Principia* to a large extent consists of mathematical formulas and equations. For two centuries it was the major guide to the world's scientific thought.

All previous thinkers had held that some continuous force was required to keep the planets moving in their orbits. In the *Principia*, Newton said that a body in motion would continue to travel in a straight line forever unless some force was applied to stop it. The planets move in circular paths because the gravitational force of the sun exactly equals the centrifugal force of their motion through space. Since there is no friction in space, no additional power is needed to keep them circling at constant speed through countless aeons of time.

Newton developed and explored his law of gravity: that every particle in the universe has a gravitational attraction for every other particle in proportion to the product of the masses of the particles and in inverse proportion to the square of their distances. He showed how to determine the mass of the sun and the planets. He established rules for calculating the orbits of comets. He proved that the gravitational force of the moon and the sun causes tides in the oceans of the earth, that spring tides occur when moon and sun are pulling together, neap tides when the forces are opposed. Such a wonderful uniformity as he found in the planetary system must, Newton said, "be allowed the effect of choice" by a Supreme Creator.

One of the greatest of all Newton's triumphs came more than a century after his death. His law of gravitation was so thoroughly accepted that when astronomers found the planet Uranus slightly out of its predicted position they did not suspect a flaw in the theory. Instead they concluded that Uranus must be affected by the gravitational pull of a planet still undiscovered. By Newtonian law, U. J. J. Leverrier in France and J. C. Adams in England independently computed the position of this undiscovered planet. Leverrier sent his calculations to the astronomer J. C. Galle in

Germany. Galle received them on September 23, 1846, went to his telescope that very night and discovered the new planet in the exact spot indicated. It is called Neptune.

Newton never married, and if there was any romance in his life, no trace of it has appeared. The hostess of his comfortable house in London was his beautiful and vivacious niece, Miss Catherine Barton. In appearance Newton was of average height, with handsome, rather sharp features, a clear ruddy complexion and flashing eyes. He was moderate in all his habits. Once when asked why he did not smoke, he replied, "Because I do not want to acquire any new necessities." He had a talent for making money, and played the stock market so successfully that he left an estate of around $160,000, which was a large sum in those days. In 1705, in a special ceremony at Cambridge, Newton was knighted by Queen Anne, the first scientist ever to be so honored.

In his 85th year, mourned by England and the world, Isaac Newton went to his last rest in Westminster Abbey, where he lies today, one of the greatest names among that company of the great. Of his life's work he had written: "I do not know what I may appear to the world, but to myself I seem to have been only like a boy playing on the seashore, diverting myself in now and then finding a smoother pebble or a prettier shell than ordinary, while the great ocean of truth lay all undiscovered before me."

Every great scientific truth goes through three stages. First, people say it conflicts with the Bible. Next, they say it has been discovered before. Lastly, they say they have always believed it.
                                                                —*Louis Agassiz*

"How did you discover the law of gravitation?" somebody once asked Newton. "By thinking about it all the time," was the answer.
                                                                —*Ernest Dimnet*

THE WISDOM OF CONFUCIUS

By Max Eastman

To us he would be rather funny-looking if he turned up in person, with his broad flaring nostrils, slanty eyes and a big bump on the top of his head. His beard and mustaches hung down in three long strands, and his costume was like a Japanese kimono. But he was tall and strong, an ardent hunter, a gifted musician and an intellectual genius. His great and subtle wisdom is little appreciated in the West, yet in the whole world his position is unique. He stands alone in history as a man who molded the mind and manners of a nation.

Confucius lived in China more than 500 years before the birth of Christ. He was one of the world's supreme teachers of the art of living—and more simply a teacher than any of the rest. He was neither a saint nor a prophet. He had no master key to the secrets of the universe. Although his teachings are often spoken of as the religion of China, he had little interest in religion or in the idea of eternal life. Yet he was fervently concerned with being good. He was the inventor of that magic formula, the golden rule, one of the most sacred jewels of our own gospel, for he summed up his teachings: "Do not unto others what you would not have them do unto you."

Confucius came so close sometimes to the Christian gospel that a whole book has been written on the similarities and contrasts between them. Similar to the Christian doctrine "Judge not, that ye be not judged," for example, was his warning that, in

judging others, we should "take our inmost self" as a standard:
might we not conceivably have committed the same sin? But in
contrast to Christianity was his answer when somebody asked
what he thought of the idea that one should reward injury with
kindness: "With what, then, will you reward kindness? Reward
injury with justice, kindness with kindness."

As a small boy, Confucius had an avid interest in all kinds of
rites and ceremonies. He loved music, too, and learned to sing
and to play the lute and zither. In mid-life he traveled to the
capital from his home in the small province of Lu, to study "the
rules of music and propriety" and become expert in all the forms
of ceremonial behavior.

When Confucius grew up, he earned his living by taking in
pupils. There was no fixed fee, and none at all if a pupil was both
poor and gifted. The teachings of Confucius have come down
to us in the form of a vast collection of disconnected remarks and
conversational episodes that his pupils recorded. Unfortunately,
they are not blended with a story of his life, as are those of Jesus,
and that makes them less readable. They also lack the eloquence
of the Christian gospels. Confucius was suspicious of eloquence.
"As to language," he said, "it is simply required that it convey
the meaning." He managed to do that in such plain prose remarks as these:

> Wherever you go, go with your whole heart.
>
> The serious fault is to have faults and not try to mend them.
>
> Don't think yourself so big that other people look small.

The bent of his mind was scientific. In his emphasis upon
flexibility of mind, upon replacing dogma with the investigation
of facts, upon suspended judgment, he was more than 2000 years
ahead of his age. He first formulated what might well be described as the golden rule of science: "When you do not know a
thing, to acknowledge that you do not know it is knowledge."
He thus swept aside the temptations of superstitions and wishful
thinking. To the same effect Confucius placed a great emphasis on

sincerity—sincerity not in speech only, but even in solitary meditation. There must be no inward self-deception if you are going
to travel in what he called "the path of truth."

And yet it was not a straight and narrow, or impossibly difficult, path that he indicated. "The way of truth," he said, "is like
a great road. It is not hard to find. The trouble is only that men
will not look for it." This does not mean that he counseled laxity
or self-indulgence. Confucius was a strict and demanding teacher.
The list of qualities toward which his pupils had to struggle makes
our seven cardinal virtues look like a course for undergraduates.
Among other things, his pupils had to be "quick in apprehension, clear in discernment, of far-reaching intelligence and all-
embracing knowledge, fitted to exercise rule, magnanimous,
fitted to exercise forbearance." They also had to learn "gravity,"
"earnestness," "faithfulness," "kindness" and "a reverent attention to business." His sayings leave me with a feeling that the
underlying idea is for everybody to be in a state of growth. He
thought there was an upward drive in us all, a wish to outdo, if
not others, then at least ourselves as of yesterday and today.

Like Plato 200 years later, Confucius drew up the blueprints of
an ideal republic, but his was very different from the regimented
one invented by Plato. For it originated in a wish that society
might function like a loving family. The idea was especially
visionary in China, because family ties were more close and binding there than anywhere else; to ask Chinese to treat all people
as members of their own family was to ask much. Confucius knew
this, but he wanted to see the world at least move in the direction
of the ideal. And the only way to begin, he thought, was to get
good and wise men into positions of power. Like Plato, again,
he made a strenuous effort throughout life to be appointed to
high executive office by one of the feudal princes. Several of his
prize pupils were so appointed, but he himself seems never to
have got much further than the position of highly esteemed
schoolmaster for such public servants.

Though he spent years wandering through China with a little

band of disciples, seeking a monarch who would give him his chance to remake the world, certain traits of his nature stood in the way of his ambition. He seems to have been too outspoken for success as a politician. To a tempestuous ruler who asked him for instruction in the art of government, he said, "First learn to govern yourself." Moreover, Confucius did not really believe in hereditary aristocracy. "By nature men are nearly equal," he said. And, though democracy had not then been invented, Confucius asserted—perhaps for the first time in history—that the true end of government is not only the welfare but the happiness of the people.

He returned at last to his hometown, a tired old man—not broken in spirit, but convinced that he was a failure. After a few quiet years of teaching he died in that conviction. His disciples mourned him as though he were their father. And since in China it was then customary for children to spend three years mourning a deceased father, they had plenty of time on their hands. They spent it reminding one another of all the vital things he had taught, and writing them down. The record of their memories became the bible of the Chinese people. More than their bible, it became their book of etiquette, their spirit of laws, the political principles toward which their good rulers aspired.

When in the third century B.C. certain brutal despots outlawed Confucianism, burning its scriptures and executing its followers, the philosophy spread like a hidden fire—just as Christianity was to spread under persecution. And, again as with Christianity, there came a more thoughtful emperor who adopted Confucianism as his belief and gave it the sanction of the state.

Books upon books were written concerning the teaching of Confucius, until a man beginning in youth and reading steadily for a lifetime could not delve through all of them. Nevertheless, the pure, high, temperate and simple art of living taught by Confucius himself shone through them all. It will shine forever, no matter how many Communists labor to replace it with their religion of state tyranny and their doctrine that the end justifies the means, no matter how bloody and evil the means may be.

PIRATE-KNIGHT

By *Donald Culross Peattie*

THE LITTLE BAY, some 30 miles north of San Francisco, is a lonely place, lovely with blowing lupine, almost unchanged from the day when Sir Francis Drake stepped ashore there nearly 400 years ago. He made friends with the Indian "king," and before sailing away he boldly posted his claim to this remote wilderness, using a plate of brass inscribed thus:

BEE IT KNOWNE VNTO ALL MEN BY THESE PRESENTS
IVNE 17 1579
BY THE GRACE OF GOD AND IN THE NAME OF HERR MAIESTY
QVEEN ELIZABETH OF ENGLAND AND HERR SVCCESSORS FOREVER
I TAKE POSSESSION OF THIS KINGDOME WHOSE KING AND PEOPLE
FREELY RESIGNE THEIR RIGHT AND TITLE IN THE WHOLE LAND
VNTO HERR MAIESTIES KEEPEING NOW NAMED BY ME AN TO BEE
KNOWNE VNTO ALL MEN AS NOVA ALBION   *FRANCIS DRAKE*

For centuries the plate remained where Drake had placed it, unknown, growing black with age. Then in 1933 a chauffeur waiting for his employer, who was hunting, came upon it. Neither man realized what had been found; the inscription was hard to read. The plate was tossed into the car and later discarded by the roadside. There, three years later, a picnicker happened on it and became curious. He took the weathered object to Dr. Herbert Bolton, head of the history department of the University of California.

That Drake, the great seafarer, had been one of the very first Europeans to land on the northern California coast no one doubted. The earliest accounts of his travels tell how, after weeks of icy gales, he found haven in a convenient cove, probably the very same one, in Marin County, called to this day "Drake's Bay." In 1936 experts tested the rediscovered plate of brass with microscope and spectroscope and found that this was indeed antique brass. Suspecting that a hole in the plate had originally been filled by a sixpence bearing Queen Elizabeth's features to act as an official seal, one of the experts inserted an ancient sixpence in the hole—and it fitted. The plate was authenticated, at least to the satisfaction of Dr. Bolton and the California Historical Society.

The man who had sailed halfway around the world to post his Queen's claim to this wilderness had the sea in his very blood. First of 12 sons, he was born about 1540 in Devon. While the boy was small, his father, an ex-mariner and poor Protestant lay preacher, was driven out of his native shire by religious fanaticism, and all the shelter he could find for his family was the hull of an old ship stranded beside the river Medway where it empties into the wide mouth of the Thames.

Across the centuries we can see the wiry, bright-eyed child striding the deck of that beached hulk, shouting defiance at passing ships. His mariner kinsman Sir John Hawkins paid for the boy's education, and in his early teens he was apprenticed on a merchant bark trading to France and Holland. So smartly did the lad learn the trade that the old shipowner willed him the craft. In his 20's, already a captain, Drake was sailing the Caribbean Sea. There the fever of adventure entered his veins, never to leave him until, some 30 years later, those storied waters closed above his leaden coffin.

And an adventurer is all that Francis Drake might ever have been but for a treacherous incident which forged him, in the white heat of anger, into a rapier for England's hand. In 1568 in a Mexican harbor a flotilla including Drake's ship was taking on fresh water, having been given promise of security by Don Martin

Enriquez, Spanish viceroy of Mexico. Suddenly, by the viceroy's order, 13 Spanish ships opened fire on the English; only Drake and Hawkins escaped to England with their vessels. The crews of the others were either slaughtered or taken prisoner. From that day forth Francis Drake declared a private war against King Philip II of Spain.

Long had Queen Elizabeth of England and her "dear brother" Philip (widower of her elder sister Mary) flirted both with notions of marriage and plots for war. Elizabeth's private secretary was Philip's paid spy, but Philip too had subjects willing to tell Queen Bess his hidden plans. One of these plans was to seize her throne for himself and take England's precious seaborne trade. As a first step he closed to English shipping all the ports in his possession— and that meant Spain, Portugal, parts of Italy, the Low Countries, most of Central and South America, the West Indies and the Philippines. For the Spanish empire then bestrode the world like a colossus.

The blood in the colossal veins was Inca gold, flowing from the mines of Peru across the seas to Philip's war chest. Not till that vein was cut would the threat to England's very life be lifted. Drake saw how to cut it. He obtained a regular privateering commission from Queen Elizabeth and returned to Central America. Scouting the Atlantic coast of Panama, he learned from Indians the route of Spanish gold. Down from the Andes it was brought, then shipped up the Pacific coast to the city of Panama. On a mule train it then crossed the isthmus to the Atlantic, where at Nombre de Dios it was loaded on the fat treasure ships that waddled, closely convoyed, to Seville.

In 1572 Drake manned two fast ships with trusty Devon boys; they were in their teens, with a few oldsters in their 20's as wiser heads. And now Drake confused the whole coast of Panama. He took and plundered Nombre de Dios. He slipped into other harbors, burning stores, carrying off treasure and dragging out Spanish galleons as prizes. Then, while the port bells were bawling alarm and messengers galloped along the coast, looking fearfully out to sea, Drake's Devon boys, with friendly natives, went creeping through the jungle of the isthmus, where the mule train plodded under its golden freight. Suddenly at Drake's lips the whistle shrilled. In a rush all was over—Drake got away, through tropic rains and treacherous coral, with the booty. That year Philip of Spain was poorer by millions.

To sap anew the golden vein of the treasure route, Drake proposed to steal into the Pacific and surprise his foes. No Englishman had ever yet attempted the trip around the southern tip of South America. Good Queen Bess said he was the very man to do it. In the same breath she warned him not to lay a finger on her dear brother-in-law's property. In the cat-and-mouse game between the two monarchs duplicity was the rule, and Drake must therefore play a lone hand.

Out of Plymouth harbor, in 1577, he sailed with a little fleet of five ships. Through misfortune or mutiny, one by one his ships turned back or were lost. Only three ships made their way through Magellan's Strait. Of these, one later foundered, another returned to England. But though all the airs of heaven combined to blow him back, Drake's flagship, the *Golden Hind*, kept slamming into the wind for 16 days till, emerging into the lonely waters of the South Pacific, he spread all sail for the north. At Valparaiso, and again at Callao, Drake struck at shipping like a duck hawk bolting from a sea cliff. When he heard of a Spanish galleon bound, with 14 days' head start, for Panama, Drake sailed her down at the equator. To disable and board her was a matter of minutes, but it took four days to transfer the monstrous booty of gold and silver, pearls and gems.

Drake now feared—and rightly—that a Spanish fleet would be waiting for him near the Strait of Magellan. He tried to sail home around North America by way of the Arctic Ocean, but howling gales drove him back. That was when he sheltered on the California coast, and posted his brazen claim. And there it was that he determined to go home by sailing right around the world. Isles of spice and sandalwood he now visited, filling out his cargo with their products. The hold of the *Golden Hind* was great with booty as it breasted the Indian Ocean, rounded the Cape of Good Hope, turned north for England. On September 26, 1580, she slid her anchor down in Plymouth harbor. Queen Elizabeth's return on her money was more than 4000 percent. Later, while Drake knelt upon the deck, she knighted the first Englishman to sail around the world.

In the grim pile of his Escorial palace, Philip raged: Twenty thousand ducats ($100,000) for this pirate, dead or alive! The quarrel of Spain and England reared up in the skies like a coming hurricane. The cold wind of its advance had already been felt when the Vatican excommunicated Elizabeth and absolved her adoring subjects of all allegiance to her. To Philip, the Pope now promised a purse of one million crowns (about a million dollars) as soon as the Spanish landed their forces on English soil.

In Cádiz an armada was readied. By April 1587 its 60 craft, guarded by galleys, lay in the outer harbor. Then into the harbor dashed a spitfire fleet of 23 English ships, led by Drake. He burned 10,000 tons of shipping. Ashore, explosions rocked white-walled Cádiz as the Devon boys destroyed stores hoarded for years. "That will singe the beard of the King of Spain!" laughed Sir Francis as he disappeared to sea.

By July 1588 the Spanish Armada had been rebuilt and doubled. The plan now was to sweep up the English Channel, convoy a Spanish army from Flanders in invasion barges. This army would march to London and there dictate peace terms—the peace of death for English liberty. In the holds of the Armada was gold enough to buy treason and collaboration. One thing, though, Philip could not buy—the pluck of the island people, tensely waiting, knowing well that the Spanish outclassed their fleet in tonnage, spread of canvas, number of soldiers. On July 19, 1588, the Spanish were sighted off Land's End. Drake ran for the docks, bawling orders, and himself bent to the oars of the dinghy towing his flagship out into the Channel.

The English were no more than well at sea when the Armada swept down—130 great ships spread out in a crescent eight miles across. From the first, the light, swift English craft sailed rings around the Armada, cutting out the Spanish ships one by one in a ten-day running battle. Drake captured one large galleon when its commander struck his colors at once on learning his adversary's name. When the Armada tried to take shelter in the harbor of Calais, the English sent in fire ships and drove the Spanish to sea once more.

Through Dover Straits the Armada fled, bound for the North Sea. Reading the skies, the weather-wise English gave up the chase at the Firth of Forth and ran for snug harbor. For to their aid came rushing the gods of storm. North around Scotland swept the Armada. Past the spouting reefs of Skye and the bellowing Hebrides reeled the floating castles from Spain, to be hurled by the gale on the thunderous west Irish coast. Into the sea leaped sailor, soldier, priest, grandee. Some filled their belts and pockets first with gold, and so bribed death to take them. A few, choking through the surf, managed to stagger to shore. Only a remnant of the Armada reached sunny Spain again, where hardly a noble or peasant family was not bereaved by the disaster.

Thus Drake saved England from Philip's Armada, and not a single ship was sunk by the Spaniards. Fittingly, the great sailor's last moments took place aboard his ship. During a 1596 expedition to fight the Spanish in the West Indies, he fell ill. He died within sight of the scene of an early triumph, the town of Nombre de Dios.

After the defeat of the Spanish Armada in 1588, a naval tournament was arranged for the victorious British seamen and, at the request of Admiral Drake, Queen Elizabeth consented to come down from London and award the prizes. The officer in charge of the arrangements proved himself one of the most tactful men in history—he issued orders that "On account of the dazzling loveliness of Her Majesty, all seamen, upon receiving their prizes, should shield their eyes with their right hand." Thus was born the naval and military salute.

A MAN TO REMEMBER

Condensed from Time

T HE SECOND Continental Congress, which met in Philadelphia in 1775 after the battles of Lexington and Concord, hesitated hardly at all in picking the man to command the American Army. At 43 George Washington was fair, broad-shouldered and huge for his day—six feet two inches, 200 pounds—with a horseman's muscular thighs, penetrating blue eyes and an impressive air of command. As a Virginian he was politically eligible. He had commanded troops; furthermore, he looked like a general. Mounted on a white charger and arrayed in red and blue uniform, he was a sight few men ever forgot. Delegates to the Congress were also impressed by his quiet good sense, his ability to bide his time, his capacity for decision.

The delegates, nevertheless, did not know how well they had chosen. Washington *became* the Revolution. His towering will, his awesome patience were often all that kept it alive. He was bitterly realistic about his country's weaknesses, but he never lost an intuitive understanding of its strength. His understanding fed the iron nerve which could risk everything on terrifying military gambles when his back was to the wall. He was also realistic about his austere figure, but George Washington had his little frailties and vanities. He imported silk stockings and silver-buckled shoes from England, and seldom missed an opportunity to have his brown hair trimmed, combed and powdered. He suffered all his life from bad teeth (he was in agony from toothache at the siege of Yorktown). He loved to dance. He fished, shot ducks and rode to hounds with reckless competence. He suffered from sunburn

and in later years was not too dignified to inspect his acres with a large umbrella affixed to his saddle.

Though a gentleman born, he was earthier, more practical, more ambitious and tougher-fibered than history might imply. Like many other upper-class Virginians of the early 1700's, his family was land-rich and money-poor. George's formal education was short and haphazard. He was tutored for a few years in reading, writing and geography; he studied mathematics. At 16 he went off as a surveyor's assistant on wild, western lands owned by a wealthy Englishman, Lord Fairfax. He burned to acquire land, wealth and, above all, honor in the eyes of his fellow Virginians. At 21, by virtue of his own eagerness and the goodwill of Robert Dinwiddie, the colony's royal governor, he set off again through the wilderness on a military mission—to warn the French not to encroach on Crown claims in the Ohio Valley.

The fur-hungry French refused to back down and Washington became Virginia's foremost soldier. He tested his courage when the British expeditionary force of General Edward Braddock was all but wiped out in an ambush in the Monongahela River forests. Washington, weak and reeling from a "violent illness," rode for 12 hours to reach the scene of battle, had two horses killed beneath him, felt four bullets tear through his clothes, but never faltered in his duty. Divine Providence, he decided, protected him.

He was given command of all Virginia troops and the responsibility for protecting every scattered settler on the state's borders. He learned hard lessons: the difficulties of recruiting Americans for military service, the harsh necessity of discipline (once he hanged two deserters to impress his troops), the jealousy and backbiting inherent in public service. Finally he quarreled with the British Army over his rank and rights as an officer. He was elected to Virginia's House of Burgesses and gave up his commission in disillusionment, to live the life of a country gentleman. But 16 years later, when the fever of rebellion swept the colonies, he wrote: "The peaceful plains of America are either to be drenched with Blood or Inhabited by Slaves. Can a virtuous man hesitate in his choice?"

British generals must be forgiven for feeling that the rebellion was merely an exhibition of rashness by excited colonials. The colonies, vaguely united and notoriously ridden by rivalry, had little industry, no military tradition, almost no military stores, no fleet, no allies and, by European standards, no army worthy of the name. They faced the wealth and trained troops of a great military power, backed by the world's greatest navy, by savage Indians and by droves of American loyalists.

At Bunker Hill, New England militiamen had already accomplished what seemed a miracle. They had proved that colonials could withstand a British charge, and that their marksmanship and ability to fight from cover were talents the British could not match. But the siege of Boston introduced Washington to his awful responsibilities. Fifteen thousand Americans camped in a great semicircle around Boston had to be fed, disciplined, taught some rudiments of military maneuvering. Few had uniforms; few had enough powder. They got noisily drunk, tore up farmers' fences for wood, quarreled with their officers. An even more horrifying phenomenon presented itself: Washington's army began melting away. Militiamen enlisted for only a few months, went home when their time was up and tried to take their muskets along with them.

He was saved from committing his unwieldy, untrained and dwindling force to an assault when long-suffering soldiers dragged heavy cannon over the snow all the way from Fort Ticonderoga on Lake Champlain. When the cannon were mounted on Dorchester Heights, the British sailed away. Washington's travail promptly began again in southern New York the next summer. His army, beaten on Long Island, escaped across the East River to Manhattan, thanks to a fog. It fought and retreated to White Plains, fought and retreated across the Hudson River and across New Jersey, then across the Delaware River into Pennsylvania. As winter deepened, only 2400 ragged, ill-fed Continental regulars were left. On December 20, 1776, Washington wrote to Congress: "Ten days more will put an end to the existence of our Army. . . ."

Then he gambled. Five nights later, on Christmas night, he took his little force across the ice-clogged Delaware. Wet, half-frozen, lashed by driving sleet, it marched nine miles to Trenton and surprised the town and its Hessian defenders. The Americans triumphed in less than two hours of fighting and without the loss of a man. Then, only a week later, they audaciously invaded New Jersey again, at Princeton. Washington, rallying his troops, rode unscathed within 30 paces of blazing enemy muskets. The country was electrified, the Revolution was saved.

That was the pattern of the war—months of defeat, discouragement and disaster—a pattern broken, when all seemed lost, by a daring stroke and a taste of triumph. It was a big war. It ranged from Georgia to Quebec, from New York to the Mississippi. In the end it involved the fleets of both England and France. It progressed slowly: months often passed without major incident. It was polite in tone: prisoners were duly exchanged, flags of truce honored, correct notes passed between opposing commanders. Washington formally returned General Sir William Howe's dog to him when it was captured by Americans at Germantown.

Yet the fighting was often bitter, even by modern standards. American volunteer squads were killed or wounded almost to a man in breaching the British defenses at Stony Point on the Hudson River. American and British troops, their flintlocks useless from rain, milled in wild combat with knife, musket butt and tomahawk at Oriskany in the New York wilderness. Cowpens, Brandywine, Germantown—all were bloody. Through it all, Washington's burdens grew. Congressmen hotly accused him of attempting to saddle the country with a military tyranny worse than that of England. It was 18 months before he was authorized to recruit an army pledged to serve for the duration. Money to pay the troops was always short.

Washington understood Congressional fears, respected its ideal of civil control, and won it over in the end with honesty—and his dogged hope of victory. He did not underestimate his army. Soldiers might desert, but they often returned to fight again. They might break before British bayonets, but they would regroup and fight the next day. Properly led, they endured incredible hardship, often without pay, without proper clothing, without proper food. The tide of war had begun to turn at Saratoga in the autumn of 1777, when Britain's plan to take the Hudson River valley came to grief. General John Burgoyne, with 8000 British and Hessian troops, came south from Canada almost unopposed. But an American army under General Horatio Gates blocked Burgoyne on high ground on the west bank of the Hudson. Trapped between a horde of fast-arriving militiamen and the northern wilderness, Burgoyne surrendered.

It was a great victory. It prompted France to contribute money, men and sea power and it enlisted the active sympathy of Spain and Holland to the American cause. But four years of fighting remained. The Americans endured Valley Forge, were stalemated in the North, almost deprived of the South by Cornwallis' campaigns in the Carolinas.

Then Cornwallis' army, badly worn by endless American harassment, moved into Virginia and took up quarters at Yorktown. Washington was in New England, contemplating an attack on New York—the French had landed 5000 troops to help him, and a big French fleet was preparing to sail from the West Indies. He decided almost overnight to move against Cornwallis instead. The French war vessels moved to Virginia, too. After five weeks of fast marching, Washington laid siege to Yorktown with 16,000 French and Continental soldiers.

Cornwallis had gone to earth on a narrow peninsula between the York and James rivers, which was a normal move for a British commander confident of sea power. But De Grasse's French fleet controlled Chesapeake Bay. Cut off, hammered night and day by artillery, Cornwallis, a fine soldier, could find no way out. On October 19, 1781, his 7000 troops marched out, bands playing a march fittingly entitled "The World Turned Upside Down," and stacked their arms. The war, for all practical purposes, was over. The rebels had won.

About to leave the Army, Washington wrote: "Having no

reward to ask for myself, if I have been so happy as to obtain the approbation of my countrymen I shall be satisfied. It still rests with them to complete my wishes by adopting such a system of Policy as will ensure the future reputation, tranquillity, happiness and glory of this extensive Empire." The man is all in that passage—his humility, his pride, his sense of honor, his vision of "this extensive Empire."

The nation, however, was not yet born, the "system of Policy" not yet constructed. All the courage and suffering of the war might be lost in the confusions of a peace without policy or system. Washington, before retirement to Mount Vernon, wrote to friends that "something must be done or the fabric must fall. . . ."

His concern was not wasted; his influence was foremost among those that prompted the Constitutional Convention of 1787, which he served as chairman. With the brilliant minds, the learned political scientists, the great prose stylists who made up that convention, Washington could not compete. He did not try. He spoke seldom, initiated little; no section of the Constitution can be called his. But the whole document belongs to him as much as to any man. His practical sense, bold vision, conservatism—all these pervade it.

There was but one choice for the first President of the United States. The office was less precisely defined than the judicial and legislative branches and it might have degenerated into a puppet Presidency. Washington defined it by stepping into it. He imparted to it the dignity of his own character.

He refused to shake hands during his eight years in office—he felt such a gesture of familiarity was beneath the Presidency—and always bowed instead. He dressed richly in velvet, rode in a six-horse coach and felt himself the equal of any king on earth. But he always thought of himself as the "Most Obed. Hble Serv.t" of the people of the United States, who, decade after decade, have borne the stamp of his character. He lived but two years after his second term was ended. In his last moments of consciousness he said, "I die hard."

And so he has.

WHAT PLATO SAYS

By Max Eastman

W HEN YOU mention the Greek philosopher Plato, people are apt to put on a pious expression as though you were going to talk about a saint. But Plato was no saint. He was a prizewinning athlete, a brave soldier, a poet, a connoisseur of race horses and an adorer of slapstick comedy. He lived to be 81, and died at a wedding feast—full of the zest for life and for conversation to the last heartbeat.

All this is important if you want to appraise his teachings as they apply to us. His times were very much like ours. He flourished in Athens in the first half of the 4th century B.C., when people were tired of wars, disillusioned with revolutions, skeptical of the old forms of faith, groping for a hold on the real values of life. Plato undertook to find that hold for them. He was as earnest about this as the Hebrew prophets, although he could not back up his findings with an appeal to divine authority. The Greek gods were a beautiful, charming, but rather selfish and hell-raising crew, who never dreamed of laying down anything like the Ten Commandments. Plato had outgrown his belief in them, and had even begun to talk of God as one being. But he did not regard this being as an authority on human behavior. He had to find both standards of conduct and the reason for adhering to them in this human world.

He would never have succeeded had he not known Socrates, the prophet of logic, the herald of sound reasoning. Plato was 20 and already getting quite a reputation as a poet when he met Socrates. But that frogfaced, pestiferous and lovable crusader for clear reason swept him right off his feet. After a few conversations with Socrates about the gigantic importance of thinking things out, of using words with a clear sense of their meaning, Plato went home and destroyed his poetry. Perhaps it was not unwise, for the poetic melody of his prose is, according to the English poet Shelley, "as intense as it is possible to conceive."

Plato adhered to Socrates as student and friend until Socrates died. He wasn't a pupil exactly, for Socrates would no more think of taking pay for teaching sound reason than Jesus would for teaching love. But Plato was one of the young men who turned up most regularly at those seminar-like meetings with Socrates at a gymnasium, the portico of a temple or the house of a friend, to have an argument about the meaning of some important idea. Their friendship meant so much to Plato that he carried Socrates with him in fancy throughout his literary life, writing practically all his thoughts in the form of dialogues—or conversations in which the figure of Socrates played the leading part.

Socrates himself had tackled the problem of what "virtue" means. He had asked why anybody should be good. And he had decided that goodness is nothing but informed and carefully reasoned conduct. Any man presented with a choice, if he knew all there was to know about it, would choose the right act. It is not necessary to believe this in order to appreciate its importance. For the first time, this teaching of Socrates gave the highest authority on moral questions to the individual human mind. It was a revolution unparalleled in history.

And Plato carried it forward. Not only is the good act the reasonable one, he said, but the good man is the man in whom reason rules. There was no science of psychology in his day, so Plato invented one. It was a pretty good one, too, and held its own for a couple of thousand years. Our conscious life, he said, is divided into three parts: a sensuous part, composed of appetites and passions; a restive part, which may be called will or "spirit"; and a thinking part, which he called reason.

Since reason is what distinguishes men from dogs and baboons, it is obviously the highest of the three parts, and its function is to rule. The function of "spirit" is to enforce the dictates of reason. The appetites and passions should obey. Where each part performs its natural function, you have virtue. Where this natural order of things breaks down, you have vice. In this simple way Plato reasserted, in a time of cynical disillusionment, the authority of the good life. Where Plato said "reason," we say "intelligence," for we realize that knowledge is not acquired merely by abstract reasoning—you have to examine the facts. But Plato's basic idea that the guidance of the mind is the essence of moral character will never become old-fashioned.

Indeed, so little in Plato is dated that you feel sometimes when reading him as though he might walk into the room. He talks of mathematical astronomy and physics as though they already existed in his day. He explains dreams, describing almost in the language of Freud how, when reason's control is relaxed in sleep, "the wild beast in our nature starts up and walks about naked." He teaches about the division of labor and the causes of it like a professor of modern economics. He is the inventor or suggester of the distinction between higher and secondary education, the necessity for specialization in science, the application of scientific method to social problems.

He spoke for the first time (so far as the records go) of the psychology of laughter, acoustics, the limitation of incomes (no family should have more than four times as much as any other). He invented day nurseries, the kindergarten method—progressive education: "Bodily exercise when compulsory does no harm, but knowledge acquired under compulsion has no hold on the mind. Therefore do not use compulsion, but let early education be a sort of amusement."

In addition to all this penetrating hard sense, Plato also had a mystical yearning in him. He wanted to escape from the world of change, from the very existence of those ever-shifting problems to which he provided so early the wise answers. He wanted a religion. Not finding any to suit him in his age and nation, he went ahead and invented one. Naturally, it grew out of that excitement about the logical relations among ideas which he had caught from Socrates. These ideas that we find so absorbing, he declared, are the true reality; the particular things we see and touch are mere shadows.

He even went so far as to say that the *idea* of beauty is more to be loved than a beautiful person—and this is the true meaning of "platonic love." Plato himself, we must add, was capable of warning against the extremes to which his belief in the superior reality of ideas could lead him. "Even the friends of ideas," he remarked in a smiling mood, "are subject to a kind of madness."

We ought to remember this when we approach another of his famously outrageous speculations, that contained in his major dialogue, *The Republic*, about the proper way to organize a state. His rapture about logic led him to think that, just as the good man is strictly disciplined by intelligence, so must the good state be disciplined by an intelligent minority.

He would classify the citizens according to their special endowments, and give his picked gang of good men the authority and armed force to keep them there. These virtuous and philosophical supermen, whom he called "Guardians," were to have no private property and no private affections. Their wives and children, as well as their property, were to be pooled. All the children of a given mating season should call all the parents of that season Mother and Father, and all the other children Brother and Sister. And since they would be removed to state schools as soon as they were weaned, no one would know who was whose. Meanwhile, the whole aristocracy, the ruling class, would keep their bodies in supreme trim by rigid diet and exercises, and their minds at the peak of penetration by constant instruction in logic, mathematics and metaphysics.

Plato did not advocate this regime for the whole state. It was a mode of life for the superior caste designed to make them really superior in mind and character. Our comment would be, "If it takes all that to produce a real aristocracy, let's get along with democracy, unwieldy as it is." But we are not living in the dawn of logic. We lack the smile of faith with which Plato followed where the argument led. Or are we blind, perhaps, to the smile of ironical humor with which he followed it so far?

The argument led him, before he got through, on one of the most famous wild-goose chases in history. He was 60 years old when he set out from Athens, on invitation, to teach Dionysius, Jr., the newly seated tyrant of Syracuse, how to establish an ideal republic. Plato entered upon his work with rosy hope, but also, alas, with prosy thoroughness. The training of the philosopher-king must begin, he decreed, with geometry. Geometry would teach him that art of close reasoning without which there is no use approaching the more intricate problems of political reform. And so it did begin: not only Dionysius but his whole court plunged into this new diversion until the palace was dusty from the drawing of diagrams in sand thrown on the marble floors.

Dionysius liked Plato, and he liked the excitement. But there was one hitch: he didn't like geometry. The anti-Platonists dug up another philosopher who could prove that tyranny is the best form of government, and do it without mathematics. In the end, Plato had to escape from the palace at night and be shipped home by a roundabout route to Athens.

Plato's life was not empty when he got home, for he had launched another enterprise many years before—he had founded a school. It was the most famous school of the ancient world and, for that matter, of all history. Its sessions were held in a "gymnasium" about a mile northwest of Athens. The city had three of these gymnasiums—immense constructions, half park, half pavilion. Each contained an indoor ball court and wrestling chamber, rubdown room, steam room, hot and cold baths, dressing rooms and an outdoor field for track events. In addition, it contained a grove with paths for educational conversation and arcades with recessed seats for those who preferred to take their education sitting down.

The gymnasium that Plato selected for his school was called "Academia"—from the Grove of Academus where it had been erected. Its sessions were probably not much more formal than those conversations with Socrates which had been the beginning of Plato's own higher education. There was no tuition fee, no required course of study, and probably a lot of fun. Indeed, it is doubtful if anything less "academic" ever existed in the name of education. But Plato's school survived almost one thousand years, and gave to all the languages of Europe the words *academy* and *academic*.

There is, to be sure, a very vital thing lacking in Plato's teaching: sympathy of one man for another, a sympathy of each man for the whole population. Plato never thought of that. That came into our Western world with Jesus and the Christian evangelists, who taught that the good man is ruled not by reason but by a passion—that of love for his fellowmen.

No need to recall how deeply this new teaching affected the world. Plato, if confronted with it, might also have been deeply affected. I think he might have said, after some years of meditation: "You are right. I failed to realize the high place occupied by sympathy, or what you call love, in the good life, and in the character of the good man. But you have only shown me that it is intelligent to cultivate sympathy. You cannot show me that self-sacrifice may not become a vice, that pity does not need, like any other passion, to be held within rational bounds. It is still reason, it is still intelligence, that rules."

Thus Plato might have demonstrated his high and abiding place in our Western philosophy of life.

Nothing in life is to be feared. It is only to be understood.
                                                   —*Marie Curie*

Plato, who opened up almost every major problem of life, always insisted that a person's life must, first of all, be a beautiful creation.   —*Rufus M. Jones*

TELLER OF TALES

By Donald Culross Peattie

IN THE CENTER of Spain, the part called La Mancha, the plain lies like a huge page open to the sky. It seems empty, save for a few villages, a few shepherds and their flocks. But if you are acquainted with the most-read work of fiction in the world you will not find this place empty. For you, too, it will be crowded with the more than 600 characters who troop across the pages of the first great novel ever written, *Don Quixote de la Mancha*.

There on the plain you can see the very windmills, centuries old now, which the knight took to be giants. Filled with splendid fury to do fine deeds, he spurred his old nag on to charge them, only to be tossed on his head. "Tilting at windmills," we call it to this day, when anyone zealously attacks an imaginary enemy. And the wonderful mad knight's name has also become part of our language, for any man may show a streak of the "quixotic." The windmill incident is only one of hundreds, some slapstick, some sadly true, some truly sad, which fill this "bible of humanity." And through all these adventures runs a vein of philosophic wisdom which was life's one real reward to the author, Miguel de Cervantes Saavedra.

You can hear his laughing voice in his self-description at the time he was writing this classic: "Of aquiline features, chestnut hair, smooth and unruffled forehead, gay eyes, nose that is crooked but well proportioned, a beard silvered now but golden a mere 20 years ago, big moustachios, little mouth, only six teeth and they in bad shape and worse arrangement, complexion light, somewhat heavy in build, and rather slow on his feet."

He came into this world, of which he was to see so much, in 1547, in the fine old university town of Alcalá de Henares, near Madrid. The family soon drifted on, however, to Valladolid, Seville, Madrid. For Papa Cervantes possessed a coat of arms and little else; his profession of apothecary-surgeon brought him few patients who paid. Miguel's first recollection was of seeing his father snatch up household gear and rush with it to the pawn-broker; then the sheriff came to clap Papa Cervantes in debtors' prison, leaving his daughters, Andrea and Luisa, and their two little brothers to weep with hunger.

Somehow the boy Miguel got schooling. He may even have attended the University of Salamanca, working his way as valet to rich undergraduates. A novelist, though, learns his trade from life itself. And in the city streets Miguel learned it as it comes, harsh, unexpected, vivid with experience. In the theater, where he spent what money he could scrape up, he learned what life is when it is turned to art. He discovered the power of make-believe, and how it can create a truth greater than actuality. All he had, at 22, was dreams, and these were now of glory.

He made his way to Italy, where Spain maintained large garri-sons, and there enlisted in the army. At last he was well dressed, in a uniform gaudy as a rooster's, and for the first time he ate regularly. These years in the service color many a later page, when the old soldier remembers with relish the fine old inns, the gur-gling Italian wine, the pretty girls. And he knew war itself. It was the Turk then who was the aggressor, and all Christendom stood in peril. A mighty Turkish fleet, in 1571, was sweeping westward through the Mediterranean. Selim II, Turkey's sultan, meant to tear the Cross from St. Peter's in Rome and raise the Crescent there. Spain sent her ships, under Don John of Austria (half-brother to her king, Philip II), to join those of the Papal States and Venice; on one of them sailed young Míguel de Cervantes.

At Lepanto, off the coast of Greece, the fleet of these allies met the Turkish navy in the bloodiest sea battle ever yet fought. Eight thousand Christians perished, 25,000 Turks, as ship after ship went down, while the soldiers fought cutlass to cutlass on the reeling decks. When the battle first was joined Cervantes lay below, tossing with malarial fever. He dashed on deck; a moment later two shots hit him in the chest, a third shattered his left arm. Yet he was with the first to board the nearest Turkish vessel. The Crescent that day sank in a bloody moonset. It was Spain's finest hour, and Cervantes' proudest.

Leaving Italy in 1575, Miguel set sail for Spain with high hopes. In his pocket he had a letter of recommendation from Don John to King Philip, which he trusted to bring him some good government post. But the luckless voyagers were overhauled by Moorish pirates and carried off into slavery in Algiers. There, though his maimed hand spared him the galleys, Miguel became the property of Dali Mami, a renegade Christian turned pirate. When this crafty master read the letter praising Cervantes, he concluded that his prisoner was a man of importance, and ordered him to send to Spain for a large ransom.

As the months dragged by, Miguel saw his fellows die in dungeons; he saw girls exposed for sale in the markets. He witnessed floggings and flayings, and beheld the dangling corpses of those who had tried to escape. Through it all he was the support and leader of his fellow captives. He fought off their despair; he organized, more than once, a break for freedom. Each time he was defeated, but when he was sentenced to death his own courage rescued him. For, cruel though these Moslem tyrants were, they admired utter bravery and, when Cervantes stood before his master with folded arms and lifted chin and defiantly took upon himself all blame for the plots to escape, he won his life. But not until he had suffered five years of captivity could his family in Spain scrape up enough to rescue Miguel. And when he finally went forth it was with a testimonial signed by Moors as well as Christians that never had a prisoner stood so unbowed.

Thus in 1580 Cervantes at last kissed the soil of Spain—and learned how soon the world forgets a maimed veteran. While he waited vain years for promotion, he tried his hand at writing. But in the attempt to be elegant his book was only artificial—a "pastoral" called *Galatea*, about stilted shepherds and coquettish shepherdesses, which brought its author just enough money to buy a suit of wedding clothes and settle 100 ducats (about $500) on his bride.

The girl, Catalina de Palacios Salazar y Vozmediano, was young, and she brought a dowry of some olive trees and vineyards, a few beehives and a share of the family farm implements. A good catch, perhaps, for some young peasant. But Catalina's new husband was nearly twice her age, and meant to scribble. He took her to Madrid and there, in the bohemian company of actors, writers and producers, she was miserable. Cervantes' plays made just enough money to encourage him to write others, not one a real success. Then onto the stage strode a young writer, Lope de Vega, who in 24 hours could turn out a box-office hit. Cervantes was crowded out of the theater, hurt and jealous.

Then, he says, "I hung up my pen," to take any employment offered. That proved to be the job of a tax collector. He was also engaged to gather supplies for the great Armada which King Philip was readying to fight England. "Spain is already singing of victory," wrote Cervantes exultantly and, in a spirit of patriotism, steeled his heart to wring from towns and villages around Seville their stores of wheat, olive oil, wine and pork. But Cervantes soon found himself behind jail bars. The trouble was that he could not do arithmetic; perfectly honest, he had got his accounts in a muddle. Though released, he was fined 6000 reals (about $750). Then, worried about carrying large sums in collected taxes, he deposited these with a Sevillian banker—who immediately went into bankruptcy. Cervantes went to jail again.

Here he learned the jargon of thieves and murderers. Looking through the bars, he sent his thoughts out over the hot white roads of Andalusia. There he had met the world going by—strolling players, princes of the Church, exiled Moors returned in disguise, venturesome girls in boys' clothing, boys from the country running away to town, horse-trading gypsies, hard-drinking muleteers—all companions of a mile or two on the road, a page or two in the book that was growing in the heart of Cervantes.

When released from prison, he was ready for his great lifework.

And Spain was at last ready to listen. For she, too, had learned. The Armada called "invincible" had sunk to the bottom of the sea; with it had perished Spain's romantic faith that she was destined to save the world her way. Time now to sear with the fire of pure laughter the wound in her pride. Time for a fantastic old knight to come riding out of La Mancha's horizon, behind him his fat servant, Sancho Panza, on a donkey. Out of the shadows around a poor writer of 58 came this immortal pair, and trooping after them hundreds of other characters—none all good or all bad, but all human.

Don Quixote is an old skin-and-bones who has read so many novels about the age of chivalry that he has come to believe he is the last knight in Christendom, and must go forth from his village to right wrongs, rescue maidens, slay giants. He sets forth in rusty armor, on a gaunt horse he fondly thinks a fiery charger. To the deluded but valorous Don all he beholds is translated into romance—a pug-nosed wench is a beauteous damsel, a country inn is a castle, a flock of sheep is a Saracen host. Though Sancho sees things as they are, he follows loyally, picking up his master each time he tumbles.

When he started this tale, Cervantes meant only to ridicule the foolish chivalric romances that all Spain was reading. But the world is so full of follies that the author soon spurred his knight on. Self-deception, false grandeur, sentimental optimism—one bubble after another is burst by the lance of laughter. On and on flies the pricking quill, while a household of women clatter and chatter beyond the door. These were his two aging sisters, his faithful niece, his difficult daughter, and Catalina, his wife, loyal to the husband she never understood.

Not even they, not even the creditors knocking at the door could distract Cervantes, for his story had run away with him. The Don now begins to command our admiration as well as laughter, and we love him for his crazy nobility of character. Sancho the servant, whom we first assumed to be only a lout, proves to be a fellow worth listening to, salty with good-hearted sense. They are, we discover, two sides of the same person—the dreamer and the down-to-earth—and that person is you or I.

Don Quixote was first published in 1605, and its fame sped over the land. The public clamored for more, and Cervantes promised a sequel. Even while he was at work on this, he learned that a sequel to *Don Quixote* was already on the bookstalls and selling briskly. Its author, who called himself Avellaneda, not only jeered at Cervantes for his poverty but besmeared the stolen characters of the Don and his squire with filthy writing. In a just rage Cervantes drove his pen to finish a true sequel, which turned out to be as good as the first part and better.

Today the two parts are printed as one, a volume that stands among the great treasures of Western culture. It has found its way into all the tongues of the civilized world. Many artists, among them Goya, Hogarth, Fragonard, Doré, Dali, have been proud to illustrate the tale. *Don Quixote* has ridden onto the stage, into opera and the movies.

Not that either fortune or personal fame ever came to Cervantes in his twilight in Madrid. When French diplomats inquired there about the author of *Don Quixote*, they were told that he was just an old soldier, poor and known to few. They discovered him in a house in the Calle del León, where he came to the door on gouty feet to receive his distinguished visitors with old-fashioned Castilian courtesy. On April 23, 1616, it was death that knocked; Cervantes was laid in a grave that is now forgotten.

Yet forever there rides onward a gallant old man who levels his lance at all that is false, his shadow lengthening across Spain, across the world, across the centuries.

It is better to light one small candle than to curse the darkness.
—*Confucius*

The human race has one really effective weapon, and that is laughter.   —*Mark Twain*

THE MacARTHUR I KNEW

Adapted from the book
By *General George C. Kenney*

I FIRST saw General Douglas MacArthur one day in 1918 in France. As the tall, handsome figure approached, I noticed the single silver star of a brigadier general and the cap set at a suggestion of an angle. As a lieutenant of the Air Corps, I couldn't help comparing him with the aviators' favorite brass hat of those days, General Billy Mitchell. They both walked with the long, quick strides of alert men who knew where they were going and wanted to get there in a hurry. Both wore their uniforms jauntily— though you wondered whether they were exactly regulation.

"That's Douglas MacArthur," said the infantry captain with me. "If he doesn't get himself knocked off by the Germans, that guy is going places. But he seems to think he's going to live forever. He goes on trench raids wearing that cap instead of a tin hat. He's already collected a couple of wound stripes, besides a flock of medals he earned the hard way."

Even Air Corps lieutenants had heard of Douglas MacArthur. The colorful son of a colorful father, General Arthur MacArthur, Douglas had been born on an Army post in Arkansas, January 26, 1880, in the days when Indians were still occasionally daubing on war paint, and he had been in the Army ever since. At 19 he had entered West Point. The story went that, shortly after his arrival,

he calmly announced that he intended to finish at the head of his class and wind up his career as Chief of Staff of the United States Army. Four years later he had made good the first goal, with the astounding four-year average of 98.14 percent.

Young MacArthur was the most self-assured and easily the handsomest cadet at the Military Academy, a good athlete, manager of the football team and a member of the baseball team. In addition, he is supposed to have gotten himself engaged to eight girls at once. (The previous West Point record was seven.) MacArthur's reputation for insisting on his rights, and incidentally for winning most of his arguments, started during his second year at the Academy. In the hospital with eye trouble, he missed some mathematics tests. Returning from the hospital, he saw on the bulletin board a notice that the "goats"—students whose records were below par—were to take a special examination the next morning. MacArthur's name was on the list. He announced that he was going to see the mathematics professor and have his name taken off the list.

"But you can't do that," protested his roommate. "You haven't permission to see the professor, and besides you can't argue about an order."

"I'm going to get my name off that list," replied MacArthur.

He put on his best uniform and called on the mathematics professor. His high marks on previous exams had given him a passing average for the course, he said; therefore he should not be included with the goats. He considered it an insult to have his name on that list. He concluded, "Sir, I will not take the test," saluted, and walked out.

His roommate remonstrated with him most of that evening, but MacArthur was adamant. "I will not take that test," he repeated stubbornly. "I know it is an order, but it is an unreasonable one. If my name is not removed by nine o'clock tomorrow morning, I will resign."

"But what will your father say?" demanded his roommate.

"He will be terribly disappointed," said Douglas, "but I believe he will approve my action."

He turned in and slept for eight solid hours. His worried room-mate hardly closed his eyes all night. Next morning an orderly brought word that the name of Cadet Douglas MacArthur had been removed from the list.

Now here he was in France, a big shot in the 42nd (Rainbow) Division, just after the first major all-American attack. Marshal Ferdinand Foch, Generalissimo of the Allies, had insisted that this St. Mihiel operation be limited to driving the Germans back to the Hindenburg Line, and General John J. Pershing had agreed.

My friend the infantry captain continued with the latest Mac-Arthur story: "MacArthur came busting into Pershing's head-quarters yesterday hot from the front to tell the Old Man that he had broken through the German lines and that there was no organized resistance ahead of him. He wanted to be turned loose, no matter what Foch had said.

"They say he told Pershing, 'Let me go and I'll be in Metz in 48 hours. Then you'll make me a major general and the President will make you a field marshal.' Pershing chased him out—but I'll bet he wished he hadn't agreed to halt the advance. This Mac-Arthur is a cocky guy, all right, but he sure is a fighting general."

Twelve years later, when President Herbert Hoover made him Chief of Staff of the United States Army with the rank of a full four-star general, MacArthur was still breaking precedents. For at 50 he was the youngest man ever to hold that position. The second of his goals set 31 years before on entering West Point had now been attained.

I used to see him often at hearings of the Military Affairs Committee. With no war clouds apparent on the horizon, many Congressmen wanted to cut all military expenditures to the bone. MacArthur, almost single-handed, fought for adequate appro-priations. He never got all he asked for, but he managed to hold on to enough to keep the framework of our national defense together.

His devotion to his mother was one of MacArthur's remark-able traits. Before returning to his office after lunch, he invariably spent an hour or so discussing his problems with her. Each had strong likes and dislikes, but in spite of the fact that they were both exceedingly positive characters, they were seldom on opposite sides of an argument. In 1935 when given the job of building a Philippine Army, MacArthur asked his mother to go with him. The General didn't know it and his mother never mentioned it to him, but her doctor had told her she would be signing her own death sentence if she went to the Philippines to live. Her devotion to her son was such that she accompanied Douglas to Manila anyway. She died there a few months later, at the age of 82.

None of our responsible military leaders, including MacArthur, foresaw the Pearl Harbor disaster which made possible Japan's early conquests. When it came to fighting, however, MacArthur's defense of the Philippines was one of the few creditable episodes of the first five months of the Pacific war; it stood out like a beacon of hope in comparison with the debacle at Singapore, the fall of the Netherlands East Indies, and the confusion in Washington. Our military history contains few stories more dramatic, more stirring, more heroic than the epic of Bataan. It is a story that America and the Philippines can be proud of for all time.

With small forces and meager resources MacArthur delayed the Japanese schedule in the Philippines for weeks. Moreover, his stubborn resistance made the Filipinos feel that we were not going to abandon them, and when MacArthur said he would return they believed it. As a result, their widespread guerrilla activity pinned down many divisions of Japanese troops throughout the war.

When in 1942 I went out to Australia to be his air commander, MacArthur looked tired, drawn and nervous, although he was in excellent physical shape for a man of 62. He had a little less hair than when I had last seen him six years before, but it was still all black. He had kept the same trim figure and youthful walk. His eyes were keen and you sensed that wise brain of his working all the time.

Often I would spend an hour or two in the evening with the General and Jean MacArthur in Brisbane. A brilliant man with a superb command of English, the General was interesting on any subject; but when he discoursed on the art of war, he was fascinating. You soon realized that here was a master craftsman at work. His analysis was so clear, so logical, so simple that you wondered why you hadn't come to the same conclusion.

Jean MacArthur was a wonderful listener. The General might be a controversial figure, but not Jean: everyone who met her sang her praises. Dark-haired, animated, neat and pretty, she was a charming hostess and an exceedingly nice person.

Working for MacArthur was fun. He demanded loyalty, but he also gave it. People who worked for him drove themselves to carry out his wishes. They felt that they must not let "the Old Man" down.

I do not remember ever having been given a direct order by MacArthur during the whole time I worked for him, but I always knew exactly what he wanted done and knew he expected me to do it. He would not tolerate disobedience or any suggestion of divided allegiance, and he was impatient with vacillation. He gave a first impression of being a pretty tough individual, and so he was. If he did not like and trust you, you did not stay around long; but if he had confidence in you, he would open his heart to you and rally to your defense instantly if you got into difficulties. An old retired colonel who served with him for years summed up the feelings of practically every soldier who ever worked closely with him: "Douglas MacArthur was a hard-boiled old softie."

MacArthur's enemies, although grudgingly admitting his ability as a general, did not hesitate to ridicule and deprecate him at every opportunity. Before World War II was over, his brilliant victories were obscured by a flood of bitter stories reflecting upon his integrity and even his courage. I have never been able to trace the origin of the name "Dugout Doug." One thing is certain: the Army did not invent it. Too many in the Army remembered his contempt for danger in World War I, and had seen him coolly sitting in the open on Corregidor while the Japanese were bombing that rock. I know that the General was never in a dugout during the whole three years I was with him in the Pacific.

Another criticism was that when MacArthur left the Philippines he took with him his family and their Chinese amah, or nurse, leaving a number of American nurses on Corregidor to be captured by the Japanese. A lot of others, the rumor went, could have been evacuated to Australia if MacArthur had not brought out furniture, wardrobes and toys for his son, Arthur—a preposterous story on the face of it.

After repeated orders from President Roosevelt, General MacArthur, his wife, his four-year-old son, the Chinese amah and several members of his staff crowded into a PT boat at Corregidor and headed south for Mindanao, where a B-17 waited to fly them to Australia. Little Arthur, who was sickly after nearly three months of living under siege conditions, protested so much that he was allowed to take with him a little red fire engine. That probably accounted for the toy story. No furniture was flown out of the Philippines. The MacArthurs had only the clothes they wore, except for what could be squeezed into small handbags.

MacArthur was with the Australian Seventh Division when they went ashore at Balikpapan, in Borneo, on July 1, 1945. Half a mile inland, the party of generals and admirals climbed a little hill. An Australian brigadier handed MacArthur a map and proceeded to point out the various places of interest. Suddenly a Japanese machine gun opened fire, snipping leaves off the bushes and kicking up little spurts of dust around them. The rest of the party hit the dirt and started sliding back down the slope, but the Aussie and MacArthur kept on as though nothing had happened.

Eventually the brigadier finished talking. MacArthur folded up the map, handed it back, and thanked him for his information. Then, pointing to another hill about a quarter of a mile away, he said, "Let's go over there and see what's going on. And by the way, Brigadier, I think it would be a good idea to have a patrol take out that Jap machine gun before someone gets hurt."

At Leyte, when General MacArthur and President Osmeña went ashore, the snap of the Japanese high-velocity bullets also sounded too close for comfort. We were warned that there might still be some snipers hiding in the trees around us. The old

Philippine marshal's cap and the corncob pipe made MacArthur a wonderful mark for a sniper as he stood there in the open. He looked younger than ever and even his trousers seemed to have preserved their crease better than ours, in spite of the fact all of us had waded ashore in water above our knees.

When MacArthur, along with President Osmeña, broadcast an announcement of the landing to the people of the Philippines, his critics back home immediately attacked his speech as "flamboyant" and "corny." But to those listening to it on the spot, it was stirring and powerful.

"People of the Philippines," he said, "I have returned. By the grace of Almighty God, our forces stand again on Philippine soil. . . . Rally to me. Let the indomitable spirit of Bataan and Corregidor lead on. As the lines of battle roll forward to bring you within the zone of operations, arise and strike! . . . For your homes and hearths, strike! In the name of your sacred dead, strike! Let no heart be faint. Let every arm be steeled. The guidance of Divine God points the way. Follow in His Name to the Holy Grail of righteous victory."

It was an emotional appeal to an emotional people, and they liked it. Every guerrilla radio station in the Philippines was turned on that day and the results were apparent immediately. We got pledges for help from all over the country.

At Tacloban, MacArthur took over a large house for his headquarters—a fact which Tokyo Radio had already announced, so we would probably soon have some attention from Japanese aircraft. As we inspected the place the General asked, "What is that mound of earth there by the porch?" Someone said it was a dugout, a superior type: besides being 20 feet underground, it had electric lights, ventilating fans, furniture and rugs.

"Level it off and fill the thing in," said MacArthur. "It spoils the looks of the lawn." Perhaps the term "Dugout Doug" was meant to emphasize an entirely opposite characteristic of the man—like calling a fat man "Skinny."

The war ended on August 15. On the 30th we flew to Japan. Less than 500 airborne infantry were there when MacArthur and his top generals landed at Atsugi airfield. Just how much of a gamble MacArthur was taking landing with a handful of troops in the midst of an armed camp of recent enemies we could not guess. But I know that at least one of the party had a few nervous moments. Japanese automobiles with Japanese drivers took us into Yokohama. Japanese soldiers, fully armed and stationed about 100 yards apart, lined both sides of the road all the way, their backs to us as we passed. It was a token of submission, but they were also guarding against the possibility that some unreconstructed Japanese would take a potshot at us.

Most of us customarily carried pistols. Just as we were getting ready to go, MacArthur suggested that we leave them behind. There would be about 15 fully armed Japanese divisions within a few miles of us. If the Japanese didn't mean what they had said about surrendering, those pistols wouldn't do us much good. MacArthur's instinct for the workings of the Oriental mind paid off. A number of Japanese told me afterward that the sight of all those officers of MacArthur's staff walking around unarmed in a country of 80 million people who only a few days before were enemies made a tremendous impression. It told the Japanese more than anything else that they had lost the war.

On September 2, the top Army, Navy and Air commanders of the Pacific and the Japanese surrender party boarded the battleship *Missouri* for the final act. At exactly the time scheduled, MacArthur appeared and walked briskly to the microphone facing the recent enemy. His hand, holding his single sheet of manuscript, trembled slightly, but his voice was penetrating and cold as steel. He was the judge pronouncing sentence. He was freedom, democracy, civilization triumphant over the despotic forces of barbarism. In both stature and dignity MacArthur towered over the Japanese that day as he spoke to them.

He finished his speech and told them to sign the surrender documents. Prince Mamoru Shigemitsu, visibly nervous, sat down at the table. Either MacArthur's speech had given him stage fright or he was affected by the significance of his task. It was the first time in the 2000 years of her history that Japan had been forced to acknowledge defeat in a war. He took off his silk hat, then his white gloves, put his hat back on, hesitated, and finally as if in desperation hurriedly put down both hat and gloves. He seemed puzzled as to which of the papers he should look at first. We watched him, fascinated, in dead silence.

"Sutherland!" MacArthur's voice startled us like a pistol shot. "Show him where to sign."

General Richard K. Sutherland stepped to the table and pointed to the dotted line. Shigemitsu nodded, picked up the pen and signed, scarcely glancing at the text. He got up, bowed to MacArthur, and resumed his place with his delegation. Now it was the turn of General Yoshijiro Umezu, Chief of the Army General Staff. Scowling, still arrogant, he strode to the table, adjusted his horn-rimmed spectacles, and signed. He stood there a few seconds, just long enough to read the last sentence of the document; then, scarcely looking in MacArthur's direction, stepped back and took his place alongside Shigemitsu.

It was now our turn. MacArthur asked General Jonathan "Skinny" Wainwright, formerly of Bataan and Corregidor, and General Arthur E. Percival, the British commander at Singapore—both of them just released from a Japanese prison camp, and ghastly thin—to stand behind him while he signed as Supreme Commander of the Allied Powers. Admiral Chester Nimitz then signed for the United States, and the other Allies followed. The whole ceremony took just 18 minutes. We had seen one of the greatest dramas of the century conducted with the perfection and timing of a great showman, who dominated the scene completely. There was no doubt about it, it was MacArthur's party.

The task of occupying Japan was something new to MacArthur. And history records very few instances of generals covering themselves with glory as administrators of conquered countries. When he landed at Atsugi airdrome a devastated, burned-out Japan was suffering from national shell shock. Everywhere things were at a standstill, the people sullen.

Unemployment and hunger were widespread and it would have

taken little to start a reactionary movement, either Communist or Fascist. The Japanese had to be given an incentive to work. They must become a self-supporting, peaceful member of the community of nations. Wise leadership was required to avoid arousing hatred, for it would be difficult to hold 80 million rebellious people in line.

A large, complex organization, part civilian and part military, was set up to assist the Japanese in learning about democracy. Freedom of speech and religion was proclaimed, and the infamous "thought control" police abolished. New elections were ordered in which women for the first time were allowed to vote. The holdings of powerful clans, like the Mitsui and Mitsubishi families, were ordered dissolved and their stocks sold to the public. The large estates, which held the greater part of the peasantry in financial bondage as sharecroppers, were broken up into small parcels. And at MacArthur's order the Japanese prepared a new constitution which elevated parliament, stripped the Emperor of his powers as the divine ruler and made him a constitutional monarch.

MacArthur's popularity with the Japanese, and it was genuine, was understandable. When the war ended they had no leader, and needed one badly. MacArthur supplied that leadership. The Japanese had confidence in him and believed that he was trying to help them. Four times a day they gathered by the hundreds outside his headquarters just to catch a glimpse of him as he entered or left. They liked his aloofness, his air of authority, even his big automobile. He got more fan mail than any Hollywood actor. The Japanese definition of democracy was probably that it was what MacArthur wanted done.

When the storm broke in Korea in June 1950, destiny beckoned again. MacArthur was the first commander of a United Nations army. Once more, with insufficient forces and resources, he was called upon to fight a well-prepared aggressor—another shoestring show to test his military genius.

The heartbreaking series of withdrawals during the summer of

1950, until his forces were pinned down in the Pusan area, stunned the world; but on September 15, after a month of hurling back the Communist hordes with bloody losses, he electrified everyone with the brilliant landing at Inchon, followed in a few days by the capture of Seoul and the liberation of all South Korea. He was acclaimed as a master strategist and the smartest general of the age.

Except for the First Marines, none of his divisions were at full strength. Additional men from the United States were not forthcoming, even to replace casualties. MacArthur's scheme was not only bold, it was revolutionary. He recruited Koreans and took 100 of them into each rifle company. Each GI was assigned a Korean to instruct in the job of being a soldier. The GIs called it the "buddy system," and the individual GI and his "buddy" solved the problem together. It isn't in the textbooks, but that is how MacArthur brought his divisions up to strength.

I talked with him in his office in Tokyo a week after the Inchon landing. "General," I said, "I had a hunch you were going to make that end run, but I thought it would be around the middle of October. Why did you advance it to September?"

"I'll tell you why," he said. "Late in August, flying over Korea, I saw one of the best rice crops the country ever had. In Tokyo they told me it was due to be harvested in October. I decided that I wanted the South Koreans to harvest that rice."

In April 1951, General MacArthur was relieved of his command by President Harry S. Truman. Though 71 years of age, the general was still tall, erect, graceful and a handsome figure of a man. His step was firm, his eyes clear and alert, his face and hands without wrinkles. He had the vigor and stamina of a man at least ten years younger. He had worn the uniform of his country continuously on active duty for 52 years. Since December 1941 until he left Japan in that spring of 1951, he had worked seven days a week without a single day's vacation.

Returning to the United States, MacArthur was given a hero's welcome. After addressing a joint session of Congress, he retired from active service to enter business. Then, on April 5, 1964, following three major operations, General of the Army Douglas MacArthur died at Walter Reed Hospital in Washington, D.C. President Lyndon B. Johnson directed that the five-star general and Congressional Medal of Honor winner "be buried with all the honors that a grateful nation can bestow."

To my mind, few men have been more selfless in service to their country regardless of the effect of their actions on their own personal fortunes. His record speaks for itself: brilliant leadership and victory in two world wars; amazingly successful administration of a conquered country after nearly four years of bitter warfare; unfaltering defense of American ideals and principles in peace and war.

No man ever sacrificed his meager command more sparingly or grudgingly. To Douglas MacArthur every American life— private to general, soldier or civilian—was something precious to be hoarded at all costs. Someday, when the complete history of his campaigns from New Guinea to Luzon is written, the world will realize the magnitude of the tasks confronting him, the paucity of men and resources he had to work with, and the true genius of the man who gained that unbroken string of victories with a relatively low casuality list. In almost four years of vicious fighting against a desperate and determined enemy, and combating the heat and diseases of tropical jungles, the war in the Southwest Pacific Area cost us about 90,000 of the 291,557 American lives expended in battle on all fronts in World War II.

MacArthur's campaigns in New Guinea, the lightning seizure of the Admiralties, the reconquest of the Philippines, furnish examples of strategy, boldness and timing that will be models for students of warfare for generations to come. He emerged from World War II as one of the "great captains" of all times.

There is no security on this earth. There is only opportunity.
—*General Douglas MacArthur*

HEROIC PREACHER

By William F. McDermott

O<small>N</small> June 17, 1963, 14 million persons throughout the world celebrated the 260th anniversary of the birth of John Wesley, whose stern rules of upright conduct earned his followers the once derisive name of "Methodists." They had occasion to think with awe of this circuit rider who spent 52 years in the saddle, sloughing through thousands of miles of muck and mire to preach from tree stumps in open fields, from slag piles near mouths of mines, from boxes on street corners. Tuberculosis threatened him, mobs stoned him, churchmen denounced him, and his own sensitive nature cringed from the roughness of the life he led. But with faith aflame he rode on to accomplish his purposes.

The historian Lecky says that the Methodist revival saved England from bloody revolution, that Wesley influenced practical Christianity more than any other man since the 16th century. Be that as it may, his shadow has lengthened into the second largest Protestant denomination in the United States; scores of hospitals, schools, colleges, churches and missions today bear the name that was once scorned.

There was little reason to suppose, during his early life, that his name would be widely known at all. At ten John Wesley was sent from Epworth, where he was born in 1703, to the famous Charterhouse school in London. He studied Greek and Hebrew, and at 17 entered Oxford. There he remained for most of 15 years as student and teacher. During this period his tuberculosis became so serious that once he stripped and plunged into a stream to stop the hemorrhage.

It was a "wild oats" era for college men. Serious-minded individuals like John and his brother Charles found themselves out of step. A small group banded together to seek refuge in religion and the discipline of rigid self-denial. They gave all but their barest necessities to the needy; they visited the sick and the imprisoned, and spent long hours in prayer. John was ordained a priest of the Church of England in 1728. When missionaries were called to go to America to serve the colonists in Georgia—most of them recruited from debtors' prisons—John Wesley responded enthusiastically. He took with him all the rituals and accessories of formal religion. He enforced ecclesiastical discipline, introduced acts of penance and emphasized the confessional. But life on the rough frontier did not live up to his exalted expectations, and presently the missionary returned to England, frustrated and somewhat embittered.

Yet one bright thing stood out in Wesley's memory—his association with the Moravians, people of tranquil faith whom he had seen aboard ship. In a storm that threatened disaster, they alone were calm. "Why be disturbed by the waves and the winds?" they had said. "God will take care of us all." This was the sort of peace he craved—and could not find.

One night in May 1738 the despairing clergyman made his way to a little room in London where the Moravians gathered for prayer. With them were other members of the Church of England who were looking for a deepened fervor. Someone was reading from the works of Luther about the change God works in the human heart through Christ. Suddenly something came alive in the soul of Wesley. "I felt my heart strangely warmed," he later wrote. It was to set off his career.

Up in Bristol, George Whitefield, the rough-and-ready son of an inn tapster, was now preaching to multitudes with the fire of a crusader. He invited Wesley to share his "ministry of the open air." Wesley shrank from it. Preach outdoors, with a pile of stones as pulpit? He was aghast. Yet there was something about the "untouchable" miners of Kingswood, near Bristol, that stirred him. They considered themselves outcasts—men completely without religion, desperate men who cursed life itself. Wesley took the plunge.

It was a motley crew of grimy-faced, cynical men—first hundreds, then thousands—who crowded about the fragile little man in church vestments. He stood only five feet four, but he seemed to tower over them. Something in that voice gripped his listeners. Quiet, but clear as a bell, the words flowed to the outer rim of the throng. With deadly earnestness Wesley drove deep into their hearts his message: "You are the sons of God, the heirs of eternal life. Lift up your heads as free men, and let your hearts overflow with joy." He pleaded with them to forsake their erring ways, he spoke of "forgiveness," "redemption" and "hope" and pointed to the road of glory ahead. He so pictured the love of God for lost men that they were transfixed as by a heavenly Presence. For weeks the crusader preached with all the flame within him. He told an inquirer: "The scene is already changed. Kingswood is no more filled with drunkenness and uncleanness, with fights and bitterness. Peace and love are there."

To expand his work, Wesley betook himself to London. Now he ignored the fine points of theology and stressed a rigid, "methodical" routine of prayer and good works. Regular societies were formed to carry on his work, with "preaching houses" manned by "Methodist" lay preachers. An abandoned cannon factory was turned into a tabernacle, and the first service drew 5000 people. When spiritually starved people of other cities besought Wesley, he began his incredible career as a parson of the saddlebags. He set for himself a strict regimen: he rose daily at four a.m., preached his first sermon at five and was on the road by six. He often made 60 to 70 miles a day and usually preached at least three times. And he demanded as much Spartan labor of his preachers as he did of himself. Any man who wouldn't gladly get up at four in the morning and be ready at five with a fresh sermon was no worker of his.

Wesley's ruthless denunciation of the immorality and drunkenness of the day aroused fierce hostility. John's brother Charles affirmed he could identify the homes of Methodists by the marks of missiles hurled against them. From bull-baiting rings vicious animals were brought to stampede crowds as they tried to worship. Men on horseback lunged into the throngs. Drunken gangs assaulted them with rocks and clubs, tore down the meetinghouses.

Once, in Staffordshire, John Wesley was stoned by a mob and slugged with a club. Beaten to the ground, he prayed with such earnestness and calm that the mob grew quiet. Suddenly the leader put his hand on Wesley's head and said dramatically, "Sir, I will spend my life for you. Not one soul shall harm a hair of your head." The man was George Clifton, prizefighter and gang leader. Completely reformed, Clifton became an ardent preacher under the Wesley banner.

Slowly, irresistibly, sympathizers were won to Wesley's crusade for decency, honesty and goodness—in the individual and in public life. He turned his guns on the evils of his day. Though slavery was protected by law and considered highly respectable, Wesley did not hesitate to fight it. His *Thoughts upon Slavery* (1774) did for England what *Uncle Tom's Cabin* did for America.

He fought the horrible prison system, exposing conditions of filth, starvation and degradation. He visited some of the vilest of the jails to minister to the unfortunates. In 1761 he was able to commend the transformation of Newgate Prison from "filth, stench and wickedness" to a place that was "clean and sweet," where prisoners were paid for their work, where free medical care was given the sick. The key to that improvement lay in the fact that the keeper of the prison was a convert of the Revival. The rough-and-tumble world in which John Wesley lived never dampened his devotion to learning. In the saddle he read the classics or made shorthand notes for his voluminous daily journal. He mastered six languages and studied their best literature.

His writings were prodigious, in range as well as volume. He wrote a four-volume history of England for the use of his followers. He compiled a *Christian Library*, comprising a wide range of devotional literature culled from the history of the Christian Church. He wrote on the habits of beasts and birds and insects. His *Compendium of Natural Philosophy* touched on sense perception, imagination and memory, understanding and will, and immortality. Years before Charles Darwin he concluded that "there is a prodigious number of continued links between the most perfect man and the ape."

His best-seller was a primitive "medical" booklet called *An Easy and Natural Method of Curing Most Diseases*. It stressed plain food, fresh air, abundant exercise and a contented spirit. Its sales netted Wesley $150,000, which he plowed back into publishing the book for free distribution. In all, some 400 publications flowed from Wesley's pen.

Says the *Encyclopaedia Britannica* of this phase of John Wesley's career: "No man in the 18th century did so much to create a taste for good reading, and to supply it with books at the lowest prices."

Wesley was the founder of England's first free medical dispensary. He set up spinning and knitting shops to give employment to the poor. He established Wesley's Benevolent Loan Fund to help finance new business enterprises, and the Strangers' Friend Society to give relief to "poor, sick, friendless strangers." He gave away $200,000—royalties from his books—but limited himself to $150 a year for personal expenses. He once said that he would give people the privilege of calling him a robber if at the time of his death he was the owner of more than $50.

Wesley lived to be 88. Even to his last he was preaching and writing daily. On his deathbed he called out, "Where is my sermon on the Love of God? Take it and spread it abroad. Give it to everyone." His burial was in keeping with his convictions about service to others. His instructions were followed to the letter: burial in nothing more costly than wool; whatever remained in his dresser and pockets to be given to his followers. As a protest against needless funeral expense, he had ordered that no hearse be employed and that six poor men, in need of work, be hired at $5 each to carry his body to the grave.

SPARK OF REASON

By Donald Culross Peattie

"I DISAGREE with every word you say, but will defend to the death your right to say it." Many attribute that famous phrase to Voltaire. It was, however, the work of one of his biographers who thus perfectly summed up Voltaire's lifelong fight for freedom of thought. "Think for yourselves!" he continually urged his contemporaries. The first modern in an age of bigotry, he turned it into the Age of Reason.

Voltaire has been called a cynic, because he insisted on your right to doubt what you cannot believe. People will assure you that Voltaire has been termed an atheist. He gives his answer not to them but to his Maker:

> O God unrecognized, whom all Thy works proclaim,
> O God, hear these my final words:
> If ever I have erred, 'twas searching for Thy Law;
> My heart may go astray, but it is full of Thee.

This is the utterance of a contrite and humble heart. Voltaire never attacked simple faith; what he ridiculed was superstitious credulity, the debasing counterfeit of faith.

The child who was to become "Voltaire" (a pen name) was born in Paris on November 21, 1694, and baptized François Marie Arouet. Motherless after his seventh year, he was delicate in health and undersized—a fiery elf of a child with an impish grin and an unnatural love for learning. At 17 he announced his intention of becoming a man of letters. Papa Arouet, a social climber and oppressively pious, thought this profession disreputable and forced him into a law office where the youngster made a showy failure. Sent in the diplomatic service to Holland, he promptly tried to elope with a girl whose family had no money, and was shipped home in disgrace. He still wanted to write. "To be a writer is to starve," cried Papa Arouet, and tried to help destiny by disinheriting his son. Within ten years young "Monsieur Voltaire" was famous.

His success was assisted by the censors who banned almost all his books and usually closed his plays on the third night. As a result, fashionable Paris packed the opening nights and memorized the most stinging lines; his books were circulated like pamphlets of some underground organization, and avidly read in foreign countries. The official charge that Voltaire was corrupting public morals did not refer to indecency; it meant what it might mean in Russia today—that to criticize the government or doubt revealed authority was the most horrible kind of "immorality." True, Voltaire's plays and fantastic novels were usually laid in exotic foreign lands; but everyone understood their political double meanings and rocked with laughter. And laughter is a flame which governments cannot extinguish. So Voltaire was clapped into the Bastille for almost a year.

Injustice to himself Voltaire could endure, but not injustice to others. When the greatest actress in France, Adrienne Lecouvreur, lay dying in agony, Voltaire at her bedside heard the priest demand she renounce her art as a shameful spectacle. But Lecouvreur proudly refused. The priest left her without religious consolation and she was buried by the police in an unmarked grave. From that day Voltaire nourished a hatred not of Christianity, as has been alleged, but of unchristian cruelty. "The man who says to me, 'Believe as I do or God will damn you,'" he warned, "will presently say to me, 'Believe as I do or I will kill you.'"

Voltaire was soon imprisoned in the Bastille a second time. Under promise to leave France he was released, and sailed for

England. In London he was astounded by the love, not fear, in which the British monarch was held. He was deeply impressed by the funeral of Sir Isaac Newton in Westminster Abbey; in France no mere scientist would have been knighted or given so splendid a burial. He marveled at the strength and independence of Parliament, and above all at the operations of British justice.

In all his life Voltaire knew only one American, Benjamin Franklin, whom he admired immensely, but how he would have loved the young man who later wrote that "all men are created equal" and have "inalienable rights" to "life, liberty and the pursuit of happiness"! For these were thoughts Voltaire had expressed long before Thomas Jefferson was born.

In 1729, Voltaire, now 35 years old, received permission to return to France. Then, shrewdly taking advantage of a government miscalculation in the issue of national lottery tickets, he formed a syndicate which bought up every ticket. This made him rich and he frankly enjoyed it. He liked comfort and fine clothes and handsome carriages. But he was keenly aware of the suffering around him, and could not, like the pleasure-mad society and luxury-loving clerics, shrug it off as "God's will." Faults he had in plenty. He was selfish and quarrelsome; when in a tight place he elaborately lied out of it, and when in genuine danger he took to his heels. Yet he had one of the most important of all moral concepts: he saw man as a free agent, responsible for his own actions, with his conscience as a bar of judgment.

He hated cruelty and intolerance, attacking them with a wit made luminous by a sense of justice—"transmuting anger into fun, fire into light." "My trade," he said, "is to say what I think." And what he thought comes to 99 volumes of plays, poems, novels and articles. He wrote about 8000 letters to famous people. Catherine the Great of Russia hoped that her replies were not so frequent as to bore him. Christian VII of Denmark apologized for not instituting all reforms at once. Gustavus III of Sweden wrote that he was trying to live up to Voltaire's humanitarian standards, and Frederick the Great, then Crown Prince of Prussia, came incognito to worship at his feet.

Voltaire's correspondents had a hard time keeping up with his addresses, for he was often forced to hide. Frequently the censor made a public bonfire of one of his new books, and all Europe could read by those flames what Voltaire thought of military brass, miracle cures, the divine right of kings, the Holy Office of the Inquisition. He could annihilate a man in a sentence: Cardinal Mazarin, he said, had been "guilty of all the good he did not do." In 1749, Voltaire accepted the long-standing invitation of Frederick the Great to grace the raw new Prussian Court at Potsdam. But soon Voltaire, indignant at the militarism of the Prussian *Junkers* and amused at the pretensions of the Court, became a thorn that sank steadily deeper in Frederick's side, till he plucked it out with a roar of anger. Voltaire now found nearly every frontier barred to him, thanks to Frederick's vengeful influence.

In 1755 the aging philosopher found refuge in the little free Republic of Geneva. Three years later he bought property in Ferney, four miles away from Geneva but on French soil. Thither almost every great man in Europe came to see him. His wraithlike body clad in a gorgeous yellow satin coat, the old elvish smile spreading across his wrinkled face, Voltaire entertained his guests with the best table talk in Europe. People came to stay three days, remained three months. "God protect me from my friends!" Voltaire sighed. "I will take care of my enemies myself."

A host of victims of religious and political persecution sought his protection. He began building houses for them, set them up in the businesses they were fitted for, from carpentry to cobbling, from dairying to weaving and pottery. Soon he had a village on his estate, and built a church and a school for the villagers' children. Voltaire's last years should have been peaceful. But his bitterest battles and his greatest work were yet ahead of him. In 1762, a time when religious fanatics still celebrated the anniversaries of the massacres of heretics, a young man was found hanged in a shop in Toulouse. Rumor asserted that he was a Protestant who had wished to become a Catholic, and that his father, Jean Calas, a feeble and gentle old man, had hanged his powerful young son. Calas, who after horrible tortures had confessed nothing, was executed.

As Voltaire became interested in this case, he began to uncover the shocking nature of criminal law as practiced then in nearly every country save England. There had been no jury; the accused had been allowed no counsel; no evidence in his favor was admitted; the accusers gave secret testimony; the judges conducted themselves as prosecutors. More, Voltaire learned that most criminal laws were not even written down, but were held in the heads of the legal profession and "interpreted" as seemed best for securing a conviction.

Voltaire swung into action with all his great influence and fortune. For three years he scarcely thought it right, he said, to take time to smile. His sleepless nights were devoted to bombarding lawyers, churchmen, kings and the entire press of Europe with a demand to reopen the Calas case. The King himself had at last to yield to an aroused public, and review the whole matter. The dead man was declared innocent. This case set rolling a reform of criminal law which governments had neglected for 800 years.

No sooner was the Calas case won than the victims of similar injustice rushed to Voltaire. One of the things that most enraged him was the power of church authorities to accuse, torture and execute laymen who had broken ecclesiastical laws. Let religion get out of politics and law, he demanded, and attend to the neglected business of things spiritual. Torrents of abuse greeted this; but step by step Voltaire cleared away the confusion between lawbreaking and sin.

This hornet of an old man adored his own country and was possessed by an intolerable desire to see his beloved Paris once more before he died. On a February day in 1778 a French customs officer stopped a carriage to see if there were any dutiable articles inside it. "There is nothing," came a thin old chuckle from inside, "no contraband except myself." The officer threw open the door. "*Mon Dieu*," he cried, "it is Monsieur Voltaire!" For the wrinkled old grin was known to millions.

Paris went wild in welcome. The National Academy, which had turned him down for years until finally electing him to membership in 1746, opened its arms. On the steps of the Comédie Française the entire cast assembled to greet the playwright. His new play was drowned in cannonades of applause that continued through the entire performance. In May the round of festivities finally brought the old man, at 83, to his deathbed. His final testament leaves to us his whole creed. "I die," he had his secretary write, "adoring God, loving my friends, not hating my enemies, and detesting superstition." Refused burial by churchly authorities, his body would have shared the fate of Lecouvreur's had not his friends, propping the corpse up between them to make the gate sentries think him still alive, rushed Voltaire out of the city to a decent interment.

But France, struggling against her tyrants, caught up at last with the man who had cried, "People, awake! Break your chains!" In 1791, when the Revolution was in full swing, the body of Voltaire was brought back to Paris and laid for one night in triumph amid the ruins of the Bastille. A quarter of a million people pressed forward between the long lines of honor guards to pay homage to his remains, before they were taken to the Pantheon, where the great of France lie buried. As the procession moved forward, a banner unrolled upon the wind. It carried these words: "He gave wings to the human mind. He prepared us to be free."

When Voltaire arrived in England in 1727, he found that feeling ran high against the French, that on the streets of London he was in grave peril. One day during a walk a crowd of angry citizens shouted, "Kill him! Hang the Frenchman!" Voltaire stopped, faced the crowd, and cried: "Englishmen! You want to kill me because I am a Frenchman! Am I not punished enough, in not being an Englishman?" The crowd cheered wildly, and provided him safe conduct back to his dwelling. —*Christian Science Monitor*

THE SULTAN OF SWAT

By Jack Sher

IT IS SOMETIMES hard for me to realize that Babe Ruth is a sports figure of the past. I somehow think of him as still at the plate, scowling at a pitcher, his big head cocked on one side, his toes turned in, his giant-sized bat waving nervously. No one before or since has ever smashed out such complete and satisfying home runs.

The Babe was colorful, lusty, greathearted, intense. The crowds loved him, and for 22 years he gave them more than their money's worth. Even when he struck out, he did it with such gigantic gusto and anger that it was a wonderful thing to watch. After the 1919 gambling scandal, when baseball hit its all-time low in public esteem, Ruth more than any other player won the fans back to the game. They knew that here was one big leaguer who would never let them down.

The Babe set many marks that still stand unchallenged. He hit the most home runs with a life total of 714. He received the most bases on balls of any man in baseball, 2056; and he struck out the most times too, 1330. His total of 60 home runs in one season, made in 1927, stood for 34 years until, in 1961, Roger Maris of the New York Yankees poled 61 homers but in a longer playing season. His lifetime batting average (.342) is among the first seven in baseball. ("Shucks," Ruth once said, "I coulda hit a .600 lifetime average easy. But I woulda had to hit them singles.")

The greatest home run ever smacked was that unforgettable one in the 1932 World Series. The score was tied at 4–4 in the fifth inning and the Cubs had been heckling Ruth, who had already hit one homer in the first. As the Babe came to the plate, a Cub player rolled a lemon out of the dugout toward him. Ruth yelled, "If that bum Root throws it in there, I'll knock it over the fence again." The Cubs jeered.

Root, the Cub pitcher, grooved one for a strike. The Babe held up one finger. Root sent another down the middle. Babe held up two fingers. Then came the most talked-of gesture in baseball history—the Babe pointed at the fence, indicating where he was going to put the next one. On the next pitch there was a solid crack and sailing through the air unbelievably straight, high and true was the home run that Ruth had called. Equally amazing was the Babe's comment when asked that evening how he would have felt if he had missed that third one. "Why," he said, startled, "I never even thought of that."

In his golden, glorious years the Babe was riding high. Money was rolling in. He endorsed endless products. He was to go on to earn a total playing salary of $872,000, plus more than a million dollars from ghostwritten stories, endorsements, barnstorming tours and movies. One year he carried around a $15,000 check from a cereal company. Whenever he went into a bar or restaurant and the time came to pay the bill, the Babe would pull it out and tell them to cash it. This, of course, could not be done, and whoever was with him had to pay the check, while the Bambino roared. And, so the story goes, he kept the check so long that when he came to cash it, the breakfast-food company had gone broke in the depression and he was out the $15,000. But Ruth took it with a grin.

Even when he got sick, Babe did it in a lavish fashion. "Saw Ruth in half," somebody once cracked at Yankee Stadium, "and you'll find half of Stevens' frankfurter concession in him." But one day in 1925, when he gorged himself with 12 hot dogs and eight bottles of soda pop, it did not turn out to be funny. Stricken with acute indigestion, the Babe was rushed to the hospital, where he nearly died. Kids sat out in the streets under his window with flowers; sports fans across the country, housewives and schoolgirls read the daily bulletins about his health and prayed for him.

He was the most accessible of all ballplayers. He had a big grin, a ready handshake for everybody, most of all for the kids. Every year thousands of grimy little hands thrust out baseballs for the autograph that sent the boys away with eyes shining. On slow days in right field he would lean against the bleacher screen and chat with them. He would pose for pictures, pat the kids on the head, ask them questions, talk man-to-man with them about baseball.

Once he learned that a 13-year-old New Jersey boy had undergone a serious operation and had failed to improve. The boy's hero was Babe Ruth. The next morning the door of the hospital ward opened and in walked Babe. Ruth sat on the edge of the bed and talked to the boy as long as the doctors would let him stay. Then he told Johnny that he was going to hit a home run that afternoon, especially for him. He did hit that homer for Johnny, just as he had promised, and the boy, his interest in life revived, immediately began to improve.

Facts about the Babe's early life are vague, but when pieced together they indicate that he began life as a pushed-around little nobody, scratching for food, unwanted by anyone. He was born in Baltimore of parents named Gearhardt or Erhardt in February 1894 or '95. Some say his mother's first name was Ruth; she died when he was very young, and his father not long afterward. When not quite seven years old the youngster was picked up on the streets and sent to St. Mary's Industrial School. Kindly Brother Gilbert took charge of him. In later years, when Ruth slipped into wild habits, Miller Huggins, Yankee manager, sometimes sent for Brother Gilbert. He was the one influence who always steadied Ruth.

There were 43 ball teams among the boys at St. Mary's. Ruth played every position, finally settled down as catcher, but in his last year switched to pitching. It was Brother Gilbert who understood that the boy was destined to become a ballplayer and got Jack Dunn, manager of the Baltimore Orioles, to have a look at him. Dunn was impressed and in the spring of 1914 the 19-year-old George Herman Ruth reported to training camp. Starting salary: $600 a year.

As Ruth walked out on the ball field, tagging at Dunn's heels, one of the coaches grinned and said, "Here comes Jack with his newest babe." The nickname stuck. Dunn sold Ruth to the Boston Red Sox, where he pitched—and won—his first big-league game on July 11, 1914. The next season he won 18 games and lost only six, to help the Red Sox win the pennant. From 1915 to 1918 the Babe was known as the top pitcher in the American League. He beat the immortal Walter Johnson six times, three of them by a 1–0 score. In a crucial game with Detroit, with the Red Sox leading by one run, he faced the Murderers' Row of that time—Ty Cobb, Bob Veach and Sam Crawford—and, with the bases loaded, struck them out one-two-three.

In 1919, Ed Barrow, manager of the Red Sox, saw that Ruth would be more valuable as a hitter playing every day than as a pitcher twice a week. Switched to a permanent outfield position, the Babe turned the national spotlight from pitchers to hitters. Up until then the great baseball heroes had been moundsmen such as Grover Alexander, Eddie Plank, Christy Mathewson. Ruth's 1919 home-run clouting—he belted 29—was considered a feat that would never again be equaled. Everywhere the Red Sox performed, the fans turned out in droves to watch him wave that big, 54-ounce stick, the heaviest one in baseball. The Babe put on great shows; his name echoed across the country.

Then Colonel Ruppert, of the Yankees, bought the Babe for $125,000. His first year in New York, 1920, Ruth rapped out 54 homers, and in return was swamped with 20,000 fan letters a week. Life became one wonderful, glorious spree for the Babe, and nobody dared break it up. Ruppert let America's new idol swing along on his merry way. "That big mug has an iron constitution," he said. "He can take it." The Babe ate ten meals a day. He bought dazzling cars, smashed them up and bought more. In 1921, training on late hours and liquids of a dubious nature, the rowdy Bambino whacked 59 balls out of the park.

The Babe's seasonal holdouts for more money were a splendid

source for newspaper copy when he was being paid $40,000, then $52,000, then the unbelievable sum of $80,000 for a season's play. None of the holdouts were phony. The Babe believed he was worth a million dollars a year, the way he could hit those homers. And his yearly clamor for more money benefited other players. A popular chant at the time, among less spectacular performers, was, "If that guy Ruth is worth $80,000, I must be worth at least a third as much!"

By 1929 the Babe had settled down quite a bit. He married a Follies girl, Claire Hodgson. A good wife, she was always a steadying influence on him. He became a proud and careful parent of his two girls, Julia and Dorothy. He was learning moderation, everywhere except at the plate. The money kept on rolling in. Ruppert was giving him a bonus for every circuit swat. He spent money lavishly, but friends forced him to buy annuities before his retirement in 1935.

Soon after he quit the game, Babe's name dropped out of the sports pages. And later, when we had a war on our hands, there were other things to think about besides baseball. Yet out in the tangled jungles of New Britain, a group of battle-worn Marines saw fanatically charging Japanese troops break into the clear, shouting a chant both unbelievable and challenging—"To hell with Babe Ruth!"

No, he was not quite forgotten. Not to the Marines on New Britain that morning, facing an enemy whose supreme insult was to curse a man who meant America to the GIs, meant it as much as the hot dogs he loved and the great game he played.

And then one day there was a charity game in Yankee Stadium, with some sort of ceremony beforehand. Walter Johnson, the great old-timer, was out in the pitcher's box warming up. Suddenly a man stepped out of the Yankee dugout. A murmur crept through the crowd. Everybody stood up and then, from every section of the stadium, there came a crashing, swelling roar that the sight of only one man could create.

It was the Babe. He had the big bat over his shoulder, a big floppy smile on a face that the years hadn't changed much. He waved at the stands. He was 48 years old, but with the sound of the crowd in his ears he must have felt ageless that day. The Babe took his position in the box. He stood the same way, feet close together, well back of the plate; broad, sloping shoulders; the old, earnest scowl on his face. And then he pointed his bat at the right-field bleachers.

Nobody believed he could still do it. It was a great gesture, though. Nobody believed him, except the old players who were there that day, the gray-headed sportswriters, the fans who had become fathers and grandfathers. Johnson wound up and threw a couple across. The Babe swung at one and missed. Nobody laughed that day. Then Johnson sent one down the middle, hard and fast. The big club came off Ruth's shoulder, there was a ringing whack. The ball sailed into the air, high, far and beautiful. There was the long "aaah." The ball dropped into the right-field stands for a homer. The Babe trotted around the bases, jogging slowly. The smile on his face was fine to see.

In 1936, the first group of players who had made major contributions to baseball was selected for membership in the National Baseball Hall of Fame at Cooperstown, New York. To nobody's surprise, Babe Ruth's name appeared alongside those of four other baseball immortals—Ty Cobb, Walter Johnson, Honus Wagner and Christy Mathewson. And on a bronze tablet which bore a likeness of Ruth and a list of his accomplishments appeared these words: *The greatest drawing card in history.*

The Babe died on August 16, 1948. His body was brought to Yankee Stadium, "The House That Ruth Built." There it lay in state while close to 80,000 fans filed past to pay their final respects to the mighty Bambino.

George Herman Ruth played in an era of celebrated stars. But no sports memory is brighter than his—and his great records are still almost intact. He was the most colorful, sincere and lovable athlete of his time. If any one man deserves the credit, Babe Ruth must go down in history as the player who made baseball the American national sport.

CRUSADER
FOR COMMON SENSE

By Max Eastman

THERE are few great men in our history who would have more
to say to us right now than Tom Paine. And there is none
who would know better how to say it. Nothing in the
history of human persuasion exceeds the achievement of this
obscure British corset maker who landed at Philadelphia in November 1774—unheralded, unknown, unpolished even in grammar—and within a year and a half had, well-nigh singlehanded,
aroused the 13 colonies to an arrogant declaration of independence
from Great Britain and her King, and kings in general.

As a thoughtful contemporary said, Paine "contributed as
much with his pen as Washington with his sword" to the making
of this republic. He foresaw its full glory 11 years before its birth
and in the darkest hour of despair for the armies whose triumph
made it possible. Replying to Lord William Howe, who had issued
a proclamation granting mercy to the defeated Americans if they
would back down, he said: "The United States of America will
sound as pompously in history as the Kingdom of Great Britain."

He was able to make that prophecy because he had fully
grasped the advantages of democracy over one-man rule. In urging independence, Paine had put as much stress on the danger of
dictatorship as the evils of autocracy. He felt we could form here
in "a cool and deliberate manner" a government suitable to sensible and responsible men. Seeing the significance of this, and
foreseeing too the size and power of the coming republic, he was

able to make a boast that is not strange in our ears today: "The cause of America is, in a great measure, the cause of all mankind."

Although the kindest of men, Paine died in bitter, almost friendless solitude. He died, to speak the appalling truth, in infamy. After a hundred years, President Theodore Roosevelt described him in a press interview as a "dirty little atheist," and refused to retract when reminded that Paine was cleanly and carefully dressed, five feet nine inches tall, and a devout believer in God. Tom Paine was a wise man and became so by devoting his days to the pursuit of understanding. "I have seldom passed five minutes of my life, however circumstanced," he once remarked, "in which I did not acquire some knowledge." That astonishing statement is the key to his character, to his sudden and great feat of genius on arriving in a land where he felt free.

He was born in the little market town of Thetford, 90 miles from London. After leaving school at 13, he learned his father's trade of staymaker, fitting whalebone corsets. Tiring of this, he ran away to sea. He made two voyages, then got a job as exciseman or tax inspector for the government. Dismissed from this post, he was a tobacconist for a while, and also taught school. Then he got back his job as exciseman. The excisemen were organizing to better their conditions, and they sent him to London with a plea to Parliament for better pay. His plea was so eloquent that in answer to it he was fired for the second time. He then moved into a garret in London and started (at 37!) to make his living as a writer.

All this is usually described as failure. But Tom had succeeded in what seems to have been a deliberately adopted purpose: to keep alive, any way he honorably could, while studying and learning all a creative thinker needs to know. It was science, mainly, that he studied, but he dearly loved to shine in debate. Besides training his mind during those seemingly aimless years, he had met while in London men like Oliver Goldsmith and Ben Franklin. Franklin perceived his genius, and suggested that he go to the American colonies where life was more fluid.

Thus in 1774 this "failure" arrived in America, widely read, variously experienced, full of roughhewn opinions. Within a few months he was writing for a new journal called the *Pennsylvania Magazine*, and soon became its editor. As editor, Paine advocated about every cause that radicals have fought for since. He denounced war, ridiculed dueling, dismissed kings and titles as outdated, condemned cruelty to animals, advocated Negro freedom (anticipating by a month the first antislavery society), urged international federation, old-age pensions, rational divorce laws, women's rights. He believed with Jefferson in the independent individual, and dreaded the morbid overgrowth of the state.

Life in the colonies turned out to be not only fluid but seething. Leaders of opinion were in a rage against the harsh and stupid colonial policies of King George III. Less than five months after Paine's arrival, there occurred the clash at Lexington between armed colonials and British regulars. Still there was hardly a murmur of disloyalty to the mother country. Franklin was assuring the British in London that no American, "be he drunk or sober," had ever expressed a wish for separation. Jefferson was "looking with fondness toward a reconciliation with Great Britain."

Tom Paine, however, knew Great Britain, and by some swift magic of kinship he already knew America. He felt, as no other man did or could, the *difference* between the old world and the new. After a few brief months on these shores, he grasped and planted in men's hearts the vision of a free, independent America:

The birthday of a new world is at hand, and a race of men, perhaps as numerous as all Europe contains, are to receive their portion of freedom from the events of a few months. . . . WHEREFORE, instead of gazing at each other with suspicious or doubtful curiosity, let each of us hold out to his neighbor the hearty hand of friendship, and unite in drawing a line, which, like an act of oblivion, shall bury in forgetfulness every former dissension. Let the names of Whig and Tory be extinct; and let none other be heard among us, than those of *a good citizen; an open and resolute friend;* and *a virtuous supporter of the* RIGHTS OF MANKIND *and of the* FREE AND INDEPENDENT STATES OF AMERICA.

Paine called his nation-making pamphlet *Common Sense*. It was published anonymously in Philadelphia on January 10, 1776. Since governments in general, he argued, are an unfortunate necessity whose sole aim is to guarantee "freedom and security" to individuals, and since King George's colonial government guarantees neither, "we pay our money for nothing. . . . There is something absurd in supposing a continent to be perpetually governed by an island. It is not in the power of Britain to do this continent justice: the business of it will soon be too weighty and intricate to be managed with any tolerable degree of convenience, by a power so distant from us, and so very ignorant of us. . . . To be always running three or four thousand miles with a tale or a petition, waiting four or five months for an answer, which, when obtained, requires five or six more to explain it in, will in a few years be looked upon as folly and childishness. There was a time when it was proper, and there is a proper time for it to cease."

Through it all ran that stubborn will to freedom, honest logic and friendly relations among men—a sort of moral common sense—which lifted these hardheaded practicalities into the realm of great literature. "As to religion," he said, "I hold it to be the indispensable duty of government to protect all conscientious professors thereof, and I know of no other business which government has to do therewith."

Tom Paine piled up the maxims of a kindly sagacity to the point where they became the platform of a crusade. His little book sold 500,000 copies. There were 2,500,000 people in the country then. That means one copy to every five persons—the equivalent in the present population of 36,000,000 copies! He turned over his royalties to the Continental Congress; he didn't want to make money, he wanted to make a revolution.

Officers read *Common Sense* to their soldiers, teachers to their classes, parsons to their congregations. George Washington was soon endorsing its "sound doctrine and unanswerable reasoning." "Never before or since," says W. E. Woodward, in an illuminating biography, *Tom Paine: America's Godfather*, "has a book of any kind had such a profound influence on human affairs."

Six months after *Common Sense* appeared, the Declaration of Independence was signed and Paine was in the army backing up his words with deeds. During the dismal retreat of the ragged colonial forces after the loss of New York, he wrote—on a drumhead by a campfire in New Jersey—the first of those 13 papers called *Crisis* which rekindled the spirit of the Revolution whenever and wherever it flagged. Its opening words became a battle cry: "These are the times that try men's souls. The summer soldier and the sunshine patriot will, in this crisis, shrink from the service of their country."

Tom Paine also served America in its darkest hour with a feat of diplomacy. At his own expense, he went to Paris to negotiate a loan. He returned with not only the money but a shipload of stores which Washington desperately needed for the campaign against Cornwallis. When he got back, he was dead broke and was too famous to find a job. He was famous for stirring people up, and the time was coming now for quieting them down. When Washington, fresh from the victory at Yorktown, came to Philadelphia to receive the congratulations of Congress, Paine was living in a rented room nearby. He wrote a letter to the General asking for help, and was allotted $800 a year to continue fighting with his pen.

Paine's subsidy ended when the war did, in 1783. In 1785 Congress voted him $3000, less than the cost of his trip to France; the Pennsylvania Assembly voted him $2500; and New York presented him with a mansion and a confiscated Loyalist farm of 277 acres in New Rochelle. He leased this place, and lived well in a small house he had previously purchased in Bordentown, New Jersey, happy to give his mind at last to his inventions. He was working on a new kind of single-arch bridge. But all he achieved was to get a committee appointed by the Pennsylvania Assembly to consider it. Franklin suggested that he try his luck with the French Academy of Sciences.

For three years Paine passed back and forth between Paris and London. In both countries liberals were in high places now; Washington was their hero, and Paine was admired and honored by men of power. But France was moving toward her violent revolution, and England toward her fierce recoil. Paine, of course, was heart and soul for a French republic. When the Bastille fell, in 1789, he went to Paris to receive its key from Lafayette for presentation to General Washington.

He had returned to England when suddenly there splashed forth on his sacred principles, like a shower of eloquent mud, Edmund Burke's *Reflections on the Revolution in France*. He knew Burke, the brilliantly gifted orator of conciliation with the colonies. And he knew the French Revolution. Forgetting his bridge—it had got built, at Sunderland, England, and had stood up very well—forgetting also a new kind of crane, a smokeless candle and a scheme for a gunpowder motor, Tom Paine sat down to say what he thought of Edmund Burke, and also what he thought of kings and lords and the true ends of government.

Of Burke's flowery praise of the English constitution and the rights it secured to a privileged minority, he wrote:

> The farce of monarchy and aristocracy, in all countries, is following that of chivalry, and Mr. Burke is dressing for the funeral. Let it then pass quietly to the tomb of all other follies, and the mourners be comforted. . . . When it shall be said in any country in the world, my poor are happy; neither ignorance nor distress is to be found among them; my jails are empty of prisoners, my streets of beggars; the aged are not in want, the taxes are not oppressive; the rational world is my friend, because I am the friend of its happiness: when these things can be said, then may that country boast of its constitution and its government.

This second book, *The Rights of Man*, written once more at fever speed, had all the eloquent lucidity of *Common Sense*. And it boosted in the same way a mounting wave of opinion. Again Tom Paine was a best-seller—and again a classic. To suppress "Paineism" was soon a major occupation of the British government. A Proclamation against Seditious Writings was issued for his special benefit, his publishers were indicted, his book suppressed, his readers deported—one man got 14 years' banishment for advising people to read him. A scurrilous biography was concocted to discredit him; men were hired to hiss, hoot and jostle him when he appeared in public.

Paine fled to France. In Calais he was welcomed with a salute of guns, and the whole town spent two days celebrating the arrival of a great French citizen. For one of the first acts of the Revolution had been to bestow French citizenship upon Thomas Paine. And now, besides, he had been elected a deputy to the National Convention. He entered that tumultuous body amid deafening cheers on the day royalty was abolished in France, the first day of the "Year One of the Republic."

I do not know any scene in history more moving, or perhaps in the long run more significant, than that in the Convention when this notorious outlaw, author and arch-agitator of American republicanism, scourge of the nobility and shaker of the throne of England, rises to defend the life of the deposed French King. He has never made a speech and moreover he does not command the French language. So he merely ascends the tribune and stands there, silent, slender, indomitable—with that glow in his eyes that no man who saw it ever forgot—while a French deputy reads his speech in translation: "My language has always been that of liberty *and* humanity, and I know that nothing so exalts a nation as the union of these two principles . . ."

Jean Paul Marat rises and shouts to the astonished deputies: "I assert that it is not Thomas Paine's opinion—it is a false translation!" "I have read the original and the translation is correct," Deputy Garran answers. Pandemonium ensues, but Paine stands calm until the reading can be finished. Marat's fierce shouts are a tribute to Paine's prestige, but they are unnecessary. The Terror is on the march, and Paine himself, for his sin of farsighted mercy, is soon in a prison cell.

The American minister, Gouverneur Morris, a reactionary royalist and long a bitter enemy of Paine, refused to intervene. Robespierre, misled by Morris as to Washington's attitude, condemned Tom Paine to the guillotine "for the interests of America as well as of France!'' Paine tells how he was saved by a miracle. The door of his cell swung outward, and it was open when the executioners marked it with a sign indicating who should be taken; when they came for their victims, Paine's door was closed— the mark was on the inside! The Terror marched past. And soon— incredibly soon—it arrived at its master, Robespierre.

Paine at the time lay unconscious in his cell, sick to his own death, it seemed, with a fever. But Morris was replaced by a democrat—the future President James Monroe—and Monroe secured Tom Paine's release, took him into his house and with his wife's help nursed him back to life.

Tom Paine was a devout man, with so austere and intellectual a religion that he thought churches superfluous and most of the Bible stories unworthy of God. When he saw religion itself being swept away in the turmoil of the French Revolution, he felt moved to lift it out of the torrent and hold it clear in its most rational form. He wrote:

> I believe in one God, and no more; and I hope for happiness beyond this life. I believe that religious duties consist in doing justice, loving mercy and endeavoring to make our fellow creatures happy. I do not believe in the creed professed by any church that I know of. Religion is not an act that can be performed by proxy. Every person must perform it for himself.

The book expounding these ideas Paine called *The Age of Reason*. It says nothing that would provoke a storm today, but it is a brusque, metallic book. Most churchmen looked on *The Age of Reason* as the rulers of England had looked on *The Rights of Man*. But they had no legal weapon with which to outlaw the rebel. Their only weapon was ostracism—and slander.

Tom Paine came home to America in 1802. He was 65 and no longer well. He was welcomed with a deafening noise in the press, platform, pulpit. Half of the noise was applause and half abuse. Paine's outspokenness about his religious faith, a faith he shared with Jefferson, Madison and Franklin, made him open game for all reactionaries. And the democrats could not march to his defense. Just now especially, when under Jefferson they were fighting to make fast their gains, Tom Paine's too lucid exposition of his unchurchly faith was a liability.

He stayed for a while as President Jefferson's guest in the White House, but saw that his presence was a political embarrassment. So he said farewell to his ever-loyal friend and moved up to New Rochelle, received as a hero by a dwindling few and by the many with a mounting torrent of abuse.

The abuse was organized, blown up into a public enterprise during the seven years Tom Paine had still to live. It did not help matters that he remained an incurable rebel to the end, refusing to retract his statements or relent from his principles. In these last years he became generally known to the public as a sot, a cheat, a lecher, an exploiter of women and children, a blasphemer of God—a man vicious in spirit, and in body too filthy to be washed.

The Founder of American Independence was denied the right to vote in New Rochelle on the ground that he was not an American citizen. He was even denied burial in a Quaker cemetery. When his body was finally interred in a grave on the farm New York had given him, the only mourners were his friend and housekeeper, Madame Bonneville; her children; two Negroes; and a Quaker named Willett Hicks. Her son at one end of the grave and herself at the other, Madame Bonneville pronounced the funeral oration: "Oh, Mr. Paine, my son stands here as testimony of the gratitude of America, and I for France!"

Reputation is what men and women think of us; character is what God and the angels know of us. *—Thomas Paine*

It is necessary to the happiness of man that he be mentally faithful to himself. Infidelity does not consist in believing or in disbelieving; it consists in professing to believe what he does not believe. *—Thomas Paine*

THE MAESTRO

By Ann M. Lingg

O N THE EVE of his famous father's 80th birthday, in 1947, Walter Toscanini was asked what the Maestro might regard as his most important achievement. "For him there can be no such thing," the conductor's son replied. "Whatever he happens to be doing at the moment is the biggest thing in his life—whether it be tackling a symphony or peeling an orange."

At 80, Arturo Toscanini was still called the World's No. 1 Musician and constantly earned the title anew. There was in him such an exquisite combination of all the qualities necessary for artistic leadership, and such a passion for perfection in music, that no orchestra player—whether he were tired, uncomfortable or merely lazy—and few listeners, however distracted, could escape his spell. He was famous in the farthest corners of the earth. A woman from Patagonia once flew 2000 miles to stand through a Toscanini concert in Buenos Aires.

Toscanini was one of the biggest money-makers in the history of musical performance. At the reopening of La Scala in 1946, tickets were quoted at 15,000 lire apiece, equal to the monthly income of a middle-class family in Italy. The theater was filled to capacity each time, while in the square outside more than 10,000 listened over loudspeakers. It is said that his fees for the broadcasts of the NBC Symphony started, in 1937, at a sum which netted him $4000 after taxes, for an hour and a half's performance. And he continued to decline Hollywood offers of more than $250,000 for a single picture (although he conducted Verdi's

Hymn of the Nations gratis for a government film during World War II). Financial inducements meant nothing to him if he was not in sympathy with the association.

Personal publicity was, to the Maestro, extremely distasteful. This feeling stemmed from a profound conviction that he himself was unimportant in comparison with the music he conducted. Curtain calls made him uncomfortable. Often, as he backed off the stage after a third call, he whispered to the concertmaster, "Go home." Immediately the orchestra rose and departed so that the Maestro would not have to accept further calls.

Almost painfully shy, Toscanini was supremely happy when hidden from the public in an invisible orchestra pit. He never made a public speech in his life. News reporters and photographers frequently irked him. "I am a private citizen," he would insist. "What does it matter how I look, where I live and what color neckties I wear?" More frequently, he referred to himself as *un contadino*—a peasant. He never tried to evade his humble origin.

Son of a poor tailor in northern Italy, Toscanini at the age of nine entered the Parma Conservatory, where his schoolmates soon called him "genius" and enthusiastically followed his lead when he organized a clandestine extracurricular band, for which all were punished. Odd jobs as a cellist in opera orchestras followed, until one night in June 1886, in Rio de Janeiro, 19-year-old Arturo was catapulted into fame.

A Brazilian conductor had been badgered by the visiting Italian opera company into resigning a few hours before the first performance of *Aïda*. Two Italian substitutes were hissed out of the pit by a patriotic public. Then someone remembered the young cellist who, on the trip over, had coached the singers, and who seemed to know a thing or two about opera. The sight of a beardless youth on the conductor's stand hushed the public. Only half conscious of the gesture, Toscanini closed the conductor's score as he gave his first cue. The audience gasped. After the first act he was a hero. He conducted 18 more operas that summer in Rio de Janeiro—all from memory.

Torrents of printer's ink have been spilled over Toscanini's feats of memory. He could learn a full opera over a weekend and remember its every detail for years. An oboist once stammered during intermission that something had gone wrong with his E-flat key. "Don't worry," said Toscanini, after a moment. "There is no E flat in the rest of your part." Once, while trying to identify an obscure piece of chamber music, he went to the piano and played the entire second movement. He had not seen the score in 62 years.

No less astounding was Toscanini's phenomenal ear. In a fortissimo of a hundred puffed cheeks and sawing bows he could detect the slightest slackening of attention by a remote second violin or double bass. Musicians gave up hope of getting away with the most minute slur. Even when the Maestro did not comment immediately, he would remark some time later, "Last Thursday you missed a 16th pause in the fifth bar," or, "You made the same mistake last year; did you think I wouldn't hear it?"

Toscanini's desperate search for artistic perfection drove him from one podium to another. A trifling incident led to a lightning resignation, accompanied by a thunderous assertion that the age could not seem to produce musicians capable of doing justice to the great composers. Hardly ever was the pure, flawless music that rang permanently in his ears played back to him by his orchestras.

When dissatisfied with a rehearsal or performance, the Maestro would ride home in stony silence and refuse to eat. If particularly displeased, he would expect his family to join in the fast. Once he called his NBC Symphony a bunch of schoolchildren and half-wits, then broke off the rehearsal and left the studio in such a sweat that he caught a severe cold. "The Old Man's doing fine," a man in the orchestra grinned broadly. "Was he mad!"

When he encountered indifference, mediocrity or immodesty he could be uncommonly rude, as in a rehearsal with a famous prima donna who responded to his corrections with the explanation that she, not he, was the star. The Maestro looked at her with supreme disdain. "Lady," he said bitingly, "the stars are in the sky. Down here we are only good or bad musicians and, so help me, you are a bad one!"

On the other hand, he made allowances for shortcomings when he sensed the true artistic spark. A soprano beloved for her heavenly voice committed a number of inaccuracies in her first rehearsal with Toscanini. Promptly he shouted at her, "You are the worst musician in the world!" Then, almost in the same breath, his voice mellowed: "But you sing like an angel."

The moment the Maestro stepped to the podium in rehearsal, his deep-set, myopic eyes flashed. The baton lashed down like a whip. Then a shrill "No, no, no, no!" interrupted the first bars of a composition the men believed they knew backward. Toscanini liked to demonstrate rather than explain. He would throw a handkerchief into the air to indicate his wish for a light, floating sound. To get a lilting effect, he would pose like a mother rocking a baby to sleep in her arms. Once he wanted a distant effect from one section of a New York orchestra. "Not too far," he specified, "about Brooklyn."

At an orchestral slip, Toscanini became a man possessed. He shook his fists, swore, broke batons, tore sheets of music, and trampled on his watch or the indispensable eyeglasses. Once, after a beautiful gift watch had been smashed, the players gave the Maestro a bulky Ingersoll inscribed, "For Rehearsals." Recordings of Toscanini rehearsals, made without his knowledge by studio engineers, were favorite party entertainment in musical circles. Those who heard them marveled that anyone would be able to follow directions given in such a red-hot gibberish of English, French, German and Italian. Out of rehearsal, however, Toscanini could be master of all four languages.

The tyrant of the podium had a soft heart in off-hours. He made a hobby of charities but tried to keep them anonymous so people would not have to thank him. After World War II he was reported to have sent 30,000 pairs of shoes to Italy. He inaugurated a pension fund for musicians of the Los Angeles Symphony by donating his services for a concert with them, even paying his own traveling expenses. In 1944, when a small boy from Brooklyn sent him a postcard requesting the "Eroka simfony by Batovon," which his father, killed in Italy in World War II, had always loved,

Toscanini not only programmed the work promptly but even advertised in a vain attempt to locate "Jimmy."

Toscanini was as precise about his person as he was about his music. No one claimed to have seen him in shirt sleeves. During performances he wore celluloid collars so that there would be no wilting when he perspired. He usually had a rubdown and change of clothes during intermission, and on these grounds once even excused himself from a summons to the royal box in London.

Despite three protracted stays in the United States, Toscanini acquired only a few typically American tastes. Among them was a weakness for Mickey Mouse movies and a definite taste for jazz. On a goodwill trip with the NBC Symphony to South America, a group of the orchestra's ace woodwind players took to holding secret jam sessions on board ship. One day the Maestro came upon them and cocked a startled ear. Later they were summoned to Toscanini's stateroom for a command performance.

The Maestro remained unenthusiastic, however, about the experimental dissonances which were offered as "modern music" and which he considered offensive to the ear. Champions of the new who berated the old gentleman for his conservative tastes would do well, nevertheless, to recall Toscanini's bold pioneering for the music that was new when he was young: of Wagner, Verdi, Brahms, Puccini, Debussy, Ravel—now accepted classics.

In April 1954 Toscanini gave a farewell concert with the NBC Symphony Orchestra in Carnegie Hall in New York. Less than three years later, as he was nearing his 90th birthday, death came to the old Maestro. Two generations of music lovers have tried to probe the source of his fascination as a conductor. Some have attributed it to a particular combination of grace and strength with the baton, others to his supersensitive ear or feats of memory. Yet each of these elements could be found in some other conductor.

While admitting with disarming frankness that no other conductor could be compared with him, Toscanini insisted that his artistic standards should be the rule rather than the exception. "It isn't true that I am the best conductor in the world," he would say with a twinkle. "The trouble is, I'm the only good one."

DISCOVERER SUPREME

By Donald Culross Peattie

To THE trudging boy the east wind brought, there on the Yorkshire road, the first word of his destiny. At the hoarse sound of the roaring surf he flung up his head to listen. Then the inland-born youngster, one of a family of seven children raised in a mud hovel, caught his first glimpse of ocean—the vast fact of it spreading to the horizon. He must have run down to the shore, plunged his hands in the cold flood as if to wash away the last clod of the potato fields where he had slaved, put his wet fingers to his lips and tasted his birthright of brine.

On that day in 1741 James Cook, aged 13, who was to become one of the greatest navigators of the greatest race of sailors in the world, had found the sea, his mistress. Apprenticed to Saunderson, a grocer and draper of the village of Staithes, young James slept under the counter at night; behind it he sold squash and gingham by day; and over it he was sometimes flung for a caning when Saunderson came home drunk. All this, and scant food, James endured in silence. For Staithes was hard by Whitby, where the ships came in.

Not that Whitby was a particularly romantic port; from it went coal, iron and stone to London and Bremen, and to it came whale oil and lumber from Norway and the Baltic countries. But nothing that concerned the sea was humdrum to the eager boy. He could not get his fill of pitch and oakum smell or of the talk of seafaring men, the creak of rigging, the mewing of gulls. Then one night Saunderson stormed in vain through his empty shop. James Cook was gone—to sea.

His first ship bore the romantic name of *Freelove*. But she was only a coal boat, grimy, sturdy, slow. The life of her cabin boy was hard, with many floggings and poor food. Yet young James Cook felt like a man among men. Ashore in winter, he lodged in the Quaker home of one of the owners of the fleet. From these friends Cook learned much of the method, the honesty and courtesy, the high ideals, that marked his later life. He rose to be deckhand, mate and at last master. The life hardened him till he could eat anything, endure any weather; it never hardened his heart or dulled his brain. He was always studying—mathematics, astronomy, geography. And always he studied men, how to obey and how to command.

In 1755, when England and France had gone to war, Cook volunteered for naval service. When four of the Seven Years' War were past, he was put in command of a sloop and sent to the siege of Quebec. In 1762 James Cook, now 34 years old, married. Elizabeth saw little of her husband, for most of his remaining years were spent at sea. She bore the anxieties, the loneliness, the children. His were the hardships, the glory, the swift end.

Before long the very stars in their courses crossed to brighten Cook's destiny. On June 3, 1769, Venus was to cross the sun's disk, an event which would not occur again for over a century. It was important to science that observations be taken from many points; by comparing the times of the transit in various latitudes, it would be possible, by triangulation, to learn the distance of the sun from the earth. James Cook was selected by the navy for an expedition to the South Seas.

The choice fell on him partly because of a fine report he had made on an eclipse of the sun, partly because of his extremely careful survey of the rugged Newfoundland coast. But above all he was chosen for his character, his burning zeal for pure knowledge. He was to take astronomical observations from the island of Tahiti (one of the few South Sea Islands then definitely known) and thence to search for new lands to enrich the British Dominion and British trade. But he did far more than he was bidden. He

spent much of his time at sea in disproving the existence of mythi-
cal lands and fictitious passageways which cluttered the maps of
the day; as a result, he was to open more real passageways and
find more actual lands than any seagoing explorer before or since.

For his trip Cook selected no frigate groaning beneath guns
that might overawe the natives. He chose a coal boat, built at
Whitby. Though broad in beam, flat-bottomed and slow-sailing,
she had plenty of stowage room and could sail over shallows
impossible to ships of deeper draft. This even-tempered vessel,
which Cook renamed the *Endeavour*, was 97 feet long. On August
26, 1768, the bark sailed out of Plymouth. On board were 94
persons, including a brilliant corps of scientists. With them they
took a natural-history library and equipment for collecting on
which $50,000 had been laid out. Thus the *Endeavour* carried the
first great seaborne scientific expedition. But the most gifted and
interesting man aboard was Cook himself. His features were plain
but his brown eyes burned with a light intense and dedicated: his
love for the life and health of every one of the sailors under his
command.

In those times pirates, reefs and hurricanes together killed
fewer sailors than did scurvy. Cook set out to fight this enemy.
Today we know scurvy is caused by a deficiency of Vitamin C.
Somehow Cook knew that the scurvy-curing value of the best
foods was stolen by cooking on the galley stove. So, to the out-
rage of his men, he dosed every sailor with molasses, apple vinegar, sassafras tea and cabbage. Old tars used to a diet of dried
salted beef, weevily oatmeal and bread spread with rancid butter—
washed down with wine—were compelled to consume quantities
of lime juice and sauerkraut. Cook's heart was filled with pride as
he dropped anchor in April 1769 at Tahiti: he had not lost one
man from scurvy, nor had one sailor spent even a day in sick bay
from that cause.

What a sailor's snug harbor was Tahiti—with shady palms,
cordial girls and feasts of roast pig and luscious fruits! There was
little danger of serious hostility from these kindly people; but
there was risk that the sailors would abuse their simple hospi-

tality. Cook immediately set up the strictest rules, and made unhappy examples of the only two cases of disobedience.

In his relations with the natives Cook showed himself a genius. He realized that among the Tahitians, as among whites, some were honest and some dishonest, some chaste and some unchaste, some peace-loving and some spoiling for a fight. When it came to blows, he used birdshot, which punishes but does not kill; thieves he dealt with by shaving their heads, making them a laughing-stock among their own people. When girls were offered by parents anxious to compliment him, he explained without priggishness that he and his crew were there not on holiday but for astronomi-cal observations. So the natives named him "Man-in-Search-of-a-Planet." As a result of his upright conduct, this island became his future base of supplies.

The transit of Venus successfully observed, Cook sailed to look for the mysterious continent believed to lie southwestward. His first important landfall was New Zealand, which he proved to be not one but two large islands. Indeed, he circumnavigated both islands, charting 2400 miles of coastline with astonishing accu-racy. Then he struck the southeast coast of Australia—where no land had been known to lie. There the naturalists discovered many plants new to science—such a haul that Cook named the inlet Botany Bay.

How big was this land? To answer that, Cook sailed along Australia's east coast. Again and again the *Endeavour* was close to disaster in these waters, now known to be among the most dan-gerous in the world. Once indeed she struck, but brilliant seaman-ship saved her. And, in five months, this little coal bark charted the whole of the treacherous east coast. On August 19, 1770, Cook took formal possession of his discovery in the name of the king. Then he sailed for home, exploring en route a great stretch of the southern coast of New Guinea. He reached England 11 months later. Cook had added two precious jewels to the British crown, Australia and New Zealand; had charted some of the most danger-ous and distant seas in the world; had found the way, by his measures against scurvy, to save more English seamen's lives than were laid down for her in the Napoleonic wars; and had written in his journals one of the world's classics of seafaring.

Stirred by his discoveries, the Admiralty sent Cook out again in 1772 to search the South Pacific for a vast continent supposed to lie there. This time Cook had two ships, the *Resolution* and the *Adventure*. These two stout vessels scoured the south polar seas for 20,000 of the loneliest leagues on the globe. Nosing his wooden prow into the monstrous ice packs, daring drifting bergs, Cook circumnavigated for the first time in history the south polar ice cap, exploding forever the myth of a habitable southern continent in the South Seas. Northeast of Australia he made the absolutely new find of such big islands as New Caledonia and Norfolk. In the South Atlantic he secured for Great Britain what we now call South Georgia Island. The trip lasted almost three years.

Whether among cannibals or semicivilized people, Cook always bore himself like a nobleman, winning, by his character, genuine love. He was careful, too, to teach respect for the Union Jack, to impress his guests with fireworks. Wherever he went he tried to stock the islands with cows, sheep, goats, horses, rabbits, ducks, geese and chickens. But these soon died of the climate or were promptly eaten by a population that saw no sense in letting a good meal run into the brush where it would be hard to catch. He planted European vegetables and cereals wherever the ground seemed promising. But the natives were indifferent. He failed to bring the people to a realization of better things. They traded in their European clothes and implements for land and women. Cannibals still refused to prefer roast beef and Yorkshire pudding to a fat enemy.

In 1776 Cook sailed a third time from England, with the *Resolution* and the *Discovery*, under orders to explore the strait between Alaska and Siberia, and hunt for a passageway around the northern end of North America. He penetrated the Bering Strait to the ice fields at the northern tip of Alaska. He could go no farther even in the Arctic summer, and thus proved that the "Northwest Passage" around our continent was not feasible as a sailing route.

On his way north, early in 1778, Cook had made the happy discovery of the Hawaiian Islands, the greatest of the far-flung Polynesian lands. In Alaska he remembered the courtesy and intelligence of the Hawaiians, the beauty of their island home, and sailed directly for that sunny archipelago. Though he was only 50 years old, he had led a life of hardships. Reaching Hawaii again in November 1778, he was a man in need of a friendly reception, a good rest.

To his dismay, the Hawaiian natives now regarded him and all his men as gods. Then, on February 4, 1779, a tremendous storm arose, springing masts, tearing sails to tatters. When it was over, Cook found the shore strangely empty. The "gods" had been found mortal, their great ships subject to the forces of nature. The high priest had placed the district under taboo.

And then the *Discovery's* cutter was stolen and later found on the beach, broken up by the natives for the sake of its nails. Cook, instead of sailing cautiously away, landed with his marines to exact reparations. Some rash sailors fired, killing a friendly chief. There was a moment of sharp skirmish on the beach, and Cook, turning to give a command, was struck from behind on the head. As he tried to rise from the water, spears were thrust into his back.

Next day a priest came out to the *Discovery* with the captain's remains wrapped in a mat. At sunset of February 15 amid the firing of minute guns, the mortal shell of one of the greatest seafarers who ever lived went home to the sea.

The larger the island of knowledge, the longer the shore line of wonder.   —*Ralph Sockman*

David Livingstone, the great explorer, wrote in one magnificent sentence, "I will go anywhere—provided it be forward."
                                                    —*Walter Russell Bowie*

PORTRAIT OF
AN OLD MASTER

By Malcolm Vaughan

M OST ARTISTS wait years for recognition. Rembrandt van Rijn, the great 17th-century Dutch painter, rose from obscurity to fame at 26. Young Rembrandt's hardworking father, a miller, wanted him to be an educated man and had saved money to send him to the nearby University of Leiden. One semester, however, made it clear that the boy wouldn't shine at book learning. He was alert, intelligent, industrious; but his time and energy went into painting and drawing.

So his parents sent him to a Leiden artist to study painting. The boy did so well that before long he was paying part of his expenses by painting "practice" portraits of Leiden men and women. To expand his opportunities Rembrandt began taking trips to the big city, Amsterdam. One well-connected art dealer there, Hendrik van Uylenburgh, suggested that the young man move to Amsterdam and open a studio in Uylenburgh's fine house. Here he would paint portraits of wealthy citizens and pay the dealer a commission. The artist jumped at the chance.

This mutually profitable arrangement might have jogged along for years. But Rembrandt fell in love with the art dealer's young cousin, a wealthy orphan, Saskia van Uylenburgh, and he wanted very much to show her how distinguished a miller's son could be. His big chance came in the latter part of 1632 when the Surgeons' Guild of the city commissioned him to do a picture for its clubroom. The subject was to be an anatomy lesson, a pictorial device whereby a number of portraits of doctors, possibly the Guild's directors, could be included. The subject was an old one in Dutch painting and had never amounted to more than a routine row of figures. Rembrandt did something totally new with it. He brought into the picture the wonder and the awe that the average person might feel if present at an anatomy lesson.

He chose for the overall geometry of his composition a simple triangular form. Within this he grouped the doctors together with dramatic intensity. To distract as little attention as possible from their spellbound faces, he painted an inoffensive moment in the lesson—study of the muscles in the forearm. The result was a notable work of art that all Amsterdam flocked to see. Rembrandt almost overnight became the most sought-after artist in Holland. In 1631 he had painted but one commissioned portrait; the next year he painted 16! He kept raising his prices until he was charging 500 guilders (approximately $250) a portrait, a great deal of money in those days. But the more expensive he became, the greater grew the demand for his pictures. Students clamored to study under him, and he took them on at the unheard-of high fee of 100 guilders per year each.

Blue-eyed Saskia, the girl he loved, had been impressed from the day they met. Rembrandt now began to make an impression on her coldhearted guardian. Within a couple of years the barriers between the wealthy, aristocratic orphan and the miller's son were swept away. He was 28, she 21, when they were married. He idolized her. She exhilarated him. The best people of Amsterdam poured in on him, sitting hour after hour for their portraits. Among them was the Prince of Orange, Frederick Henry, "the George Washington of Holland." Rembrandt also painted his beloved Saskia's portrait again and again, and a whole series of Biblical scenes and historical allegories in which she served as model. These pictures tell us that she was not only his treasured wife but his ideal of womanhood.

He bought a magnificent mansion—at least he made the down payment on it—then blithely moved in. He furnished it with beautiful antiques, hung the walls with old masters, scattered expensive ornaments and curios through the rooms. The fact that he was spending more than he earned did not bother him: money was rolling in. Why shouldn't they live recklessly? Then in 1642 Saskia died after childbirth, leaving a sickly infant. One grief piled upon another. The artist's creditors pounced on him. A huge group portrait on which he'd been at work for a year—the now-famous "The Night Watch"—was unveiled and greeted with silence. Rembrandt's portrait commissions began to drop away, and for 14 years he kept on losing ground financially. Finally he was evicted from his house. His furnishings were sold at auction; they brought less than enough to satisfy his creditors.

Artists, it is said, must suffer, must know anguish and despair before their art can take on depth, strength, universal appeal and the powerful impact of simplicity. It seems a cruel requirement. But in Rembrandt's case it proved to be true. As his burdens grew heavier his art grew greater. Out of his pain came forth some of the greatest masterpieces the world has ever seen: "The Old Woman Cutting Her Nails"; "The Mill"; "Aristotle Contemplating the Bust of Homer"; Christ at Emmaus"; "The Descent from the Cross." What a tremendous career was launched with the young painter's fabulous first success, "The Anatomy Lesson"!

Joseph Duveen, the art dealer, had a loving regard for the masterpieces that passed through his hands. To him they were not mere canvas and paint, but something almost human. One day a millionaire came to his gallery to buy a painting. Duveen, who had never seen the man before, showed him around. As he did so, he learned that the other had just started collecting and owned only a few pictures of minor importance. They stopped in front of a Rembrandt, and the man asked: "How much?"

"$100,000," said the art dealer.

"All right. I'll take it."

"Oh, no," gently protested Duveen. "I couldn't possibly sell it to you. Rembrandt would be lonely in your collection!"

—*E. E. Edgar*

THE RAIL-SPLITTER

Condensed from Meet Abraham Lincoln

By G. Lynn Sumner

FIVE EVENTS—only remotely related in time and place—made Abraham Lincoln President. Not all his qualities of character, his eloquence or his political sagacity could have placed Lincoln at the head of the nation in its greatest hour of peril had not chance circumstances conspired to make it happen.

What were these circumstances? An invitation to deliver a lecture for a fee of $200. The failure of a young man to pass his entrance examinations at Harvard. A sudden sense of showmanship by a politician in Decatur, Illinois. The failure of a printer to keep his promise. And, finally, a midnight political conspiracy in a hotel room. If all this seems incongruous and at variance with commonly accepted history, let us look at events—veiled *then* by the surface excitement of political turmoil and dimmed *now* by the passage of time—and see how Lincoln really rose to power.

First, let us look in on a discouraged man sitting in a shabby law office in Springfield, Illinois. It was the fall of 1859. Lincoln was 50 years old. For more than 20 years he had been practicing law, earning about $3000 a year, although recently his firm had received a few substantial fees. His worldly possessions consisted of the house he lived in, 160 acres of land in Crawford and Tama Counties, Iowa, and some lots and a little acreage near Council Bluffs, Iowa, taken on a note. His cash resources were meager and of his credit he later wrote, "I could not raise $10,000 if it would save me from the fate of John Brown."

Some of his associates were beginning to talk about him as a candidate for the Presidency. He deprecated these suggestions. Why, he asked, should the Republican Party consider him when it had such conspicuous leaders as William H. Seward of New York, and Salmon P. Chase of Ohio? Yet he wanted to be President and curiously enough turned to the lecture platform, perhaps as a means of keeping himself before the public. But he also needed the extra income, and was interested in an offer of $200 and his expenses for a lecture at Plymouth Church in Brooklyn. The offer appealed to him for another reason. It would bring him East near his son Robert, who had gone to Cambridge that fall, expecting to enter Harvard. But in the entrance examinations Robert had failed in 15 out of 16 subjects, and had therefore gone to Phillips Exeter Academy in New Hampshire to complete his preparations. Lincoln was now anxious about his son's progress, and he seized upon the lecture engagement as a means of visiting him.

After arrangements had been made for Lincoln's appearance at Plymouth Church, the lecture people, learning that he was to speak on a political subject, changed the meeting place to Cooper Union, in New York City, which could hold a larger crowd. Although the night of February 27 was stormy, about 1500 people came, and at 25 cents admission the door receipts amounted to $367. New Yorkers had been hearing more and more of this lanky lawyer from the West, and were curious to see him.

Even Lincoln's friends feared the impression he would make. "But," writes one who heard him, "he held the vast meeting spellbound by his logic, and at the close, the audience broke into wild and prolonged enthusiasm." Next day the New York papers carried the address in full, with the result that Republican leaders throughout New England urgently appealed to Lincoln to speak along the route of his visit to Exeter. In the week that followed, he delivered 11 addresses in Connecticut, Rhode Island and New Hampshire, and made an impression that cannot be overestimated in considering the events that followed. Robert Lincoln always maintained that, but for his failure in the Harvard entrance examinations, his father might not have visited New York and New

England that winter, and might never have become President.

Let us return now to Springfield with a Lincoln who felt for the first time that his nomination for President was possible. Seward, the outstanding popular Republican leader, with great prestige throughout the country, was already strong in Illinois. So Lincoln began writing to influential party workers throughout the state. He knew that, unless he could go into the national convention with his own state delegates, his cause was hopeless. He wrote to Norman B. Judd, northern Illinois member of the Republican National Committee, asking, "Can you help me a little in your end of the vineyard?" Judd managed so well that he obtained the national convention for Chicago.

Lincoln had another warm friend in Richard J. Oglesby of Decatur, who had a sense of showmanship rare in the frontier country of the Sixties. The state convention was to be held at Decatur, and Oglesby's aim was to rally the delegates to pledge the state to Lincoln.

Oglesby had heard that only a short distance from Decatur, Lincoln, in his youth, had split rails with John Hanks, who still lived in the vicinity. Oglesby went to Hanks and asked him whether any of the rails they had split were still in existence. Hanks said he remembered well a fence they had built on a farm ten miles west of town, with rails split from locust and black-walnut logs. So Oglesby took old John Hanks in his buggy and drove to the farm, where they found the rail fence still in service. They took two of the rails, lashed them to the buggy, carried them back into Decatur, and hid them in Oglesby's barn. A week later, at a strategic moment in the state convention, Oglesby rose and announced that a former Democrat desired to make a contribution. Whereupon old John Hanks appeared upon the stage, carrying the rails that he and Lincoln had split in 1830. They bore a large sign:

> ABRAHAM LINCOLN
> THE RAIL-SPLITTER
> CANDIDATE
> FOR PRESIDENT IN 1860

The convention went wild. The Seward forces were snowed under. Then and there, Illinois went on record for Lincoln. Not only that—John Hanks and his rails became a feature of political gatherings everywhere. "Abe Lincoln, the Rail-Splitter" became a national political slogan.

But two more fateful events in this play of destiny were still to happen: The Republican national convention met at Chicago on Wednesday, May 16, 1860. On Thursday, the platform was adopted. That evening the candidate was to be nominated. There seemed no possible doubt of the result. Seward was the outstanding choice. Straw votes taken among the passengers on four trains entering the city showed Seward with 860, Lincoln 144, all others 288. The vote of the delegates seemed merely a formality. And had it been taken that Thursday evening, Seward would certainly have been nominee and President.

But the tally sheets which a printer had promised to deliver by nine o'clock did not arrive. After a while, messengers were sent out to get them. In half an hour, they had not returned. The delegates grew restless, and at last two of them moved that the convention adjourn until ten o'clock the following morning. The motion carried. Thus an obscure and unreliable printer became an instrument of destiny. For the hours of that night were to see the course of history changed.

When the convention adjourned, Lincoln's friends went feverishly to work. They argued that if Seward were nominated he could not carry Pennsylvania, Indiana and Illinois, and without at least two of those states and New Jersey the Republican cause would be lost. This argument was effective with many wavering delegates. But whole blocks, not single votes, were necessary— and the night was passing. In separate hotel rooms, two of Lincoln's political managers began dickering for state delegations. Lincoln, 150 miles away in Springfield, must have suspected it, for he sent them a message: "Do nothing that will bind me." The bargainers were astounded. Wrathful at first, they made a swift decision: "We'll pretend we never got it." And, between then and dawn, they drove two bargains. On their pledge of two posts in the Cabinet, Pennsylvania and Indiana agreed to vote for Lincoln.

Next morning when the convention met, Seward led strongly on the first ballot while many state delegations cast their votes for favorite sons. On the second, Pennsylvania and Indiana led the swing to Lincoln. On the fourth, Ohio joined them, and the battle was over. Of 466 votes on the final ballot, 354 were cast for Lincoln. The Republican nomination assured him the great office, for the Democrats, hopelessly divided on the question of slavery, split and nominated three candidates. In November, with 40 percent of the popular vote, Lincoln was elected to the Presidency.

Thus, a strange series of unrelated events conspired to place him in the White House. But was it an accident? Was it merely political intrigue? . . . Or was it fate? Is it not just possible that that momentous day the hand of Destiny rested upon the shoulder of Abraham Lincoln?

The story is told that during the Confederate attack on Fort Stevens, President Lincoln came out from the White House to make a tour of inspection of Union defenses. The task of piloting him about fell to one Oliver Wendell Holmes, aide-de-camp to the general in command. Lincoln wanted to know just where the enemy were, and Holmes pointed them out. The President stood up to look. Standing, and supplemented by his high plug hat, Mr. Lincoln was a target of exceptional visibility, and from the rebel marksmen there came a snarl of musketry fire. Grabbing the President by the arm, the young officer dragged him under cover, saying, "Get down, you fool!"

Admittedly this was not the approved style for an officer to employ in addressing the commander in chief of the armed forces of his country. The youthful aide's relief from worry came when, just as Lincoln was quitting the fort, he took the trouble to walk back. "Good-bye, Colonel Holmes," he said. "I'm glad to see you know how to talk to a civilian."

—Alexander Woollcott

EMPERORS OF THE WALTZ

By Donald Culross Peattie

O F ALL the rhythms that ever set foot to tapping, the headiest is the waltz, which swung into its most glorious outburst some hundred years ago. Once a beat for rustic stamp and twirl, the waltz suddenly flashed forth like a diamond polished to fiery brilliance, exciting the world's most musical city and delighting an emperor's court. Its dazzling triumph was the work of a father and son, both named Johann Strauss. Today a Strauss waltz still echoes the mood of that vanished Vienna—a gaiety half mad, half melancholy, and dizzying as champagne.

The first of these masters of light music was born in a Vienna slum in 1804 to the keepers of a wretched inn. Before the sickly infant was a year old his father was found drowned in the nearby Danube River, perhaps because of despair. The struggling mother turned to another innkeeper who, as time went on, took to her tempestuous child, with his black hair and lively eyes. Observing how the little boy liked to beat time or pretend to play a violin, the stepfather got him a fiddle. Even in school the child could not keep his fingers from the strings. One of the teachers listened to his self-taught performance and told the parents what a great talent it promised. But to them a musician meant a good-fornothing who wandered from tavern to tavern picking up a meal for a tune. They apprenticed Johann to a bookbinder.

The frustrated boy made havoc of glue and paper, got beaten, ran away and finally overcame all opposition by sheer unhappy rage. So, at 15, Johann was playing the viola in a third-rate orchestra. Near his curly dark head shone the blond one of Joseph Lanner, also stuffed with melodies. When Lanner formed a group of his own, Johann joined him. Their success mounted rapidly, for Lanner's sentimental dance tunes were much in demand. But jealousy flamed when Johann's first composition was performed under Lanner's name, and Strauss resigned in a rage. With him went 14 of Lanner's best musicians; they became the nucleus of the first Strauss orchestra.

On his own, and married now to Anna Streim, as gypsy-dark and headstrong as himself, Johann felt the whip of ambition. He took lessons in composition from a friend of Beethoven and began to write waltzes with a freedom and elegance never before heard. His orchestra was constantly in demand. By the time he was 26 he had 200 musicians, and the finest ballroom in Vienna was his concert hall. Soon all Europe was impatient to hear his breath-catching, heart-lifting waltzes. In the next few years he and his men made a series of tours gathering triumphs in Germany, Holland and Belgium. They conquered Paris and, in 1838, crossed the Channel for the coronation of 19-year-old Victoria as Queen of England.

Under the warm onslaught of his singing strings Victorian prudery melted into romance. The waltz, thought shocking a few years before, filled every ballroom, and to meet his engagements Strauss crisscrossed the land at a pace as reckless as the melodies he incessantly composed. As though drunk with his own music, Strauss drove his men on by his dramatic performance, now bending low to his violin, now holding it high to draw from it the last exquisite pleasure. Such intensity made impossible demands on his health. In several cities he played with a high fever. In Calais he collapsed but refused to rest. In Linz, delirious, he stumbled into the street in his nightclothes. At last, near death, he arrived in Vienna.

To a nervous convalescent the Strauss flat became a prison. His wife hung onto her temper and hushed their five children. But one day the invalid heard the ghost of his own music—a Strauss waltz played on a violin. Mystified—for his children had been forbidden this instrument, though granted piano lessons—the sick man went to see. There before a mirror, swaying to his fiddle in typical Strauss style, drawing forth lilting Strauss fire, stood his eldest son, Johann. The enraged father demanded an explanation. Coolly the boy gave it: by teaching piano to younger children he had earned the money to take violin lessons himself. Strauss senior angrily locked up the violin, but the boy's mother smuggled him another from his father's collection. When Johann I bundled Johann II off to business school, the lad deviled the school into expelling him.

Now the Strauss family was divided into two camps. The bitter father deserted the family for a trivial milliner named Emilie. For all his successes the spendthrift elder Strauss could not support two homes, and the burden of one fell upon young Johann. Better schooled in music and better disciplined in character than his father, the boy was ready at 19 to make his debut as an orchestra leader. A hall as fashionable as his father's was promised him. The newspapers, seizing upon the challenge of son to father, broadcast wide publicity. Strauss the elder, irate, hoped aloud to die before his son's concert.

By early evening every seat was filled, and soon every foot of floor space. Strauss senior was conducting a concert of his own that night, but his manager led a squad of troublemakers to sit close to young Johann. Pale, sturdy, and calm but for his blazing eyes, the young man opened his program with four waltzes of his own composition. The boos and whistles of his father's friends were applauded down. A polka and a quadrille were followed by more of the younger Johann's caressing, winning melodies in three-four time until, at the close of the concert, his enemies were clapping and shouting with the loudest. Nineteen encores were demanded of the bowing young conductor—more than ever had been asked of his father.

Suddenly Johann signaled his men, and into the silence floated a final number not on the program: the greatest of all the waltzes written by Strauss the elder, "Strains of the Lorelei and the Rhine."

When the last note died softly, the audience rose, cheering, and rushed the stage to bear the generous young man out on exultant shoulders. In a glow of pride and affection, father and son were reconciled.

But in 1849, on the day of a great banquet at which he was to have conducted, old Johann collapsed with scarlet fever. Almost no news of this leaked out until his death, when his wife and son discovered his corpse abandoned in the house of his mistress. Emilie had taken everything, including the bedclothes, and departed. This brought young Strauss not only grief but horror, for all his life he had an uncontrollable dread of the dead. When, a few years later, he lost his mother, he fled the city and did not return until after the funeral. This darkness of soul was the reverse of the bright gaiety in him. You can hear in his waltzes both the lighthearted rapture and the melancholy beneath it which he seems always trying to wash away with sparkling melody. In this he was a typical Viennese of his day.

With the death of Johann I, all Strauss enthusiasts of both factions united to applaud the new waltz king. Johann's music became big business, requiring the help not only of his brothers Joseph and Eduard but of a corps of orchestrators and several dance bands. Johann was caught on a treadmill of engagements. He would dash about the city from one orchestra to another, leading each for a couple of numbers, then turning it over to one of his brothers. He became that rare thing, a rich musician, and was faced with all the dangers of success.

From these he was saved by a wise marriage. Henrietta ("Jetty") Treffz, ten years his senior, was warm of heart, steady of head and knowledgeable about both music and contracts, having sung with the Dresden Opera. She put a stop to Johann's feverish spending of his strength, and in the relaxation and depth of his happiness with Jetty he found the power that flowered in the many great waltzes, which despite a million repetitions, still sparkle and shimmer for us today.

Sensuous, brooding, breaking with a lilt in the beat from reverie to reckless, pulsating joy, these waltzes were composed not for the dance floor but for the concert hall. There is a symphonic beauty in each—"On the Beautiful Blue Danube," "Artist's Life," "Wine, Women and Song," "Tales from the Vienna Woods," "Emperor Waltzes." For nearly 100 years we have been drinking in their intoxicating melodies.

In the summer of 1872 Boston was staging a World Peace Jubilee, and offered Strauss an irresistible fee to conduct there. When he arrived he found that the concerts had been planned on the belief of "the bigger the better." In a vast hall with wretched acoustics he was to conduct, from a high platform, by means of 100 assistant conductors, each leading his own orchestra (a total of 1087 instruments) or part of the 20,000-voice chorus. A cannon shot was the signal for the chorus to burst into "The Blue Danube." Horrified though Strauss was, he nevertheless met with such success that to satisfy his admirers' demands for a lock of his raven hair he had to keep a pocket full of clippings from the coat of his shaggy Newfoundland dog. But he never again came to America.

Back in the lighthearted, opulent world of 19th-century Europe, Strauss found every condition favorable for his work. And now into his hands came a French farce which at once set alight his restless and sensitive imagination. He shut himself away, forgetting to eat, turning to melody this giddy riot of masked balls, mistaken identities and popping champagne corks. He worked night after night and, in a little more than one month, completed the delicious, taunting and haunting music which is *Die Fledermaus*, the brightest jewel that ever flashed in that brilliant age of light opera. From the opening night of April 5, 1874, to our own day it has frolicked and glittered on stages all over the Western world, and its lovely, laughing strains will ever wake new audiences to applause.

Still triumphantly successful, Johann Strauss was halted in full career by the sudden death in 1878 of his beloved Jetty. He raised her cold hand to his lips in a last kiss, then in his old horror of mortality he quit the city, leaving his brother Eduard to make the sad final arrangements. A few distracted weeks later he found himself married again. Angelika Diettrich had a pretty face, a mediocre singing voice and, as her husband soon discovered, no morals. Many years his junior, she made of her youth an instrument of torment to him. Strauss began to look old; his music lost its sparkle. One operetta after another, flawed by the horror at the center of his life, failed dismally. The kindest thing Angelika ever did for him was to run away with one of her lovers.

But at 58 Johann fell in love again, love true and rewarding. Adele Deutsch, whom he married after divorcing Angelika, was more beautiful than Angelika, and as wise and devoted as Jetty. She gave him back his youth, his gaiety, his art. Under her guiding hand he found his way back to fame with *The Gypsy Baron*, an operetta even more melodious and varied than *Fledermaus*. With a Hungarian setting and many kindling Magyar rhythms, it did more to unite the dual monarchy of Austria-Hungary than Franz Josef had done in 37 years of rule by sword and spy.

Strauss was now king not only of the waltz but of all the realm of light music of two continents. In May of the last year of the brilliant 19th century, Vienna heard that the beloved composer was ill. The Strauss orchestra was giving a concert on June 3 when a messenger stepped up to the conductor with a note. The conductor read it, halted the orchestra abruptly and then softly began another melody in which all joined, strings muted in sorrow. It was "The Blue Danube." Vienna understood.

George Gershwin, who was never happier than when playing his songs on the piano, reserved one unpublished little waltz tune for affairs of the heart. "You're the kind of girl who makes me feel like composing a song," he would tell the enraptured lady of the moment, and lead her off to his suite. We would follow on tiptoe to hear him "compose" the familiar tune for her. "It will be dedicated to you," he would conclude soulfully.
—*Bennett Cerf*

THE GREAT DISSENTER

By Beverly Smith

AMERICANS, busy with the conquest of a continent, frequently tended to honor their men of action rather than their thinkers. From this, perhaps, grew the idea that thinking was tiresome and unprofitable and the thinker a dull theorist. This tradition diverted some of the best young American minds into "practical" pursuits. Nowadays, however, we are beginning to believe that we should be better off if less energy had been devoted to action and more to thought.

The life of the late Justice Oliver Wendell Holmes, generally conceded to be one of the greatest Americans of the 20th century, ought to dispel the foolish idea that thinking is "dull." Holmes has shown that thinking can be a glorious and exciting adventure. "To think great thoughts you must be heroes as well as idealists," he, who knew so well the heroism of the battlefield, once wrote. "Only when you have worked alone—when you have felt around you a black gulf of solitude more isolating than that which surrounds the dying man, and in hope and in despair have trusted to your own unshaken will—then only will you have achieved the secret, isolated joy of the thinker, who knows that a hundred years after he is dead, men who never heard of him will be moving to the measure of his thought."

Holmes's influence upon all who knew him cannot be explained by his ideas alone. With all the weight of his learning, he was one of the gayest, wittiest men who ever lived. There was about him a personal charm as strong as magic. It resided partly in his physical presence. The tall, soldierly figure, only at the last a little stooped with age. The snowy whiteness of his hair, the bushy eyebrows, his jauntily flowing mustaches. The aquiline features, the gray-blue eyes, now stern, now snapping with inner laughter. His manner had the courtliness of a vanished day, a flattering assumption, even to the very young, that you were his equal, man to man.

The magic worked upon all kinds of men—Theodore Roosevelt, the British historian and statesman Lord Bryce, Charles Evans Hughes, Louis D. Brandeis. His village neighbors at Beverly Farms, Massachusetts, where Holmes passed his summers from boyhood, idolized him. They were proud of his eminent visitors, but somehow he made them feel that he liked his old neighbors just a little bit more than his distinguished guests.

James Emo, watchman at the railroad crossing near Justice Holmes's summer home, told me how the justice stopped every day to chat with him. He spoke of him not as a celebrity, but as a friend whom it had been great good luck to know. "The Justice was interested in Rex, my dog," Mr. Emo explained. "He always asked about Rex's health and habits. Wanted to know whether Rex could tell from the whistle which way the train was coming." From the way Mr. Emo's face lighted up, I could see that Holmes's inquiries had given him a new and special interest in Rex. Just so, throughout his long years, the vividness of Holmes's interest in life kindled the interest of other men.

Justice Holmes was born in 1841, son of a young Boston physician later to be noted as the author of *The Autocrat of the Breakfast Table*. In 1841 America was a rural nation of some 18 millions, its cities scattered chiefly along the Atlantic seaboard. Chicago was hardly more than a small town and the West a wilderness. But Boston was already coming into its golden age. Emerson, Longfellow, Hawthorne, Whittier walked its streets and hobnobbed with Holmes, Sr., at the Parker House. It was in such a tradition that young Holmes grew up.

He graduated from Harvard in 1861, and that summer marched away for Virginia with the 20th Massachusetts Regiment. He was wounded twice at Ball's Bluff, the second bullet missing his heart by half an inch. The surgeons guessed the wound as mortal, but he recovered and was invalided home. Back again, he was shot through the neck at Antietam and left for dead, but was picked up and nursed back to life. Back once more with his company, at Chancellorsville, his foot was shattered by shrapnel. There was talk of amputation, but the foot healed, and still again he returned to the front.

After the war, he was the young hero, an officer, tall, dashing, debonair. The ladies doted on him, men sought him as a drinking companion. And Holmes liked it. But the war had given him something he could never have found in the genteel Brahmin tradition of the old New England families. "In our youth our hearts were touched with fire," he wrote. "It was given us to learn that life is a profound and passionate thing."

He knew well that the law could be dry and technical, its practice a sordid scramble for clients, winning cases that were better lost. But he knew too, as he said, that "Every calling is great when greatly pursued." This idea was central in his philosophy: Whatever you do, do it with all your might.

Thus it was, during the next 15 years, that Holmes flung himself into the law. His friends were afraid he was working himself to death. He wasn't content to learn the rules; he tracked down their origin to see if they had outlived their usefulness. He came to believe that the law was not sacredly drawn from dead precedents, but was based on experience, living and growing to serve man's changing destiny. His greatest service of all perhaps was to give judges everywhere this new approach to the law. His book *The Common Law*, embodying these teachings, was published in 1881, and still stands as a classic. In 1882 his state honored him for it (he was then 41) by appointing him justice of the Supreme Court of Massachusetts. He remained on the court for 20 years, the last three as chief justice.

Conventional Boston was puzzled by the new justice. Unquestionably an aristocrat, he consorted with all kinds of people. He believed the rights of labor were as important as the rights of property. Invariably courteous, nevertheless he sometimes only half concealed a biting impatience with pomposity and verbosity.

He once advised a long-winded attorney to read *risqué* French novels, and thus learn the value of innuendo. The bar was also scandalized to learn that the justice sometimes went to a burlesque show. On one such occasion, after a particularly lurid joke, Justice Holmes murmured: "Thank God I am a man of low tastes."

In 1902, President Theodore Roosevelt appointed Holmes a member of the United States Supreme Court. In farewell to the members of the Boston bar association, he said of his new task: "Gentlemen, it is a great adventure, and that thought brings with it a mighty joy. The chance to do one's share in shaping the laws of the whole country brings the hush one used to feel when awaiting the beginning of a battle. . . . We will not falter."

Nobly he fulfilled his high resolve. His influence was always on the side of individual freedom of thought and speech—"Not free thought for those who agree with us, but freedom for the thought we hate"—and in favor of allowing considerable freedom of experiment in legislation. Because of the brilliance of some of his dissenting opinions he has sometimes been called the Great Dissenter. As a matter of fact, he disagreed with the majority of his colleagues in only about one tenth of the cases in his 30 years on the Supreme Court. Holmes saw change as the law of life and growth and wanted only to see that it came about in an orderly fashion and "according to the rules."

One great piece of good luck Justice Holmes had. He found in Miss Fanny Dixwell, whom he married in 1872, his match and true companion. Her wit and high spirit were the equal of his own. She died in 1929, after 57 years of a marriage which their friends said was like a honeymoon to the end.

After their marriage they lived for two years with his parents in Boston, then moved to a flat over a drugstore. Later she was hostess at the most brilliant dinners in Washington, but never did the dignity of the Supreme Court put a damper on her spirits. She liked to go to fires. In their early days in Washington, when a fire engine came past the house, she would say, "Come on, Wendell, let's go." And they would race hand in hand after the engines. She kept her husband amused and guessing to the last. She did not hesitate to call him sharply to account occasionally. All his suits, she declared, had been purchased before the Civil War. The routine glitter of official Washington appealed to neither of them, and it was to their simple, unconventional life that Holmes owed the extent of his accomplishment.

The range of his reading was incredible. When you read hungrily every day for 80 years you cover a lot of territory. He had absorbed the literature of the Greeks and the Romans, Dante, Rabelais, Shakespeare, Montesquieu and Darwin—and Ernest Hemingway, Milt Gross, Anita Loos and other popular authors of his day shared his interest with heavy tomes of philosophy, psychology and the law. As befitted a student of words and an old soldier, he had a striking artistry in the use of profanity when among intimates. But he yielded the palm to the Confederates. "Young feller," he said to a friend one day, "you will never appreciate the potentialities of the English language until you have heard a Southern mule driver search the soul of a mule."

He was intensely patriotic, and had a deep feeling for the romance, power and spirit which carved this nation. He wanted America to be, truly, the land of the free and the home of the brave. He liked young people, and each year he had a new secretary, a young man selected from the honor graduates of the Harvard Law School. A year with him was a liberal education, eagerly sought after. And Holmes, indeed, seemed to learn as much from these young men. They were his connection with the future. And he demanded the best of their energies.

On his 90th birthday, March 8, 1931, the justice was persuaded to speak briefly on the radio. "To express one's feelings as the end draws near is too intimate a task," he said. "But I may mention one thought. The riders in a race do not stop short when they reach the goal. There is a little finishing canter. The race is over, but the work is never done while the power to work remains. It cannot be, while you still live. For to live is to function. That is all there is in living.

"And so I end with a line from a Latin poet: 'Death plucks my ear and says, *Live, I am coming.*'"

THE MAGICIAN OF
LIBERTY HALL

Condensed from The Electrical Genius of Liberty Hall
By Floyd Miller

T HE United States immigration officer grimaced as he sized
up the next applicant in line. It was June 1889, and the
French ship *La Champagne* had just disgorged a new batch
of immigrants from its steerage. Few of them looked like much
after the exhausting, comfortless trip, but this candidate appeared particularly unpromising. Almost a dwarf, he was less than
five feet tall, and his frail body was deformed by a large hump on
his back. His head was overlarge, his hair unkempt, his face
bloated from a bad head cold, and his pince-nez eyeglasses jig-
gled precariously with each wheezing breath. Suspecting an un-
pleasant duty ahead, the official armored himself with gruffness.

"Name?" he barked.

"Karl August Rudolf Steinmetz," the little man said.

"Profession?"

"*Ich bin Mathematiker und Forscher.*"

Into the form went the words "mathematician and researcher."

"Do you have any money?"

The little man did not reply, but his threadbare clothing told
the answer.

"Do you speak English?"

"A few," came the hesitant reply.

"No English," the official grunted, making the entry. "Do you have a job in America?" He waited, then repeated the question in German.

"*Nein,*" the little hunchback said softly.

The official walked over to consult his superior. Pointing back at Steinmetz, he reported, "No English, no money, no job. Besides, he's sick—and a hunchback."

The superior nodded. "Refuse admission."

The official waved Steinmetz toward a door marked DETENTION PEN in five languages. Attempting dignity, Steinmetz moved obediently on his spindly legs. He knew this meant deportation, and in his case something more—prison. He had fled his university in Breslau, Germany, in the middle of the night, because of political activities offensive to the government of Bismarck, the Iron Chancellor. He had barely escaped arrest and was a wanted man in his homeland. He was halfway to the detention pen when a voice called, "Karl! Karl! *Wo gehen Sie?*" Hurrying toward him came his traveling companion, a big, blond Dane named Oscar Asmussen. This was the man who had persuaded him that he should come to America and who had financed the trip. Steinmetz shrugged sadly but without bitterness. "I am to be deported," he said.

"Nonsense!" the Dane exploded. "We'll change that in a hurry."

As Asmussen bore down on the immigration office, he had several advantages over his small friend: he spoke excellent English, he was handsome and sophisticated, and he had money. He now tackled the officials with supreme self-confidence; after a brief, spirited argument, there was a reshuffling of papers, a signature or two, and the decision on Steinmetz was reversed.

"What did you say?" Steinmetz asked wonderingly as, a few minutes later, he found himself on a Manhattan street with his friend. Asmussen pulled out a large roll of bills and waved it gaily. "I told them that you were a distinguished and wealthy German scientist," he said, "and that I was keeping your money for you."

This mild deception, which saved Steinmetz and his great genius for America, was to have an incalculable effect on the growth of the country's infant electrical industry. But it by no means solved Steinmetz's problems of the moment, the most pressing being his dire need of a job.

Asmussen's relatives in Brooklyn provided Steinmetz a place to live, and he applied at a number of machine shops for work as an electrician. The answer was always no. A friend back home had given him a letter of introduction to Rudolf Eickemeyer, who owned a plant in Yonkers which manufactured hat-making machinery. It seemed a most unlikely place for a mathematician to find work, but Steinmetz had nowhere else to turn.

When Steinmetz entered the factory office and timidly asked to see Mr. Eickemeyer, he was taken to a tall and formidable man with a patriarchal beard who stared at him sternly. In heavily accented English, Steinmetz began his carefully rehearsed speech. "I am Mr. Steinmetz. Do I have the honor of addressing Mr. Rudolf Eickemeyer?"

Unexpectedly Eickemeyer began to smile. He said gently, "*Sprechen Sie Deutsch?*"

The little hunchback gratefully reverted to his own language and produced his letter of introduction. Eickemeyer read it and began to question Steinmetz about the latest electrical developments abroad. They talked for two hours about politics and philosophy and literature and mathematics, and finally about hat-making machines. At the end of the time Steinmetz had a job as a draftsman at $12 a week.

Rudolf Eickemeyer was himself an inventive, quick-minded man. The hat-making machine he manufactured was his own device, and he had prospered with it. But by the time Steinmetz arrived, a good deal of Eickemeyer's interest had shifted to electric motors, and Steinmetz was soon taken off the drafting board, given a small laboratory and put on this project. At the moment Eickemeyer was trying to perfect a large trolley motor, but almost invariably the models he built overheated and stalled. The trouble was caused by the effect of magnetism on the motor's iron core, but the laws governing this effect were completely unknown. Mass production of large motors was, of course, impossible under these conditions.

Steinmetz tackled this problem. Unlike Edison, who worked largely by concrete experiment, Steinmetz's approach was theoretical. His only tools were a tin box of pencils, reams of paper, a canister of cigars (to which he had become addicted shortly after arriving in America)—and his mind. The report which came from this search some two years later ran to nearly 200 pages of the most complicated mathematical calculations. But Steinmetz had found what he was looking for: the unchangeable law which governs the loss of power by alternating magnetism. He called it the law of hysteresis.

Such a discovery could hardly thrill the public, but when Steinmetz read the first section of his paper before the American Institute of Electrical Engineers in January 1892, there was great excitement. Steinmetz was immediately acclaimed and his mathematical genius recognized as of the highest order.

He was then just 27 years old. He had decided that his name of Karl was much too Germanic and had changed it to Charles. Already he had begun to acquire a reputation for warmhearted, and even quixotic, eccentricity. On a bitter winter day one of the plant engineers climbed the three flights to Steinmetz's small laboratory to consult him on a problem. He was surprised to find the lab's potbellied stove without a fire and the little scientist working in overcoat, fur cap and boots. The engineer couldn't help saying, "Mr. Steinmetz, I can't understand why in the world you don't build a fire in your stove."

Steinmetz blinked and looked around as if aware of the cold for the first time. "Well," he said, smiling apologetically, "a mouse had some babies in there and they are not yet old enough to move."

Hardly less quixotic were his early negotiations with the General Electric Company. This concern, organized three years after his arrival in America, was determined to hire the best brains in the industry. Company officials had heard of the young mathematician who worked for Eickemeyer, and they dispatched E. W. Rice, Jr. (later the company's president), to report on the advisability of hiring him. On Rice's recommendation, General Electric offered Steinmetz a job and enormously expanded research facilities. The little man was delighted at first, but a week later announced regretfully that he could not accept the offer.

"But why?" demanded Rice. "You were ready to take it last week."

"Mr. Eickemeyer does not wish me to leave," Steinmetz said simply.

"Now, look here, Steinmetz, we're ready to bargain. We can raise your salary over our first offer . . . say, another two thousand?"

"Money has nothing to do with it. If you offered me ten times as much, it would change nothing. Mr. Eickemeyer gave me a job when I needed it badly. If now he needs me, it is my duty to stay with him."

Rice did not give up, and the following month two other General Electric officials arrived in Yonkers to examine the Eickemeyer books and analyze his patents. Shortly thereafter General Electric bought the entire Eickemeyer company, liquidated most of it and transferred Steinmetz to their new plant in Schenectady. It was the only way they could get him.

After this move, which occurred in 1893, Steinmetz was to spend the next 30 years in Schenectady grappling with the mysteries of electricity. Elated by his laboratory and extensive research facilities, he went to work with a fierce and joyous energy. Soon he became the keystone of a brilliant engineering staff; he was the flame that ignited enthusiasm, inspired the extra effort needed to achieve the impossible.

He was so unerringly correct in his visions and calculations that the General Electric management began referring to him as "the Supreme Court." Whenever an engineer sought to develop some pet new project, he was told, "Go to the Supreme Court. If Steinmetz says it will work, you can have the money."

One of Steinmetz's greatest triumphs, and one which was to send the electrical industry forward in mighty strides, was achieved shortly after he came to General Electric. The only electricity then readily available was direct current. This flowed in one direction only, had constant characteristics and was easily controlled. But it had one big drawback: it could not be practically transmitted farther than three miles. Steinmetz believed that the problem of transmission could be solved by the use of alternating current. As its name indicates, it flows first in one direction, then the other, alternating directions with great frequency, usually at the rate of 120 times per second.

At last Steinmetz announced he had solved the problem by the application of pure mathematics. It had been a staggering task. So intricate was his reasoning that at first few of his colleagues could understand it. Many engineers doubted that his theory would work, but General Electric decided to give it a test. In 1894 at Niagara Falls they built an alternating-current generator to see if it could transmit current to Buffalo, 26 miles away. When the switch was thrown, the generator hummed, the wires sang, and a great city had electricity produced for the first time at that unheard-of distance. In the face of this demonstration all opposition from the direct-current partisans melted away, and soon power was transmitted, not just 26 miles, but thousands of miles across the continent. The electrification of the nation had begun.

Realizing the significance of his work, newspapers began to make a celebrity of Steinmetz, ranking him with Edison, Marconi and Bell. He was awarded complete freedom to conduct any research he chose, in his own way and in his own time—with the result that he tried to crowd even more work into his already overlong day.

During his first four years in Schenectady, Steinmetz lived in a boardinghouse. In 1897, however, he rented a gloomy three-story Victorian dwelling, installed a complete laboratory so that he could continue his researches at whatever hour, and moved in, bringing with him some of the bachelor engineers who had become his cronies. All the inmates of Liberty Hall, as it was called, put in long overtime hours in the laboratory, and held endless scientific discussions; nevertheless, the whole atmosphere was raffish and marked by juvenile horseplay. Practical jokes flourished, and unwary visitors found themselves accepting exploding cigars, grasping wired doorknobs that gave off a shock or being victimized by an easy chair so rigged that static electricity caused their hair to stand on end.

Steinmetz firmly denied himself the right of marriage. He was the third generation of hunchbacks in his family and was convinced his genes were too strongly twisted for him to take a chance on having children. He decided to end his family line with himself. Perhaps the harshness of this fate influenced his choice of pets for Liberty Hall. In any case he now acquired a menagerie containing some of nature's most unlovely misfits, including a Gila monster, several alligators and two crows, outcasts of the bird world.

Whatever his relations with the grownups, Steinmetz went to endless efforts to make friends with the neighborhood children. He took them through his laboratory and menagerie when they were brave enough, and always stopped to talk to them on the street. He added a big dog to his household and let it be known that if the dog ran away he would pay 50 cents reward for its return. It became a neighborhood game to lure the dog to the next block, then decide he was lost and take him back to his master. Although this would occur a dozen times a week, Steinmetz always paid the reward and sat on the front steps to talk to the child.

In 1901, after he had been at Liberty Hall for five years, Steinmetz bought some land on Wendell Avenue at the edge of the city. Eventually he was to build a house there; at first, however, he merely erected a two-story laboratory, but one so lavishly equipped that he began to do nearly all his work in it.

General Electric, recognizing in Steinmetz one of its greatest assets, was much concerned about his health and the relentless way he drove himself. Since no amount of management pressure could slow his pace or divert him from a problem, the company tried to conserve his strength by surrounding him with half a dozen "lab boys" as assistants. These were young engineers just out of college; they were to perform the master's routine research, construct what apparatus he required, clean and stock his laboratory and do whatever other chores he gave them. The assignment was much prized, and the young engineers went about their work in an aura of dedication, hero worship and comradeship.

Steinmetz developed a great fondness for all these assistants. But there was one lab boy who claimed his special affection. Joseph LeRoy Hayden understood Steinmetz's loneliness, listened with sympathetic interest to his stories about undergraduate days in Germany, and of all the little scientist's associates seemed to sense most clearly what it was like to be a hunchback. For two years they worked in close harmony and growing intimacy. When Steinmetz revealed his plan to build a home of his own on the ground next to the laboratory, Hayden helped him draw up the plans. The place, which was to be a huge, three-story, Elizabethan-style brick structure, was obviously much too big for one man, but neither of them mentioned this fact.

One April day in 1903 Hayden made a disturbing announcement. "I am planning to be married," he said. "You have already met the girl—Corinne Rost. Would it be all right if I took a week off for the honeymoon?"

Steinmetz agreed that the request was reasonable.

"I have asked Corinne to find an apartment near the lab," Hayden assured his boss, "so this won't affect our work together." Steinmetz smiled and nodded absently.

The young people were married in May, and took their brief week of honeymoon. On the first afternoon of their return, Steinmetz dropped by the new apartment and knocked hesitantly. When Hayden answered the door, he broke into a warm grin of welcome. "Honey, guess who's here," he called over his shoulder to his wife.

"Mr. Steinmetz," came the reply, and if the bride's tone was slightly acid the groom did not notice it.

"Come in, come in," he boomed. "I've been wondering how things are going at the lab. Did you finish charting that last arc phase?"

"Yes, and I must say some remarkable characteristics were revealed," Steinmetz said. "I have been anxious to discuss them with you."

The two men sat down, lighted cigars and filled the tiny living room with smoke and talk. Immersed in the technicalities of this work, the two friends lost all track of time; as it grew dusk, the bride finally interrupted briskly, "It's suppertime."

The men looked up with momentarily blank faces. Steinmetz glanced at his watch, then climbed reluctantly to his feet, murmuring, "I had no idea I had stayed so long."

"Darling, do we have enough food so Mr. Steinmetz could stay for supper?" the groom asked.

The question revealed the innocent obtuseness of the male, for this was the very first night in their own apartment, the meal the very first prepared by the bride's loving hands. Corinne Hayden stood stiffly silent for a few moments, trying to suppress her annoyance. Then she relaxed, smiled and said gently, "Of course, Mr. Steinmetz must stay for supper."

During the meal the two men resumed their earnest conversation, directing scarcely a word to her. And for the newlyweds the occasion set the pattern for much of their new life together; it became a fixed routine that Steinmetz had supper with them every evening.

Corinne Rost Hayden was a handsome French-Canadian girl possessed of a clear, no-nonsense view of life. She knew from the first that Steinmetz was going to be a problem in her marriage, and she suspected that the vast house he was building was simply a trap. On the day it was completed she was not surprised when the little scientist took the young couple on a tour of the many rooms, then turned to her and said, "Why don't you and LeRoy come and live with me?"

Her refusal was instinctive and automatic. "It is kind of you," she said, "but our apartment is quite adequate." That disposed of

the matter for that day, but it was not the end. Her husband was
soon pointing out the rough logic of Steinmetz's suggestion. The
house *was* large, and the two men *did* work late at night, and how
convenient to live so close to the laboratory! They could never
afford to live in such fine style on their own—why not take advantage of the generous offer?

When Corinne eventually saw that surrender was inevitable—
how could she hold out against the two men?—she determined to
obtain the best terms she could. She went to Steinmetz and said
bluntly, "If we move in with you, I want it understood that I run
the house as I see fit."

Struggling to conceal his elation, Steinmetz said, "Of course,
my dear."

"The meals will be served on time. You and LeRoy will leave
the laboratory when they are ready."

"Certainly."

Steinmetz no doubt made his promises to Corinne in good
faith, but some of them were simply beyond his power to keep.
When he and LeRoy were in the midst of an engrossing experiment, for example, it was obviously impossible to drop everything, wash up and sit down to eat merely because it happened to
be mealtime. Steinmetz found a hundred ways to give them luxuries they themselves would not dream of buying. One day he
marched into the kitchen and with a combination of bravado and
guilt asked Corinne to come outside. He had something to show
her. It was an electric automobile. An elegant affair of sleek black
enamel, cut-glass flower vases, plush upholstery and silk shades
dripping with tassels, it stood in the carriage drive, tall, square and
ponderous with dignity. Corinne was impressed despite herself
and clapped her hands. Steinmetz grinned happily.

"Who is the car for?" she demanded sternly after recovering
herself.

"Oh, I thought we . . ." He paused and corrected himself. "I
thought that I needed one."

"But you don't drive."

He waved away the objection. "Someone will drive it."

Corinne stood speechless, completely unable to cope with this sort of indirection. Finally she shrugged and went into the house. It took her a long time to realize that Steinmetz had almost no use for money except to bring happiness to others, and that the gifts he forced upon her and her husband were not bribes but the acts of a generous and loving heart.

The final change in the relationship between Steinmetz and Corinne came when the Haydens had their first child. Steinmetz came into Corinne's upstairs bedroom and, after admiring her son's lung power and marveling at the mechanism of his tiny fists, he set himself to say something which was evidently not easy for him. "Mousie," he said finally, after squirming uncomfortably in his chair. The nickname, begun as a joke, was now used in whimsical affection. "Mousie, I want to adopt your husband as my son, legally."

LeRoy had told her of Steinmetz's wish the night before, and they had discussed it at length then. But now that the little hunchback was making his humble request in person, she was filled with inarticulate emotion.

"I . . . I've talked to LeRoy, and it's all right with him," Steinmetz continued, "but I won't do it unless you approve."

She looked up from her son and smiled at the anxious little man. Then she held out her hand. "I approve—Grandpa."

The adoption papers were soon drawn up and filed, and at last Steinmetz had a family of his own. Which (though nobody ever quite knew for sure) was apparently just what he had in mind when he built that tremendous house.

The next few years brought the Haydens two more children. The three offspring, Joe, Midge and Billy, grew up in a family which contained three adults—Mother, Father and "Daddy" Steinmetz. Except that there was some doubt in their minds that Steinmetz really was an adult. He was no taller than Joe at nine years and, when they sat down to dinner, with Father and Mother at the head and foot of the table, four heads barely cleared the plates. The fact that one of them wore a beard didn't seem to make him any less childlike.

The secret and magic world of children is not easy to penetrate, but Steinmetz was at home in it. Unlike most adults he did not question the existence of elves and enchanted forests, and his enthusiasms were as inexhaustible as the children's own. He liked to invite the neighborhood moppets into his laboratory. The mere entrance into this place with its massive electrical equipment, vials of chemicals, Bunsen burners, retorts, test tubes and slightly sulfurous smell, left them excited, awed and a little frightened.

"How about some fireworks?" Steinmetz would then suggest. And, egged on by the shrill cries of assent, he would reach into a supply cabinet, take out a jar of innocent-looking white crystals and sprinkle a few of them into a pail of water. As the sodium came into contact with the water, hydrogen was released in explosive bubbles that burst into colored flame. The children loved it and clapped their hands.

Steinmetz installed slides and swings on the front lawn, and the cries of the neighborhood children as they played there seemed never to disturb his work. Indeed, all contacts with the young appeared to refresh him, and his bedtime stories to the Hayden children became such an important ritual that nothing was allowed to interfere with it.

One time Henry Ford, then at the first flush of his fame as creator of the Model T, came to Steinmetz with a problem. His automobiles had headlights that ran off a magneto, and this source of power was reliable enough when the engine was racing but faded away to nothing when the motor idled. For all his mechanical genius, Ford had been unable to lick this problem.

The famous man was invited to have dinner with the family, and afterward he and Steinmetz retired to the study. They were deep in the problem, their heads together, when the door burst open and in tripped Midge in her pajamas. "It's bedtime, Daddy," she said brightly.

Steinmetz nodded, stood up and said to Ford, "It's time for a bedtime story. I'll return in half an hour."

Ford was shocked. He was not accustomed to interruptions, especially from small children, and he immediately revised his estimate of Steinmetz downward. If there had been a train out of town that moment, he would have taken it. Instead, he walked the streets of Schenectady for half an hour, then reluctantly returned to the Wendell Avenue house. It was fortunate for him that he did. When Steinmetz came back downstairs he quickly sketched on a pad of paper the solution he had devised for the lighting problem.

Steinmetz's zest for young people was strikingly evident at Union College in Schenectady, where for ten years, beginning in 1903, he taught a class in electrical engineering. Only the most brilliant students could understand more than a fraction of what he taught, but he was far and away the most popular man on the faculty. Just as he was a child with his adopted grandchildren, he was in many ways an undergraduate on the campus. He shared the students' cults and never missed an athletic game. Moreover, his humor was on their level, and hardly a week passed without some new Steinmetz quip being delightedly passed around the student body.

One baffling problem which engaged Steinmetz at General Electric was that bane of the power industry, lightning. This implacable enemy melted power lines, burned out transformers and even traveled back to generators to melt vital parts. Every storm meant a power failure somewhere, often for days. How were power systems to absorb the sudden tremendous thrust of electricity from the skies? The problem was complicated by lightning's elusiveness, which made experiments with it almost impossible. Steinmetz tried erecting a tower on a hill which over the years had been repeatedly scarred by lightning. He attached all sorts of meters and instruments and had shifts of scientists watch them around the clock. Lightning never came near the hill all summer long.

But one day in the spring of 1920 nature gave Steinmetz an assist. He and Emil Remscheid, one of his lab boys, had driven out to his summer cabin at Camp Mohawk. They found it had been all but wrecked by lightning. Steinmetz surveyed the chaos with delight. "Drive back to town and get the camera," he told Emil. "I want to photograph every detail."

By the time Emil returned with the camera, Steinmetz had reconstructed the event. A bolt of lightning had struck the tall tree next to the front porch. It ran down the tree, shattered a window to hit the metal lamp on his worktable. From there it followed the wiring system, melting wires as it went, and entered a long outside extension cord that was draped outside the building. The cord was hung on a wooden peg and wound in a dozen loops; when the lightning got to this point the loops acted as a condenser to increase the voltage many times. Finally it was discharged through the cabin wall and onto the silvered back of the bedroom mirror inside.

Steinmetz looked down almost lovingly at the mess of scattered glass. "Emil, that mirror is our most important clue. Don't come in here until I finish putting it back together." He spent the rest of that weekend on hands and knees searching out the tiniest slivers of glass and carefully putting them back together like a great jigsaw puzzle. When at last it was done, he placed the reconstructed mirror between two large plates of clear glass and sealed the edges with tape. On the mirror's silvered back was burned the bold pattern of the bolt.

"Look here, Emil! The picture of a bolt of lightning. See where it struck? And see the melted ribbons where it ran to the edges. We will now be able to calculate the potential of lightning by measuring the distance from the point of impact to the end of the melted streamers."

From this start Steinmetz began a quest which was to last for two years. It involved reams of calculations, massive, strange-looking apparatus and puzzling, seemingly unconnected research projects for the scientists assigned to him. The whole city knew that something big was afoot. Just how big became apparent when word seeped out that he was actually trying to create lightning. He was bent on learning how to produce it artificially, to control it and to direct its course.

The city reacted variously to this news. Fundamentalist preachers decried what they considered an unwarranted invasion of God's province. The city fathers wondered if Steinmetz was not creating a terrible hazard to life and property. Other men, some of them scientists, questioned the usefulness of man-made lightning. The tense and difficult experiments continued, and in the winter of 1922 were crowned with success. Steinmetz invited Thomas A. Edison and other notables as well as reporters, photographers and high company officials to witness a demonstration.

On the appointed day the visitors were admitted to the laboratory to find a monstrous, strange machine—a lightning machine! It towered two stories high, and carried rack on rack of large glass plates covered with foil. These served as condensers to build the electrical energy to extremely high voltage. The voltage of the local power system was stepped up through transformers, then rectified through glass tubes known as kenetrons, which in turn charged the glass-plate condensers. When the current was turned on, the power would build until all the condensers discharged simultaneously. Two ominous-looking brass domes, called sphere gaps, were positioned to carry the bolt of lightning when it exploded.

The visitors stood behind a protective wire screen to view the machine with awe and speculation. There was a buzz of conversation but this ceased abruptly when Steinmetz entered. He greeted the viewers with brisk cheerfulness, conferred briefly with his associates to see that all was ready, then turned to the newspaper photographers. "How do you propose to photograph the lightning?" he asked. They told him in some detail. He then suggested changes, specifying the exact settings for their lens openings and shutter speeds. As a final bit of drama, a model village, complete with church steeple and tree-lined streets, was produced and placed between the sphere gaps. It was to be struck by lightning!

At last everything was ready, and a hush fell on the assembly. Steinmetz gave a small nod, and an assistant threw a switch. There was a slight hum as the condensers began to gather their charge of electricity. The spectators braced themselves, and some of them apprehensively placed their hands over their ears. Then it came—a blazing flash of lightning followed by a thunderous crash of sound that shook the room. The air filled with dust and the odor of ozone. As soon as the reporters recovered their breath they looked for the model village. It was gone . . . vanished . . . atomized!

Steinmetz began speaking matter-of-factly. "In our lightning generator we get a discharge of 10,000 amperes, at over 100,000 volts; that is, a force of over a million horsepower, lasting for a hundred-thousandth of a second. This gives us the explosive, tearing and shattering effects of real lightning."

After this Steinmetz soon developed an effective lightning arrester. Operating with the speed of lightning itself, this invaluable device automatically opened a path by which the lightning bolt could jump harmlessly to the ground instead of entering the power system. This meant everything to the power industry, but to the public it was a less impressive achievement than the ability to create artificial lightning. As newspapers around the world announced after that first demonstration: MODERN JOVE HURLS THUNDERBOLTS AT WILL.

The Hayden children were now in their teens—Joe 17, Midge 15, Billy 13—and had developed a fiercely possessive and protective attitude toward Steinmetz. For his part, he continued to spoil them with ever larger and more expensive gifts. When the American Institute of Electrical Engineers invited him to speak at their annual convention in Del Monte, California, in October of 1923, Steinmetz saw in the trip a chance for a family vacation. "What do you think, Mousie?" he asked Corinne. "Don't you think we should all go? It would be a chance to see the country."

"But the children will be in school."

He dismissed this as of no consequence. "Seeing the Great Plains, the Rockies, the Grand Canyon and Hollywood will all be educational. Come on, Mousie, let's do it!"

She sighed. "If I know you, you've already told the children, and I'm outvoted."

The trip west turned out to be an extended, triumphal tour. At every stop, crowds milled about the train waiting for a glimpse of the "modern Jove." Mayors and governors jostled one another to be photographed with him, and invitations to speak poured in from every city on the itinerary. Starting with Denver, Steinmetz accepted several such invitations, always speaking to packed auditoriums.

In Hollywood he was entertained by the reigning royalty, the famous motion-picture stars Douglas Fairbanks and Mary Pickford. In Del Monte his speech before the engineering convention received a rousing ovation, a tribute from men who realized that their careers had been created largely by him. And in Salt Lake City, the Mormon Tabernacle Choir gave a special recital for him and his family. Altogether the "vacation" lasted for six stimulating but exceptionally strenuous weeks. On October 12, when he returned to Schenectady and the familiar home on Wendell Avenue, Steinmetz complained mildly of being tired.

"Next year we'll take a cruise to the Mediterranean," he assured Corinne slyly. "There won't be so much walking." Then he went to bed.

Next day he was still tired, and a doctor was summoned. General exhaustion, the doctor said, and prescribed that the little man should stay in bed for a complete rest. Steinmetz grumbled but complied. On the morning of October 26, 1923, young Billy went to his grandfather's room with a breakfast tray, to find him dead. His face was serene, without a trace of pain or worry. His heart had run down and stopped as easily as an electric motor deprived of current. He was 59 years old.

Steinmetz had had no formal religion, yet his whole life had been an avowal of love, a sustained testament of faith. He had had ample opportunity to accumulate riches, but the estate he left was surprisingly small. He left the house and a modest amount of money to his adopted son, established a trust fund for a sister, and remembered close friends and other relatives with small sums. Aside from that, his legacy was to the world of science, to the users of electricity, to the students at Union College and to the children.

ARISTOTLE,
THE MASTER MIND

By Will Durant

WHEN, in his 49th year, Aristotle established his school at the Lyceum, or gymnasium, of Athens, so many students flocked to him that it became necessary to make complicated regulations for the maintenance of order. The students themselves determined the rules, and elected, every ten days, one of their number to supervise the school. But we must not think of it as a place of rigid discipline; rather the picture that comes down to us is of scholars eating their meals in common with the master, and learning from him as he and they strolled up and down the walk along the athletic field from which the Lyceum took its name.

The Lyceum was devoted above all to biology and the natural sciences. Alexander instructed his hunters, gamekeepers, gardeners and fishermen to furnish Aristotle with all the zoological and botanical material he might desire; and at one time we are told that he had at his disposal a thousand men, scattered throughout Greece and Asia, collecting for him specimens of the fauna and flora of every land. With this wealth of material he was enabled to establish the first great zoological garden that the world had seen.

Where did Aristotle derive the funds to finance these undertakings? He was himself a man of spacious income; and he had married into the fortune of one of the most powerful public men in Greece. It is related that Alexander gave Aristotle, for equipment and research, the sum of 800 talents (some $4,000,000). Such works as the digest of 158 political constitutions, drawn up for Aristotle, indicate a considerable corps of aides and secretaries. In short we have here the first example of the large-scale financing of science by public wealth.

Yet we should do Aristotle injustice if we were to ignore the almost fatal limitations of equipment which accompanied these unprecedented resources and facilities. Of all our mathematical, optical and physical instruments he possessed only the rule and compass, together with the most imperfect substitutes for some few others. Moreover, all the facts on which the physical theories of modern science are based were wholly, or almost wholly, undiscovered. Indeed, it was in industrial and technical invention that Greece fell furthest below the general standard of its unparalleled achievements. Perhaps the very cheapness of slaves made invention lag; muscle was still less costly than machines. So Aristotle could seldom appeal to experiment; the best he could do was to achieve an almost universal and continuous observation. Nevertheless the vast body of data gathered by him and his assistants became the groundwork of the progress of science, the textbook of knowledge for some 2000 years—one of the wonders of the works of man.

Aristotle's writings ran into the hundreds. Some ancient authors credit him with a thousand volumes. What remains is but a part, and yet it is a library in itself. Consider the scope and grandeur of the whole. There are, first, the Logical works, dealing with correct thinking: "Categories," "Topics," "Prior Analytics" and "Posterior Analytics," "Propositions" and "Sophistical Refutations." Secondly, there are the Scientific works: "Physics," "On the Heavens," "Growth and Decay," "Meteorology," "Natural History," "On the Soul," "The Parts of Animals" and "The Generation of Animals." There are, thirdly, the Esthetic works: "Rhetoric" and "Poetics." And fourthly, the more strictly Philosophical works: "Ethics," "Politics" and "Metaphysics." Here, evidently, is the Encyclopedia of Greece: every problem under the sun and about it finds a place. Here is such a fusing of knowledge and theory as no man would ever achieve again till Herbert

Spencer's day, and even then not half so magnificently; here was a conquest of the world. If philosophy is the quest of unity, Aristotle deserves the high name that 20 centuries have given him—The Philosopher.

Aristotle built the terminology of science and philosophy; we can hardly speak of any science today without employing terms which he invented: faculty, mean, maxim, category, energy, actuality, motive, end, principle, form—these indispensable coins of philosophic thought were minted in his mind. Aristotle almost entirely by his own hard thinking created a new science—Logic, the art and method of correct thinking. It is a science because to a considerable extent the processes of right thinking can be reduced to rules like physics and geometry, and taught to any normal mind. It is an art because by practice it gives to thought, at last, that unconscious accuracy which guides the fingers of the pianist over his instrument.

Before Aristotle, science was in embryo; with him it was born. Earlier civilizations than the Greek explained every obscure operation in nature by some supernatural agency; everywhere there were gods. It is one of the many glories of Aristotle that he was broad and brave enough to bring together a magnificent body of organized science.

Aristotle was born in 384 B.C. His father was physician to Amyntas, King of Macedon and grandfather of Alexander. He studied under Plato, who recognized the greatness of his pupil. Aristotle spent money lavishly on the collection of books (manuscripts); he was the first, after Euripides, to gather together a library, and the foundation of the principles of library classification was among his many contributions to scholarship. Some biographers tell us that Aristotle founded a school of oratory. Later, Philip, King of Macedon, called Aristotle to the court at Pella, to undertake the education of Alexander. It bespeaks the rising repute of our philosopher that the greatest monarch of the time, looking about for the greatest teacher, should single out Aristotle to be the tutor of the future master of much of the world.

Philip was determined that his son should have every educational advantage, for he had made for him boundless designs. His people were vigorous peasants and warriors, as yet unspoiled by city luxury and vice. Here was the combination that would make possible the enslavement of over a hundred petty city-states and the political unification of Greece. Philip had no sympathy whatsoever with the individualism that had fostered the art and intellect of Greece but had at the same time brought about the disintegration of her social order.

In all these little capitals he saw not the exhilarating culture and the unsurpassable art, but the commercial corruption and the political chaos. He saw insatiable merchants and bankers absorbing the vital resources of the nation, incompetent politicians and clever orators misleading a busy populace into disastrous plots and wars, factions cleaving classes and congealing into castes. Philip said he would bring the hand of order down upon this turmoil, and make all Greece stand up united and strong as the political center and basis of the world.

These problems are not so very dissimilar to those confronting many of our governments today! And perhaps we should now have more adequate solutions to these problems had the world, during the past 2000 years, been able to produce more men of the mental caliber of Aristotle, of whom Plato once said, "He is Intelligence Personified."

At a turbulent public meeting once I lost my temper and said some harsh and sarcastic things. The proposal I was supporting was promptly defeated. My father, who was there, said nothing, but that night, on my pillow, I found a marked passage from Aristotle: "Anybody can become angry—that is easy; but to be angry with the right person, and to the right degree, and at the right time, and for the right purpose, and in the right way— that is not within everybody's power and is not easy."

—*Arthur Gordon*

OLD HICKORY

By *Donald Culross Peattie*

THE WAR OF 1812 gave birth to a legend that took the form of a man; and it made a man who became a legend. The legend was "Uncle Sam." The man was Andrew Jackson, seventh President of the United States. Legend and man came to stand for many of the same things, and finally even to look alike.

The battle skies of 1812 lowered black indeed. Things were going wrong. Parts of the country were against the war, and giving less than no help; the whole country was unprepared. Worse, the Administration was backing a lot of incompetents, passing over able men. One of the able ones was Andrew Jackson, who pestered the Administration with plans for campaigns that were thrown into the wastebaskets, and with demands to be allowed to fight that were considered ridiculous for a man with a dueling bullet lodged so close to his heart it could never be removed.

The Administration knew something about this Jackson of Nashville, but the reports were mixed. He had been an excellent general in the Tennessee militia, a successful lawyer and a good frontier judge; one of the delegates who had helped make the constitution of the new state of Tennessee, he was the first Congressman from that state, and later a Senator. He had voted *against* paying off the Algerian pirates and *for* the construction of frigates to fight them. He had a gentlemanly taste in horse racing, and an uncanny knack of bringing in "the tavern vote" in local politics.

He was a Jeffersonian democrat who thought the radical Mr. Jefferson wasn't half radical enough. He had a temper like a fighting cock's and reputedly would fight a duel with a man for tread-

ing on his toes. He was ill-educated, self-made, an incurable land speculator, and involved in some old scandal which it had already cost one man his life to mention. His troops adored him and would obey no orders contrary to his.

When, during the War of 1812, the Creek Indians, egged on by British agents, attacked murderously from Mississippi Territory, Tennessee's governor called out the state militia and gave Jackson command. On the march, sleeping on the swampy ground with his men, eating the same slim rations, Jackson had acquired a nickname. "He's tough as hickory," his rugged frontiersmen said, and the name "Old Hickory" stuck. The Creeks were the most powerful Indian confederation in the southern states. Jackson's troops were unpaid and ill-provisioned. Old Hickory himself, having contracted violent dysentery, was reeling in his saddle. But on March 27, 1814, he caught the Creek braves at the Horseshoe Bend of the Tallapoosa River, in what is now Alabama. In point of numbers engaged, this was one of the greatest Indian battles in history, contested with unsurpassed ferocity. When night fell the Creeks were broken, their dead lying in heaps.

Now the War Department, faced with the most serious threat of the war, sent the man they had passed over as a crank to meet a British attack on New Orleans. Ten thousand strong, the enemy troops were disciplined Redcoats and Highlanders, veterans who had beaten Napoleon's armies. Creole New Orleans had not so much as thrown up a rampart for its defense when Jackson arrived. Its spectacle-loving habitants at first were disappointed in this outsider in the campaign-stained uniform, who thrust aside their famous cooking for the hominy on which he lived. Jackson soon found it necessary to declare martial law, under which he put a member of the legislature in jail. When a high judge issued a writ in favor of the offender, he arrested the judge too. Then, with his backwoods boys, New Orleans volunteers, and patriotic pirates of the Laffite crew, he set about ordering his defense. He had an old score to settle with the British as he watched their bayonets emerge out of the morning fog at Chalmette plantation on January 8, 1815.

Andy was born near the line between North and South Carolina. (He always gave South Carolina as his home state.) When only 14, he joined the Revolutionary Army and was captured by the British, along with his wounded brother. When Andy refused to clean an officer's boots, he was struck with a saber that cleft his scalp and cut his hand to the bone. Bleeding, he was marched without food or water to a prison camp at Camden, South Carolina. When the boys contracted smallpox, their widowed mother secured their release. The sicker boy she put on a horse. Coatless, barefoot, in an icy rain, Andy staggered 40 miles home, fell into bed delirious. He lived, but his brother died and, less than a year later, his mother also. He was on his own in the world.

Now, almost 48, he saw again the glitter of British bayonets, and the steely look that men were to learn and fear came into his blue eyes. The end of that day found the British driven from the field in a stinging defeat. It was the most glorious battle of the war for America, its glory undimmed by the fact that a peace treaty had been signed—but not ratified—at Ghent in Belgium two weeks earlier. From that hour New Orleans adored Jackson. So popular was the nation's new hero that when the judge he had arrested fined Jackson $1000 in revenge, a purse was pressed into the general's hand to pay the fine. He turned that over to the widows and orphans of the battle, and paid the fine out of his own pocket.

Resigning his military commission in 1821, Old Hickory hoped to spend the rest of his life at his beloved estate, The Hermitage, near Nashville. But he could not hide from destiny. In 1824, Jackson's friends ran him for President against three other candidates, including Henry Clay and John Quincy Adams. Without himself campaigning, Jackson polled the majority of popular votes. But because there was no clear majority for any candidate in the Electoral College, the election was decided in the House, where Clay's influence sent Adams to the White House.

But Jackson's friends persisted and pushed his candidacy for 1828. The campaign against him was unprecedented in American politics for slanderous personal attacks. A Jackson legend was started—one still found in many history books—of a man of low personal morals, a murderer, an ignoramus, an opportunist with no fixed political principles. Worst of all, for General and Mrs. Jackson, was the airing of an old misfortune. Rachel, when young Andrew first met and loved her, was the estranged wife of Lewis Robards of Kentucky. Robards publicly started divorce proceedings, quietly dropped them, then permitted a story to circulate that he had obtained his decree. Jackson trustingly married Mrs. Robards. Two years later the startled couple learned that Robards only then was obtaining a divorce on the grounds that his wife was living in adultery with another man.

The fierce publicity given this old story during the campaign of 1828 killed Rachel Jackson—at least, so thought her adoring husband as he stood beside her grave. The din of victory at the polls fell on his deaf ears; no sadder man ever entered the White House. And his health, broken by dysentery, had declined into tuberculosis.

But duty to country called Old Hickory into action. Sixty-two, hair gone snowy now, his figure soldierly though gaunt, he did not ride in state to the Capitol, but walked there from his hotel. Chief Justice John Marshall, who privately believed Jackson would ruin the country, administered the oath of office. Outgoing President Adams refused to ride back to the White House with Jackson. But a mob stormed it to congratulate him. The diplomatic corps came to dinner, prepared to sneer at the ignorant boor whom the base populace had selected; but they found a deeply courteous old man who provided the best table talk and wines in Washington. Political wiseacres who came to advise him were kept waiting while he rode horseback with a cavalcade of children. "They are the only friends I have," he explained, "who don't pester me with advice."

Foreign observers believed that a bloody revolution was about to take place. It was indeed a further chapter in the American revolution that had begun when the first settlers came to this country. A new era in our economic life had dawned, the beginning of the machine age. Between 1820 and 1840, factory workers increased 127 percent, or more than any other group in the country. And we had no governmental control over industrialists. Much of "the old governing class," ousted by Jackson's success, was bound by its bank accounts to this ungoverned new power. The Bank of the United States, operating under government charter, was unlike any we have today; it was a private bank but in it were deposited all of the government's reserves. The man whom America had sent to the White House saw danger in this. "The Bank of the United States," Jackson thundered, "is in itself a government. The question between it and the people has become one of power."

So hot did the battle grow that Nicholas Biddle, the Bank's president, and the forces that backed him threw the issue into Jackson's campaign for a second term, confident of defeating him. For the moneyed interests had everything at their command — most of the press, many of the most famous pulpits, a majority in the Senate. Jackson was represented as trying to ruin business, tearing up the Constitution, violating Heaven's laws. But most of the people of the United States were with him. Carrying hickory poles, chanting the magic name of Old Hickory, they swept him into office a second time.

When Congress voted to recharter the Bank, Jackson vetoed the measure and the veto was upheld. When Jackson tried to remove the government deposits from the Bank, two successive Secretaries of the Treasury refused to do so. Finally, Roger Taney, later appointed by Jackson as Chief Justice, did the job. When Biddle called in all loans, a nationwide panic resulted. Jackson was stormed by frightened or angry delegations, begging him to appease the Bank. Old Hickory never budged. "Go to Biddle for your redress," he told them grimly. But Biddle could not stand up to the Administration. With the withdrawal of U. S. funds his Bank died. With it died the rule of money that had boasted it ran the government.

Together with the Bank battle rose the crisis of states' rights. The issue was brought to a head by the enactment of new high tariffs drawn up by Senator Henry Clay. Designed to protect the manufacturing interests of the North, they bore hard on the South, which exported raw material for a living and bought almost all its manufactured goods. A cotton planter himself, Jackson may have hated the tariff laws. But law they were, and when Jackson's native South Carolina declared the tariff within her borders "null, void and no law," she reckoned without her greatest son. Jackson looked ahead in history with piercing eyes. "The tariff was only the pretext," he said, "and disunion and a Southern Confederacy the real object. The gallows ought to be the fate of all who involve their country in civil war." When the Nullifiers began to arm, Jackson at one time promised to march 200,000 troops into the rebellious state. And nobody doubted he would come at the head of the columns. Desperately the Nullifiers grasped at the straw of a slightly lower tariff and repealed their ordinance.

Jackson, who believed that government is best which spends least, left the Treasury richer than he found it. In his administration old barriers to foreign trade were broken down. He pursued an open expansionist policy. His methods were rough-and-ready, but Americans of his day roared approval of the way he forced Spain's hand in the sale of Florida, of the way he kept pushing the Indians westward, and of the annexation of Texas accomplished by his devoted followers.

Jackson left the White House a poor man, ruined by his lavish hospitality and charity, by the neglect of private business for public duty. But he left the White House stronger than he found it, just as Marshall had raised the Supreme Court from impotence to mighty power. Jackson made the Presidency one of the three great powers of our government.

After his death on June 8, 1845, at his home near Nashville, Tennessee, Andrew Jackson was buried next to the grave of his adored Rachel. There in The Hermitage garden stand six towering shagbark hickories. Every foot of their grand American hardwood growth symbolizes the leader who sleeps beneath them. Old Hickory was not a flawless man, but a *man* he was, every sound inch of him, a people's President, a great American.

THE SOLDIERS' ANGEL

Condensed from A Lost Commander

By Mary Raymond Shipman Andrews

MANY OF US have read in Dickens about Nurse Sairey Gamp, who took a drink "when she was so dispoged." Not all of us know that less than a century ago Sairey Gamp, the drunken, the ignorant, the immoral nurse, was real and was multiple. Around 1870, in Bellevue Hospital, New York, there were plenty of her. In those days, says an eminent physician, "some of the nursing in Bellevue was done by drunken prostitutes, who were given the option of going to prison or to hospital service. They were often found in sleep under the beds of their dead patients whose liquor they had stolen."

A bad kettle of fish that seems to us, who trust our lives unhesitatingly to the comfort and service of hospitals. Yet such was the deplorable state of nursing, not alone in this country but in England, around 1850, when Florence Nightingale—destined heroine of the Crimea—was fighting for her future. Nurses were "all drunkards without exception; but two nurses whom the surgeon can trust to give the patients their medicines"—such is a doctor's account of a London hospital. Toward such a world of drunkenness and immorality and misery did this daintily raised society girl steadfastly set her steps. In between London and country house parties she was studying anatomy and visiting hospitals. That her family opposed her, tooth and nail, is not remarkable.

Yet by 1852, in spite of family opposition, she had grown

steadily in wisdom and judgment in her chosen field. On the Continent she had received nursing training at the institute for Protestant deaconesses in Kaiserswerth, Germany. In 1853 she obtained permission to study Paris hospitals managed by the Sisters of Charity. Finally, back in London that summer, she went into her first "situation" as superintendent of the "Establishment for Gentlewomen During Illness" in Harley Street. Her task was extremely difficult: she had to manage the nurses, assist at operations and hold down expenses of coal cellar and food larder. But that year in Harley Street, with experience as organizer, manager, nurse, diplomat, led directly into the responsibilities of the Crimean War.

In 1854 England, France and Turkey were at war with Russia; British troops were landed in the Crimea, and six days later was the battle of the Alma River. After rejoicings of victory came a shift to bitter resentment. "No sufficient preparations have been made for the care of the wounded," read a dispatch. "Not only not sufficient surgeons; not only no dressers and nurses; but not even linen to make bandages." The newspaper indictment stirred England. The writer told of the French: "Their medical arrangements are extremely good; they have the help of the Sisters of Charity who have accompanied the expedition; these are excellent nurses." Next day was a letter in the *Times* of London: "Why have we no Sisters of Charity?" Florence Nightingale was urged to take out nurses, but she wanted official sanction. She submitted a plan to Sidney Herbert, Secretary at War.

Englishwomen nurses in the army! A woman in any position of public responsibility was at that time a subject for prejudiced talk. Herbert knew that military jealousy and opposition would occur. Now, however, public indignation over the scandal in the Crimea was so aroused that Herbert, with the approval of the Cabinet, appointed Florence Nightingale to select and lead a group of nurses.

On an autumn day in 1854 Sir Alexander Moore lay wounded in the Barrack Hospital at Scutari on the shore of the Bosporus. Balaklava had been fought, and the wounded from the cavalry engagement had just been brought by ship across the Black Sea.

Moore's cot was near a window; he had a view into the central courtyard of the hospital—a view that was to haunt him the rest of his life. The operating room was opposite, and out from its window came flying, making an ever-increasing pile on the pavement, amputated arms and legs. From their beds wounded men watched. On this day, when Sir Alexander was trying to sleep, trying to forget the bloody things which came tumbling endlessly, the officer in the nearest cot spoke: "Moore," he said, "I believe that English nurse has come."

Sir Alexander lifted his head and looked out. An army mule cart was carrying off the mass which had lain rotting. The English nurse had indeed come! Florence Nightingale and 38 nurses had landed the afternoon before. There was no excitement, yet already her organizing power was beginning to be felt.

Each side of the hospital was nearly a quarter of a mile in length. There were several stories of galleries and corridors on three sides of the building, enough to make, if continuously extended, four miles. In these corridors, closely packed, without decencies or necessities, lay men with terrible wounds, sick with hideous diseases. "The hospital had been transformed from a barracks by the simple process of whitewashing, and underneath its imposing mass were sewers of the worst possible construction, from which the wind blew sewer air up into the corridors where the sick were lying. Wounds and sickness, overcrowding and want of proper ventilation added to the foulness of the atmosphere. At night it was indescribable. The wards were infested with rats, mice and vermin. Even the commonest utensils for cleanliness, decency and comfort were lacking," Miss Nightingale wrote.

"Not a basin, not a towel, not a bit of soap or a broom," she noted. "The cooking was done in large coppers at one end of the vast building, and it took three or four hours to serve the ordinary dinners."

Such was the hell into which this highbred, soft-voiced woman walked eagerly. "Before she came," a soldier's letter said, "there was cussin' and swearin', but after that it was as holy as a church." "After that" many things changed. "Six shirts washed a month" for 2000 sick, dirty heroes did not fit with Florence Nightingale's training. And the bedding, when washed, had been washed in cold water. In a week a laundry was started. Miss Nightingale, "using her own funds, took a house, had boilers put in, and employed soldiers' wives to do the washing."

Within ten days she had three diet kitchens making and serving delicacies for those so desperately ill that they were unable to eat the food that came to them. With supplies she herself had provided, she set up a storeroom from which the surgeons were thankful to get necessaries. For there was a lack of these, even when they were actually in Scutari. Soldiers lay in blood-soaked garments of the battlefield, while three bales marked "hospital clothes" were in Scutari and nobody dared open the bales till a "board" had "sat upon" them! An important person of the board was away; the board could not meet without him; so the men continued to lack the clothes.

She was charged with officiousness in supplying needs. She preferred to obey rules, but between rules and her soldiers the rules went to the wall. There was jealousy from military and medical officers; a "female" with power assigned by the government, with ability to use her power—it was unendurable. Some officers sulked; others threw obstacles. Yet reforms went forward like armored tanks plowing over machine-gun nests of jealousy and red tape. She set up a money-order department to receive the money of any soldier who wished to send it home, and in the next six months over $350,000 "rescued from the canteen," she said, went to families in England. She started another rival to the canteen, the Inkerman Coffeehouse, and drunkenness among the soldiers was automatically reduced. She established classrooms and reading rooms, and people back in England eagerly sent out books, games and music. She trained orderlies and educated her nurses. Beyond that, she wrote endless letters, chiefly to officials.

By the miracle power of busy people she had time to do all these things. But the greatest of her miracles was the accomplishment of the supreme object of her life, nursing. Not merely organizer and purveyor and schoolmistress and correspondent and thorn-in-the-flesh to dozing officials, she was with her own hands intensely a nurse. She was known to pass eight hours on her knees, dressing wounds and comforting the men. Sometimes she stood 20 hours at a stretch, assisting at operations, distributing stores, directing work. She had an utter disregard of contagion. "The more awful any particular case, the more certainly might her slight form be seen bending over him, seldom quitting his side till death released him," a report stated. The men worshiped her, and at night, as she passed down the long rows, lamp in hand, pausing here and there to give comfort or assistance, they would kiss her shadow as it fell across their pillows.

The treaty of peace was signed at Paris in March 1856. All England was on fire to meet Florence Nightingale. The government offered her a man-of-war to come home on, but she declined; and one day early in August, "Miss Smith" slipped quietly into London unrecognized, missing the bands, the triumphal arches and addresses that had been planned for the "Lady-in-Chief." She was utterly tired—but more than that, her health was seriously impaired.

To Florence Nightingale the two years in the Crimea were an episode; really, they were an enormous and far-reaching starting point. One movement which she had not directly thought of serving, she had served: the position of women as people instead of as females. "Mark what, by breaking through customs and prejudices, Miss Nightingale has effected for her sex," Lord Stanley, the 15th Earl of Derby, said about that time. "She has opened to them a new profession, a new sphere of usefulness."

The country wanted to do something for the soldiers' angel, already doomed to invalidism for the rest of her life. It was understood that the wish of her heart was a school for nursing, and a fund was started. In a year the fund was over $200,000, and in 1859 Florence Nightingale began, at St. Thomas's Hospital, the first lay training school for nurses. From her invalid's bed in South

Street she gave much time to the new institution. The first class of 13 was graduated in 1861. With those 13 girls in brown frocks and white caps there opened a new profession which has reached to many countries. That little school at St. Thomas's reformed the pauper hospitals of all England and finally the public hospitals of the whole world—redeeming them from the drunken, immoral nurses, from the Sairey Gamps.

Meanwhile, lying on a sofa in South Street, Florence Nightingale read and worked and wrote without end. Her life of 90 years was crammed with action almost to the end, despite nearly half a century of invalidism. In a land where women were almost chattels, she acted as ultimate court of appeal on large public questions, and as unquestioned adviser to high government officials. Her fame grew to international proportions, and she was consulted on hospital administration during our own Civil War, and again by the French during the Franco-Prussian War.

Today, a figure of Florence Nightingale stands, lofty, on a pedestal in mid-London, and all England seethes about in the streets below. That is as it should be; but it is not all. Her truest monument, not made with hands, is one not always associated with her name; it is the far-reaching outcome of that school of 13 young women in brown and white, housed and guarded in a wing of old St. Thomas's Hospital. It is the hope of help to which the world turns in trouble, a fitting, enormous monument—the modern profession of nursing.

Life always needs beauty. Something deep within the spirit goes unsatisfied unless it can go from time to time and bathe itself in that atmosphere which breathes from lovely things. Florence Nightingale, desperately ill of fever in the Crimea, left a record of the fact that the thing which wooed her back to convalescence was the sight of a single rose.

— *Walter Russell Bowie*

THE GRAND CARUSO

Based on Enrico Caruso *by Dorothy Caruso*

By George Kent

ANNA CARUSO had 21 children; only three lived beyond infancy. One of these, the 18th child, became perhaps the greatest singer of all time. He made his American debut on the stage of the Metropolitan Opera House in New York in 1903, and sang his last aria on the same stage in 1920. Eight months later he was dead. Millions of men and women, in many countries, wept, and thousands donned mourning. He had been not only a great voice but a great and dearly loved human being.

In Enrico Caruso's day broadcasting was unknown, and there were no talking pictures. If you wanted to hear him sing, you bought a ticket and heard him as a man in the flesh, or you cranked the Victrola and heard his voice come out through the trumpet horn. The total audience was small compared to today's millions of radio listeners and television viewers, yet for sheer public acclaim there has been little in the history of idol worship to equal that accorded to Enrico Caruso.

His singing was chiefly arias from French and Italian grand opera—regarded then as today as highbrow stuff—yet so extraordinary were his range and his power, and so effectively did he transmit his emotion, that he overwhelmed all audiences, often leaving them in tears. He himself was so strongly affected that sometimes after a performance he would sit sobbing in his dressing room.

His home stage was, of course, the Metropolitan, but his fame was equally great in every world capital from Buenos Aires to Moscow. Wherever he went crowds milled about him. In restaurants, people rose and cheered when he came in. To avoid the clamor he ate at home, or in a cheap New York West Side spaghetti house, where he idled away the afternoons playing cards with the proprietor. Every mail brought him gifts—candy, food, jewelry, his own portrait embroidered on silk or wool.

Thousands of commercial articles, from cigars to soap, were named for him. A chain of restaurants was called Caruso. A spaghetti and a line of canned goods still bear his name. Someone called a race horse Caruso and the singer faithfully bet $10 each time the horse ran. The horse never won.

Financially, Caruso established records in that distant era which have never been equaled. The money came to him solely from singing on the stage and from phonograph records. He never asked the Met for more than $2500 a performance, but in Cuba he got $10,000 and in Mexico, $15,000. He once refused an offer of $250,000 for a two-month swing through Latin America. In his lifetime he earned close to $10,000,000.

At least a part of his popularity was due to his greatness as a man. He had a peasant's naïveté, impelling him to warmhearted gestures which endeared him to the public. One night in Brussels there was a great deal of noise outside his dressing-room window. Caruso opened the window and discovered a crowd of several thousand standing there unhappily because every space in the theater had been sold. It was a gala performance, with royalty in attendance. Caruso thought a moment, then sang to the people in the street all the principal arias of the opera he was about to appear in on the stage.

One day as he sat signing checks for the more than 200 persons he helped to support, his wife murmured, "Surely all these people aren't deserving." "You are right, Doro," he replied, "but can you tell which is and which isn't?"

In Cleveland, one morning, he was walking with Bruno Zirato, his secretary. "It isn't right," he said suddenly. "We come here, we take the money—and we go away. We must leave some here."

They happened to be passing a display of china in a shopwindow. Caruso plunged inside and bought the entire contents of the store. He had everything shipped to New York for distribution among his needy friends. Thereafter he always managed somehow to plow back into every town some of the money he received for singing.

At the peak of his career he was a plump, middle-sized man who wore a size 18 collar and whose hair was growing thin on top. He was clean to the point of fanaticism. He bathed twice a day, meanwhile studying music from a special rack fitted to the tub. The door stood open, and in the next room an accompanist ran through the score on the piano. Each morning he was shaved, massaged, pedicured and manicured, again to the piano accompaniment for his next role.

He was utterly intolerant of people not as fastidious as himself. Of a diva, to whom he was required to make love on the stage, he complained: "It is terrible to sing with one that doesn't bathe, but to be emotionated over one who breathes garlic is impossible!"

Enrico was born in Naples, Italy, the son of a factory mechanic. He went to school only a few years. His father wanted him to become a mechanic like himself, and by dint of beatings managed to get a little work out of him. But Caruso wanted one thing only in life, to be a singer. In this he was constantly encouraged by his mother. His first hearing before a music teacher was not successful. The professor, Giuseppe Vergine, known now chiefly because of the episode, said to him after the trial, "You have a voice like wind in the shutters." But Caruso obtained permission to remain and listen to the instruction. Of his poverty in those days, he had this to say to his wife:

"My black suit had turned green so I bought a little bottle of dye and dyed it before I went to the class. I cut my shirt fronts from paper so I would look nice. I had to walk very far every day to get there, and shoes cost money, so I sang at weddings and funerals to make enough to buy a pair. The soles were cardboard.

Halfway to the Maestro's house came the rain. When I got there I put them by the stove to dry. They curled up and I walked home on bare feet."

At the end of the term, there were tests and Caruso begged for permission to take them. Signor Vergine conceded that he had made progress but was not impressed. Nevertheless he obtained for Caruso one or two small engagements, and finally a job in opera as understudy to the tenor of a small traveling company: One day they arrived at a place where Caruso had friends. Reasonably certain that he would not be called on, he joined his cronies, and together they sang old Neapolitan songs and drank large quantities of wine. Enrico was a little tipsy when a messenger arrived to summon him because the tenor at last had fallen ill. Caruso rushed to the theater. He sang well, but to the dismay of the management and the delight of the audience, he bumped into people, stumbled and generally made a mess of things. The audience roared with laughter, shouting, "*Ubriacone*," or drunkard.

The manager fired Caruso the moment the act ended, and a very disconsolate 19-year-old youth went back to his little room. His first opportunity had come and he had missed it. But the messenger again broke in to tell him breathlessly that the audience had booed the other tenor off the stage and was stamping and roaring for the *Ubriacone*. Caruso went back and triumphed. From then on he progressed steadily. During the next ten years he became one of the best-known tenors in Italian opera, and sang in many countries in Europe. Then he was invited to sing at the Metropolitan Opera House in New York, making his debut in *Rigoletto*.

The requisites of a great singer, Caruso explained one day, were "a big chest, a big mouth, 90 percent memory, ten percent intelligence, lots of hard work and something in the heart." He had all these attributes, intellectual, emotional, moral and physical. His chest was enormous, and he could expand it nine inches.

Before going on the stage, he followed a strict procedure of his own invention. First he gargled deeply with warm salt water, then he inhaled a little Swedish snuff to clear his nostrils. After that came a wineglass of whiskey, a glass of charged water and finally a quarter of an apple. Into the pockets of his costume he slipped two vials of warm salt water for use if his throat became clogged during the performance. When that happened, he would turn his back to the audience, quickly swallow the contents of one of the vials, and continue without anyone out front knowing what had taken place.

Caruso was always sensitive to criticism. When Boston critics condemned a performance, he swore he would never sing there again—and he never did. Generally, however, he bubbled with good humor. He loved joking, which he called "making a funny," and his "funnies" are remembered even today. During a performance of *Tosca*, in a scene in an artist's studio, baritone Antonio Scotti stooped to pick up a paintbrush that had fallen beneath the easel—and found it immovable. Caruso had nailed it to the floor.

David Ewen, in *Listen to the Mocking Words*, tells of an occasion when Caruso and Geraldine Farrar were recording a duet from *Madame Butterfly*. The session with the recording machine was long and arduous, and Caruso dashed across the street for a bit of stimulation at the corner bar. When he returned and began again to sing with Farrar, the prima donna mischievously interpolated into her aria: "Oh, you've had a highball!" And Caruso sang back: "No—I've had *two* highballs!" That record is now a collector's item.

Perhaps the tenderest passage in this extraordinary life is the story of his marriage. He was 45 and at the height of his career when he met Dorothy Park Benjamin, a shy, unworldly girl in her early 20's, not many years out of a convent school. He courted and won her despite the disapproval of her conservative, old New York family. Their brief, three-year life together was an idyll. The fact shines forth in the biography she wrote of him, but even more in his letters to her. These letters are unique, their very errors in English enhancing their charm. Here is a passage, selected at random:

"My heart jomping so strong I think he want to fly to you, never more, never more I will leave you. . . . I wish you were in myself to see how I love you. What can I do to let you be certenly of that? I think I done all my best to show you my love and I am steel trying do things to let you be convinched of it. Be sure that your Rico adore you. . . ."

The couple led a quiet life together in a suite in a New York hotel. Caruso did not like to go out, because crowds disturbed him. They would sit at home, he in gold-rimmed glasses, pasting stamps and clippings, she reading. Often at midnight he would get hungry and send for a loaf of bread and some minute steaks. He would cut the bread in half the long way, insert the steaks and eat them as a sandwich. When Caruso did accept a dinner invitation he invariably sent a message to the hostess, saying he must sit next to his wife. "Tell her," he would instruct the messenger, "I married my wife to be with her. If I have to be away from her I stay home."

In December 1920, as Caruso was singing an aria in the first act of the opera *L'Elisir d'Amore*, a blood vessel burst in his throat. He insisted on going on until the act was finished. A New York *Times* reporter told the story: "His own reddened handkerchief he had discarded, and one after the other, members of the chorus found opportunity to come close to him and deftly give him another and slip away. One after another he used them until they were stained scarlet, and now and then little flecks of blood would show upon his lips." In the front row, Dorothy Caruso sat imploring him to leave the stage.

On Christmas Eve he returned once more to the Met, but again he collapsed. Seven operations were performed for abscesses of the lungs, but he never sang again. In the summer of the following year, he sailed for Naples. There in a small hotel looking out on the Bay of Naples, he died, aged 48.

In her book, Dorothy Caruso wrote: "I have been sitting by the radio, listening to his recorded voice singing gloriously on a memorial program. He would have liked this tribute. He would have said: 'So kind of them to remember after so long.'"

PEARY OF THE POLE

By Jo Chamberlin

O N SEPTEMBER 5, 1909, a blackened, thick-hulled little ship named the *Roosevelt* steamed proudly into Indian Harbor, Labrador, from the north. On board was Robert E. Peary, who seven times previously had tried in vain to reach the North Pole. Now, from the little town's wireless station, he sent this revealing message to his wife: I HAVE MADE GOOD AT LAST. Then to the press he sent five simple words that he felt would electrify the world: POLE REACHED, ROOSEVELT SAFE, PEARY.

Proceeding down the Labrador coast, the *Roosevelt* anchored in Battle Harbor, and there a chartered ship, its decks almost awash with newspaper reporters, came alongside. Immediately the reporters shouted to Peary for his comments on "the big row."

"Row? What row?" asked Peary. Why, between him and Cook. Didn't he know that Dr. Frederick A. Cook had reached the North Pole *first*, in April 1908, a year ago; that Dr. Cook had only recently managed to return to the outside world and had announced his achievement just *five days* before Peary sent his message from Indian Harbor? Two men reaching a goal that had been sought for three centuries and announcing it almost simultaneously—why, it was the biggest story of the decade!

Peary appeared unimpressed. Yes, he had been given wireless reports about Cook and his claim a few days before at Indian Harbor but he had dismissed the claim as unthinkable. After all, the Pole was in the center of the ice-jammed Arctic Ocean, 400 miles from nearest land, and Eskimos who had been with Dr. Cook on his Arctic "hunting trip" (which he now asserted was when he made his journey to the Pole) had later assured Peary that they had never been out of sight of land.

Peary held a press conference that afternoon and told the reporters his own story without flourish. He and his men had left New York in the *Roosevelt* on a blistering July day in 1908. At Cape York, Greenland, he began picking up the Eskimo helpers he had learned to know intimately during his years in the north. "You are like the sun," they said. "You always come back." They were glad to help him again. They piled aboard with their wives, children, skin tents, sledges and dogs.

Peary was 52 years old at the time. Twenty years he had devoted to seeking the Pole—ever since that sunny afternoon in Washington, D. C., when he had chanced to pick up a volume on Arctic exploration and the spell of the north had seized him. Thereafter he had endured untold hardships and repeated defeats. He had sacrificed to his quest a promising career in the engineering corps of the Navy. But even his heartbreaking 1906 expedition, from which he and his men had barely returned alive after getting within 174 miles of the Pole, the sudden death of his principal financial backer, and the flat failure of his last book had not swerved him from his purpose. He was determined to reach his goal this time or die trying. It was his last chance.

Foot by foot the *Roosevelt* worked its way from Baffin Bay into the narrow channels between Greenland and Ellesmere Island, almost to the polar sea itself. There they spent the winter, the *Roosevelt* locked in the ice. Meanwhile the Eskimos built sledges and hunted for extra food—musk-ox, caribou, polar bear and seal. Matt Henson, the husky Negro who had been on Peary's expeditions for many years, built sledges of a type which Peary had perfected. The Eskimo women sewed fur clothes, which Peary had found warmer and more durable than any civilized man's garments. The explorers toughened themselves for the job ahead in temperatures as low as 60 degrees below zero.

Since the Pole was presumed to be in the center of the ice-jammed Arctic Ocean, the problem was one of dashing from Cape Columbia to the Pole and back again—about 1000 miles round trip—with the least possible weight. All equipment for men and dogs had to be sledged and, counting every ounce, it was just possible to carry enough for a few men to get to the Pole itself. The plan, therefore, was to organize several advance parties who would break trail, deposit food supplies and build igloos for shelter. Then a picked group would follow their prepared trail at top speed, with no heavy burdens, to within 150 miles of the Pole. There the last supply party would turn back, while the fresh, picked group would make a lightning dash to the Pole, having to get back before spring tides broke up the ice. It was a race against time, weather, water and death.

Before the winter night had lifted, the polar dash began—on Washington's birthday, 1909. For six days the men were held up by open water or "leads" caused by the drifting ice pack. When the ice closed, they hurried on—only to meet more open water. Their camp was almost destroyed in the night by a lead opening right between their igloos. The men scrambled to safety. Had Peary not insisted that they wear Eskimo clothes, in which they could both work and sleep comfortably, in place of the clumsy sleeping bags used by most explorers, the men would surely have drowned. The ice closed again and they hurried northward.

Captain Bob Bartlett, with the last supply sledge, turned back on April 1, just 133 miles from the Pole, to keep the return trail open. Peary pushed on, with Henson, who was a splendid sledge driver, and four picked Eskimos. There was just enough food for the round trip. Haste was essential across this icy waste. Their marches lengthened to 25 and 30 miles a day.

And at 10 o'clock in the morning of April 6, 1909, the party reached the North Pole. Peary shook hands with each of his men. Photographs were taken; Peary cached a record and took possession of the region for the United States. Five flags were planted, one of them being the tattered silk emblem of which a piece had been left at the northernmost point of each of Peary's previous attempts. During 30 hours at the Pole, Peary took 32 observations from points several miles apart.

But getting back presented a problem. They must travel even

faster than on the way north. The spring tides would soon break up the ice. Peary increased the distance covered each day over the return trail. Spare clothing was cast aside. Rations were diminishing. Periodically they slept a few hours in igloos built on the way up, then pressed on. They reached a dreaded big lead and crossed it, as it was forming, on moving cakes of ice.

Cape Columbia at last! There they ate and slept for two days before getting back to a hearty welcome at the *Roosevelt*. The commander and his party had lost about 30 pounds each during their forced marches. But, for the first time in years, Peary could sleep at night. He had at last justified himself! He had claimed the North Pole for the United States. He looked forward to patriotic approval at home—and then to peaceful days of retirement.

And now, here at Battle Harbor, Peary found instead of peace a humiliating controversy. He had known Dr. Cook well; Dr. Cook had been a surgeon on one of his early expeditions. But Peary was sure that Dr. Cook had not been able to overcome the countless hazards of polar conquest. To the reporters he explained why, with scientific detail. To his dismay, some of the reporters weren't interested in scientific proofs; they wanted a "story." Had Peary fought with polar bears? Had he been attacked by wolves or musk-ox? No, he hadn't. Well, Dr. Cook had. Gradually the truth dawned on Peary. After a lifetime sacrificed to one great ambition, his priority at the Pole was now being denied, his personal integrity questioned! Well, as he had battled a lifetime for the Pole, he would now battle for the recognition that was due him.

At the time Peary's announcement was made, Dr. Cook was in Copenhagen where he had stopped off on his way back from the Arctic. There he had been received by the King and had a hero's wreath of roses placed on his head. His word had been accepted. When asked for a comment on the Peary news, Dr. Cook said shrewdly, "If Peary says he reached the Pole, I believe him." When Peary bluntly declared Cook had sold the country a gold brick, Cook replied, "There is glory enough for all." On Peary lay the burden of the poor-sport and also-ran.

Dr. Cook had a head start for home. In New York harbor he

was met by a welcoming boat with 1000 admirers aboard. Triumphal arches were erected, banners hung in the streets. He began a rapid lecture tour, with nightly fees as high as $10,000. He got $24,000 for his newspaper story, $400,000 for all his enterprises. Peary got $4000 for his newspaper story, $40,000 and a moderate pension for book and magazine material.

When challenged to produce scientific proofs of his exploit, such as comprehensive solar observations, Dr. Cook said that he had left these valuable records with a wandering friend! When critics found errors in his newspaper narrative, he said he had not been able to read proof and that his book would prove everything.

By the time Peary arrived in New York, the Hudson-Fulton Centenary celebration was in full blast. As the *Roosevelt* steamed up the Hudson, there were boos, catcalls and insulting remarks from Cook sympathizers. Peary did not reply. At first he refused honors until the two claimants should present their evidence to some acceptable tribunal and a judgment should be rendered. But it became apparent that this would never occur. He did present his evidence to a committee of the National Geographic Society; it was carefully scrutinized and approved. He addressed various scientific societies, but never accepted pay.

A Pittsburgh newspaper took a poll of readers' sympathies. The result was 10 to 1 for Cook. Powerful newspapers supported him vigorously. Two months of profitable lecturing for Cook passed before he submitted data to the University of Copenhagen (which he considered unbiased) to prove he had been to the Pole. His proof was flatly rejected.

Gradually the tide turned. People came to side with Peary because of his dignified conduct and readiness to produce his proofs. The Gettysburg of the great controversy occurred during the Congressional hearings on a bill to retire Peary with the rank of Rear Admiral. At first, instead of receiving the thanks of a grateful nation, Peary heard himself denounced by Cook supporters in Congress. Nevertheless, he answered the most insulting and irrelevant questions with care. The hearings dragged on for weeks until his hecklers finally gave up. Peary was winning out.

Another attack came from certain hostile officers in the Navy. Peary's promotion, they said, would break seniority rules. It was pointed out, too, that due to his long absences (marching to the Pole) he had not taken the official Navy walking tests! So Peary (who had lost all his toes but the little ones when both feet had been frozen on an earlier expedition) stretched his legs and walked 25 miles in six hours. Next day he walked the same distance in seven and one-half hours. His critics were silenced.

Finally, two years after his Arctic exploit, he was retired with the rank of Rear Admiral and placed on the retired list as of April 6, 1909, the day he had reached the Pole. His achievement was officially recognized by Congress and the President of the United States, as it had already been by most scientific societies. Peary had won his last fight!

Dr. Cook had further adventures. During the height of the controversy two New York men, one a sea captain, swore they had been hired by Dr. Cook to furnish solar observations to prove he had been at the Pole. Edward Barrill, the guide who had been with Dr. Cook on a reportedly successful climb of Mt. McKinley in 1906, and others in the party declared Dr. Cook had never reached the top. Dr. Cook went on lecturing, disappeared to South America for several months, then returned to this country and gradually dropped from public sight. In 1923 he was sentenced to 14 years in prison for using the mails to defraud in connection with an oil swindle. After serving five years of his sentence he was paroled, and in May 1940 received an unconditional pardon from President Franklin D. Roosevelt. Dr. Cook died less than three months later.

After the controversy subsided, Peary really did enjoy the quiet family life he had longed for. During the summer of 1917, when he was delivering wartime lectures, he began to suffer from anemia. He maintained stoutly that this was just one more battle to win, but it was a losing one. On the 19th of February, 1920, he lapsed into a coma, and early in the next morning the light of his courageous spirit flickered and went out.

MR. ALICE
IN WONDERLAND

By Lancelot Robson

URING my boyhood it was my good fortune to meet the author of *Alice in Wonderland* often, for the Reverend Charles Lutwidge Dodgson, who wrote his children's fantasies under the name of Lewis Carroll, was a close friend of my father. Both were clergymen and both were mathematicians.

I remember Dodgson as a tall, slim figure, with pale face, dark wavy hair and a peculiar high-pitched voice. His dark-blue eyes met a child's with a kindly twinkle. Whatever the weather, he never wore an overcoat over his clerical blacks—but he always wore a tall black hat. And, winter and summer, he invariably wore knitted black wool gloves. Meeting him in the street, you would not have just noticed him, you would have looked twice.

One day we were having a children's party and unexpectedly "Mr. Alice in Wonderland," as we called him, came in to see my father. How delighted we were! He asked us if, in our school, we added up sums. A chorus answered, "Yes." There was a little pause, then Lewis Carroll said, "I am afraid you go to a very poor school. I never add up sums; I always put the answer down first and set the sum afterward."

There was silence. Then he continued, "We will do some sums." He wrote some figures on a piece of paper, and gave it to my stepmother, saying, "That will be the answer to our sum when we have set it." Then he wrote 1066 on another piece of paper. Choosing a little girl, he let her put down any four figures she

liked under his 1066. Then he put down four figures under hers and a small boy contributed another line. Lewis Carroll added a fifth line, so the column stood:

1066	Lewis Carroll
3478	Little Girl
6521	Lewis Carroll
7150	Little Boy
2849	Lewis Carroll

A rather perky youngster was allowed to add it up, and he pronounced the answer to be 21,064. My stepmother then read the figures on the paper Lewis Carroll had given her: 21,064. There were cries of "Oh!" from the children.

Actually, it was not so intricate as it first appeared. Whatever figure a child wrote, Carroll each time added a number that made both lines total 9999. Thus no matter what numbers the children wrote, the total of the five lines would be known to him in advance; it would be 20,000 more, less 2, than the number he originally wrote down at the top of the column.

We begged him for another trick, so he asked a little boy to write the number 12345679. He surveyed it in silence, then said, "You don't form your figures very clearly, do you? Which of these figures do you think you have made the worst?" The boy thought his 5 was poorest. Lewis Carroll suggested he should multiply the line by 45. The child laboriously worked it out and to his surprise found the result was 555555555. "Supposing I had said four, what then?" the boy queried. "In that case we would have made the answer all fours," Carroll replied. He would have told the boy to multiply by 36, another multiple of nine. But he did not attempt to explain "mystic nines" to us.

It was in 1862 that Lewis Carroll first told the story of "Alice's Adventures in Wonderland." By that time Charles Dodgson, who had spent a happy childhood inventing games, mathematical puzzles and puppet plays for seven adoring younger sisters, was teaching mathematics at Oxford as an ordained deacon of Christ Church College. From his window the lonely young man watched three little girls playing in Dean Liddell's garden. Their friendship started by his introducing them to "castle croquet"—his own variation of the game, involving ten balls, ten wickets, five stakes and other complications. Soon the children were regularly invading his rooms at story time. Picnics on the river followed, with stories "that lived and died like summer midges, each in its own golden afternoon."

One day the picnic party went ashore to have their tea in the shade of a hayrick. "The children clamored for a story: and then the miracle began. Straight down the rabbit-hole went the most lovely, the most confused, and the most appealing little girl that English literature has produced—'Alice'—to meet the fantastic, wistful, ludicrous creatures that peopled her Wonderland," wrote Warren Weaver in *The Princeton University Library Chronicle*.

The story of "Alice" didn't die, because her namesake, Alice Liddell, begged Mr. Dodgson to write it out for her. And her friend sat up all night to recapture the spontaneous flow of verses and stories. The little handwritten book lay on the Liddell table for visitors to see. They urged publication upon the reluctant author. It wasn't until Sir John Tenniel, the famous *Punch* artist, agreed to do the illustrations that Dodgson decided to add several chapters and arrange with Macmillan to publish it "on commission"—which meant at the author's expense. It was not signed by Charles L. Dodgson, Oxford don and author of such works as *Curiosa Mathematica* and *The Formulae of Plane Trigonometry*, but by Lewis Carroll, a blither spirit who had occasionally contributed poems to a literary paper.

Alice appeared in 1865 and was taken immediately to England's heart. Even Queen Victoria loved her, and invited the author to Windsor Castle. At the close of his visit she said, "And now, Mr. Dodgson, you must send me a copy of the next book you write." True to the royal command, he did so. It must have been a great disappointment to the Queen, for it was a treatise on an abstruse mathematical problem.

The acclaim showered on *Alice's* creator would have turned a lesser man's head. But Carroll, always shy with all but his intimates, fled whenever his work was praised; he refused to read reviews because such reading seemed to him "unhealthy"; and he objected to being invited to dinners or other social engagements.

In his suite of rooms at Christ Church he led a contented and happy life, his many odd ways seeming to his friends but delightful additions to his charming personality. Florence Becker Lennon, in *Victoria Through the Looking-Glass*, tells of his horror of drafts. "His theory was that there could be no drafts if the temperature was equalized all over the room. Accordingly, he had a number of thermometers about the room, and near each one an oil stove. Periodically he made a round of the thermometers, adjusting the adjacent stove according to the reading. All cracks under doors were boarded up with coats and rugs. . . .

"Dodgson," Mrs. Lennon also relates, "was a meticulous traveler. He had two pocketbooks, each with labeled compartments. Exact change for every contingency was placed in one of the compartments." This planning extended to his correspondence—he made an abstract of every letter he wrote or received, and cross-indexed each (the last entry was numbered 98,721).

His wit and charm won him the friendship of the great Victorians, including Ruskin, Tennyson and Rossetti. Yet he preferred the company of children. Carroll was more than a friend to the many children who played in the stage version of *Alice*. He saw that they got the best education and coaching possible, took them for country walks and entertained them at dinner in his Oxford rooms. There he had a wardrobe full of costumes for "dressing up." Always there was something new to engage a child's fancy. There was a vast collection of puzzles, clockwork mice and frogs, and a toy bat which would fly around the room. And, after dinner, the happy little girl would sit on Carroll's knee before the fire, while he made the animals in the hearth tiles come alive through the stories he told her.

Carroll undertook personally to teach Isa Bowman, a well-loved stage "Alice," geography (with the aid of jigsaw puzzles), arithmetic and Biblical knowledge. Langford Reed, in his charming *Life of Lewis Carroll*, quotes Miss Bowman as saying that these lessons continued for years. When her mother took her to America to play children's parts in Shakespearean repertoire, the lessons continued by mail. Just before Isa left England, Carroll took her to see a panorama of Niagara Falls. She tells how the panorama had, in the foreground, the model of a little dog accompanying the wax tourists who appeared to be gazing at the Falls. "In a moment, the academic Dodgson, intent on geographical instruction, was effaced by Carroll, who began relating a story about the dog, which, he said, was alive but trained to stand motionless.

" 'If you watch ever so carefully,' he declared, 'you will see his tail move slightly.'

" 'I do!' I cried excitedly, and I really thought I did. Mr. Carroll told how, if we waited long enough, we would see an attendant bring him a bone. Suddenly he began to stammer, and looking up I saw that a dozen grownups and children had gathered around to listen. It was not Mr. Carroll but a very confused Mr. Dodgson who led me quickly from the scene."

One of Carroll's nephews tells of another occasion when Lewis Carroll embarrassed the Reverend Charles Dodgson. He had been invited to a children's party. Entering the house, he dropped on all fours and went into the drawing room growling like a bear. But the children's party was next door. He found himself confronting an astonished women's party . . . and fled.

Of all the stories about Lewis Carroll, I like best one my father used to tell. In Guildford there was a shop called Bretts, where the well-to-do took morning coffee or afternoon tea. The windows were filled with luscious cakes and pastries. On a cold winter morning Carroll noticed a group of poor, ill-clad children gazing longingly at the fairy-tale display. He watched the group for a moment, then went up to them and said, "I think you all ought to have cakes." And into the shop he led the little band, where all were asked to choose the confections they fancied most.

One of the thousands of playful letters he wrote to his young friends ends charmingly, "Give my love to any children you happen to meet." And that is precisely what the shy old mathematician did all his life.

ACKNOWLEDGMENTS

*The condensations reprinted in this book are used by permission of,
and special arrangement with, the publishers holding the respective copyrights.*

LIVES OF THE GREAT, by Fred Eastman, cond. from *The Christian Century*, pub. by Christian
Century Press. THE ADVENTURES OF MARK TWAIN, by Jerry Allen, cond. from the book, © 1954,
Jerry Allen, pub. by Little, Brown and Company. THE STEADY LIGHT OF HELEN KELLER, by Ishbel
Ross, cond. from *Journey into Light*, © 1951, Ishbel Ross, pub. by Appleton-Century-Crofts. THE
VICTORIOUS MADAME CURIE, by Eve Curie and translated by Vincent Sheean, cond. from *Madame
Curie*, © 1937, Doubleday, Doran & Company. KING OF THE ROAD, by Joe McCarthy, cond. from
Holiday, © 1957, The Curtis Pub. Co. THE F.D.R. LEGEND, by Hamilton Basso, cond. from *Life*,
© 1947, Time Inc. BULLDOG WARRIOR, by Robert Lewis Taylor, cond. from *Winston Churchill*, ©
1952, Robert Lewis Taylor, pub. by Doubleday and Company. GREAT LIBERATOR, by Thomas
Rourke, adapted from *Man of Glory: Simón Bolívar*, © 1939, William Morrow and Company, Inc.
ROUGH-RIDING PRESIDENT, cond. from *Time*, © 1958, Time Inc. THE MIDNIGHT RIDER, by
Esther Forbes, cond. from *Paul Revere and the World He Lived In*, © 1942, Esther Forbes, pub. by
Houghton Mifflin Company. ALL THE WORLD'S HIS STAGE, cond. from *Time*, © 1960, Time Inc.
HER BOOK BREWED A WAR, by Forrest Wilson, cond. from *Crusader in Crinoline*, © 1941, Forrest
Wilson; by special arrangement with J. B. Lippincott Company. CONQUEROR OF THE SEAS, by
Stefan Zweig and translated by Eden and Cedar Paul, cond. from the book, © 1938, The Viking
Press. A GENTLEMAN OF VIRGINIA, by Robert W. Winston, cond. from *Robert E. Lee*, © 1934,
Robert W. Winston, pub. by William Morrow and Company. THE WIDOW OF WINDSOR, by
André Maurois, cond. from *The Edwardian Era*, © 1961, D. Appleton-Century Company, Inc.
SAM HOUSTON'S MAGNIFICENT LAST STAND, by John F. Kennedy, cond. from *Profiles in Courage*,
© 1955, John F. Kennedy, pub. by Harper and Brothers. HE KNEW THE WORLD WAS ROUND, by
George Kent, based on *Admiral of the Ocean Sea*, by Samuel Eliot Morison, © 1942, Samuel Eliot
Morison, pub. by Little, Brown and Company and the Atlantic Monthly Press. OUR UNKNOWN
EX-PRESIDENT, by Eugene Lyons, cond. from the book, © 1948, Doubleday and Company, Inc.
HE'D RATHER BE RIGHT, by John F. Kennedy, cond. from *Profiles in Courage*, © 1955, John F.
Kennedy, pub. by Harper and Brothers. A MAN TO REMEMBER, cond. from *Time*, © 1953, Time
Inc. THE MACARTHUR I KNEW, by General George C. Kenney, cond. from *The MacArthur I
Know*, © 1951, George C. Kenney, pub. by Duell, Sloan and Pearce. THE SULTAN OF SWAT, by
Jack Sher, cond. from *Sport*, © 1946, Macfadden Publications, Inc. THE MAGICIAN OF LIBERTY
HALL, by Floyd Miller, cond. from *The Electrical Genius of Liberty Hall*, © 1962, Floyd Miller, pub.
by McGraw-Hill Book Company. THE RAIL-SPLITTER, by G. Lynn Sumner, cond. from *Meet
Abraham Lincoln*, © 1946, G. Lynn Sumner, pub. by Harper and Brothers. THE GRAND CARUSO,
by George Kent, based on *Enrico Caruso*, by Dorothy Caruso, © 1945, Dorothy Caruso, pub. by
Simon and Schuster. THE SOLDIERS' ANGEL, by Mary Raymond Shipman Andrews, cond. from
A Lost Commander, © 1929, Doubleday, Doran & Company, Inc. THE GREAT DISSENTER, by
Beverly Smith, cond. from *The American Magazine*, © 1933, The Crowell Pub. Co.

Excerpts: Page 42, *This Week*. Page 49 (bottom), *Collier's*. Page 107 (top), an address at Smith
College; (bottom), *Man, the Unknown*, pub. by Harper & Row. Page 118, *This Week*. Page 174,
African and European Addresses, pub. by G. P. Putnam's Sons. Page 179, *The Paderewski Memoirs*,
pub. by Charles Scribner's Sons. Page 205, *Good Housekeeping*. Page 213 (third from top), *Man,
the Unknown*, pub. by Harper & Row. Page 254 (top), *Living Under Tension*, pub. by Harper &
Row. Page 277, *Little Golden America*, © 1937, Holt, Rinehart & Winston. Page 297, *The Case
of Miss Cavell, from the Unpublished Documents of the Trial* (1920). Page 302, *The Laugh's on Me*,
pub. by Doubleday & Company. Page 344, *Life*. Page 348, "Truth" from *Poems by John Masefield*,
pub. by The Macmillan Company. Page 373, *Negro Digest*. Page 406, *Mark Twain, a Biography*,
pub. by Harper & Row. Page 418 (bottom), *The Art of Thinking*, pub. by Simon and Schuster.
Page 442, *New Eyes for Invisibles*, pub. by The Macmillan Company. Page 501 (top), *Now to Live!*,
pub. by Abingdon-Cokesbury; (bottom), *On Being Alive*, pub. by Charles Scribner's Sons.
Page 510, *The Atlantic Monthly*. Page 516, *The Saturday Review Treasury*, pub. by Simon and
Schuster. Page 543, *Together*, © 1963, The Methodist Publishing House. Page 556, *On Being Alive*,
pub. by Charles Scribner's Sons.

Theodore Roosevelt

Mark Twain

J. S. Newton   A Einstein

Franklin Roosevelt   Rembran

Helen Keller   Charles A. Lindberg

M. Curie

A. Lincoln   Picas

Ludwig van Beethove

Thomas A Edison   Daniel Boone

Carl Sandburg   Andrew Jackson